Thomas Holcroft's Revolutionary Drama

D1598132

TRANSITS
LITERATURE, THOUGHT & CULTURE, 1650–1850

Series editors:
Miriam Wallace, New College of Florida
Mona Narain, Texas Christian University

A landmark series in long-eighteenth-century studies, *Transits* publishes monographs and edited volumes that are timely, transformative in their approach, and global in their engagement with arts, literature, culture, and history. Books in the series have engaged with visual arts, environment, politics, material culture, travel, theater and performance, embodiment, connections between the natural sciences and medical humanities, writing and book history, sexuality, gender, disability, race, and colonialism from Britain and Europe to the Americas, the Far East, the Middle/Near East, Africa, and Oceania. Works that make provocative connections across time, space, geography, or intellectual history, or that develop new modes of critical imagining are particularly welcome.

Recent titles in the series:

Thomas Holcroft's Revolutionary Drama: Reception and Afterlives
Amy Garnai

Families of the Heart: Surrogate Relations in the Eighteenth-Century British Novel
Ann Campbell

Eighteenth-Century Environmental Humanities
Jeremy Chow, ed.

Political Affairs of the Heart: Female Travel Writers, the Sentimental Travelogue, and Revolution, 1775–1800
Linda Van Netten Blimke

The Limits of Familiarity: Authorship and Romantic Readers
Lindsey Eckert

"Robinson Crusoe" after 300 Years
Andreas K. E. Mueller and Glynis Ridley, eds.

Transatlantic Women Travelers, 1688–1843
Misty Krueger, ed.

Laurence Sterne's "A Sentimental Journey": A Legacy to the World
W. B. Gerard and M-C. Newbould, eds.

For more information about the series, please visit www.bucknelluniversitypress.org.

Thomas Holcroft's Revolutionary Drama

RECEPTION AND
AFTERLIVES

AMY GARNAI

BUCKNELL
UNIVERSITY PRESS

LEWISBURG, PENNSYLVANIA

Library of Congress Cataloging-in-Publication Data

Names: Garnai, Amy, 1957– author.
Title: Thomas Holcroft's revolutionary drama : reception and
    afterlives / Amy Garnai.
Description: Lewisburg, Pennsylvania : Bucknell University Press,
    [2023] | Includes bibliographical references.
Identifiers: LCCN 2022010615 | ISBN 9781684484447 (hardback) |
    ISBN 9781684484430 (paperback) | ISBN 9781684484454 (epub) |
    ISBN 9781684484461 (mobi) | ISBN 9781684484478 (pdf)
Subjects: LCSH: Holcroft, Thomas, 1745–1809—Criticism and
    interpretation. | Holcroft, Thomas, 1745–1809—Influence. |
    English drama—18th century—History and criticism.
Classification: LCC PR3515.H2 Z68 2023 | DDC 822/.6—
    dc23/eng/20220909
LC record available at https://lccn.loc.gov/2022010615

A British Cataloging-in-Publication record for this book is available
from the British Library.

⊖ The paper used in this publication meets the requirements of the
American National Standard for Information Sciences—Permanence
of Paper for Printed Library Materials, ANSI Z39.48-1992.

www.bucknelluniversitypress.org

Distributed worldwide by Rutgers University Press

Manufactured in the United States of America

For Anne Steiner

Thomas Holcroft's Revolutionary Drama has been many years in the making, and I have accumulated debts of gratitude to institutions, colleagues, and friends that it is now a pleasure to acknowledge. The first extended research for the book was carried out with the help of a fellowship at the Humanities Research Centre of the Australian National University. I am indebted to the fellows and staff at the Centre for making my visit so enjoyable. An evening spent in Canberra with Gillian Russell, David Worrall, and Georgina Lock discussing Holcroft's play *The Man of Ten Thousand* exemplified, memorably, scholarly conviviality. The award of a travel grant from the Lewis Walpole Library of Yale University gave me the opportunity to work with its wonderful collections; I want to thank Nicole Bouché and Susan Walker for so graciously receiving me and librarians Scott Poglitsch and Kristen Macdonald for their knowledgeable and generous assistance during and after my visit. I wish to thank the librarians at the Yale University Libraries in New Haven, especially Richard Boursy at the Yale Music Library, who found Holcroft resources whose existence was previously unknown to me. I am grateful to Wolfson College, University of Oxford, and its then president, Professor Hermione Lee, for granting me a visiting scholarship. My time in Oxford and at the Bodleian Library was crucial for this project, in particular working with the Holcroft side of the Godwin-Holcroft correspondence in the Abinger Papers. My thanks go out to the Bodleian staff for their helpfulness. I am grateful to the American Philosophical Society (APS) for two Franklin Research Grants, which were essential for carrying out research in the United States and the United Kingdom. Special thanks go to Linda Musumeci of the APS for her ongoing encouragement and support. I am also indebted to the staffs of many other institutions: the National Library of Australia and the National Film & Sound Archive of Australia in Canberra; the British Library, the Victoria and Albert Museum Theatre and Performance Archives, the British Film Institute (where I spent a memorable afternoon watching the 1913 film *The Road to Ruin*), and the Guildhall Library in London; the Chawton House Library in Hampshire; the Marshall Library in Glasgow; the Beinecke Library and the Yale Music Library at Yale University; the Pierpont Morgan Library and the New York Public Library in New York City; the Huntington Library in San Marino, California; and the Folger Shakespeare Library in Washington DC. The Folger Library's generosity in granting—even to short-term visitors—ongoing home access to electronic resources was a godsend, especially as the COVID-19 pandemic entered our lives and the world closed down. At the Kibbutzim College of Education, I wish to thank the Inter-Library Loan staff for its helpfulness in delivering material during lockdowns and Yosi Mishan for his help with technical and logistical issues.

Many friends and colleagues accompanied me on this journey. Jon Mee, Pamela Clemit, David Worrall, Georgina Lock, and Gillian Russell were generous with their knowledge and inestimable in their support and encouragement. Others kindly responded to queries and questions when I approached them as a stranger: James Vigus, Matthew Sangster, Jenny MacCauley, Liz Denlinger, and Steven Howe. Closer to home, Galia Benziman and Sonia Weiner have been perceptive listeners and valued friends. Any errors that may appear in what follows are, of course, my own.

It was an honor to speak about Holcroft at the Centre for Eighteenth-Century Studies at the University of York, and to return to that beautiful city where I had been a British Academy fellow many years earlier, at which time, in the King's Manor Library, I had read my first Holcroft play.

I also wish to thank Rivi Carmel and Beverley Topaz, chairs of the English Department at the Kibbutzim College during the years in which I wrote this book, as well as colleagues and students at the College for their support and goodwill.

At Bucknell University Press I want to thank Suzanne Guiod and Miriam Wallace for their initial and ongoing support of the manuscript and Pamelia Dailey, who has patiently guided me through the later stages of transforming the manuscript into a book. I also thank the anonymous readers for Bucknell University Press for their thoughtful and incisive comments and suggestions that helped make this a better book.

Thomas Holcroft's Revolutionary Drama could not have been written without the encouragement of my family, Nati, Erez, and Anat Garnai, who have always been my strongest supporters. The book is dedicated to my sister, Anne Steiner, who patiently listened to me talk about Holcroft, literally, for years.

* * *

A section of chapter 3 was originally published in a slightly different version as "'A Lock upon My Lips': The Melodrama of Silencing and Censorship in Thomas Holcroft's *Knave, or Not?*" *Eighteenth-Century Studies* 43, no. 4 (summer 2010): 473–484, © 2010 The American Society for Eighteenth-Century Studies. Reprinted by permission of Johns Hopkins University Press.

Amy Garnai
January 2023

CG   Covent Garden Theatre

Clemit   Pamela Clemit, ed., *The Letters of William Godwin, Vol. I:*
            1778–1797 (Oxford: Oxford University Press, 2011); *The Letters of*
            William Godwin, Vol. II: 1798–1805 (Oxford: Oxford University
            Press, 2014).

DL   Drury Lane Theatre

Genest   John Genest, *Some Account of the English Stage from the Restoration*
            in 1660 to 1830. In ten volumes. (Bath: H. E. Carrington, 1832).

GD   The Diary of William Godwin, edited by Victoria Myers, David
            O'Shaughnessy, and Mark Philp (Oxford: Oxford Digital Library,
            2010). http://godwindiary.bodleian.ox.ac.uk.

LA   Larpent Collection of Manuscript Plays, The Huntington Library,
            San Marino, California

Life   *The Life of Thomas Holcroft Written by Himself Continued to the*
            Time of His Death from His Diary Notes and Other Papers by
            William Hazlitt and Now Newly Edited with Introduction and
            Notes by Elbridge Colby. In two volumes. (1925). Reprint. (New
            York: Benjamin Blom, 1968).

NF   Thomas Holcroft, *A Narrative of Facts Relating to a Prosecution for*
            High Treason; Including the Address to the Jury, Which the Court
            Refused to Hear: with Letters to the Attorney General, Lord Chief
            Justice Eyre, Mr. Serjeant Adair, the Honourable Thomas Erskine,
            and Vicary Gibbs, Esq. and the Defence the Author Had Prepared, If
            He Had Been Brought to Trial. (London: H. D. Symonds, 1795).

Ransom   London Playbills and Programs Collection. Harry Ransom
            Center. University of Texas at Austin. http://norman.hrc.utexas
            .edu/playbills/index.cfm?prod=1533.

Thomas Holcroft's Revolutionary Drama

IN SEPTEMBER 2002, THE ORANGE TREE Theatre in Richmond, United Kingdom, staged a revival of Thomas Holcroft's 1792 play, *The Road to Ruin*. The play received favorable reviews, with critics noting the effectiveness of Holcroft's humor before a twenty-first-century audience, the fine acting of the roles he had crafted, and through the story of the Dorntons—the banker facing financial collapse and his profligate son—the continued relevance of Holcroft's exploration of the "malign influence of the cash-nexus."[1] Common to these reviews was the notice of the play's origin in a distant Georgian past; not staged for many years, it was commended as worthy of revival.[2] Holcroft's own history was briefly acknowledged: writing in *The Guardian*, Michael Billington noted that the playwright was "a pivotal member of a radical group that welcomed the French Revolution and that was indicted for high treason in 1794." In *The Times*, Benedict Nightingale also remarked on the politics, as well as on another relevant aspect, the play's echoes of the suicide of Holcroft's son.

This book examines the life, times, and dramatic writing of Thomas Holcroft (1745–1809), playwright, novelist, literary critic, translator, and reforming activist, viewing his work for the theater as it intertwines with a political engagement still recalled and cultural pressures yet acknowledged, its resilience evident in the Orange Tree production of his work, and those revivals that preceded it in the nineteenth and early twentieth centuries. This confluence of literature and politics, reception and afterlives, revival and remembrance will be examined through the successes of some plays, particularly *The Road to Ruin* and the pioneering melodrama, *A Tale of Mystery* (1802), and in the failure of others, as well as in the drama of Holcroft's own life story. While his first play, an afterpiece, was performed in 1778 and he had dramatic successes throughout the 1780s, I focus in this study on the Holcroft plays produced between the years 1792 and 1806, a period concurrent with and defined by the French Revolution and the Anglo-French wars that ensued. Holcroft's dramatic writing and his experience as an activist during these years was a drama in itself, shaped by the cultural tensions that informed the work of the theaters and by the political aims of the Pitt government, primarily. These two dimensions of the "revolutionary drama"—as theme and form in writing and as the gripping and sometimes valiant actions of life itself—form the substance of this book.

The censorship of the theater during these years and the pressures exerted on the production of plays have been well documented.[3] Censorship had been in place since the Licensing Act of 1737 and would continue until 1968; between the years 1778 and 1824, John Larpent held the position of Chief Examiner for Plays in the Lord Chamberlain's office, assisted unofficially by his wife Anna Margaretta Larpent. Those plays submitted to the censor containing passages or themes deemed too controversial were returned to the theater managers with the offending passages crossed out, or with the instruction "Out!" written in the margins of the manuscript. As a result of the Larpents' vigilance, outright references to the French Revolution, or any overt criticism regarding contemporary social issues, were generally kept to a minimum on the British stage. Moreover, the staging of earlier plays with strong topical resonances, such as Shakespeare's *Julius Caesar*, Addison's *Cato*, and Thomas Otway's *Venice Preserved*, was prohibited at times when political tensions were high.[4]

Frequently more severe than the Larpents were the "juries" of public opinion[5] that viewed, deliberated over, and responded to theatrical productions—the spectators in the patent theaters, the critics who reviewed the plays for newspapers and periodicals, and the readers of those reviews, as well as readers and reviewers of later published editions of the plays. These audiences and readers were particularly watchful for, and critical of, antigovernment and oppositional content and in their capacity as unofficial censors, called anxious attention to "transgressing" passages that had earlier been approved. These observers were sensitive to the implications of a rights discourse influenced by the values and the rhetoric of the French Revolution and what sometimes followed, an antiwar sentiment which was seen as especially pernicious following the outbreak of hostilities between Britain and France. Examining Holcroft's plays and their reception enables a view of the change in political sentiment as the revolutionary decade progressed. Through this progression we can discern the limits of what the censor, but even more importantly, the mainstream British public, was willing to tolerate, as the consensus moved from support of the Revolution to suspicion, fear, apostasy, and compliance. This change can be illustrated, for example, by observing the inclusion of a prologue praising the Revolution that did no harm to Holcroft's success with *The Road to Ruin* in 1792 and then a comment on the "uselessness of gentlemen"[6] in his *Love's Frailties* two years later, which set off something of a furor in the theater and in reviews of the play that followed.

During these years, Holcroft was cognizant of his life as a revolutionary drama, most notably so during his experience as a defendant during the Treason Trials of 1794. There his "embodied practices,"[7] to use James Epstein and David Karr's term, announced a radical performance, as when he turned himself in to the authorities on the basis of an unserved warrant for his arrest. This was a conscious practice manifested as he expounded an agenda of truth, sincerity, transparency, nonviolence, and the promotion of a social ethics, whether as a member of the radical Society for Constitutional Information, or during the Trials, in an aborted attempt to address the startled officers of the court and the courtroom audience immediately after his release without trial. To be sure, it was not only these physical or aural manifestations that constituted Holcroft's revolutionary drama. His life, from modest beginnings, its achievements and setbacks, the ascent to fame and the fall to notoriety were perceived as remarkable and in many ways viewed as a real-life drama. This was the case especially in regard to his rise from obscurity, as recorded, for example, in the seemingly astonished account appearing in the *European Magazine* after his first major success with his play *Duplicity* in 1781, where Holcroft is described as having "a strong mind, and a perseverance which is not often found . . . he appears remarkable for a degree of fortitude in pursuing anything he undertakes, which nothing can overthrow."[8] This recognition of the remarkableness of his accomplishments once again emerged to grip the public's imagination years after his death with the publication of his *Memoirs* (1816), whose first person account of childhood poverty exhibits the buoyancy of his efforts, the degree of his achievement, and the obstacles overcome. It was in this context, but especially regarding Holcroft's radicalism and involvement in the Treason Trials, that Elbridge Colby, later to be Holcroft's twentieth-century biographer, expresses his admiration for Holcroft and his fellow radicals: "for the ideal of liberty and reform these men worked. They dared daylight and looked the world in the face."[9]

Thomas Holcroft's Revolutionary Drama is not a cradle-to-grave biography; rather, the biographical material appears alongside close readings of a selection of his plays accompanied by literary, cultural, and historical analyses and the examination of newspapers, letters, diaries, account books, and manuscripts. Through these sources I stress the reception of Holcroft's work as it appeared in the original responses of critics, general readers, and audiences, and then throughout the years. Three chapters of the book do center on biographical topics. Chapter One, following a brief account of theatricality and the Revolution debate, presents a summary of Holcroft's early years and a discussion of the Treason Trials of 1794 and those efforts that had so captured Colby's imagination and admiration. Chapter Four deals with Holcroft's life writing—his short-lived diary and some of his letters written while abroad—with Chapter Six examining his final years, his death, and the lives of his family in its aftermath. Although these chapters include short discussions of some of his dramatic works, the other chapters engage with his plays more at length: Chapter Two discusses *The Road to Ruin*; Chapter Three delves into Holcroft's plays written immediately preceding and then following the Treason Trials; Chapter Five presents an analysis of his melodramas.

In exploring these subjects, I assume a wide-ranging readership. Some readers might already be familiar with Holcroft's work; others might be knowledgeable of the literature and political thought of the 1790s or of Romantic-era writing; still others might be coming from the study of memoir, biography, and life writing, or from history or theater studies more generally. Among them may be those who, probably like many in the audience at the Orange Tree Theatre in Richmond, will be meeting Holcroft with no prior knowledge of his life and work. What may be common knowledge to some regarding, for instance, the Burke-Paine "war of ideas," the Treason Trials, or the birth of melodrama, may be new to others. I have tried to balance my narrative so as to accommodate these different audiences. An account that charts well-worn territory to some readers may still appear, I hope, with new perspectives or emphases to consider, focalized now through Holcroft's experience.

Having introduced my subject as the convergence of Holcroft's dramatic writing and the politics of the revolutionary decade, I should now explain my decision to concentrate on his plays rather than his novels. Like many of the topics discussed in this book, my interest in genre is bound up with reception. A good illustration of the differences between drama and novel writing as it was perceived around the turn of the nineteenth century—and which acknowledges reception—appears in an essay by Holcroft's contemporary (and close friend) Elizabeth Inchbald, published in Prince Hoare's periodical *The Artist*. Consisting mainly of advice for writers of novels, Inchbald's essay also distinguishes between different genres: "The Novelist is a free agent. He lives in a land of liberty, whilst the Dramatic writer exists but under a despotic government."[10] Her discussion acknowledges, briefly, the role of the censor of plays as opposed to the "freedom of speech" (16) enjoyed by the novelist and in a more extended manner, the role of the audience and the critics in the reception of drama. "The will of such critics is the law," Inchbald asserts, "and execution instantly follows judgment" (16). Inchbald's use of legal vocabulary—law, judgment, execution and later, juries (17)—ostensibly refers to theatrical taste, innovation, and originality (and she criticizes the lack of it); the political referentiality discreetly appears in her use of these very terms. Inchbald also stresses the immediacy of performance: she represents the dramatist as the "slave of the audience" (16), suggesting a proximity (and an anxious one, at that) between creator and audience that is lacking in the world of the novelist.

The distinction between genres is also apparent in the meeting of manuscript, performance, and print. The Larpent manuscripts allow us a view of the censorship of drama in practice and of the work of revision even before a play reached the stage, as offending passages were marked and excised. A heightened response following a premiere, with revisions sometimes made the following night and later alterations included in the printed editions of plays, frequently connected to politics, was a drama in itself. Novels, to be sure, are extremely valuable for enabling detailed attention to the arguments, ideas, philosophies, and cruxes of the cultural moment, in their capaciousness and freedom to do so, as Inchbald had it, and very much valuable work has been done on what has often been called the "Jacobin" novel.[11] The study of the theater helps to illuminate something more immediate—the burden of cultural transmission when the text and its reception are instantaneous and danger may be imminent; the energy of the creative endeavor meeting the pressures of public engagement. That reception, the force of that dramatic encounter but also, crucially, the power of print media that amplified it, is a major focus of this book. Certainly, Holcroft was attuned to that power. Throughout his life he believed in the eminence of print, what Jon Mee calls "print magic";[12] the reformers' belief in the power of the written word to shape ideas and to change the world. This was true when Holcroft welcomed Paine's *Rights of Man* (as we will see in Chapter One), in his own writings and later when he responded, in print, to the danger he confronted in his life.

Danger was indeed often near, and Holcroft's political engagement brought performance, print, reception, and action into close, tense interplay. How can we define that radicalism, which eventually brought him to indictment and imprisonment? The radicalism referenced in this book appears as an ideological positioning similar to the one described by John Barrell regarding the two leading progressive political societies in London in the first half of the 1790s, the London Corresponding Society and the Society for Constitutional Information (the group in which Holcroft was a member). As Barrell explains, the societies' agendas included the support of universal manhood suffrage and annual parliaments; of Thomas Paine and his followers, the ancient constitution, and elective monarchy. The members of these societies, Barrell continues, were "republicans, at least to the extent of supporting the Republic of France and hoping for—rather than working for—the end of hereditary monarchy in Britain."[13] Holcroft's commitment shares these values while specifically partaking of his close friend William Godwin's own contribution to radical discourse as most prominently articulated in *An Enquiry Concerning Political Justice* (1793). In that seminal text of philosophical political anarchy, Godwin described and delineated the search for and adherence to truth, for social and economic justice and equality, the belief in perfectibility accompanied by transparency of action, the suspicion of institutions, the rejection of punishment, and, centrally, the belief in communities of conversation. Together these ideals would lead to the creation of a world defined by political justice and achieved through a gradual nonviolent effort.

Those various elements in Godwin's philosophy as utilized by Holcroft are crucial for understanding his literary oeuvre and his life, and will be expanded upon throughout this book, for example, in trying to make sense of Holcroft's proceedings in the period of the Treason Trials. There, in what seemed to some observers as eccentric decision making, he enacted through personal example his conviction that the Godwinian ideology could change political systems and the world. His valorization of perfectibility—that belief in continual improvement through the ability to recognize and act upon truth[14]—elucidates what have some-times been perceived as unsatisfying conclusions to his plays and novels and explains why the villains are never punished but choose to reform instead. My use of the word "radical" throughout this book references, then, both the more gen-eral beliefs and activism identified by Barrell in regard to the reforming political societies and in particular the Godwinian inflection characterizing Holcroft's work as it defines, accompanies, and sometimes modifies those aspirations and values.

Holcroft's friendship with Godwin lies at the heart of this book. Their con-versations, their reading and criticism of each other's work, along with their shared social interactions, helped shape Holcroft's ideological beliefs, which were then embedded in his writing and actualized in his social transactions and public nego-tiations as a writer, an activist, and a citizen. Holcroft and Godwin met in 1786, and their friendship quickly developed, along with their shared political engage-ment that commenced with the start of the French Revolution. The strength of their connection included and was sustained by their intellectual and political grap-pling, wars of ideas, collaboration, conversation, and argument. They successfully accommodated disagreement and dispute up until the final rupture in 1805, four years before Holcroft's death. Godwin had called Holcroft one of his "four prin-cipal oral instructors,"[15] and Holcroft learned much from Godwin as well, as he applied their shared philosophical and political ideas in his imaginative writing and in his life.

The friendship between Holcroft and Godwin was importantly linked to the wider social networks that influenced and shaped their writing and their contri-bution to the Revolution debate. Mark Philp's pathbreaking study of Godwin exhibited how the practices of community in Godwin's own life enabled him in *Political Justice* to posit his anarchic vision as a "practical political possibility in Britain in the 1790s," one which allowed its participants to "believe that their beliefs and values were widely shared."[16] The enlightened community of their own expe-rience became for Godwin and Holcroft a reachable ideal for the wider world, a template grounded in lived experience and applicable for cultural formations in general. In characterizing the Godwin milieu, Philp further explains that "God-win's circles are an instance of both a counter-culture and an emergent social class . . . by virtue of their critical attitude to the political and social *status quo*, in their rejection of the norms of the dominant culture" and in the "professional and semi-professional men and women" who made up their ranks.[17] For Holcroft, the membership and central role in the influential circle and the affinity with its social and ideological ideals, indeed the embodiment in his own life of both emergent social class and counterculture allegiance, enabled him to navigate his cultural, literary, and political endeavors; the strength of this identity and his belief in the group's values and certainly his deep friendship with Godwin enabled him to confront both outright and insidious threats and pressures.

The interconnectedness of ideas, philosophies, social groups, and texts such as those exhibited in the writings and lives of the members of the Godwin-Holcroft circle calls attention to the idea, and value, of sociability in the late eighteenth and early nineteenth centuries on a larger scale. Gillian Russell and Clara Tuite characterize sociability as "a fundamental part of the self-definition of Romantic writers and artists"[18] and argue that viewing the cultural production of Romanticism through the traditional focus on isolated and solitary experience must be challenged by the recognition of its "sociable other."[19] Discussing the social interactions of the Godwin milieu and of other figures of the period, the essays in Russell and Tuite's collection, *Romantic Sociability*, also identify instances and occasions in which a heightened sociability led to pursuit and persecution, such as in the case of the lawyer John Frost, whose political argumentativeness in a tavern led to his eventual incarceration in Newgate prison, or the poet Robert Merry, whose radicalism was regarded by his former friends and other observers as increasingly destructive when linked to his association with working-class political writers and agitators.[20]

Sociability as a practice was not enough, as John Frost, Robert Merry, and countless others learned, to avert the confrontation with hegemonic power and a dominant political ideology. Resisting government repression and possible legal retribution was the key challenge faced by Holcroft and other like-minded men and women who opposed the Pitt government in the 1790s. In *Unusual Suspects*, Kenneth R. Johnston details the fates of many writers and intellectuals during Pitt's "Reign of Alarm," which was characterized by the quashing of reform and the accompanying reactionary backlash.[21] Johnston explains the processes whereby lives and careers were changed and ruined by government counteraction and in which sociability reversed into ostracism. Distinguishing between "usual" and "unusual" suspects, he devotes his book mainly to the latter, to those "bystanding sympathetic fellow-travelers for reform who did not expect to get into trouble for their liberal sympathies, but did."[22] Holcroft, in contrast, is identified by Johnston as a "usual suspect"; that is, as a defendant in the Treason Trials, he achieved prominence as one at the center of events rather than in the status of a sympathetic onlooker with a lesser degree of public prominence. It is hard to say if he meets Johnston's other criterion—that of not expecting "to get into trouble": as a member of the Society for Constitutional Information, a group infiltrated by spies, he had opted to join its secret committee of conference. Yet he minimized the sense of danger at various points, with the Godwinian belief in truth, transparency, and conversation propelling him onwards in his convictions. Moreover, he was never completely ostracized. Despite getting into serious trouble with the authorities, he always had access to the powerful managers of the patent theaters and to publishers and other leading cultural figures.

With the historical turn in literary and cultural studies, much groundbreaking work has been done that introduces, revisits, and recovers the writers and writing of the revolutionary decade within this deep historical ecology of revolution, activism, repression, and creative endeavor, illuminating various aspects of the work (and reception) of canonical writers, as well as those who have at various points fallen off the scholarly radar.[23] As far as William Godwin in particular is concerned, there has been a wealth of new studies and resources published in recent years, including the online digital edition of Godwin's Diary edited by Mark Philp, Victoria Meyers, and David O'Shaughnessy, without which my own book could not have been written as it is. As Jon Mee asserts, "we seem to be living through a critical moment for William Godwin,"[24] one which includes, in addition to the launch of Godwin's Diary, the first two volumes (of a projected six-volume work) of Pamela Clemit's edition of Godwin's letters and other books and essays examining his life and writing.[25] *Thomas Holcroft's Revolutionary Drama* takes part in and celebrates the Godwinian moment, while also aspiring to include Holcroft vigorously within it, to make it his moment as well.

There was an earlier historical period—the first decade of the twentieth century and on through World War One and its aftermath—which likewise privileged the revolutionary era in Britain as a significant historical phenomenon. To be sure, throughout the nineteenth century Holcroft and Godwin never really disappeared entirely from view. In his biography of Godwin, Peter Marshall concludes by documenting the strong influence of Godwin's writings on nineteenth-century social movements such as Owenism, Chartism, and the National Union of Working Classes, showing how, following the Reform Bill of 1832, his ideas "helped form the powerful British libertarian tradition in British history and thought," while also shaping political thinking worldwide.[26] Holcroft, less the philosopher than Godwin, was remembered and his life summarized as new productions of *The Road to Ruin* premiered, after new editions of his *Memoirs* were published, and sometimes when his poem "Gaffer Gray" (discussed in Chapter Six) was anthologized. At the same time, the beginning of the twentieth century saw an increased scrutiny of the 1790s as a period worthy of attention. Many writers contributed detailed scholarly studies of the period of the French Revolution and the reform movements in Britain, including discussions of Godwin and Holcroft, echoing perhaps the pulse of their own era—the "explosion of intellectual and artistic energy" that characterized the Edwardians and that "swept Britain into the modern world."[27] After the long reign of Queen Victoria and with the start of a new century, the contemplation of Britain's past, present, and future gripped the public imagination and found expression in works of social history such as C.F.G

Masterman's *The Condition of England* (1909).[28] Important Edwardian works looked carefully back through history to examine reform movements in 1790s Britain, for example, G. S. Veitch's *The Genesis of Parliamentary Reform* (1913) and Philip A. Brown's *The French Revolution in English History* (published in 1918, after his death in the trenches of the Great War), books which are sympathetic to the reformers.[29] This is also the case with Henry Noel Brailsford's *Shelley, Godwin and Their Circle* (1913). There he characterizes Holcroft's behavior at the Treason Trials as typical of the Godwin circle in his "naïve courage [and] doctrinaire hardihood" and the trials as a "monstrous attempt" at interpreting the law of high treason; the greatest danger to English liberties in modern times.[30] Edmund Blunden was a Great War poet but also a prolific editor and critic, with much of his work done on the Romantic writers, notably, Shelley, Keats, and Charles Lamb. In 1931 he produced a volume, *Tragical Consequences, or A Disaster at Deal*, which was a copy of the letter sent by William Godwin to John Fenwick in 1789 relating the suicide of William Holcroft, and now presented with editorial apparatus and an epigraph from Spenser's pastoral elegy, "Daphnaida." While elucidating some of the details appearing in Godwin's letter, Blunden also includes his own appraisal of the event and records his opinion of the severity of Godwin and Holcroft as fathers; he viewed the latter's behavior as possible cause for William Holcroft's suicide.[31] It was certainly a subject—perhaps a lifelong guilt—that Holcroft carried with him; it was to be the trigger that led to the end of Holcroft and Godwin's friendship in 1805.

Two of the most significant voices to appear in the early twentieth century in regard to the 1790s reform movements and in relation to Holcroft in particular, came from across the Atlantic. Allene Gregory's *The French Revolution and the English Novel* (1915), written with a vigorous economic-materialist approach, devotes a chapter to Holcroft.[32] There, Gregory foregrounds Holcroft as a "truer representative of Revolutionary idealism" ("truer" that is, than Godwin) and who presents a "saner, kindlier and more comprehensive" distillation of their philosophical principles, unencumbered by the burden of Godwin's Calvinist background.[33] Gregory's detailed discussions of Holcroft's novels would have reminded her earliest readers of this aspect of his literary output at a time when he was both overshadowed by Godwin in the general studies of this period and remembered primarily on account of his plays, owing to the frequent revival of *The Road to Ruin*. Elbridge Colby wrote extensively and fairly exclusively about Thomas Holcroft rather than about the revolutionary era in general and edited a modern edition of Holcroft's *Memoirs*. Colby was both an academic in the field of English literature and an officer in the United States Army. In the same years he was writing about Holcroft and editing the *Memoirs*, he published an article in *The Nation*, "Justice in Georgia" (1926), in which he protested the murder of a Black soldier by a white man who had demanded that the soldier step off a sidewalk; the murderer was later acquitted by an all-white jury. Colby's intervention seriously damaged his military career. Members of Congress censured him, and the Army did not step up in his defense.[34] Colby's remark cited above, where he praised those 1790s activists who "looked the world in the face," can be turned back at him to define his own courage. Researching Holcroft might have provided a degree of comfort by presenting him with a like-minded fellow traveler. In his preface to the *Memoirs*, he privileges Holcroft's "radical activities" as the accomplishment by which his name will "be remembered," singling out also his "sensitive pride and his strong opinions . . . 'sometimes so strange and sometimes so good'" (*Life*, 1:ix).[35]

Unlike Gregory, I do not rank Holcroft against Godwin, and, as opposed to Colby, I do not view all Holcroft's plays as "mediocre" (*Life*, I:ix). My book owes, however (and almost needless to say) much to these pioneering scholars, who had recognized a century ago that Holcroft is worthy of a study that places him at the center of attention. My own contribution offers a more sustained examination of many of his plays and personal convictions, as well as a detailed view, informed by the wealth of recent scholarship, of the social and cultural developments accompanying those dramas and the drama of his life as it unfolded. Politics, literature, sociability, and theatricality—for Holcroft was both a writer for the theater and a man caught up in his own self-fashioning—meshed together as a lived experience of revolutionary idealism.

As both Holcroft and Colby knew well, ostracism and subtle (or not-so-subtle) attacks find expression in varied ways. Holcroft acknowledged many of the attacks against him as they played out in a variety of media—in books, journals, and newspapers, or in more ephemeral forms such as the handkerchiefs whose designs etched him as a traitor following the Treason Trials.[36] This book, in documenting Holcroft's experience, presents an illustration of how political unorthodoxy was identified, threatened, and punished not only in major actions but also in seemingly minor ones that are far from innocuous when viewed in their aggregate. Alongside the ongoing assault, we will see the success of Holcroft's career in the theater, as even in the toughest of times he continued to premiere new work, for example the play *The Deserted Daughter*, in May 1795, half a year after his release from Newgate. In this tense period, he also saw revivals of earlier plays such as *The Follies of a Day* (1784) and *The School for Arrogance* (1791) both in June 1795, and *The Road to Ruin* (among its very many revivals) on 8 January of that year, a little over a month after his release from prison. In his triumph, too, he featured in print and ephemeral culture. As a counterpoint to the censuring handkerchief, lodged in Holcroft's memory but lost to present-day observation, a fan representing scenes from *The Road to Ruin* is preserved at the British Museum and is available to view on its website.[37]

Holcroft was well aware of the pressures he was up against in presenting new work so soon after his release from prison. How far did his beliefs sustain him against these attacks? Evidence from his diary, letters, and published accounts suggests that he persevered and believed, but felt the pressure and rethought at times the power of truth and transparency. This was the case when menacing reports followed him abroad to his exile in Paris, using the name "The Road to Ruin" as a kind of veiled threat. However, in untangling Holcroft's response to the pursuit of hostile adversaries and certainly in examining his life story, it is clear that we cannot know everything. The main challenge in writing a biographical account and especially the story of an individual enmeshed in and dependent upon a culture censorious towards oppositional opinion, is of course in accepting that some facts remain hidden. In writing about Holcroft, I share the eminent biographer Hermione Lee's fascination with both the "secret places of reserve"[38] as well as with the "ambivalence, self-consciousness and self-contradictions . . . [and the] unreconciled double-ness" of the biographical subject himself or herself.[39] These contradictions and ambivalences will appear throughout this study—for example in such issues as the vexed public or private nature of Holcroft's diary, the insistence on conspicuous performance and self-fashioning during the Treason Trials, the unfortunate and inexcusable anti-Semitism and complacency towards slavery that appear alongside (and taint) his otherwise valiant struggle for equality and social justice, and the "secret places" still impenetrable. In exploring these issues through a discussion of many of Holcroft's published plays and aspects of his life, I thus acknowledge those elements of his life half or wholly hidden, the tensions surrounding them, and the attempt to retrieve what can be discovered about them.

THOMAS HOLCROFT AND THE TREASON TRIALS

T HERE IS A WELL-KNOWN ACCOUNT of the first printing of Thomas Paine's *Rights of Man* that centers on a note, now held at the Bodleian Library, which Thomas Holcroft wrote to William Godwin upon the occasion: "I have got it—If this do not cure my cough it is a damned perverse mule of a cough—The pamphlet—From the row—But mum—We don't sell it—Oh, no—Ears and Eggs—Verbatim, except the addition of a short preface, which, as you have not seen, I send you my copy—Not a single castration (Laud be unto God and J. S. Jordan) can I discover—Hey for the New Jerusalem! The millennium! And peace and eternal beatitude unto the soul of Thomas Paine."[1] The event portrayed here, which finds Holcroft posing as a conspiratorial bookseller, shows him as he partakes of, and stages, the early energy of the revolutionary moment. The vocabulary I use to describe it—"posing" and "staging"—foregrounds his political engagement as it aligns with theatrical consciousness and careful self-fashioning in the early 1790s, at a moment when, despite the secrecy surrounding the book's publication, the reformist vision seemed attainable and could be celebrated in an enthusiastic rhetorical performance.

Conversation, community, theatricality, and sociability are never far from view amidst the dramatic events that defined this period and that shaped Holcroft's life; the excitement emerging from his note to Godwin is evident also in its sociable energy. The claim of ostensible denial, "but mum—we don't sell it—oh no," as if he (and Godwin) were really booksellers themselves, enables through the idea of a shared deception a view of the close friendship of Holcroft and Godwin, while also illustrating Holcroft's proximity to circles of bold political action and his affiliation with an "in-group" of radical men of letters. As Harriet Guest observes, this note exhibits a "supportive social network" that encourages and facilitates an "intensity of engagement," a "homosocial immediacy and intimacy of exchange."[2] Although there are anecdotal accounts that Holcroft was a member of a committee that shepherded the book through publication, these have not been substantiated.[3] Nonetheless, considering his identification with the principles expounded in *Rights of Man*, Holcroft's enthusiasm is certainly in place. The strength of his ideological investment, as well as his perspicacity regarding the importance of Paine's book, is clearly evident: his use of religious and millennial terminology, which is both ludic and at the same time heartfelt, appears as Paine is anointed to radical, reformist sainthood. The power of Paine's text, moreover, is acknowledged to be not only secularly spiritual but also physically restorative: if the publication of *Rights of Man* doesn't cure Holcroft's cough, nothing apparently will.

Throughout *Thomas Holcroft's Revolutionary Drama*, we will see many examples of the intensity of Holcroft and Godwin's political and cultural pursuits, illuminating a fierce friendship but also leading at times to disagreement and anger. This was certainly the case as they navigated a public sphere increasingly policed by repressive government authority as well as by popular lay vigilantism. Those developments would lead to actual incarcerations for publishing and selling radical reformist texts; among those arrested in later years were publishers J. S. Jordan and Joseph Johnson.[4] In that sense, the whimsically complicit, somewhat fanciful, "we don't sell it—oh no," appears as a privileged moment before the political, social, and cultural storm set in.

This chapter examines Holcroft's political engagement from the early excitement evident in his note to Godwin to the repercussions of his activism culminating in the Treason Trials of 1794. Whereas in other chapters of this book, I examine how politics entered the theater through contentious play texts, audience involvement, and (or despite) various configurations of censorship, in this chapter, I examine the ways that theater entered into politics. Part I of the chapter points to some intersections of politics and theatricality in the writings of Burke and Paine that illustrate the reach of the theatrical idea throughout the early 1790s. In Part II, I turn back to Holcroft's early years, before examining his engagement with the Revolution debate, in particular his embrace of Godwinian political philosophy. Part III examines Holcroft's involvement with the Society for Constitutional Information and the lead-up to his arrest and incarceration in Newgate Prison. In Part IV, I conclude the chapter by discussing the 1794 Treason Trials; Holcroft's arrest and his ordeal during that judicial test included his own studied performance of his ideological beliefs. The outcome of his political involvement and its aftereffects would shape the remainder of his life, as he continued to perform on the most prominent and public of stages.

* * *

In their roles as secretive booksellers whose exhilarated, euphoric pose anticipates the enlightened age of reform, Holcroft and Godwin are playing their part in its emergence. In doing so, Holcroft's note acknowledges, even if implicitly, the enmeshment of politics and theater—theatrical rhetoric, imagery, symbolism, and performance—in the revolutionary decade. That the theatre was a powerful, culturally crucial and much-beloved institution in Britain throughout the eighteenth century, is a point that hardly needs to be mentioned. Beyond the actual stage, Gillian Russell has shown how it offered linguistic analogies for the political discourse of this period but also provided the source for a repertoire of performative possibilities.[5] Its ubiquity is apparent in the variety of theatrical possibilities adopted by the 1790s activists—in their speeches, symbolic actions, sociable arrangements, and in the functioning of the reform societies. The events leading up to the 1794 London Treason Trials, the trials themselves, and Holcroft's place within them gestured to the theater and became a site of performance and were represented as such in reportage of events. One gets the sense that the reformers, at crucial, defining moments of their lives, saw themselves as performing on a vast stage, using metaphor, cultural citation, and physical exploit; through gestures, actions, allusions, vocabulary, and rhetoric.[6] This is the case, for example, in the Scottish radicals naming their 1793 gathering the "British Convention of the People"; in the way they addressed each other as "citizen"; in the manner in which they proceeded to the trial of the Scottish activist Maurice Margarot, carrying "a twenty-foot tree of liberty"; in Joseph Gerrald's revolutionary dress in his own trial; in the concluding of their reports with the French revolutionary song, "Ça Ira"; in the salute of Thomas Hardy, one of the chief defendants of the London trials, to his fellow prisoners at Newgate as he was taken each morning to the Old Bailey, when he pronounced: "Farewell, Citizens! Death or liberty."[7] A few years later, in debating the passage of the Treasonable Practices and Seditious Meetings Bills (the "Two Acts"), which limited freedom of assembly and speech, one of the bills' supporters referred, in a debate in Parliament, to the political clubs as "political theatres, and made the vehicles of sedition." The speaker then extended the analogy by referencing a previously legislated means of limiting free speech *specifically* in the theater, the 1737 Licensing Act, which "disables any theatre unlicensed . . . which has not the King's previous approbation."[8]

In his stirring response to the publication of *Rights of Man*, Holcroft had immediately foreseen that it was to be a crucial event, a pivotal moment, in the movement for reform in Britain and in the discursive engagement which had commenced with the publication of Edmund Burke's *Reflections on the Revolution in France* (1790). *Rights of Man*, written in clear, accessible language and focusing, as its title proclaims, on natural rights, as opposed to Burke's privileging of precedent, became amidst the variety of responses to Burke the most influential and the most celebrated, the target of government scrutiny on one hand and the motivating force for the present and emerging reform societies on the other.[9] Initially prepared by the publisher Joseph Johnson in February 1791, the printed text was withdrawn because of fear of government action. A month later, *Rights of Man*,

Part I was finally brought out by the radical publisher J. S. Jordan. *Rights of Man, Part II* was published in the following year, in February 1792, and then, three months later, in May, a cheap edition appeared, including both parts of Paine's treatise.[10] Now affordable for the widest swaths of the reading public, the book became even more dangerous in the eyes of the authorities.[11] Paine was subjected to the direct force of the government's response, escaping to France and then tried in Britain in absentia in December 1792. Holcroft, too, would become a target of government repression as one of the defendants in the London Treason Trials in the autumn of 1794. With these trials yet in the future—the literal ones emerging from the heightened anxiety regarding the reform movements, but also the figurative trials manifested in the ongoing confrontation with the "court" of public opinion—Holcroft's optimism at the initial publication of *Rights of Man* was as yet unhindered or untested in the crucible of personal experience.

Holcroft's emotional investment in Paine's book and his dramatic and dramatized note to Godwin following the news of its publication key into a wider cultural awareness, as writers who took part in both sides of the Revolution debate recognized the importance of the theater and the power of its attendant vocabulary in articulating their response to developments such as this. Thus, the pervasiveness of the theatrical allusions in Burke's *Reflections on the Revolution in France* and Paine's *Rights of Man* indicates how, in David O'Shaughnessy's words, the "theatrical aspect of political discourse was thrown into relief."[12] Burke, for example, decried the "great change of scene . . . magnificent stage effect . . . [and] grand spectacle" by which Revolutionary activists and supporters valorized the events in France and the energy of revolutionary actions.[13] In the same vein, the members of the National Assembly in France were portrayed as "comedians in a fair before a riotous audience . . . the gallery is in the place of the house."[14] This theatrical vocabulary underscores for Burke his consciousness of a world turned upside-down; the proceedings of that changed world are what he struggles against in his privileging of continuity, precedent, and tradition. In their disruption of the old order—the gallery in place of the house—the events in France are the "great drama" of *real-life* theatre in which, shockingly for him, all-too-real tragedies are played out. The tears generated by fictitious dramas acted by "Garrick formerly . . . [and] Siddons not long since" pale in comparison.[15] The near execution of Marie Antoinette in October 1789 manifested itself for him as the ultimate real-life tragedy, while the telling of it also became what Steven Blakemore calls "Burkean theatre."[16] Burke constructed a sympathetically sentimentalized, highly effective, and affective melodrama (before melodrama became known as such), which culminated in the famous retelling of the Queen's escape from "a band of cruel ruffians and assassins . . . to the feet of a king and husband, not secure of his own life for a moment."[17] His famous description of these events resonated widely and became, as history would prove, one of the most dominant and durable accounts of that tumultuous period in the autumn of 1789, when the monarchy and aristocracy lost their power to the revolutionaries and the National Assembly.

Thomas Paine similarly used the theatrical imagination and its associated vocabulary to critique Burke and the present monarchical system but also to align the theater with a new order characterized by openness and clarity. In both Part I and Part II of *Rights of Man*, theatrical symbolism is used to critique Burke's argument in general and specifically in relation to the events in Versailles and Burke's "dramatic license of putting the King and Queen in their places."[18] Paine also employs allusions to the theater in reference to his own political program. Thus, he asserts in Part II that the monarchy, "a silly, contemptible thing," is "something kept behind a curtain, about which there is a great deal of bustle and fuss, and a wonderful air of seeming solemnity; but when, by any accident, the curtain happens to be open—and the company see what it is, they burst into laughter."[19] Paine has turned absolute monarchy into a farce and, as Joseph M. Butwin has shown, *Rights of Man* is saturated with the language of comedy which Paine "invoked . . . as a corrective to aristocracy and monarchy."[20] In contrast to this "staged" comedy of absolutism, Paine argues, the "representative system of government . . . presents itself on the open theatre of the world in a fair and manly manner."[21] Paine's famous phrase suggests a transparency of action generated by a transformative reforming endeavor. As Gillian Russell explains, Paine "postulated a 'manly' theatre of the people" in which "the audience would not be subordinate to the performer but would in fact become the performance."[22]

Reforming activists embraced this possibility of being performers in their own drama. As shown earlier, a discourse saturated in theatrical vocabulary and symbolism accompanied their actions of daily life and at times of political momentousness, such as in the calling of each other "citizen." The activists' style (at least regarding some of them) was viewed pejoratively by E. P. Thompson as "self-dramatization"[23] and examined in a less critical way by James Epstein and David Karr as the "style and modes of theatricality."[24] Russell has shown how the practice of political performance took place on both sides of the ideological aisle; her revealing discussion of an incident in which Burke threw down a dagger in Parliament on 28 December 1792 during a debate on the Alien Bill exhibits how a gesture, a prop, and a performance opportunity are available as symbolic markers outside the theatre per se.[25]

Theater practices pervade culture as a whole; gestures, style, and studied actions would become crucial for the political developments of 1793–1794, in general, and in relation to the Treason Trials in Scotland in 1793 and in London in 1794, specifically. There, the connections between enactment, intent, and meaning, between words and actions, between stated desires and real outcomes, were interrogated.[26] These concerns would have wide-ranging implications as legal proceedings against the activists commenced. What William Godwin would later distinguish as "moral" and "tendency"—the tension between an author's intended instruction and the actual effect of the text on a reader, one that is difficult at the outset to predict—would be key to the judicial process when radical activists were put on trial.[27] In evaluating loyalty, protest, and possibly rebellion, intent and meaning were seen to have, by those with judicial authority, divergent and potentially sinister effects.

Questions of actions, intents, and meanings as understood and articulated by judges, juries, and publics, shaped the lives of the 1790s activists when they became the defendants at the Treason Trials, acting as major players in the great drama of their lives. Holcroft, among them, had a life story that included an abundance of real-life drama, preceding and culminating in his experience in the Trials, and he was indeed aware of it as such, as remarkable (*Life*: 1:8).[28] Along, then, with those detailed discussions of the later period of his life that are at the heart of this book, a brief biographical survey of Holcroft's early years is also in order.

* * *

Thomas Holcroft was born in London on 10 December 1745, the son of a shoemaker. At the age of six, his relatively comfortable working-class existence was shattered, as his father's finances collapsed and the family began to traverse the countryside as itinerant peddlers.[29] In the first seventeen chapters of his *Memoirs*, dictated as he lay bedridden at the close of his life, Holcroft vividly details these early years, with the energy, resourcefulness, and intelligence of the autodidact captivating his readers. After enduring much deprivation, he eventually found work as a stable boy at Newmarket, and then subsequent employment as a shoemaker, a teacher, and a personal assistant to the churchman and abolitionist Granville Sharp. From there, and indulging his love of drama, he applied to the provincial theaters, finding work—briefly and unsuccessfully—under Charles Macklin, then with Samuel Foote and in strolling theater companies, meeting, among others, Elizabeth Inchbald and the famous siblings John Philip Kemble and Sarah Siddons. Holcroft settled in London and in addition to acting, began to write. Among his first pieces were the play "The Crisis, or Love and Famine" (1778, not printed), the novel, *Alwyn, or the Gentleman Comedian* (1780), which was loosely based on some of his experiences as a traveling player, and an account of the Gordon Riots (1780) published under the pseudonym William Vincent. He also wrote poetry, including an elegy marking the death of Samuel Foote,[30] in addition to the hack work he did as a writer of short journalistic pieces and translations.[31] He later achieved marked success with his plays *Duplicity* (1781), *Seduction* (1787), and especially with his translation of Beaumarchais's *The Marriage of Figaro* as *The Follies of a Day* (1784).[32] We can imagine his sense of accomplishment in meeting the applause of the audience as he played the role of Figaro at the Covent Garden premiere.

Holcroft's domestic life is also worth briefly noting here. He was married four times and had ten children; his son, William, committed suicide in 1789, after running away from home with some of his father's money and possessions. His other children, whom we will encounter at various points throughout this book, were Ann (later Harwood), with his first wife, whose name, unfortunately, is lost; Sophy (later Cole) in addition to William, with his second wife, Matilda; Fanny, with his third wife Dinah; and six children with his fourth wife, Louisa Mercier: Villiers, Louisa, Thomas, Harwood, Henry, and Ellen.

Holcroft's collaboration with Covent Garden manager Thomas Harris, which began with *Figaro*, would continue throughout his life, and together with his earlier acquaintance with the Haymarket theater manager Foote (acknowledged in the publication of his poetic tribute) were markers of his participation in developing professional and sociable urban networks. Some of those persons, whom he met in his early London years, would remain Holcroft's lifelong friends, among them the musician William Shield; the future editor of the *Morning Chronicle*, James Perry; and the chemist William Nicholson. A biographical sketch of Nicholson, written by Nicholson's son in 1868, presents an appealing view of this circle in these early London years. "I have often heard my father talk about Porridge Island [a dining area in eighteenth-century London]," writes the younger Nicholson, "and I remember he and Holcroft laughing together about some joke or adventure at the island." Meeting at one of the cook shops there, the two friends and their companions would retire to a large upstairs room to eat, drink, talk, laugh, and relate anecdotes, their conversation displaying, as Nicholson, Jr. described it, "wit and intellect"[33] and surely the confidence and optimism of those who were in the process of becoming self-made men.

It was during this period when Holcroft was establishing himself as a writer that he met William Godwin, who was to be, for many years, his closest friend. *An Enquiry Concerning Political Justice*, Godwin's contribution to the Revolution debate published in February 1793, was shaped in part through conversations with Holcroft, which in turn influenced Holcroft in his life and writing. The *Enquiry* offered a broad survey of the state of British society and its injustices, along with a wide-ranging program for its philosophical, economic, legal, civic, and moral repair. Rather than an aggressive or belligerent overthrow of current systems, Godwin envisioned an ethical revolution that would emerge from the nonviolent exercise of "private judgment and the pursuit of the public good," which would then bring about universal reform.[34] Reform is gradual, and will occur when men and women abandon the doctrine of self-love; privileging the common good takes precedence over the promotion of individual and intimate concerns. "What magic is there in the pronoun 'my'"?[35] Godwin memorably asks, as he dismisses the allure of personal, self-directed motivations, focusing instead on working for the benefit of the larger community, promoting what Mark Philp calls "first-order impartiality."[36] The emphasis on gradualism is crucial; change is effected by nonviolent means, through conversation and learning, leading to perfectibility through the pursuit of truth, which in turn generates the ideal society. Social practices such as oaths, promises, punishments, laws, and, in the first edition of *Political Justice*, marriage are unnecessary, indeed hostile to the growth of such a society, as they bind to outdated circumstances rather than leading forward to organic change and improvement. In the ideal communities of conversation that Godwin envisions, government itself is as a result unnecessary; in its place he posits a philosophical anarchy, which, he states, "is generated by the hatred of oppression. It is accompanied with a spirit of independence. It disengages men from prejudice and implicit faith."[37] Eventually it leads to political justice.

Holcroft and Godwin had many conversations while Godwin was writing *Political Justice* between September 1791 and January 1793. As Godwin's diary shows, the two friends met very frequently during this period, almost daily—and frequently twice a day—for dinner, tea, and/or supper, most often following Godwin's morning work of writing and revision, and quite certainly discussing, among their many subjects, either just between themselves or with assorted company, the ideas appearing in Godwin's treatise as it was being written. To cite just a few of the many examples appearing in the diary: he started the New Year on 1 January 1792 by dining at Holcroft's and discussing with him and John Fenwick the subject of government and the law. On 13 May 1792, Holcroft and Godwin had supper with William Nicholson and discussed "immortality, abstraction, causation, majorities [and] promises." On 22 September 1792, at tea in the home of Alexander Jardine, Godwin, Holcroft, and others (among them Mary Wollstonecraft) talked of sympathy, perfectibility and self-love (GD). On these three occasions, Godwin had worked on his book in the morning; these subjects were surely on his mind. Many of them also resonated in Holcroft's texts; perfectibility in particular stands out as a concern that appears repeatedly in his writing. The idea prominently emerges through the fact that there are little, if any, punitive outcomes for wrongdoing in his plays and novels; appearing instead is the hope for, and conviction of, improvement. Writing of his own situation in his *Narrative of Facts Relating to a Prosecution for High Treason* (1795), the detailed, self-reflective account he published following his release from prison, Holcroft similarly differentiated between a "man," who may err but can correct himself and the "mistake" that should always be condemned: "the mistake is past recal [sic], but the man may amend" (NF, 80). This assertion appears as a kind of refrain in *Thomas Holcroft's*

Revolutionary Drama (and I reference it again later in this book), perfectly encapsulating Holcroft's belief in and implementation of Godwinian philosophy in his fictional work and in his own life.

*   *   *

Holcroft's public engagement would have extreme consequences as he sought to put Godwinian ideals into practice. He was, of course, part of a wider groundswell of groups, organizations, and individuals that seized upon the revolutionary moment to promote the reform of Parliament and British society, very often through a communal and sociable framework. There were many debating and political clubs in London at the close of the eighteenth century, as well as important and influential reforming organizations in other cities and towns such as Sheffield and Norwich. I focus here on the two most prominent reform societies located in the capital which were active in the 1790s, the London Corresponding Society (LCS) and the Society for Constitutional Information (SCI).[38] These associations were the crucial players in the struggle for parliamentary reform and in the events of the 1794 Treason Trials that later unfolded. The London Corresponding Society was in many ways the key organization of the period. It was composed mainly of artisans, tradesmen, and shopkeepers, what its leader, the shoemaker Thomas Hardy, called "the lower and middling class of society called the people."[39] This social makeup of its membership was what made it a new and compelling—and for many in the establishment, dangerous—force on the political landscape. Its members met to discuss and debate the politics of the day in public houses and taverns, at a membership fee of a penny per week. The Society of Constitutional Information, which Holcroft joined in 1792, was founded in 1780 by Major John Cartwright and reactivated in the early 1790s under the leadership of John Horne Tooke. It was more "polite," its dues at least one guinea a year, excluding a working-class membership.[40] It was comprised of landowners and urban professionals such as lawyers, journalists, and nonconforming ministers. The class distribution within the two political organizations, however, was not fixed and absolute. Gentleman radicals such as the lecturer and poet John Thelwall, the writer and reformer Joseph Gerrald, and the physician James Parkinson were members of both the SCI and the LCS, providing, especially in the latter organization, a kind of intellectual leadership.[41]

Change in class and status at the intersection of activism, community, and sociability is a crucial element in Holcroft's story.[42] Class movement, the awareness of which was always indelibly present for Holcroft and recognized by his supporters and detractors alike, is apparent also in the stories of other progressive activists—and just as Holcroft aspired upwards in his membership in the SCI, others privileged a different class flow. Let me digress then for a moment to offer another example of the permeability of class and status through the story of the poet and playwright Robert Merry, 1755–1798 ("Della Crusca"). Merry's career illustrates these fluid social boundaries as they received expression in the political societies and other activist associations in the 1790s, as well as affording a glance at how this class movement and flux was perceived by the public at large. Merry had commenced his political activism as a member of the elite Whig reform group The Friends of the People, before moving on to the Society for Constitutional Information, and finally becoming associated with a more radical working-class circle. For many observers, it was that latter development which left its impression. The newspaper *The True Briton*, for example, looking back on Merry's life, wrote that his radical political opinions caused him to "unite with people far beneath his talents, and quite unsuitable to his habits."[43] These comments evince the widespread anxiety over the dislodging of traditional class perimeters, of the sense that, as Jon Mee puts it, one could "become detached from a sense of belonging to the dominant culture of eighteenth-century Britain."[44]

Just as Merry's sociable association with men "beneath his talents" caused this upper-class unease, it was the idea of an actual working-class recruitment en masse into radical political activism—"the gallery . . . in place of the house"—that certainly frightened the establishment the most. That anxiety resonated in Burke's infamous comment in the *Reflections* about a society in which the nobility and clergy lose their preeminent place—when learning would be "trodden down under the hoofs of a swinish multitude."[45] That assertion resulted in the establishment of radical publications proudly acknowledging their own "swinishness"—*Hog's Wash* and *Pig's Meat*, to name just two[46]—the very retort to Burke celebrating the porcine nomenclature as a measure of resistance and self-worth. In the end Merry, regardless of his class identification and like so many other radicals, was frozen out of employment; he eventually emigrated to the United States in 1796 and died there two years later. Holcroft's career represents a move in the opposite direction, although he, too, would later go into (temporary) exile. He had been born into the working class and had known poverty; at times he had been close to starvation. By joining the SCI, he quietly embraced his upward mobility and the professional status he had earned through his writing and had acquired over the years, carving his identity as a man of letters in polite society, while meeting important contacts, including Captain (later Colonel) Harwood, the future husband of his daughter, Ann.[47]

The variances of political affiliation and class membership within and between the London Corresponding Society and the Society for Constitutional Information were accompanied by a sameness of purpose that is indicated in the different collaborations between the two societies during the heyday of their activities, in the period 1792–1794, when they frequently exchanged missives and statements of support. More concretely, as the SCI had made it its mission to publish and then disseminate *Rights of Man* throughout the country, the LCS began in the spring of 1792 to raise funds for Paine's defense, following his arrest in absentia.[48] Almost two years later, the SCI arranged for the printing of 40,000 copies of the speech of one of the LCS members, the radical attorney John Martin, who, in his "Address to the People of Great Britain and Ireland," had energetically articulated the idea of holding a British Convention. This vigorously worded address aroused the government's suspicion of what was perceived to be the societies' treasonable intentions.[49] The forming of a Committee of Conference made up of members of the LCS and the SCI to plan that convention would be construed by the authorities as part of that treasonous endeavor. The preoccupation with Paine, in all events, reflects the societies' recognition of the importance of his book and, together with the printing of Martin's speech, exhibits the shared understanding of the crucial role of print culture itself; motions announcing the specifics for wide dissemination of their writings and decisions are features of almost all meetings of the reform societies.

The alignment of print and reform is underlined in another dimension: Mee has shown that there was "a notable overlap" in SCI membership and involvement with the Literary Fund, an organization set up for the welfare and benefit of writers and literary professionals.[50] As Mee evocatively puts it in acknowledging the phenomenon more generally, the societies were under "the spell of print magic . . . a faith that print could liberate mankind simply by bringing ideas into printed circulation."[51] The idea that print could liberate was a key tenet of Holcroft's own beliefs; his life's project was dictated by his faith in print magic. His reformist principles were consciously promoted in his published work—his plays, novels, and, many years later, his autobiography (although he didn't live to see its publication)—where the first person narration stresses the political and didactic value of his message. Thus, for example, he remarks in the *Memoirs* on how the portrayal of his triumph over childhood hardship could serve as a "school of instruction, to bring forth hidden talent" (*Life*: 1:38); in his diary he acknowledges some "facts" that may "turn to use" (*Life*: 2:207); in the prefaces to the print editions of his plays *Knave, or Not?* (1798) and *The Lady of the Rock* (1805), he asserts the aim of affording "improvement to morals" and the conveying of a "public moral."[52]

Many years before these publications appeared, in 1791, Holcroft had recognized the weightiness and urgency of print magic with his excitement over the publication of Paine's *Rights of Man*. The following year, 1792, was a kind of annus mirabilis for him, as far as his engagement with print was concerned, with two of his most notable works appearing, the novel *Anna St. Ives*, which showcased his reforming ideas through the epistolary mode, and *The Road to Ruin*, which would become his most popular and well-known play and in which political ideas likewise appeared, albeit in a more subdued form.[53] *The Road to Ruin* was almost universally praised at its premiere and in later revivals, and its popularity was mostly detached from, and thus withstood, Holcroft's Treason Trials ordeal. *Anna St. Ives* also garnered critical attention although, at least in regard to the first reviews, its reception depended on the ideological propensity of the reviewing journal.[54] The wide attention to the reforming message of the novel in prominent literary journals underscores at the same time the popular reach of Holcroft (and Godwin) who, as Miriam Wallace puts it, conceived "their fiction as a way to engage common readers . . . with political reform through affective storytelling."[55]

It is clear, however, that through his membership in the Society for Constitutional Information Holcroft also sought to put reform into practice beyond the writing of politically inflected fiction and drama. He joined the SCI at the height of his authorial success, first attending a meeting on 12 October 1792 (*Life*: 2:27, n.1). In this case, it is important to note that his political activity represented a divergence from that of Godwin, who was highly suspicious of organized societies; the idea behind such organizations was in opposition to his vision of an organically emerging political and philosophical anarchy.[56] This extension of Holcroft's political engagement was accompanied by nervousness on his part. In the tense political climate of late 1792 and in the years that followed, his anxiety was certainly justified and would have extreme consequences for him.

The period of heightened suspicion effectually commenced with the establishment of the Royal Proclamation of May 1792, which called on "all loyal subjects to resist attempts to subvert all regular government"[57] and which was instituted in part as a response to the publication of *Rights of Man*. The Proclamation backfired in the immediate aftermath. It motivated Paine to publish his book in cheap editions and the London Corresponding Society to raise money for his defense when he was later charged. Membership in the Society for Constitutional Information increased. At the same time, the Proclamation did alert public opinion to the presence of radical activity and to "subversive propaganda."[58] As the year progressed, the tide turned against the reformers, especially in the provincial towns but also in London, with the events in France, such as the establishment of the Republic in August 1792 and the September massacres in the following month surely not helping the cause of the Revolution's British supporters. William Hazlitt, in recounting Holcroft's association with the SCI, vividly describes the social and political climate in this period following the Proclamation:

> Associations were formed, and the danger of the constitution, from the wicked attempts of republicans and levellers, became the cry of what was called the aristocratic party. So active were these self-declared friends of government . . . that quiet people began to partake of the fears of these agitators; [. . .] Men even of respectable characters and honest intentions now thought it an heroical act of duty, to watch the conduct of their intimate friends, excite them to utter violent or seditious expressions, and afterwards to turn informers . . . [People] supposed themselves watched by the very waiters [in the taverns where they congregated]. (*Life*: 2:36–38)[59]

Holcroft's friend, the author Amelia Opie, recalled a similar climate of suspicion in her native Norwich, which likewise illustrates the situation more generally: "To such a height had party-spirit reached on both sides, in my native city and elsewhere, that even innocent men were accused of treasonable intentions and practices, who *talked*, when excited by contradiction, the fearful things they—would never have thought of acting [emphasis in the original]."[60]

The apprehension described by Hazlitt and Opie was exacerbated for Holcroft by his fear for his livelihood as a writer. Frequently described in other contexts as assertive, argumentative, dynamic, and forceful,[61] in the SCI Holcroft is seen to be more reticent and subdued. In the *Narrative of Facts* he describes his time in the Society: "I never framed a single resolution, or excited others to the publication of any thing except of those facts that I believed would conduce to the well being of man. When questions were put, I sometimes voted; and sometimes spoke, to declare my opinion, but was much oftener silent; occasionally because I thought them frivolous, but more frequently because they were in my apprehension such a mixture of right and wrong as to leave me undecided (NF, 6)." Notwithstanding the fact of his inconspicuousness in the SCI and his ambivalence regarding the topics discussed there, Holcroft *was* present at the majority of meetings; his first attendance occurred, as noted, on 12 October 1792. That meeting was held, as they all were, at the Crown and Anchor Tavern, and it discussed British radical Joel Barlow's letter to the French National Convention.[62] Despite his emphasis on the limited extent of his participation, Holcroft took part, and voted, in meetings in which important motions with wide ramifications, such as support for a British convention, were affirmed. He was also, crucially as it turned out, a member of the doomed Committee of Conference, which was set up together with the London Corresponding Society with the aim of planning that convention. As John Barrell explains, the committee was "made up of six members of each society . . . the existence of this committee, [and] participation in [it] would be represented" at the Treason Trials in October as "an overt act of imagining the king's death,"[63] that is, an act of treason itself. Together with the authorities' claim for evidence of arms gathered to defend the convention, that threat of treason and insurrection would be deemed justifiable for indictment and trial by the authority of the law.[64]

In the end, the Committee of Conference appears to have met just twice,[65] and Holcroft was present at only one of those meetings. There, rather than deliberating over the minutiae of organizing a British convention, he took the opportunity to speak about a favorite subject of his—the powers of the human mind—and to stress the need for a peaceful resolution to war and conflict. As he later explained in the *Narrative of Facts*, directly addressing Attorney General John Scott: "I appeared at [the committee meeting] but once, and you had evidence that I then 'talked a great deal about peace; of my being against any violent or coercive means . . . that I urged more powerful operations of philosophy and reason, to convince man of his errors; . . . man might disarm his greatest enemy by those means, and oppose his fury, because truth is all powerful' (NF, 90)."[66] Holcroft notes here that his fellow committee members seemed to agree: "no person opposed my argument; and this conversation lasted better than an hour" (NF, 90). The "evidence" Holcroft refers to is that given by his friend, the engraver William Sharp, who was questioned by the Privy Council. Sharp had been among those arrested in the spring of 1794; he was released on bail in exchange for providing information.[67] Sharp presented a strictly factual account of Holcroft's actions and words; how, for example, his speech in the Committee of Conference addressed "the more powerful operation of philosophy and reason" and "was against violence of all kinds" (NF, 130). Comparing Holcroft's belief in nonviolence to that of a Quaker, he added that Holcroft, however, "did not believe in the secret impulses of the Spirit" (NF, 131). This account was presented to Holcroft following his request to Sharp for information regarding this interrogation. He recognized the exculpatory nature of Sharp's report, and the two men remained friends following the event.

Notwithstanding Sharp's evidence for the willing, energetic, authentic, and ideologically motivated oratorical contribution of Holcroft—his plea for nonviolence and peace—we can also see in Holcroft's actions surrounding the Committee of Conference a kind of diffidence, or reluctance, when it came to promoting the society's agenda outside the dimension of abstract talk. Thus, Holcroft missed one meeting of the Committee—the only delegate to be absent—(*Life*, 2:69) and, additionally, voiced an unwillingness to hold a conspicuous position in its proceedings, "as he did not wish further to injure himself in the Public Opinion by taking so open a part"(*Life*, 2: 69). This contradictory behavior—a noticeable speech (abstract though it was) at the Committee of Conference along with a stated reluctance *to be more active* in its deliberations—together with what he himself mentioned as an ideological uncertainty regarding various SCI motions more generally, is not easily resolved. Why call attention to oneself and then begrudge, or fear, that attention?

This inner conflict regarding his membership on the Committee, moreover, crucially anticipates Holcroft's later surrender, in October, to government authorities. William Sharp had been but one of over thirty individuals apprehended in May, June, and July of 1794. Beginning with the arrests on 12 May of Thomas Hardy, secretary of the LCS, and Daniel Adams, his counterpart at the SCI, members of five reform societies were charged with treason. This number included all the members of the Committee of Conference; one of these men, Thomas Wardle, evaded arrest, but the others, including John Horne Tooke, a prominent member of the SCI, and John Thelwall were detained. Tooke and Thelwall, along with Thomas Hardy, were the ones ultimately put on trial. The warrant for Holcroft, as a member of the Committee of Conference, had thus been written at this time as well but was *not* served.[68] In the *Narrative of Facts*, Holcroft would later claim, improbably, that he had actually been under suspicion because of an altercation with a police officer who was insulted because Holcroft had remarked that "violence was always a vice" (NF, 201).[69]

John Barrell argues that Holcroft's warrant, whatever the circumstances of its issuance, had been ignored because the government did not view his position seriously.[70] In all events, Holcroft lived his life anxiously but nonetheless in a routine manner in the period between May and October 1794. The specter of the unserved warrant always before him, during what he calls "the summer of the memorable 1794" (NF, 17), he decided to remain in London, taking care "to appear publicly, that it might be ascertained I had no desire to evade inquiry" (NF, 18). Even so, he received a hostile reception: "The timid shunned me, the moderate regarded me with an evil eye, and the violent never mentioned me but with virulence and odium" (NF, 62).[71] Tension had increased that summer with the suspension of habeas corpus on 7 May 1794. The fear arose that those arrested might not have their day in court; that evidence could be flung at them but not be subjected to judicial scrutiny.[72] The sociability of the "Godwin circle" nonetheless continued its course. Evidence from Godwin's diary shows that he and Holcroft continued to meet regularly, almost daily, and frequently to dine and sup together. They were joined by Robert Merry on a few occasions during this period for supper at Holcroft's home. Godwin frequently visited the detainees or their relations that summer—Thelwall and his wife, but also Joseph Gerrald, who was convicted of treason following the Scottish treason trials held earlier in the year and was in Newgate and later in the prison ship hulks awaiting transportation to Botany Bay.[73]

Godwin also took two trips outside of London that summer and fall, and it was on the second excursion, when he was in Warwickshire visiting the educator and minister Samuel Parr that he read in the *Morning Chronicle* of Holcroft's arrest.[74] Holcroft later explained that after days of conflicting rumors, he had finally heard that his name was read in the Bill of Indictment and he ran to "face [his] accusers" (NF, 22–23, 28). The *Chronicle* quotes at length Holcroft's remarks at the dramatic moment of his surrender to the authorities. Thus, he announced as he entered the Grand Jury meeting room at the Clerkenwell Sessions House:

> Being informed that a Bill for High Treason has been preferred against me, Thomas Holcroft, by his Majesty's Attorney general, and returned a true Bill by a Grand Jury of these Realms, I come to surrender myself to this Court, and my Country, to be put upon my trial; that, if I am a guilty man the whole extent of my guilt may become notorious; and, if innocent, that the rectitude of my principles and conduct may be no less public. And I hope, my Lord, there is no appearance of vaunting in assuring your Lordship, this Court, and my country, that, after the misfortune of

having been suspected as an enemy to the peace and happiness of mankind, there is nothing on earth, after which, as an individual, I more ardently aspire than a full, fair, and public examination.[75]

Barrell explains that Chief Justice Sir James Eyre tried to save Holcroft from himself, from "compromis[ing] his claim of innocence"; the judge repeatedly questioned the equivalence of name to person after he (Holcroft) identified himself as *the* "Thomas Holcroft" that had appeared on the indictment.[76] Nonetheless Holcroft disregarded Eyre's hints, insisting that it was he who had appeared on the bill. As a result, he was detained and sent to Newgate Prison. The *St. James Chronicle*, also reporting on the event, sought to explain Holcroft's behavior by implying that he was "not in any very imminent danger" and that he was "fond of speechifying," furthermore insinuating that, in turning himself in, he "had the idea of obtaining the reputation of a martyr at an easy rate."[77]

Why indeed turn oneself over to the authorities and then be arrested, if the warrant had been ignored by those very authorities? Why seek unnecessary trouble, especially when the charge is one for a capital offense? It was as if Holcroft knew, according to this account, there was not really a case against him; as if he knew he would not have to stand trial; as if, at this crucial moment, he imagined himself on stage, giving a speech in a performance. This appears to be the same pattern of behavior we saw earlier with the Committee of Conference, the membership in which brought Holcroft to this situation in the first place. It is as if he is caught in the realm of abstract ideas and their conspicuous expression without the necessary attention to their practical, real-world implications. He can indulge in an hour-long speech at the Committee of Conference on his favorite topic—the powers of the human mind—seemingly oblivious to the fact that the very forum in which he is speaking is supposed to be planning a radical British convention and most likely has been infiltrated by spies. Later, when trouble came, he can attribute the warrant for his arrest to the "vindictiveness" of an ostensibly insulted police officer, supposedly taking offense because Holcroft claimed that violence was a part of that officer's profession. Finally, in October 1794, facing Chief Justice Eyre, he presumably desires to go on trial, asserting that there is nothing more important than to "ardently aspire [for] a full, fair, and public examination." And in preparing for that examination, that trial, he can consider it, as he wrote to Godwin at the beginning of his incarceration, an event "that may be productive of so much general good"; a "nobler purpose" at which Holcroft and Godwin should aim (Clemit: 1:107).[78]

Holcroft wishes to promote a "general good" and a "noble purpose," even if ultimately it must be done through the dangerous, politically conspicuous gesture of turning himself in to the authorities and being imprisoned in Newgate. He "ardently" desires to perform his innocence—through words and deeds—as he strides into the jury meeting room, stubbornly reiterating his true identity to a judge who wants to save him. His subsequent imprisonment in Newgate may also be viewed as a kind of performance. Regarding the Newgate political prisoners, Iain MacCalman notes the way "newspapers probed intimate details of prison visitors, routines, and private life"; their incarceration increased their visibility. MacCalman quotes Lord George Gordon, imprisoned for his role in the 1780 riots that bear his name: "I am become one of the shows of London for strangers and foreigners to stare at."[79] The general awareness that they had become "one of the shows" features in Holcroft's and his codefendants' prison ordeal, showing the ubiquity of the theatrical imagination as it underpinned their judicial experience.

* * *

The pervasiveness of theatrical discourse and exploit in the public, political sphere has been influentially discussed and expanded upon with particular attention to the Revolution debate and the "war of ideas" in the 1790s, as shown earlier by Russell, Epstein, Karr, and others. These scholars note the prevalence of theatricality and performance-conscious actions, ranging from the deeds and writings of the members of the radical societies with their salutes and salutations to the dramatic actions of Edmund Burke in Parliament. In addition, Judith Pascoe has examined how a sense of literary performance characterizes, especially, early Romantic poetry, from Mary Robinson and the Della Cruscans to Wordsworth and Coleridge, while also devoting a chapter of her book to the 1794 London Treason Trials, where she discusses the "theatrical modes of representation" that feature prominently there.[80] More recently, John Bugg has expanded our understanding of Romantic poetry's theatricality to include the poet-prisoners during the Treason Trials, John Thelwall, John Augustus Bonney, and James Montgomery, noting how they "theatricalize their poetic utterances as though they are addressing an audience."[81] John Barrell and Jon Mee add the popular eighteenth-century genre of trial literature to this catalogue of 1790s literary performance-conscious writing. This genre included different mediated and edited accounts of legal proceedings, including subgenres of crime literature, often "breathless accounts" of dramatic topical events and, especially relevant for my discussion, another subgenre, that of "speeches that were never made," prominent among which is Holcroft's *Narrative of Facts*, including his "Address to the Jury, which the Court Refused to Hear."[82]

Newspaper reportage of the Trials was certainly crucial in foregrounding and intensifying the theatrical inflection that informed the proceedings, as well as in conveying essential information to the public. Amelia Opie, then the young Amelia Alderson, was highly sympathetic to the defendants, yet she referred to the trials as the "prospect of entertainment opening before [her]."[83] The lead attorney for the defense, Thomas Erskine, brilliant barrister as he was, was known also for the performative elements with which he conducted his cases, with popular publications emphasizing his "histrionics" and his ability to "win over the crowd," his occasional fainting and the melodramatic mien in which he conducted his defense.[84] The fact that, to use Pascoe's words, the trials were, "before all else, performances"[85] is underscored, moreover, in the way that those witnessing and recording events—and also those taking part in them—often presented their narratives as a kind of dramatic manuscript, with speakers' names or functions set off from the text, often followed by a colon or dash, and sometimes with stage directions and even asides added in parenthesized italics. In the final section of this chapter, I examine some of those various intersections of theatricality and political and judicial action as they appear in the Treason Trials, briefly addressing the course of the Trials themselves, as well as Holcroft's actions throughout the proceedings.

Let us take, for example, the account of Holcroft's release as presented in the *Morning Post* of 2 December 1794. His discharge from custody on 1 December followed the acquittals of Thomas Hardy on 5 November and then John Horne Tooke on 22 November, when Erskine used not only his forceful presentation of the faulty evidence but also his dramatic skills as he discredited the testimony of the government spies.[86] It became clear to the authorities that the case against the remaining detained men was untenable, except for the one against John Thelwall, against whom the loyalist press claimed for evidence that was "unusually compelling."[87] The others in the meantime were released. In reporting the discharge of Holcroft, along with John Augustus Bonney, Stewart Kyd, and Jeremiah Joyce, the *Morning Post* presents the events through the dialogue that ensued between Chief Justice Eyre and Holcroft. Thus, it relayed the proceedings:

> The jury immediately pronounced a verdict not guilty—and Messrs. *Bonney*, *Kyd*, and *Joyce* retired.
>
> MR. HOLCROFT:—GENTLEMEN of the Jury—
>
> CHIEF JUSTICE: You have been acquitted; and after such an acquittal, Mr. Holcroft, I do not see that there is great room afforded for observation. I should think it the best way to follow the example of those who have just retired.
>
> MR. HOLCROFT: Every man, my Lord, must act according to the best of his judgement; my judgement tells me that it is my duty to address a few words to the Court, thus openly in the face of my country, upon the hardships I have so undeservedly suffered.
>
> CHIEF JUSTICE: You have no right to address a word, Sir, to the Jury, after being acquitted in the manner you have just been; but I do not wish to hold you to that right, conduct yourself properly, and I shall have no wish to stop you.[88]

Chief Justice Eyre's leniency here derives most probably from the fact that he had anticipated just a few words from Holcroft. Upon hearing of Holcroft's plan for a speaking time of no "more than half an hour," his mood changed.

> CHIEF JUSTICE:—Half an hour! that is quite out of the question."
> MR. HOLCROFT: After having suffered the injustice and cruelty which I think I have suffered.
> CHIEF JUSTICE: You have been dealt with most honorably by the Attorney General. You ought not to complain of injustice, because, in doing so, you accuse your Country, who have put you on your trial. You can have no extraordinary hardship to complain of, you voluntarily brought yourself into custody, and have been treated mildly and honourably by the Attorney General. You must withdraw, Sir.
> [Here was a general cry of *Withdraw*][89]

After a further elaboration by Holcroft, the Chief Justice continued:

> CHIEF JUSTICE:—You had better take care, Sir, you may bring yourself into another scrape, after having been extricated from this.
> MR. HOLCROFT:—I am very willing to suffer in what I think right.
> *(Mr. Holcroft then retired, and sat among the Auditors in the Court.)*[90]

These proceedings were likewise reported in the other newspapers that day, but without the theatrical embellishments such as the verbal exchange mapped out as a play script and the speakers arranged as dramatis personae offering their parts, or their movements presented through added stage directions.[91] At the same time, the *St. James Chronicle* included in its report a related allusion: "the Playwright then, in the true theatrical spirit of his friend *Puff* the Critick, declared, as he could not speak, he would 'print the whole, and shame the rogues.'"[92] The aftermath of the charged dialogue between Chief Justice Eyre and Holcroft was preserved in artistic and historical memory by the painter Sir Thomas Lawrence. His sketch of Holcroft and Godwin side by side at the proceedings (see figure 1.1) following the Chief Justice's rebuke, "taken on the spot," as William St. Clair relates it, "vividly catches the spirit of earnest defiance with which they faced the greatest crisis in their lives."[93] I have chosen to use Lawrence's sketch also for the cover of this book—the "earnest defiance" exhibited in the courtroom and then memorialized by Lawrence, encapsulating the essence of Holcroft's revolutionary drama.

As with his speech at the Committee of Conference and again when turning himself in to the authorities at the Clerkenwell Sessions House, Holcroft embraces in this courtroom a performance opportunity, seemingly sidelining the danger of his situation when the alternative was to actualize his ideological iden-

Figure 1.1 Sir Thomas Lawrence, *Thomas Holcroft; William Godwin,*
© National Portrait Gallery, London

tity in front of an attentive audience. And once again he extolls the value of print
magic when vowing to "print the whole" of his intended speech, which he did, as
the *Narrative of Facts*. Characteristically, he promotes the power of truth, now,
as in the earlier instances, at a high degree of risk to himself. This was not "speechifying," to use the *St. James Chronicle*'s term of almost two months earlier regarding

Holcroft's surrender to the authorities, but *speaking*, promoting truth, putting into practice his deepest beliefs. Pascoe joins other commentators on these events when she views Holcroft's actions as "a duty . . . carried to a humorous extreme," while claiming that she doesn't mean to "belittle him," recognizing also the urgency and authenticity with which he "translate[s] private suffering into public performance."[94] Yet her apophasis (saying she is not belittling Holcroft but pointing in that direction) also signals the way his actions—the depth of his Godwinian belief in truth, transparency, communication and conversation, and the willingness to implement that belief at this and other critical junctures—clash with our own (non-Godwinian) judgments and sensibilities and, unintelligible to the uninitiated, appear incongruous and thus potentially humorous when actually put into practice.

The Trials concluded only following the acquittal of the final defendant, John Thelwall on 5 December, when again Erskine managed to discredit key witnesses. Although Thelwall's literary and public pursuits were mostly different from Holcroft's—he was a lecturer, a charismatic public speaker, a poet, and, later in life, an elocutionist—he and Holcroft shared an understanding of the power and possibilities of performance, as well as those of print magic, in their engagement with reform.[95] In his publication, *The Tribune* (1795), in the volume published some months after his release from prison, Thelwall recalls his arrest on 13 May 1794, the day following that of Hardy and Adams, and presents the event as a highly charged drama, which it really was, even without the later thespian inflection. That night, following an emergency meeting of delegates of the LCS, as Thelwall was leaving his house, he was met by the spy, James Walsh, and other persons.[96] Thelwall describes the encounter:

> WA: Mr. Thelwall, I believe, *[offering his hand.]*
> TH: The same.

Upon which the rest (among whom were *Tims* and *Schaw* the Messengers *King*, secretary to *Dundas*, and *Carpmeal*, one of the Bow Street Runners) came up.

> TIMS: Then Sir, you are my prisoner *[Tapping me on the shoulder.]*[97]

Thelwall intersperses other "theatrical" dialogues later in this account, including a meeting with a mysterious, high-ranked gentleman while he was held at an office in Downing Street, a development which adds an additional degree of suspense and a gothic flavor to the narrative. Moreover, as it turns out, following his imprisonment, trial, and acquittal, he also wanted, like Holcroft, to address the court. "'I'll be hanged if I don't,' he told Erskine; 'You'll be hanged if you do,' was Erskine's reply."[98]

Neither Thelwall nor Holcroft was hanged, although both men continued to experience the aftereffects of their experience. In addition to his trial, Thelwall's role in the protest against the Two Acts in 1795 led to increasing hostility toward him and eventually to an internal exile, his profession as a public speaker also damaged as a result of the Acts' prohibition of large gatherings.[99] Holcroft left Britain for exile in Germany and France in 1799, and remained there until 1802. To their detriment, the public who read their books and listened to their arguments (and in Holcroft's case, attended his plays) had a good memory, and a long one. Holcroft's anxiety in the spring of 1794 regarding possible damage to his career, the fear of "further . . . injur[ing] himself in the Public Opinion" as a result of his political activity was thus a correct assessment in hindsight, with the arrest and court experience creating a far greater notoriety and inflicting far more damage than he would have first imagined when commencing his SCI involvement. After the heights of success in 1792 with *Anna St Ives* and especially *The Road to Ruin* (which, however, continued to be performed), it would be many years before the return of that public praise, finally coming when his play *A Tale of Mystery* (1802) became a huge success on the London stage and the aesthetics of melodrama, a new theatrical genre, captured the public's attention.

A Tale of Mystery was a stage melodrama. The moral and ethical struggle accompanied by the heightened and extreme response that melodrama captures and characterizes had earlier been present in a more diffuse sense in the 1794 Treason Trials, their buildup and aftermath. That event in itself had been preceded by a general embrace of the vocabulary and gesture associated with the theater, from the beginning of the British response to the French Revolution and the publication of the two major texts that most prominently articulated the key issues and values at stake: Burke's *Reflection on the Revolution in France* and Paine's *Rights of Man*. The ongoing engagement with the Burke-Paine debate and its different variations seemed to privilege the theater as conducive, through its vocabulary and repertoire of actions, for expressing the key tenets of this war of ideas and their manifestations in the public sphere. Of course, the engagement with drama as real-life activity, or with real-life activity as drama, was not limited to the 1790s. Writing in *Middlemarch* (1871–1872) of another age of reform, the period leading up to the passage of the Great Reform Bill of 1832, George Eliot observed that "they are fortunate who get a theatre where the audience demands their best."[100] I doubt that Holcroft considered himself fortunate as he struggled against the charge of treason, against the ultimate penalty, and through the remainder of a life in which he strove to rehabilitate his career. He *did* face, however, an exacting audience which demanded "his best," and he performed on the stage on which they viewed him with an energy of conviction that aimed to supply it. Although many observers failed to hide their disdain, or conceal their smirks, at what appeared to be his clear disavowal of caution or probability, he nonetheless represented a particular radical system of belief as a noticeable and memorable public presence. This resolve would face numerous challenges throughout the coming years, and would mainly be played out in the original and central arena for the expression of theatricality, which is, to be sure, the theater itself. But before we consider Holcroft's dramatic writing in the aftermath of the Trials, it is necessary to go back to examine his most illustrious and durable success, *The Road to Ruin*. Just as the Treason Trials experience signaled the start of his notoriety, that play ensured his ongoing fame.

THE ROAD TO RUIN AND ITS AFTERLIVES

IN OCTOBER 1905 *SAINT GEORGE,* a periodical subtitled "a national review dealing with literature, art and social questions in a broad and progressive spirit," published an essay, "A Group of Revolutionaries," which sought to recover for its early twentieth-century readers some of the leading radical literary figures of the 1790s. In words that seem to foreshadow the critical endeavor of opening up the literary canon that emerged at the *end* of the twentieth century, the writer of the piece, A. M. Williams, argues that the "effect in this country of the theory and practice of the French Revolution is familiar enough to the general student of literature who knows his Wordsworth and Coleridge, his Southey and Scott, but there are obscurer names of that troubled period which deserve to be rescued from oblivion."[1] Williams focuses on William Godwin, Mary Wollstonecraft, Robert Bage, and Thomas Holcroft as those members of that "group of revolutionaries" worthy of his readers' attention. He presents biographical and literary summaries with quite interesting presumptions (for a twenty-first-century reader) as to his contemporaries' knowledge of the texts mentioned in his survey, while exhibiting varying degrees of sympathy with the writers under discussion. Williams's treatment of Godwin is singularly harsh: he asserts that "the works by which he [Godwin] hoped to secure remembrance [have] fallen from esteem and almost from knowledge" while Godwin himself maintains "a parasitic immortality" due solely to the efforts of the "Shelley cult."[2] He is much more sympathetic to the other authors appearing in the essay. Thomas Holcroft receives an especially favorable account, one which extends, in marked contrast to his close friend Godwin, to the assumption of popular approval. Williams proclaims Holcroft "a remarkable" man, "whose name at least is known to playgoers as the author of the lively comedy, 'The Road to Ruin.'"[3] Williams's essay thus represents one later view of the 1790s struggle for reform and its intersection with the history of drama, theater, and performance, marking the ongoing shift in the collective cultural memory of what survives and what has been forgotten, of what is valued and what is disparaged. A glance at the current twenty-first-century view of these two writers reveals a different hierarchy of familiarity and reception. Godwin is widely known and studied as a pathbreaking philosopher and novelist; Holcroft is much less visible in the field. We cannot assume, as in 1905, knowledge of him amongst "playgoers," or general acquaintance with *The Road to Ruin*.

A. M. Williams recognizes *The Road to Ruin* as Holcroft's greatest achievement, as a play known to all who attend the theater, and Williams himself might have seen one of the many revivals produced at the close of the nineteenth century. But what made the play so beloved? A key to its popularity lies most certainly in the fact that although far from oblivious to the French Revolution, the play's politics were nonetheless much more subdued than in Holcroft's other works of the revolutionary decade. His more general critique of financial corruption and greed, along with the play's theme of intergenerational strife and reconciliation, engaged universal concerns. A former actor himself, Holcroft knew well how to craft roles for the stage, and *The Road to Ruin* was a vehicle for much-loved and well-remembered performances. The play's success ensured that for the most part it rose above the animosity directed towards Holcroft in the years following the Treason Trials, although it also functioned—such was its success—as a synecdoche for him in perilous contexts.

In examining *The Road to Ruin* as a major theatrical success, my argument has both a synchronic and a diachronic focus, as I discuss the play in the context of its original performances, as well as its afterlife within a broader theater history. I first look closely at the play itself, its original reception and its engagement with contemporary and universal themes, calling attention along the way to Holcroft's use of stock dramatic characters such as the amorous older woman and the stage Jew. I then trace its revival throughout the nineteenth and early twentieth centuries, concluding with its adaptation into silent film. In doing so, I suggest a cultural-historical development whereby the radical theater of the late eighteenth century would come to be inscribed as the "old English comedy," innocuous, comfortably nostalgic, at times fashionably melodramatic, but nothing more. Yet this arc of success has at the same time a limited trajectory. Holcroft *did* eventually recede from view, and we can no longer assume, with A. M. Williams, that his name "at least is known" as the author of *The Road to Ruin*. Nonetheless, through the study of his most famous play emerges a surprising longevity recovered from the historical record, and with it, a new view of Holcroft's dramatic legacy, the afterlives of the revolutionary drama and, to a certain extent, the 1790s reform activism and its place in cultural memory.

* * *

In my discussion of *The Road to Ruin* I employ Jacky Bratton's concept of "intertheatricality," which she defines as a theatrical intertextuality that seeks to articulate the mesh of connections between all kinds of theatre texts, and between texts and their users. It posits that all entertainments, including the dramas, that are performed within a single theatrical tradition are more or less interdependent. They are uttered in a language, shared by successive generations, which includes not only speech and the systems of the stage . . . but also genres, conventions, and, very importantly, memory. The fabric of that memory, shared by audience and players, is made up of dances, spectacles, plays and songs, experienced as particular performances—a different selection, of course, for each individual—woven upon knowledge of the performers' other current and previous roles, and their personae on and off the stage.[4]

An obvious example of intertheatricality would be attendance at a performance to see a specific actor play a particular role on the basis of ongoing reputation and collective cultural memory, just as much, if not more, than to view the play itself, an eighteenth-century instance being the way the public flocked to see Sarah Siddons perform the role of Lady Macbeth.[5] This tendency is apparent in *The Road to Ruin* as well, as spectators queued up to see actors such as William Lewis or Charles Mathews perform Goldfinch, Holcroft's brilliant comic creation, or to view Joseph Munden play Old Dornton, the ardent and benevolent father, a performance memorialized by Charles Lamb in the Elia essays.[6] The actors themselves, aware of the popularity of these roles, often chose them for their benefit night performances (Genest 7:103, 106). The theatrical customs and practices surrounding *The Road to Ruin* were robust and, to use Bratton's terminology, "intertheatrical": a critic for *The Academy* wrote in 1873 that, "to the acting of this work, there are attached countless traditions, so that the players find themselves the inheritors of ready-made parts, which it is undoubtedly their business to alter and improve as they can."[7] When some years later the actor and theater manager Edward Compton played a "double"—the role of Goldfinch as well as that of the young male lead, Harry Dornton—he was surely seeking to foreground his acting credentials and to place himself in a comic tradition; the blurb on the playbill of 26 March 1886 for his company's production of *The Road to Ruin* at the Grand Leeds Theatre proclaimed that Compton's acting was "[i]mmediately pronounced by the London Press and Public to be the most remarkable 'double' successfully attempted." This advertisement enticed potential spectators through the promise of witnessing artistic prowess just as much, if not more, than in its offering the opportunity to experience the plot, themes, and ideas of the play itself. The assertion that Compton's performance is "the most remarkable double" references that feat—the "double"— as one with a history and tradition of its own, knowable to the readers of the playbill.

Just as it marks continuities, I am also interested in what intertheatricality can tell us about divergences and digressions—what has been retained in theatrical tradition but also what has been erased. A telling example of discontinuity in relation to 1790s radicalism on the stage would be George Washington's attendance at two performances of another very successful reformist comedy, Elizabeth Inchbald's *Every One Has His Fault* (1793), in Philadelphia in 1794. There is no record that the president was anything other than oblivious to the play's noted radical tendencies, which were later clearly acknowledged back in Britain in a performance of that play in which a group of Portsmouth soldiers rioted.[8] An instance of the same kind of dislocation is apparent in the 8 January 1795 production of *The Road to Ruin*: Holcroft had been released a little over a month earlier, on 1 December 1794, from Newgate Prison, after the collapse of the government's case in the Treason Trials. The seriousness of the charges against him and the prominent attention given to the trials did not stop Covent Garden manager Thomas Harris (himself closely associated with the Pitt government) from staging the play or the public from going to see it.[9] This is likewise the case with the 3 June 1794 performance of the play, a time when many of Holcroft's associates had been arrested and he was in a kind of limbo, waiting for his own warrant to be served.

The Road to Ruin was performed regularly throughout the remainder of Holcroft's life, and through the first part of the twentieth century, in London, in the provincial theaters, and around the world. Three weeks before his death in March 1809, there had been a production of the play in Bath (Genest 8: 156). Such was the fame of *The Road to Ruin* that the mesh of connections between this text and its users—again to use Bratton's formulation—did not often extend, within the context of its production, to include any acknowledgement of Holcroft's political activities. The production of the play at Covent Garden in January 1795 seems to have taken place in a performance space that by the evidence of a successful box office take—£221.11. 6—was oblivious of or at least willing to ignore his political notoriety.[10] As Judith Milhous has shown, £167 was the break-even point for the theater box office at the beginning of the 1790s, and we can assume that it had not risen too substantially above that figure by mid-decade; a London audience was clearly happy to view the play.[11]

At the same time, the political connection *was* established elsewhere, outside of the theater. Robert Dighton's *Five in the Morning* (1795), one of a set of four prints illustrating a dandy's life at various points of the day and night, shows the young man, inebriated and disheveled, helped into his carriage by three members of the Watch (see figure 2.1).[12] Appearing against the backdrop of the Covent Garden arcade, the man steps on a playbill, ostensibly a remnant from that night's performance, advertising: "At Covent Garden on Wednesday December 1, 1794 The ROAD to RUIN." The phrase "the road to ruin" was often used as a catchphrase for the overindulgence in and addiction to drinking. (Today there is a "Road to Ruin" walking tour in London in which the public is invited to "discover the relationship of Londoners and their alcohol."[13]) In that sense it might be an apt

Figure 2.1 Robert Dighton, *Five in the Morning*, © The Trustees of the British Museum

allusion to the dandy's condition. Holcroft's *Road to Ruin* was *not* performed, however, on 1 December 1794. Instead, Frederick Reynolds's comedy *The Rage* was the main piece at Covent Garden that evening, followed by Byrn's *Hercules and Omphale* (Ransom). 1 December 1794 was the day, rather, when Holcroft, with other defendants, was released from prison and the charges of treason against him were dropped. Why choose 1 December for the fictional playbill? Could this date have been chosen by chance? If so, it establishes an eerie coincidence. Or perhaps it was intentional—and in connecting the play with physical and moral decrepitude, Dighton is likewise acknowledging the zeitgeist of 1795 and alluding to a personal, sinister "road to ruin," the ruin being Holcroft's own.

The play's name reappeared, now explicitly invidious as a shorthand for Holcroft himself, in *The Times*, on 26 January 1802, while Holcroft was living in a self-imposed exile in Paris. Announcing to its readers the presence in Paris of "one of the *'soi-disant'* twelve Apostles of Liberty" (the twelve defendants in the 1794 London Treason Trials), the newspaper furthers its identification by stating that this "Informer, who though once in the *road to ruin*, is now in the high way to fortune."[14] Holcroft recognized the allusion, and wanted to take legal action against the newspaper. That incident will be discussed later in this book; for now, it is important just to note the seamlessness of the identification between the "apostle of liberty" and the "road to ruin," as it straddles theater and politics, life and art, past triumph, and present distress. In positing the interchangeability between Holcroft and his best-known work, *The Times* seems assured that its readers would make the connection in the aftermath of the Trials and amidst the climate of suspicion and retaliation.[15]

A more benign though likewise telling connection between the playwright and his play appeared in Holcroft's obituary. On 27 March 1809, the *Morning Post* concluded its brief account of his life by noting "his literary efforts, which are many and respectable. *The Road to Ruin*, however, is the only dramatic production of his pen that experienced much success. His political sentiments are well known."[16] This obituary calls attention to how Holcroft's theatrical legacy and his politics are both linked and disengaged in cultural memory. Just as he assumes the general public's familiarity with Holcroft's radical past, the writer for *The Morning Post* also acknowledges the resounding success of *The Road to Ruin* and its durability in the theatrical repertoire. Although this obituarist does not make an explicit connection between politics and drama, their proximity in his account exhibits both the power of the theater and the equally strong persistence of a radical reputation and thus, once more, the linkage between them.

* * *

The Road to Ruin is no longer universally known, so a brief plot summary is in order. Mixing social satire with sentimental domestic drama, the play tells the story of Mr. Dornton, the owner of a successful London banking house, and his son Harry, whose extravagant lifestyle and excessive gambling threaten to bring financial ruin to his father's bank. Made aware of the imminent collapse of the bank and the severity of the threat to his family's name and livelihood, Harry tries to rectify the situation by mercenarily marrying the rich Widow Warren, although he is actually in love with her daughter, Sophia. At this time, it also transpires that a will had been made by the widow's late husband, which would take away her share of the inheritance should she remarry, leaving the fortune instead to Sophia and to his natural son, Milford, who is Harry Dornton's friend. This will was mistakenly delivered to Mr. Silky, an unscrupulous moneylender, ostensibly a Jewish man, instead of to Mr. Sulky, the legitimate executor and Dornton's partner at the bank. Complicit in this financial intrigue is Goldfinch, a Newmarket jockey who joins forces with Silky and Mrs. Warren to complete the deception by marrying the widow himself. (She herself is more receptive to the opportunistic advances of young Harry.) Eventually the plan is exposed, and all ends happily: Harry is united with Sophia and reconciled with his father, and the bank is saved from ruin.

The Road to Ruin was favorably received at its premiere on 18 February 1792. As opposed to the intricacies of the financial plot, what stood out to reviewers and audiences was the sentimentality of the father-son relationship, along with the critique of gambling and conspicuous consumption amongst the social elite. The character of Goldfinch also received wide attention, soon becoming the talk of the town. As Elbridge Colby put it, Goldfinch's catchphrase, "that's your sort," "resounded in all the drawing rooms of London . . . and drew applause and laughter from theatre audiences for over a hundred years" (Life: 1: xxvii–xviii). The role of Goldfinch offered actors a vehicle in which to showcase their comic abilities, and, in fact, in a larger view, it can be said that this is an actor's play. Elizabeth Inchbald wrote in her remarks for Longman's The British Theatre that The Road to Ruin excelled in what she calls the "dramatic science," which crafts "character, scenes and dialogue" rather than spectacle.[17] Indeed, the acting of the original cast was universally praised in the first reviews, the London Recorder or Sunday Gazette remarking that "with such acting . . . [the play] will prove the Road to Wealth to the Manager—and we hope also to the Author."[18] Yet offering the opportunity to view good acting was but one aspect that preserved the popularity of this work. Thematic concerns such as the pernicious effects of gambling and the presentation of an emotionally charged intergenerational relationship also enabled the play to transcend its original moment, while the echoes of a revolutionary awareness, as well as the presence of the problematic characters of the widow and the stage Jew, plant it firmly on the eighteenth-century stage.

I wish now to briefly consider Holcroft's portrayal of the amorous older woman and the avaricious Jew, the two stereotypes that cast a pall on his otherwise benevolent, compassionate, and exuberant story of reconciliation and reform and thus to acknowledge those who are left out of his revolutionary equation. Holcroft's construction of the widow and the Jew indicates his reliance on standard character types linked to pervasive prejudices, showing him, in this respect at least, simply to be a man of his time. The Saturday Review, in a commentary on a revival of *The Road to Ruin* that appeared many years later, would note the "Wanton Widow" as one of many "stage types and conventionalities" that Holcroft used in the play,[19] a type that had its source in works such as Thomas Betterton's *The Amorous Widow* (1670). As Barbara J. Todd has observed, most stage widows were "drawn as foolish, pathetic characters . . . who anxiously sought a husband at any cost." However, theirs was also a paradoxical situation: as unmarried women they were a threat to the patriarchal order, and were expected to remarry, but if they did so, they were likewise criticized. A remarrying woman reminded men of the possibility that when they died, they too would be replaced by another.[20] (The Widow Warren's late husband, who stipulated in his will that she should lose her share of the inheritance should she remarry, is anxiously acknowledging that possibility.) These attitudes were part of a larger cultural ambivalence. Devoney Looser has examined the many stereotypes associated with older women—both single women and widows—in the eighteenth and nineteenth centuries. Among many other examples, she discusses the public fascination with the epistolary relationship between an older Hester Thrale Piozzi and the young actor William Augustus Conway. The possibility of a love affair between the octogenarian Piozzi and the twenty-seven-year-old Conway and the debate about their letters "titillated" readers for decades.[21] Holcroft's depiction of the Widow Warren's attraction to young Dornton, many years her junior, would have drawn upon the same fascination and anxiety, which would have had an outlet in the same titillation and laughter. It is worth noting here that, in his treatment of Sophia, the widow's daughter, who is Harry Dornton's true love interest, Holcroft also presents a somewhat stereotypical portrayal of a kindhearted young woman, spirited yet blissfully naive. The character was well received throughout the years, with Anne Brunton Merry garnering praise for her performance in that role in the original production.[22]

Holcroft's depiction of the moneylender, Silky, once again relies on culturally entrenched stereotypes. Identified repeatedly as a Jew (but denying it himself), Silky is the crucial figure who puts into motion the financial deception; the documents which should have gone to Mr. Sulky, in a mix-up caused by the similarity of names, arrive to him instead. Silky is one of many "stage Jews" that appeared from the mid-eighteenth century on the British stage. Michael Ragussis has brilliantly analyzed this phenomenon, arguing that the proliferation of these characters resulted from two competing cultural developments. On one hand, from the beginning of the eighteenth century, "a new, secular, sanitized image of the Jew was installed at the heart of a specific ideology about Englishness and commerce" and was central to England's identity as a nation of "liberty and tolerance." Yet in 1753, the proposed legislation of the "Jew Bill," which would have made naturalization easier for foreign-born Jews, led to a "national hysteria"; an outcry "at the thought of being overwhelmed by Jewish influence in every sphere of life." The "Jew Bill" led to a reactionary discourse that infiltrated print media and found a presence on the stage as well, leading, in the final decades of the eighteenth century to a wide range of representations of Jews in the British theater.[23] Holcroft's Silky joins many other "money-mad stage Jews" as markers of English anxieties over finance and commerce, upward mobility and national identity.[24] But Silky is not alone in Holcroft's oeuvre. In *Duplicity*, which also deals with the issues of gambling and financial speculation, there are a number of derogatory references to Jewish moneylenders. In *The Vindictive Man* (1806) there is a Jewish character who is treated more kindly but whose heavy, stereotyped accent is central to his presentation as a comic figure. Holcroft's novels *Anna St. Ives* and *Hugh Trevor* also include passing, stereotypical references to Jews. In his travel narrative *Travels from Hamburg, through Westphalia, Holland and the Netherlands to Paris* (1804) Holcroft includes some unflattering descriptions of Jews he met during his journey.

Holcroft had begun his career in the theater as an actor in the company of Charles Macklin, the actor and playwright, who, Ragussis argues, is the central figure through which to understand "the politics of ethnic identity in the Georgian theatre and Georgian culture generally."[25] Macklin not only memorably performed a wide range of ethnic characters on stage (including a groundbreaking Shylock) but also, as a writer, was influential in interrogating the newly heterogeneous British culture. His *Love à la Mode* (1759) was crucial to the development of the "multiethnic spectacle": in the play, he assembled a cast of ethnically diverse characters (Scottish, Irish, English, and Jewish) together on stage—as suitors vying for the hand of the heroine, in what is a farcical reworking of act one, scene two in *The Merchant of Venice*.[26] Holcroft's close association with Macklin at the formative stages of his thespian career must have influenced his own use of multiethnic stereotypes, including his troubling presentation of Jewish figures. Conversely, his close friends Godwin and Inchbald responded much more positively to the subject, displaying sympathy towards Jews, rather than prejudice.[27]

Play scripts from later revivals of *The Road to Ruin* have not survived, and it is difficult to know how this issue was represented on stage in the late nineteenth and twentieth centuries. The text for the 1949 BBC radio drama *is* extant and is housed in the BBC archives. In that production Silky's religion is not debated, but after his refusal to lend Goldfinch money, the latter says, "then some other Jew must."[28] The line is jarring, and incongruous with this otherwise sprightly adaptation, which keeps all the main scenes and speeches. Much of the dialogue is truncated, however, and the political awareness, appearing mainly in the scene with young Dornton's creditors, and which stood out even in later productions, is subdued.

Holcroft's Jewish characters emerge from the wider social landscape of late eighteenth-century Britain and its fraught financial ecology. In Todd Endelman's words, "the mania for gambling [during this period] sent scores of well-connected young men in search of Jewish moneylenders."[29] Gambling was a central concern for Holcroft. It was the catalyst for the dramatic events in *The Road to Ruin*, and the subject was also addressed elsewhere in his oeuvre, such as in *Duplicity*, in his novels *Hugh Trevor* (1794–1797) and *The Memoirs of Bryan Perdue* (1805) and in his own *Memoirs*, where he provides a detailed account of an early experience when, as an apprentice at Newmarket, he had been led to bet on the horses; looking back years later he remembered well his feelings of "anguish" and "despair" at losing a substantial sum of money (*Life*, 1: 110).[30] As Marilyn Morris has shown, gambling was a much-discussed subject in the late eighteenth century, its prominence as a topic of contemporary discourse deriving in part from the widespread reportage of the Prince of Wales's financial difficulties and extravagant lifestyle. The financial affairs of the royal family were often presented in the print media as a domestic drama with "George III as a bourgeois paterfamilias and his sons as aristocratic libertines."[31] *The Road to Ruin's* topical referentiality in this context would have been heightened with the inclusion of the character of the Newmarket jockey, Goldfinch. The Prince of Wales had been caught up in a turf scandal in 1791, the previous year, following which he never raced at Newmarket again.[32] And yet none of the newspaper reviews of *The Road to Ruin* acknowledged a connection between the play's condemnation of financial profligacy and the royal family, perhaps because the young Dornton is portrayed consistently as a loving and affectionate son, despite his faults, thus distancing the character from the prince. Instead, reviewers concentrated on the criticism of gambling in general.[33] In this sense, *The Road to Ruin* contributed to a wider social critique whereby, as Morris puts it, "[t]he danger of ruin from . . . living beyond one's means became a staple of plays, fiction, satire, and proscriptive literature."[34] So strongly was this critique of gambling presented in the play that the *St. James Chronicle* referred to Holcroft as a "stern moralist [who] applies the lash of satire with a determined and heavy hand."[35]

Several elements within the manuscript "The Road to Ruin" and its paratexts shed light on Holcroft's engagement with this and other relevant contemporary political concerns. The Larpent copy of the manuscript play (LA 935), held at the Huntington Library, exhibits many erasures, although it does not seem likely that they were all dictated by the censor; in fact, they most probably indicate Holcroft's own stylistic editing and revision. Whatever the motivation for their removal, some crossed-out passages were later returned to the published play and marked by inverted commas, a practice favored by Holcroft.[36] One erasure stands out, however, in its political connotations and seems to relate specifically to the Prince of Wales. It appears in the manuscript in Act I when, after the elder Dornton and his associate, Sulky, discuss Harry Dornton's profligate lifestyle, the latter remarks upon the young man's "lords and his ladies, his court friends and his Newmarket friends, his women of wit and his men of soul, his blue stockings and his black legs!" (LA 935, 4). "Black leg" was a term used to describe a swindler (*OED*), often referring in the eighteenth century to a sharper on the turf. Together with the references to "court friends" and "Newmarket," it would have immediately called to mind the Prince's racing scandal of the previous year and thus would have exhibited a timely political critique. Whether crossed out by the chief examiner, Larpent, or by Holcroft himself in an act of preemptory self-censorship, these lines reappear in the printed text with the inverted commas to signal their status as a political message, and a risky one to a certain extent.

Another dimension of the cultural-political underpinnings of *The Road to Ruin* appears in the projection of Holcroft's belief in perfectibility, in personal, individual amendment, an idea he regularly expressed in his plays and novels. The idea of perfectibility is a crucial, consistent feature of his plot resolutions and one he would implement in his own actions two years later during the period of the Treason Trials. As he wrote in the *Narrative of Facts*, "the mistake is past recal, but the man may amend" (NF, 80). The reconciliation that concludes *The Road to Ruin* showcases this idea whereby a flawed individual is given a reprieve and misjudgments and crimes are cast aside without recourse to punitive justice or retaliatory consequences. This notion of amendment—underscoring a Godwinian, and specifically a *Political Justice* subtext in which faults are pointed out so as to lead to personal improvement rather than punishment—is represented in the conversation between the elder Dornton and Mr. Williams, the philosophical hosier, one of Harry's creditors:

> DORNTON: [*Shakes him by the hand*] You are an honest fellow! An
>   unaccountable—!
> And so Harry has been your friend?
> HOSIER: Yes, sir; a liberal-minded friend; for he lent me money, though I was
>   sincere enough to tell him of his faults.
> DORNTON: Zounds, sir! How came you to be a weaver of stockings?
> HOSIER: I don't know, sir, how I came to be at all; I only know that here
>   I am.
> DORNTON: A philosopher!
> HOSIER: I am not fond of titles, sir—I'm a man. (RR, 56)

Equality, truth, sincerity: the ideas that emerge in this dialogue illustrate the currency of the play as articulated through the Godwinian-Holcroftian vocabulary of reform. This dialogue was in fact acknowledged in later years as an indication of Holcroft's ideological positioning. (Interestingly, in his obituary of Holcroft, Godwin wrote that it was he—Godwin—who recommended changing this character, originally intended to be a shoemaker, into a hosier.)[37]

For *The Road to Ruin*'s first audiences, the play's political relevance would have been emphasized even before the action commenced, with the speaking of the prologue, which presents a supposedly extempore recitation resulting from the actual prologue having been mislaid by the prompter. The speaker (the actor John Fawcett, who did not appear in the play itself) mentions the play's author, who had "a smart touch or two, about Poland, France, and the—the revolution":

Telling us that Frenchman, and Polishman, and every man is our
    brother:
And that all men, ay, even poor negro [*sic*] men, have a right to be
    free; one as well as another!
Freedom at length, said he, like a torrent is spreading and swelling,
    To sweep away pride and reach the most miserable dwelling: To
        ease, happiness, art, science, wit, and genius to give birth;
    Ay, to fertilize a world, and renovate old earth! (RR, n.p.)

This prologue had been submitted to Larpent together with the manuscript play and was approved by him. This "spontaneous," authentically hesitant ("the—the revolution") but in reality, carefully planned preamble, seemingly disconnected from the play, also through the fact that Fawcett, the speaker, was not a member of its cast, suggests Holcroft's desire to invite the audience to view his portrayal of a flawed society in need of reform as a contribution to the Revolution debate. Although as Allardyce Nicoll writes regarding this prologue that "few, even in such a jesting strain, dared to be so explicit,"[38] there are no reports in the newspapers of any kind of audience response to it, critical or otherwise. Rather, it was at the performance of *Macbeth* that took place at Drury Lane the same night as the premiere of *The Road to Ruin* at Covent Garden that the audience intervened, as the revolutionary song "Ça Ira" "was loudly called for from the pit and gallery."[39] (This action exhibits how political interruptions at the theatre could come from both sides of the ideological spectrum.) The night of 18 February 1792 provides a telling example, then, of the presence of the French Revolution on the British stage. Whereas at Drury Lane it is shown through the explicit intervention of spectators from the pit and gallery, at Covent Garden it appears in actual stage oratory, exhibiting, as Gillian Russell has written regarding prologues in general, the "here and now"[40] of the play, and, certainly, its political provenance, in a very distinct way. It is important to note that the speaking of this prologue was stopped after twenty-one performances,[41] although it was included in the published text of *The Road to Ruin* through the twelfth edition of 1796. The prologue was also published separately in *The London Chronicle* and *The Diary, or Woodfall's Register* two weeks after the premiere.[42] The theater spectators who saw *The Road to Ruin* in its first twenty-one performances or those who attended later but with the memory of having read the prologue would have experienced the play through the intertheatricality of enmeshed texts and contexts that framed it with a revolutionary energy.

* * *

Just as I call attention to this revolutionary context, it is crucial to note that this was not what made *The Road to Ruin* a success. We might even say that the play succeeded *despite* its political foundations, rooted as they were in a particular place and time. Rather it was the play's heightened comedy and expressive sentimentality that truly engaged its audiences, in particular the character of Goldfinch and the relationship between the Dornton father and son, with the tension it displays between intergenerational struggle and deep filial love. A key moment in the play in which this tension is memorably expressed appears at the conclusion of Act I, when Harry Dornton insists on hearing his father wish him a good night even as he continues to disobey paternal orders:

> HARRY: Bid me good night, sir. Mr. Sulky here will bid me good night, and you are my father!—Good night, Mr. Sulky.
> SULKY: Good night.
> HARRY: Come, Sir—
> DORNTON: *[Struggling with passion]* I won't!—If I do—!
> HARRY: Reproach me with my follies, strike out my name, disinherit me, I deserve it all and more—But say Good Night, Harry!
> DORNTON: I won't!—I won't!—I won't!—
> HARRY: Poverty is a trifle; we can whistle it off—But enmity—
> DORNTON: I will not!
> HARRY: Sleep in enmity? And who can say how soundly?—Come! Good night.
> DORNTON: I won't! I won't! *[Runs off]*
> HARRY: Say you so?—Why then, my noble-hearted dad, I am indeed a scoundrel!
> *Re-enter* Mr. Dornton
> DORNTON: Good night!
> HARRY: Good night! And Heaven eternally bless you, Sir. (RR, 16)

William Hazlitt, Mary Russell Mitford, and Charles Lamb remarked upon this interchange, with Mitford writing that "perhaps no scenes have ever drawn so many tears as those between the father and the son . . . the famous 'Good Night' is truly the one touch of nature that makes the whole world kin; and although I have seen it played as well as anything can be played by Munden and Elliston, I have always felt that the real merit belonged to the author."[43] Lamb's comments are in the same vein: "I have seen [Munden] . . . in old Dornton, diffuse a glow of sentiment which has made the pulse of a crowded theatre beat like that of one man."[44] These reflections (both from the revival of *The Road to Ruin* at Drury Lane, 1819) underscore Holcroft's success in writing for his actors, just as Mitford's emphasis on his ability to bring forth the "many tears" shed during the performance acknowledges a universal theme and its emotive power when presented in well-crafted dialogue, which, as both Mitford and Lamb noted, brought the audience together as one. The "Good Night" scene, as well as all of the father-son interactions, would have been even further heightened emotionally for those audience members who had known of Holcroft's personal tragedy, his son William's suicide, which had received newspaper coverage at the time.[45] Today's reader, reading Old Dornton's exclamation, later in the play, "Oh, who would be a father!" (RR, 92), with William Holcroft's suicide in mind is perhaps equally moved by this projection of what "might have been" and the play's conciliatory resolution as opposed to the real-life tragic outcome of William Holcroft's death. In its review of the 2002 Orange Tree production, *The Times* still noted Holcroft as the "object of sympathy" in this regard.[46]

Yet just as much, if not more, than its sentimental appeal, the key factor for the play's popularity in the early years was Goldfinch. This was a new and original figure, not crucial to the development of the plot as such, but remarkable and memorable for the linguistic energy he brought to the stage, his staccato phrasings exhibiting the anxiety and edginess that accompany the effort of social mobility. Let us look briefly at one of his characteristic speeches, given in response to Harry Dornton's remark that he is a "high fellow":

> To be sure!—Know the odds!—Hold four in hand!—Turn a corner in stile!—Reins in form—Elbows square—Wrist pliant—Hayait!—Drive the Coventry stage twice a week all summer—Pay for an inside place—Mount the box—Tip the coachy a crown—Beat the mail—Come in full speed!—Rattle down the gateway!—Take care of your heads!—Never killed but one woman and a child in all my life—That's your sort! (RR, 30–31)

At the play's premiere, with this and many other speeches in the same style, Goldfinch "provoked incessant laughter and applause," in the words of one of the original reviewers; years later Hazlitt would note that "nine persons out of ten who went to see the Road to Ruin, went for the sake of seeing Goldfinch . . . It was a compendious receipt for being witty, to go and see Goldfinch, and repeat after him, "*That's your sort.*"[47] The political topicality—the parallels with the royal family and the revolutionary resonances—were occluded by the hearty laughter generated by his stage presence.

Fourteen years later, in 1806, Holcroft attempted to revive Goldfinch in *The Vindictive Man*. Roundly condemned by the critics, it was a sad shadow of his earlier triumph. This attempt at revival marks the centrality of Goldfinch to Holcroft himself, in his own assessment of his career. The productions of *The Road to Ruin* in the years that followed saw, in contrast, the enduring success of this character in its original context. Remarkably, both Drury Lane and Covent Garden produced the play on the same night, 2 November 1819. The former theater seems to have had the more successful performance because of its all-star cast, with Robert Elliston and Joseph Munden as the Dornton son and father (the acting that Mitford had been so moved by) and John Harley as Goldfinch, who "set the house in a roar," according to the *Morning Post*.[48]

Although productions in the London patent theatres were less frequent from the mid-1820s, *The Road to Ruin* continued to be regularly performed in provincial theaters in Britain and throughout the world. The play was ubiquitous on the theatrical landscape. It was often taken up for amateur theatricals, and we find mentions of amateur performances in such diverse places as British Calcutta in 1837, in Geelong, Australia, for a hospital benefit in 1853, and by a Norwegian American theater group in Chicago in 1870. There was a performance under the auspices of the Colonel and Officers of the First Warwickshire Rifle Volunteers in Birmingham in 1871, and one by a group of amateur thespians associated with the Birkbeck Institution in London the following year.[49] Echoes of *The Road to Ruin* also appeared in nontheatrical contexts, the most prominent example being Charles Dickens's *The Pickwick Papers* (1837) and the character Jingle. With the same disjointed associative speech and the same obsessive drive for a shortcut to upward mobility, the connection between Jingle and Goldfinch was in fact acknowledged. One early observer noted that "if Dickens did not borrow Mr. Jingle from Holcroft's sportsman Goldfinch, then it is a curious literary coincidence."[50] Other more minor echoes include a report of a road accident in 1889 that was compared to Goldfinch's own carriage mishaps, or a serial story in *The Boy's Halfpenny Journal* in 1879, called "The Road to Ruin in Six Steps." There, the gambling character responds to a comment on his behavior with "that's your sort."[51]

Perhaps the later, casual familiarity with the play as exhibited in these last two examples emerges from the series of revivals that appeared from the late 1860s and on through the end of the century. In this later series of productions, the play was now rebranded as the "old English comedy" and associated with a cozy but distant theatrical past. Yet the movement from currency and contemporaneousness to "old English comedy" had begun even earlier. The writer of the playbill for an 1843 revival of *The Road to Ruin* at the Haymarket added the information "period of the play, 1792," apparently feeling that something in the play—the kind of carriage travel shown there, the costumes of the characters, or maybe even the veiled references to the Prince of Wales—needed to be announced and clarified. This Haymarket playbill is thus an important indicator of a middle, transitional period for *The Road to Ruin*, no longer contemporary but not yet antiquated or nostalgic.

*   *   *

The "pastness" of *The Road to Ruin* in 1843 was not only limited to its representation of fashion or conveyance but was also connected to the wide-ranging developments and changes that were taking place in theater culture, particularly in the metropolis. From the beginning of the nineteenth century the London theater was undergoing a major transformation, as the Drury Lane–Covent Garden monopoly became increasingly vulnerable to the rise of the illegitimate theater and alternative sites of performance. Whereas the spoken drama had been limited by law since the time of Charles II to the two patent theaters (as well as later to the Haymarket during the summer season), the minor theaters were becoming increasingly popular from the beginning of the nineteenth century. As Jane Moody and David Worrall have each shown, this "illegitimate theatre" provided a heterogeneous repertoire of burletta, pantomime, and spectacle to growing and increasingly diversified audiences and was accompanied by the gradual emergence of the spoken word on the nonpatent stage, a practice that had been strictly prohibited when the monopoly was at the height of its power.[52] The theater world in which Holcroft had worked was transformed by these developments, which included the enlargement of theatrical spaces, the growing use of special effects, and the changing nature of many of the dramatic pieces presented to the public, including, most prominently, the emergence of melodrama, to the success of which Holcroft had of course contributed. The many very popular adaptations of Pierce Egan's *Life in London* ("Tom and Jerry") introduced, additionally, a much more explicit representation of sexual themes and the expanded use of what was deemed to be improper language.[53] These adaptations would have made Holcroft's mildly salacious material in *The Road to Ruin*, in particular some of the dialogues with the Widow Warren, seem quite tame indeed.

These new developments led to a campaign to revise the existing theater laws. The attempt to relegislate theater production was initially begun in 1832, the year of the Great Reform Bill, highly significant as a watershed moment in which the reform of the nation and the reform of the theater were perceived as intertwined.[54] At the instigation of Edward Lytton-Bulwer (later, better known as Bulwer-Lytton), a select committee was formed to inquire into the condition of the British theater, its practices, the viability of the Drury Lane–Covent Garden monopoly, and the state of the drama itself. In Katherine Newey's words, "this agenda was of a piece with other moves for political reform . . . a clearing-out of the accumulated injustices of outmoded aristocratic and corrupt practices of preferment and protectionism" while also promoting the aesthetic and moral legitimacy of the national drama.[55] The proposed Dramatic Performances Bill, which resulted from the committee's deliberations and which, in addition to deregulation, also upheld the state censorship and extended it to the minor theaters, was defeated in the House of Lords in 1833. The Theatre Regulation Act, which ended the monopoly, was ultimately passed only in 1843, although censorship of the theater remained in place until 1968. In all events, with the vigorous political discussions leading up to, and surrounding, the legislation of the Great Reform Bill in 1831–1832, the struggles for reform during the 1790s seemed to belong to a distant past, and the government's attempt to suppress them at that time were now viewed as disproportionate to the threat that they had been seen to represent.[56] Holcroft was no longer that defendant of the Treason Trials who, in spite of the success of *The Road to Ruin*, had been ostracized by the cultural establishment and whose later plays had been hissed and booed. *The Road to Ruin* lost all vestiges of its own participation in the revolutionary drama *as* a revolutionary drama, as social critique. It became historical, "sterling," innocuous.

It was the desire to experience a cherished theatrical tradition and a shared cultural heritage that led to the practice of reviving the "old English comedies," beginning from the late 1860s. Audiences thronged to these productions, which offered a different theatrical experience from the usual fare of spectacles, melodramas, and sensationalist productions, although *The Road to Ruin* became, in certain productions, tinged with a melodramatic flavor. I want now to briefly discuss some major revivals of the play that appeared during these years, available to us through a number of very thoughtful reviews that accompanied them, before concluding this chapter with a glance at the silent film adaptations. *The Road to Ruin* was performed at the St. James Theatre in London in February 1867, starring a young Henry Irving as Harry Dornton. A review of the play appeared in *The Times* on 11 February; because this piece inaugurates the criticism that accompanied the later period of revival—with the focus on acting and interpretation coinciding with the mildly disparaging view of the play itself that most of the reviews had in common—it is worth discussing at length.[57] The *Times* critic opens by remarking on the play's status within the dramatic canon: "Everybody of a certain age has seen it at some time of his life or other, everybody is acquainted with its general outline and with the broad characteristics of its leading personages . . . [n]evertheless . . . when it is seen again, after a lapse of some years, one is astonished to find how much it contains with which one is not familiar." This recognition of familiarity *and* strangeness is opposed to the perception of Richard Brinsley Sheridan's *The School for Scandal* (1777) (with which *The Road to Ruin* was often linked in the discussions of its revival) in which "the majority of elder playgoers could almost prompt the actors." This reviewer is astute in noting Holcroft's dramatic affiliations with Elizabeth Inchbald and in placing his work within the influence of the

Figure 2.2 Guy Little Theatrical Photograph, *Road to Ruin,* Vaudeville Theatre, 1873, © Victoria and Albert Museum, London

French Revolution, remarking at the same time that the only "democratic twaddle in the whole play is made by Williams, the hosier." These reflections underscore the fact that for the theater spectator of the Victorian era, *The Road to Ruin* is a "relic" of a particular historical moment, the only dramatic work that continued to be performed from the dynamic cultural production of the 1790s in general and from the work of Holcroft and Inchbald in particular. So vibrant, so well-known, and so controversial in their own time, the politics of their work is now reduced to a brief "twaddle." The critic for *The Times* concludes this piece with another reflection on datedness and universality. He notes the irrelevance of Goldfinch, who had been the "life and soul of the play" in earlier times, but now "the least interesting." At the same time, he calls attention to the "unchangeable feelings of human nature" embodied in the Dornton father and son, with Irving's performance of Harry Dornton "excellently conceived" through the nuanced portrayal of the young man's conflicted situation. The praise of the other actors in the cast once more points to the fact that Holcroft knew well how to write for his actors; the acting itself was able to transcend time and succeed in engaging audiences despite the perceived obsolescence of many of the characters and themes.

The Road to Ruin began its extended run at the Vaudeville Theatre (see figure 2.2) in London on 1 November 1873, replacing Sheridan's *The School for Scandal*, which had been performed over 400 times.[58] The reviews were favorable, focusing mainly on the Dornton father-son relationship and the standout performances of William Farren and Charles Warner, respectively, in these roles, as they brought a surprising "intensity" to the portrayal of the filial bond. The "Good Night" exchange, which had moved so many spectators in the past, was again acknowledged and praised.[59]

Like the St. James production six years earlier, Goldfinch receives short shrift from the reviewers, as the audiences were drawn especially to the popular Warner, who later re-created the role of Harry Dornton at Sadler's Wells in 1880, revived it at the Vaudeville in 1886, and starred in it again at the Argus Theatre in Melbourne, Australia, in 1888. In the Sadler's Wells production he received a colder reception from the critics, with the *Pall Mall Gazette* writing that his "chief fault is want of depth."[60] In this insightful and detailed review the critic once again places *The Road to Ruin* in a wider historical context, mentioning Holcroft's laboring-class background, as well as the singularity of his theatrical success: "[T]he fact that he has written a play which ninety years after its first production has still vitality enough to run for between one and two hundred nights before sophisticated audiences is highly creditable . . . Not half a dozen English dramatists has the eighteenth century supplied whom a similar honour has befallen." This critic also acknowledges the play's politics, mentioning again the scene with Williams the philosophical hosier, claiming (improbably, or perhaps tongue in cheek) that this speech may have been one factor leading to Holcroft's arrest for treason![61]

Yet, fascinating as its perception of the 1790s may be, the bulk of the *Pall Mall's* review focuses on the acting of Warner. And while there are perfunctory remarks about other members of the cast, there is no mention of Goldfinch. As in 1873, the focus in 1880 is on Warner's melodramatically inflected interpretation of young Dornton, keying in to the wide popularity of this genre in these years, as well as to the fact that since his first appearance in *The Road to Ruin*, Warner had risen to stardom through his work in melodrama, in particular in the lead role in Charles Reade's *Drink* (1879), an adaptation of Emile Zola's *L'Assommoir*. And although in the 1880 *Road to Ruin* revival at Sadler's Wells, Warner's performance was criticized as "too loud and pronounced in style,"[62] he seems to have recuperated his more finely tuned interpretive skills in the 1888 production in Melbourne. There as the Melbourne *Leader* asserts, he "display[ed] his consummate powers as an artist." "Viewed by the light of the text," the critic continues, "Harry [Dornton] seems little better than a rake . . . in the hands of the artist he becomes a hero."[63]

As opposed to the emphasis that Warner (and the companies he worked with) placed on the sentimental and melodramatic aspects of *The Road to Ruin*, another revival that began in the 1880s focused on its comic dimensions. This was the production of the play by the Compton Comedy Company, led by Edward Compton. It has been suggested that Compton, who had gone prematurely bald as a young man, chose to focus his company's efforts on the old English comedy for purely personal reasons, so that he could wear "a white wig instead of a toupee."[64]

This troupe toured extensively in British cities and towns for over twenty years (they were more successful in the provinces than in the capital) with *The School for Scandal*, *Davy Garrick*, and *The Road to Ruin* as central plays in its repertoire. Along the way, Compton promoted a view of eighteenth-century comedy as "pure, wholesome and worthy entertainment" and portrayed himself as a "Strolling Player . . . in the cause of old comedy."[65] In contrast to the revivals of *The Road to Ruin* at the Vaudeville and Sadler's Wells, Compton foregrounded the part of Goldfinch, as seen by the way he cast himself as this character and gave it the lead billing. However, as opposed to the earliest productions of the play, and perhaps with the memory of Irving's and especially Warner's performances in mind, audiences were expecting a different emphasis. As the *Saturday Review* commented, "the hero of the piece is not Goldfinch, but Harry Dornton; and Harry Dornton is only to be played by an actor with a touch of genius."[66] The Compton Company's actor, Burton, cast in this role, simply had no chance of success when his acting was viewed in comparison to his auspicious predecessors. The situation did not improve when Compton at times played the "double" by acting the role of Harry Dornton as well as that of Goldfinch. This practice seems to have been a way for Compton to showcase his acting skills and comic versatility but must have come at the expense of the exploration of the darker and more complex side of young Dornton, as well as of the verisimilitude of the theatrical event as a whole.[67] Even before the immense popularity of Warner's Dornton, audiences had been receptive to the sentimental father-son drama; we recall the tears the "Good Night" scene elicited from the spectators. It is not surprising that, notwithstanding the blurb from the Leeds playbill that I quoted earlier—"the most remarkable 'double' successfully attempted"—Compton's performance, which most certainly minimized the effect (and affect) of this scene and others like it, fell flat in London.[68]

It is clear that the London revivals, as well as its frequent performance by the Compton Comedy Company mostly in the provincial cities and towns, ensured that *The Road to Ruin* was familiar to theatergoers at the end of the nineteenth century. A. M. Williams's comment, with which I opened this chapter, that Holcroft's "name at least is known" to these audiences, is borne out by the evidence of his play's steady presence in the theatrical landscape. In looking back over a century of performance, we can imagine the different productions: the tears elicited by Munden and Elliston, Farren and Warner; the laughter accompanying the Goldfinches of William Lewis, Charles Mathews, Compton, and the great American actor Joseph Jefferson; in the earliest performances, the once-suggestive revolutionary allusions. These can only be our imaginings. These performances are now, in Nina Auerbach's evocative words, "vanished in the mists that engulfed the world before film preserved it."[69]

In 1930 Amy Cruse, in *The Englishman and His Books*, attempted to reconstruct a late October 1802 Covent Garden revival of *The Road to Ruin*.[70] She populated her account with, among others, William and Mary Jane Godwin, Mary Russell Mitford, Charles and Mary Lamb, and Holcroft and his daughter Fanny as spectators, with the cast of the original production—Munden and Joseph Holman acting the Dornton father-and-son roles, and Lewis as Goldfinch. Cruse has an actor read the prologue, which elicits, of course, different political responses from the pit, the gallery, and the boxes. Cruse's book, pathbreaking in its time in its book-history focus on reading practices and reception, makes use of published accounts such as those written by Lamb and Mitford to re-create this cultural moment. In actual fact, however, there was no performance of the play at Covent Garden in October 1802 (although it was performed in September and December of that year, at Covent Garden and the Haymarket, respectively).[71] If there had been, the prologue would not have been spoken, as it was discontinued after twenty-one nights back in 1792. Moreover, one would have been hard-pressed to find ardor for the French Revolution or the open expression of support for it in the theatres in 1802, although the Peace of Amiens, which commenced in March 1802, had brought with it a robust renewed cultural exchange with France. Godwin, present in Cruse's account, recorded in his diary his real-life attendance at later revivals of his friend's play. He attended ten performances of *The Road to Ruin* over the course of more than forty (!) years—including the opening night at Covent Garden on 18 February 1792, the 2 November 1819 performance (at Covent Garden rather than the much-lauded one at Drury Lane), and in 1835, a half year before his death (GD).[72]

Despite these inaccuracies, Cruse's readers, reading from 1930 onwards, were shown the significance of *The Road to Ruin* as a well-loved play, and her depiction of the status-conscious audience in the theater who gathered to view it would have reinforced the occasion of its performance to be perceived as an important cultural event. These readers themselves might have been familiar not only with the late nineteenth- and early twentieth-century productions of the play but also perhaps with even later revivals, such as that of the Birmingham Rep in 1926, in which a young Laurence Olivier played the role of Harry Dornton's friend, Milford.[73] Perhaps some readers would later see in London the Ambassadors Theatre production of 1937 (in which Hay Petrie, playing Goldfinch, memorably forgot his lines) or hear the radio adaptation on BBC Radio's Third Programme on 29 May 1949 mentioned earlier, in which Goldfinch was played by Maurice Denham.[74] Likewise, they might have seen, or known of, two film adaptations, both produced in 1913. One was a British production directed by and starring George Gray, a copy of which is held at the British Film Institute in London. As the BFI website describes it, this film is a "drama of a weak Oxford undergraduate halted on the downward path by a loving mother."[75] Specifically, the film tells the story of George Wyndham (played by Gray) a student at Oxford, and his decline into a sordid world of gambling and debt. Much of Wyndham's decline is portrayed through an extended dream sequence in which events move from bad to worse. Wyndham's continuous gambling and reckless behavior lead, in this sequence, to alcoholism, eviction, and the near starvation of his wife and daughter. In one of his drunken frenzies, he kills his wife. After jumping from a window in the attempt to end his own life, he awakes. The film concludes with George receiving his honors degree upon graduation. As this brief synopsis makes clear, the link to the original Holcroft play is somewhat tenuous. Besides the sentimental depiction of a parent-child relationship under duress (the song "Don't Forget Your Mother" is repeatedly heard at crucial moments), we also view a corrupt horse-racing scheme and much attention to the various manifestations of the perniciousness of gambling in general. However, there is no plot of financial duplicity, nor any comic characters or situations. And then there is the Australian *Road to Ruin*, directed by W. J. Lincoln and set in Melbourne, which starred Roy Redgrave, the founder of the famous acting dynasty. This film is about the son of a magnate who makes a fortune from speculation, borrows too much, faces ruin, is involved with fraud, and is then bailed out by his father. This film was shown in Australia but is now considered lost.[76]

Whatever the extent to which these films are consciously based on Holcroft's play, I think we can safely assume that the moviegoers of 1913, whether in the United Kingdom or in Australia, were oblivious to the revolutionary energy that informed the original 1792 production. Likewise, almost certainly, were the audiences at the Vaudeville, Sadler's Wells, the St. James Theatre, and the countless provincial venues visited by the Compton Comedy Company; the hospital benefit committee at Geelong; the amateurs at the Birkbeck Institute; and, of course, so many more. It is clear that at the end of the eighteenth century and throughout the nineteenth century, *The Road to Ruin* had a ubiquitous cultural presence, appearing in countless prints and other material forms, such as the fan with etchings of selected scenes from the play mentioned in the Introduction to this book. For most, if not all, of its history, it is also clear that at the conclusion of a performance of *The Road to Ruin*, it was *not* the revolutionary awareness but the comedy and the sentimentality—the roars of laughter and the tears shed—that accompanied the spectators on their departure from the theater and that made the play memorable for them. Would these theatergoers have known of Holcroft's activity as a reformer, of his arrest for treason? Would the spectators at Covent Garden on 8 January 1795, with the Treason Trials still fresh in the public mind, have cared?

In Chapter Five of this book, I discuss in detail Holcroft's melodramas— those plays explicitly or implicitly presented as such—and argue for his centrality in introducing this influential genre to the British stage, a development which *The Road to Ruin* benefited from for many years in its later revivals. This is the case *because* Holcroft's understanding of his own cultural moment anticipated the changing world and shifting values that melodrama sought to explain, as critics such as Peter Brooks and David Mayer, among others, have argued in regard to the genre more generally.[77] Finally, although *The Road to Ruin* became dissociated from some of the contexts that made it notable in the first place, other contexts continue to be highly relevant today. The perceptive remarks of the Australian newspaper *The Argus* on 11 October 1913 regarding Lincoln's now-lost film succinctly sum up this relevance, regardless of whether the film is a faithful adaptation of the play or not: "[*The Road to Ruin* is] a true vignette of life . . . It discloses the luxury of life, the temptations of the weak and . . . the complex conditions that surround humanity in the race for wealth and position."[78] In our present moment, defined as it is by conspicuous consumption, debt, financial speculation, and economic anxiety, we too can relate to *The Road to Ruin*'s themes, a fact that may explain the play's durability while, looking further back, its own specific performance history may also open new ways of looking at the revolutionary drama and its afterlives.

AFTER THE MAJOR SUCCESS OF *The Road to Ruin* and after a rare
year, 1793, in which he did not publish plays or novels, Thomas Holcroft returned
in 1794 with new work for the British stage. During the next four years, eight,
perhaps nine, new plays by Holcroft were performed in the London theaters.[1] Following his release from prison, plays which he presented as his own work were
censured by audiences and the press while those submitted under another name,
or through a third party, were more successful. Central to all these works is Holcroft's critique of class hierarchies and unearned privilege, whether discreetly, in the
presentation of a sentimental comedy such as *The Deserted Daughter* (1795), or
through a more directly polemical attack on society, as in *Knave, or Not?* (1798).
This chapter examines four Holcroft plays written and performed between 1794
and 1798, both before and after his arrest, in order to view his promotion of a
reforming, if not radical, agenda on the London stage. This body of work engages
much more directly with politics than *The Road to Ruin* but, following the Treason Trials, it is also more pessimistic. The idea of truth—that central concept in
the Godwinian philosophy of reform and a key element in Holcroft's ideological
work—is complicated in these later dramas, both by the prevalence of disguise
and concealment within the plays and in Holcroft's efforts in bringing them to
the stage. It is different in this context from the treatment of truth that had
appeared in some of Holcroft's earlier works, such as *Duplicity*. There the elaborate deception carried out against the protagonist, Sir Harry, by his good friend
Osborne is a didactic lesson in the dangers of gambling and a subterfuge to which
those closest to Sir Harry are recruited. In the later plays discussed in this chapter,
the dissimulations feature as efforts of resistance against something more than a
bad habit, destructive as it may be, challenging instead institutional structures—
patriarchy in *The Deserted Daughter* and class hierarchies in *Knave, or Not?*—even
as they lead to a belated kind of justice.

Holcroft had learned from Godwin the value of truth as a political ideal but from his own experience had seen its limitations. Textual and authorial practices illuminate Holcroft's ongoing negotiation of the often-conflicting issues of truth, politics, sincerity, authorship, and the desire for the success of his dramatic works. Success was not easily, or often, achieved during these years. That this was an anxious and fraught authorial endeavor is evident also in the fact that, unlike *The Road to Ruin*, only *The Deserted Daughter* (among the plays written between the years 1794 and 1798) had any real afterlife to speak of. Rather, the response of the audience and, what was at times equally vigorous, that of the print media, to what was perceived as politically contentious material, led to runs on the stage that were notable often only in the fractiousness they called forth. More than a half century later, Mary Russell Mitford looked back at the final years of the eighteenth century and perceptively described the reception of Holcroft's dramatic works during that time: "The demon of party hatred was evoked. . . . Every fresh play was a fresh battle; and a battle, whatever be the issue, is in itself fatal to a great success."[2]

My discussion of Holcroft plays in this chapter centers on *Love's Frailties* (1794), which exhibited a reformist outlook and was written and performed before Holcroft's arrest; *The Deserted Daughter* (1795), notable as a relative success and an anticipation of melodrama, whose authorship was at first unknown; *The Man of Ten Thousand* (1796) and *Knave, or Not?* (1798), both appearing under Holcroft's name and showing (in addition to a contentious reception) a pessimism that challenges his earlier philosophical belief in a gradual organic emergence of truth and perfectibility. In examining the "battlefield" that was Holcroft's relationship with the late eighteenth-century British stage, I pay close attention to two dimensions that concurrently define it. On one hand, I foreground the materiality of this engagement and the web of connections—the reciprocity—between texts, authors, performers, audiences, economic outputs, reviewers, and venues, what David Worrall has theorized as a social assemblage—a "connected social network or assemblage of production and reception" with an extensive cultural reach.[3] Evidence for the interconnectedness of this network appears, for example, in newspaper and journal commentary; in advertising; in actors' memoirs; and in the workings of the Drury Lane and Covent Garden theaters, where audiences included "elite and increasingly influential middle-class theatre-goers" who made up specific "networks of cultural dissemination."[4] To a twenty-first-century observer these now-forgotten Holcroft plays may seem to represent simply obscure moments within, or brief footnotes to, a period of wide-ranging cultural production. Yet the strength of cultural dissemination and the material connections informing a play's dramatic life show how the brevity of its run on the stage belies the fact that in its own time any play would have had palpable resonances deriving from the power of the theater as a crucial cultural force. Hence, the significance of such plays was expanded beyond the statistical evidence of a brief performance run. A viewer would discuss the play, for example, with fellow members of the audience and later with friends and family; conversation about it might be continued after seeing advertisements, playbills, and reviews in the daily newspapers, as well as the plays' prologues, which were frequently reprinted in the papers separately a few days later. When the plays were later published, as they most often were, public interest was revived with a printed text to be read and reread; "every one" reads works of this kind, one commentator on the print edition of a Holcroft play asserted.[5] In the case of publication, periodical journals included in their dedicated theater sections reviews accompanied by substantial and often quite-detailed textual and cultural commentary. This second round of reviews was published in influential, opinion-shaping periodicals such as the *Monthly Review,* the *European Magazine,* the *Analytical Review,* *The Anti-Jacobin Review,* and *The British Critic.* Holcroft himself often directly addressed his audiences in the "advertisements" to these published plays, adding another layer of engagement to the dramatic text and additional commentary to that of the periodicals' reviews.

The second dimension of my discussion focuses on the politics. In examining Holcroft's work for the theater in the second half of the 1790s and in acknowledging its political resonances, this chapter focuses on the climate of oppression during the 1790s (especially the latter half of the decade) and its implications for literary production. Holcroft's work for the theater in these years provides additional evidence for John Bugg's account of the pervasiveness of censorship and self-censorship that followed the legislation of the Two Acts (the Treasonable Practices and Seditious Meetings bills) of 1795.[6] These bills were a result of government anxiety over increased political agitation and were formulated and legislated immediately following the stoning of the king's carriage as he was on his way to the opening of Parliament. Frequently referred to as the Gagging Acts, they severely restricted antigovernment speech and writing. Meetings of over fifty people convened for public discussion and debate were subjected to strict discretionary control, and the right to petition was severely curtailed.[7] The response to the Two Acts in literary texts is evident, as Bugg puts it, in "performed or registered breakdowns in communication . . . representations of characters who are afraid to speak," silence as the "focus of discourse," and the necessity of "alternative modes of communication."[8]

I want to return to Kenneth R. Johnston's understanding of "usual and unusual suspects" as, likewise, key to positioning Holcroft's work within the anxious climate of the mid- to late revolutionary decade. The "suspect" writers of the 1790s are those who suffered varying degrees of ostracism and punishment—exile, harassment, silencing, neglect, and other forms of insidious persecution—for their support of reform.[9] Johnston's distinction between "usual" and "unusual" suspects places the former group as those more directly involved in punishable offenses;

they were the victims of over one hundred state trials for treason and sedition during "Pitt's Reign of Terror." The latter group, conversely, who were less (if at all) involved as actual defendants in legal proceedings, nonetheless suffered indirectly as a result of their political activities, such as loss of work, loss of inheritance, loss of literary fame, and loss of prospects.[10] For Johnston, Holcroft, a "usual suspect" is also "the major victim"[11] of what had happened when the repressive social and political consensus met theater culture. Most obviously, this repression, as it emerges from the meeting between politics and drama, is lodged in the work of Chief Examiner of Plays John Larpent, who determined whether a play would be licensed and staged and if so, with what, if any, modifications to the manuscript text. Yet in many ways the power of the theater in anxious times was exhibited more subtly and perhaps even more powerfully through audience and press enforcement of hegemonic norms *after* a play had reached the stage.[12] The major, ongoing success of *The Road to Ruin* was an anomaly in the context of this narrative insofar as Holcroft was concerned. The general opprobrium attached to him following his release from Newgate Prison did not affect the later success of that play, did not lead to riots in the theater, nor did it discourage future performances throughout the nineteenth century.

The plays on which I focus in this chapter tell a different story. There was a popular and critical success among them (*The Deserted Daughter*), but that play was submitted anonymously. Another relatively successful play from this period, which I just briefly acknowledge, *He's Much to Blame* (1798) was submitted under the name of Holcroft's friend, John Fenwick. The other plays in my selection, presented under Holcroft's own name, faced the fate of immediate failure and later obscurity, victims of the alarmist times in which they were produced. In the discussion that follows, I will be attentive to the various divisions that can be located in this later group of Holcroft plays. Thus, I distinguish between plays that appeared before and after his incarceration. While the later plays underscore Bugg's awareness of the increased anxieties over political expression in the aftermath of the Two Acts, they also, even more decidedly, acknowledge the 1794 Treason Trials as another dividing line of the revolutionary decade. Thus, although E. P. Thompson identifies a "brief moment of 'glasnost'" following the acquittals of the Treason Trials and before the passing of the Two Acts, in which a climate of optimism appeared,[13] for Holcroft there seems to have been no participation in this shared sanguinity, no renewed sense of possibility. As the case of *The Deserted Daughter*, written and performed during this period, makes clear, there was no respite from the hostility that followed him post-Newgate. In calling attention to the differences between works submitted under Holcroft's own name and one in which his authorship is obfuscated, I also consider the idea of "truth" as it is exhibited within these plays. Dissembling is a key indicator of Holcroft's recognition of the need to survive professionally and financially during this period, in which the very efficacy of truth succumbs to the pressures of things as they are. Holcroft wrote for the stage as a "usual suspect," yet, despite the various disguises onstage and off, he nonetheless continued to present a reformist, and a Godwinian, agenda to the public within a cultural space—the theater—in which it was dangerous and surely self-destructive to do so.

A further element of my argument that should be noted at the outset concerns the shift between sentimental comedy and melodrama, a genre with which Holcroft is frequently credited for bringing to the British stage. Although my main discussion of melodrama appears in Chapter Five and focuses there on the beginning of the nineteenth century, the roots of Holcroft's engagement with the form appear during the period following his release from prison and before his self-imposed exile on the Continent in 1799–1802. Later productions of *The Road to Ruin* had also exhibited sentimental elements appropriated as melodrama, especially in the later nineteenth century and when in the hands of actors associated with and trained in that genre. The "swerve of melodrama," to use Diane Hoeveler's phrase,[14] is further present in *Knave, or Not?* and is anticipated in *The Deserted Daughter*, underscoring the political underpinnings of that genre and its origins in the aftermath of the French Revolution as it articulated the anxiety over changing values, hierarchies, and belief systems.

* * *

While all Holcroft's plays produced in the mid-to-late 1790s display aspects of his reformist endeavor, *Love's Frailties, or Precept against Practice* (CG, 1794)[15] stands out in its optimism for the possibility of reform in the months before the Treason Trials. Premiering on 5 February 1794, it predated not only Holcroft's own arrest in October of that year but that of the major defendants five months earlier, in May.[16] The prologue to the play, coauthored by Holcroft and John Thelwall, one of those defendants, exhibits a mixture of exuberance and anxiety that also portended what was to come with the arrest of both men later in 1794.[17] Using the genre of the prologue itself as their subject matter, Holcroft and Thelwall use a series of military metaphors to view the theater and its audience as a battlefield to be negotiated. They conclude:

> Here let us pause: for ah! 'tis but too true,
> Cassandra like, in black prophetic view,
> I see the massacres that may ensue!
> Wit, humour, character, are put to rout!
> The prompter breathless, and the actors out!
> Quibbles and claptraps in confusion run!
> Slain is a sentiment! Down drops a pun!
> Nay, plot himself, that leader far renown'd,
> Oh shame! dare scarcely stand another round!

"How shall our general dare such danger meet?
"Were it not better, think you, sirs, to treat?
"War honours grant then, as he files away;
"So may he live and fight another day."[18]

Lines such as "I see the massacres that may ensue" (Holcroft) and "So may he live and fight another day" (Thelwall, acknowledged as the writer of the lines in inverted commas [LF, vi]) are perspicuous in anticipating the eventual course of events, whether immediately—the virulent objection to *Love's Frailties* by members of the audience that same night—or later, with Holcroft's tenacious perseverance in nonetheless continuing to write politically contentious plays in the years that followed.[19]

 Love's Frailties (loosely based upon O. H. Gemmingen's *Der Deutsche Hausvater* [1779])[20] tells the story of a brother and sister, Charles and Louisa Seymour. In their romantic attachments to partners ostensibly of a lower status and class, they oppose their imperious uncle and guardian, Sir Gregory, a Burkean figure yearning for the return to an age of chivalry, although he is far from chivalrous in his own personal actions. (We soon discover his hypocrisy when it emerges that his servants procure women for him.) Charles has rebelled against traditional hierarchies when falling in love with Paulina, the daughter of Craig Campbell, a penniless artist, who, unknown to all, is also the brother-in-law of Sir Gregory himself, disinherited because he had married Sir Gregory's sister against his— Sir Gregory's—wishes. In contrast to Paulina's belief, shared by the other young people, that there is "no true inequality, but between virtue and vice" (LF, 46), the older generation, including the disinherited Campbell, stubbornly clings to rank and privilege. At the same time, it is Campbell who receives the most radical lines in the play, which William Hazlitt later noted, had "excited the most violent resentment" (*Life*, 2:94): "I was born to the most useless and often the most worthless of all professions; [Campbell asserts] that of a gentleman" (LF, 66). Holcroft's belief in the possibility of change at this time (before his arrest) appears most prominently through the character of Lady Fancourt, Paulina's rival for Charles Seymour's affections. Observing the love of Charles and Paulina, she withdraws her claim, finally acknowledging that "riches, rank and power are feeble arms, as opposed to the energies of mind and virtue" (LF, 73).

 The noblewoman's conversion, which succinctly sums up the theme of the play, exhibits optimism for social change that is reinforced in Paulina's closing words: "Why this is true delight—love, friendship, and benevolence, catching and spreading from mind to mind, from heart to heart; modeling the young, melting the old, and harmonizing all. May the principle and the practice become universal!" (LF, 79). This vision of social harmony and universal benevolence may have accompanied the Covent Garden spectators as they exited the theater, yet it is safe to assume that those who attended the first night's performance were even more forcefully under the impression of the altercation that had erupted earlier with Campbell's "worthless gentleman" speech. *The World* called attention to the "manifest . . . dissatisfaction" of the audience[21] that night, and the *European Magazine*, writing after the play had concluded its run, reminded its readers that Campbell's remarks on the uselessness of gentlemen "provoked a loud and continued expression of disapprobation and disgust, which for a few seconds interrupted the performance, and damped the effect of the scene."[22] As the prologue had foretold, amidst the confusion the "sentiment" had been "slain."

The play's call for "love, friendship and benevolence" was clearly *not* the message emphasized or even acknowledged to the wider public in the newspaper reviews that immediately followed the first performance. The *St. James Chronicle* devotes but a few lines of its commentary to the play's theme—"the tyranny of parents, avarice and the pride of rank"—focusing instead on its tense reception and the impossibility of articulating "general maxims of morals and politics" in the current cultural climate.[23] Interestingly, this reviewer, who is not overtly hostile, takes Holcroft to task for attempting to employ the genre of comedy "as a vehicle of general maxims" but also leaves it in the public's hands to decide whether the play will continue its run. The commentary in the *Times* of 15 February was, not surprisingly, more biased. "'Love's Frailties', in spite of all the puffs of *Constitutional Friends*, has at length expired, though not without many a bitter groan. The truth is—the piece was fairly damned the first night."[24]

In fact, *Love's Frailties* might have been damned even earlier. In a piece included in his publication, *The Tribune*, in 1795, the following year, John Thelwall remarked upon the play, noting that it contained "a variety of just and moral sentiments which were obliged to be struck out, for political reasons." Referring to Paulina's assertion that there is no inequality "but between virtue and vice," Thelwall states:

> This was a sentence not to be endured, and every thing of the kind was expunged before it was permitted to be performed; and after all, it being reported that the author was a man who professed patriotic sentiments, a conspiracy to damn it was formed at the Percy Coffeehouse (the same house in which the conspiracy was formed against Citizen Frost;) and though they could not effect this, such an opposition was made to it as to prevail with the managers after a few nights to lay it aside.[25]

Thelwall's commentary acknowledges the climate of repression in the 1790s as he links the fate of Holcroft's play to the fate of another radical, John Frost, who was brought to trial and imprisoned for speaking "seditious words" during the course of a political argument. It is noteworthy for him that the man (Frost) and the play (*Love's Frailties*) were both "damned" in the same coffeehouse. In examining the

Frost incident, James Epstein states that "Frost's case provides a point of departure for thinking about the nexus among sites of sociability, politics and law, and the behaviour and language appropriate to each."[26] Thelwall's linkage of Frost and Holcroft inserts theater into this array of connections. Through his continued involvement with drama, Holcroft would experience the effects of this nexus of power throughout the rest of his career; he (and, of course, Thelwall) were damned, and then, repeatedly, damned again.[27]

In an attempt to counter the powers of enforcement that emanated from sites such as Percy's coffeehouse, Holcroft directly addresses those persons "offended" by his play, "violent [but] few," in his advertisement to the printed edition of *Love's Frailties*. From the outset he informs his readers that he has included in italics "passages . . . omitted on the first representation," while also noting that one speech that *was* spoken on the stage (Craig Campbell's remark on the uselessness of gentlemen) is given in capital letters. He then calls on the reader

> who has not quite lost his understanding [to] examine what there
> is in them injurious to truth, or the good of mankind, and find
> it, if he can. In different times, and under different feelings,
> it will appear astonishing that any one of these passages were
> suppressed, from any apprehension of political resentment: but
> such was the fact. That the one unwarily retained should incite the
> anger which was testified is still more astonishing (LF, iii).

Invoking transparency and a self-evident truth, Holcroft invites his readers to consider a text whose very print layout calls attention to caution, revision, and censorship, graphically displayed for all to see and judge through a patchwork of standard type, italics, inverted commas, and capital letters. When he singles out the Craig Campbell speech as the "one unwarily retained," we may ask—retained by whom? By the censor (it is unmarked in the Larpent copy[28]) or by Holcroft himself? Had both Larpent and Holcroft been "unwarily" remiss in their censorial or self-censorial practices? Certainly, Holcroft's willingness to (re) present and emphasize these omissions in print shows his own acknowledgement of the relatively safer space of page than stage, although print would become increasingly vulnerable with the passing of the Two Acts at the close of 1795. Be that as it may, the spirit of this preface and the play that follows it with its energetic and optimistic conclusion would soon come under duress with the Treason Trials and the events leading up to them. The lines in the prologue of "liv[ing] to fight another day" would soon take on a more ominous cast.

* * *

Holcroft's next play, *The Deserted Daughter* (CG, 1795) appeared over a year after *Love's Frailties*. Much had happened in the interim: his arrest for treason, his incarceration in Newgate, and the eventual acquittal without trial. He would continue throughout his life to suffer the aftereffects of his involvement in the Treason Trials. He was repeatedly reminded of his status as a former prisoner of the Crown; the epithet of "acquitted felon" that was frequently flung at him was especially stinging. Holcroft's experience of the "many small, mean ways in which political heterodoxy was punished" (to use Kenneth R. Johnston's words)[29] even after he had been subjected to, and acquitted, by the state legal processes, is reflected in his open letter to Secretary of War William Windham after the latter had used the "acquitted felon" term in Parliament. In the letter, Holcroft first acknowledges "[t]he spirit of unrelenting animosity, with which I and my fellow sufferers have been pursued . . . so bitter, so absolutely unmixed with any compunctions of benevolence, so disappointed in its appetite for vengeance and blood, and so fanatically pertinacious in continuing its attempts."[30] He then elaborates:

> [A]fter the persons accused [of treason] had been acquitted by an unequivocal and beyond all example deliberate verdict of Not Guilty, and the prosecution dropped in despair; still, the men tried and acquitted, in this extraordinary and unheard of manner, are pronounced "acquitted felons." This is the unintelligible principle you maintain! Sir, the mind turns with loathing from the rancour of such an assertion, the wickedness of such a prosecution, and the errors of such prosecutors. Was it not enough to have suffered imprisonment, defamation, loss of property, loss of character, and the hazard of loss of life? To have been hawked about the streets like Tyburn malefactors? To have been sung in ballads as Jacobins and Cannibals? To have been exhibited on handkerchiefs as traitors, caged in the cells of Newgate? To have been kept in the most awful suspence, from the fatal and horrid sentences that were likely to follow; not because of our guilt, but of the prejudiced and angry state of the public mind, which had been inflamed to this excess by artifices so flagitious and abominable as these? (*Letter*, 14–15).

It was surely the desire to circumvent this acrimony and prejudice that led Holcroft to forego truth and transparency and to submit *The Deserted Daughter* anonymously; the play was given to the censor on 17 April 1795 and originally titled, "'Tis a Strange World" (LA 1077).[31] The force of his experience, and the continual attempt to pursue him ("fanatically pertinacious," as he had put it) had left its mark not only on his view of society but also on the self-evident nature of truth and on its ability to forge a benevolent society, a better world. The decision to conceal his authorship arguably contributed (at least at the outset) to the play's more marked success. It ran for a respectable sixteen performances in its original run, far more than the plays submitted under his name during these years. At the same time, its popularity was also probably due to the fact that the political criticism in the play is less openly articulated than in *Love's Frailties* or in the later *Man of Ten*

Thousand and *Knave, or Not?*. Rather, the affective sentimentality of the family drama is what appealed to spectators and readers, holding their attention, even as Holcroft's authorship was hinted at and speculated upon again and again.

The Deserted Daughter, loosely based upon Richard Cumberland's *The Fashionable Lover* (1772),[32] premiered at Covent Garden on 2 May 1795. The play tells the story of Mr. Mordent, who is besieged by the impending collapse of his finances, by the breakdown of his marriage, and by the crisis that emerges with Joanna, the eponymous "deserted daughter." Joanna's mother, Mordent's first wife, had died in childbirth, and seeing the child as an obstacle to his remarriage to the wealthy and socially prominent Lady Anne, he conceals her, leaving her fate in the hands of his villainous associates. In order to pocket the 1,000 pounds meant to secure Joanna in a trade, these associates, Item and Grime, convey her, unbeknownst to her father, to a house of prostitution. There she catches the attention and admiration of Mordent and his friends, who happen upon the establishment and are unaware of her true identity. Among these friends is Cheveril, Mordent's ward, who has just reached his majority. Cheveril's desire to live the life of a man of fashion—as a "rake"—is repeatedly confounded by his genuinely benevolent principles and his developing love for Joanna. Eventually the financial embezzlement is revealed as a result of Item accidentally misplacing his secret accounts book. Joanna's identity becomes known as well, when she escapes the house of prostitution disguised as a man. She accepts the love of Cheveril and is welcomed as a daughter by Lady Anne and by Mordent, whose marital reconciliation concludes the play.

The Deserted Daughter was well received by critics and the public. The *Oracle or Public Advertiser*, perhaps unaware of Holcroft's authorship, praised it as "the work of a reflecting mind, knowing in stage effects and human passions, and actuating both to the best of purposes."[33] The *Whitehall Evening Post* concurred in the praise, while also acknowledging the "decided approbation" of the audience. This newspaper *was* aware of the identity of the play's author: ". . . though not *avowedly* from the pen of Mr. Holcroft, [the play] has too many of those bold and forcible appeals to the passions which characterize this gentleman's works, to be mistaken for that of any other writer" [emphasis in the original].[34] Later reviews of the published text of *The Deserted Daughter* likewise acknowledged, if conditionally, Holcroft's authorship, a fact which may also have dictated their approval or disapproval of the play according to their political leanings. Thus, the conservative *British Critic* presents a negative commentary, its brief review stating that "everything is hurried and unfinished," while the *Analytical Review* declares that the play "is entitled to high commendation."[35] On the other hand, the *Pocket Magazine* would note both the assumption that the author is "the famous Mr. Thomas Holcroft, lately tried for high-treason" but also that the play is "so very far superior to any thing which ever before came from his busy pen," in a commentary that reinforces the persistent connection between Holcroft's later publications and the inescapable yoke of his political notoriety.[36] Significantly, the review in the *Analytical* is the only one to acknowledge a political awareness in the play itself, calling attention to its author's representation of "the mischievous effects of the present systems of law."[37] This reviewer's further remark that Mordent views "nature [as] a system of evil,"[38] also indirectly (and astutely) acknowledges, in its attention to the nature of "systems," a Godwinian philosophy of reform tucked away fairly unassumingly in the play. Presenting a critique against institutions in general, Mordent declares that "knaves and fools engender each other; together they make rulers; rulers make laws; laws make villains and villains sanctify and perpetuate the use of prisons, chains, ropes and racks."[39] Another passage, originally included in the manuscript but struck out in the Larpent copy, has Mordent, reviewing his tense domestic and financial situation at the beginning of the play, announce: "The whole town would ring my name. Title pages, handbills, and advertisements, posts, walls and windows."[40] This passage strikingly replicates Holcroft's own experience in the aftermath of the Treason Trials as expressed in his letter to Windham—hawked in the streets, sung in ballads, exhibited on handkerchiefs.

Noteworthy as his critique of institutional systems may be, Mordent is, to be clear, neither a Godwinian anarchist nor a disciple of *Political Justice*. Although he exhibits and embraces the idea of perfectibility in his eventual reform, for most of the play he is presented through the lens of his self-serving depravity. The anarchistic allusion, however, was evident to the writer of the section on the Georgian drama for the 1932 edition of the *Cambridge History of English Literature*, who noted that "[t]he play manages, in melodramatic form, to portray the doctrines of the Godwin circle . . . [Holcroft] champions the new belief in the perfectibility of man."[41] Alongside these Godwinian undertones *The Deserted Daughter* exhibits a readjustment of other aspects of the worldview that had appeared in the pre–Treason Trials *Love's Frailties*. In a reversal of the critique of aristocracy that had featured in the earlier play, Lady Anne, Mordent's long-suffering wife, is the object of our sympathy as the victim of the intractable social mores of her family. In the end it is she—the noblewoman—who is the redeemer rather than the redeemed, in her unconditional forgiveness of her wayward husband and her affectionate acceptance of his daughter. Moreover, chance plays a key role in the plot resolution: the exposure of the fraud which leads to the successful conclusion of events results from the villainous Item's misplacement of his accounts book and thus from a matter of accident rather than from the availability of the self-evident truth to which the aristocratic characters of *Love's Frailties* were eventually recruited.[42] The idea of truth under pressure is also exhibited in the crucial role of disguise—the costume Joanna dons as she executes her escape, as well as, outside the text, Holcroft's concealment of his authorship. Clearly, the more generous portrayal of nobility, chance as a crucial element in the plot, and the issue of dissembling in its various dimensions indicate that *The Deserted Daughter* is a far more politically subdued work than *Love's Frailties* and others that would follow it, darker and less exuberant than *The Road to Ruin*.

Yet *The Deserted Daughter* exhibits more than politics. In a different dimension, the play can be seen as illustrative of a development within the eighteenth-century sentimental comedy. The character of Mordent, "tormenting and tormented" (as the *Analytical Review* puts it)[43] acknowledges something beyond comedy, in fact, a mixture of genres that led the play's original reviewers to call it "a grave and sentimental drama" or to note that the production "caused the mingled emotions of smiles and tears."[44] Among modern critics, both George Taylor and Diane Long Hoeveler note *The Deserted Daughter's* status as an eighteenth-century sentimental comedy, but one at the edge of the genre; in Hoeveler's words, it is an example of its "exhaustion and limitations," on the verge of becoming melodrama.[45] Hoeveler argues that "the evolution of melodrama is predicated on lower—and middle-class women as forces to be reckoned with in an increasingly secularized society"; women who "are the voice of moral and social authority." Her main examples of this type of woman are the servant Fiametta and the daughter Selina in Holcroft's *A Tale of Mystery* (1802). These women, she argues, who actively determine the outcome of tumultuous events and articulate the voice of moral authority, appear in opposition to Joanna in *The Deserted Daughter*, who is saved by her good looks and her innocence rather than by any concerted action of her own.[46] Hoeveler's depiction of Joanna thus locates this character as a central factor in placing *The Deserted Daughter* on the cusp of the genre divide: although the play is not a true sentimental comedy, it is not yet melodrama. We will return to *A Tale of Mystery* and to Hoeveler's analysis in a later chapter, and I will not dwell here on Joanna at any great length. That said, I believe that she is not as passively innocent as Hoeveler suggests. She knows well the physiognomic studies of Johann Caspar Lavater and uses his principles to define her father's face. "I don't quite like him. . . . He's a wicked man," she exclaims when shown his portrait at the house of prostitution (DD, 18).[47] Despite years of neglect, however, she ultimately, in true, sentimental, domestic spirit, falls at her father's feet and "rapturously" kisses his hand (DD, 81). At the same time, she also exhibits a degree of resourcefulness and an energetic directness, qualities that in the view of some of *The Deserted Daughter's* original critics, point to a kind of *im*perfection. As opposed to the twenty-first-century view of critics like Hoeveler, they were taken aback at Joanna's impropriety. *The Oracle* remarked, "We grieve that a child must tell a father, though unknown, that he has an artful, cruel and betraying face."[48] Even more directly, Elizabeth Inchbald, in her preface to the play for Longman's *The British Theatre*, notes "the unfeeling and ill-bred manner with which [Joanna] tells her friends they bear signs of guilt in their feelings."[49] The perceived nonconventional behavior of Joanna noted by Holcroft's contemporaries marks an awareness of the play as a departure from what can be called the "classic" sentimental comedy, introducing a nuanced and, for some observers, questionable form of female resistance.

The inclusion of *The Deserted Daughter* in Longman's compilation of British drama suggests institutional approval; the play was deemed worthy of being anthologized and deserving of entry into the British canon.[50] It also had a fairly robust afterlife. It met with success in the United States and was performed in Philadelphia, New York, and Boston.[51] Back home, the Queen's Royal Regiment, stationed at Lymington in October 1796, performed the play soon before its departure for the West Indies.[52] The regiment's choice of *The Deserted Daughter* is somewhat surprising, as Holcroft's plays were often, along with those of Elizabeth Inchbald, the cause for riot by members of the military in many provincial locations, as Gillian Russell has shown.[53] The performance at Lymington is an intriguing, perhaps ironic, coda to the conclusion of the play's original run, another aspect of which is summarized in a poem published under the name of "Miss Churchill" in the 28–30 May 1795 edition of the *Whitehall Evening Post*:

EXTEMPORE

ON NOT SEEING AS GOOD A HOUSE AT A LATE
REPRESENTATION OF THE DESERTED DAUGHTER
AS THE COMEDY DESERVED
By Miss Churchill

The town—not knowing whose the pen—
    With approbation smil'd—
    For the *Deserted Daughter* then
        Was—the *Adopted Child!*
But now—since known her FATHER'S name—
    Tho' late she did succeed—
The Daughter—surely to our shame!—
    Deserted is, indeed!

If attendance fell at performances of *The Deserted Daughter* as the result of the later knowledge of Holcroft's authorship, then this little poem clearly illustrates the process of "damning" that accompanied his career in the mid- and late 1790s, such as had appeared in *Love's Frailties* and with even more force after the Treason Trials. But did the play really fail? Evidence from the Covent Garden account books suggests that Miss Churchill's claim was not borne out by fact. (I have not been able to further identify Miss Churchill.) The ledger records earnings of £143.19*s* (a fairly low sum) for 9 May, but the very respectable £216.12*s*.6*d* two days later, on 11 May, and £161.14*s* (just slightly under Judith Milhous's break-even box office figure of

£167 for the early 1790s⁵⁴) on 15 May. After the poem was published, the play earned £178.3s for the night of 1 June, and £163.10s.6d for 15 June. This was not really a loss at the till; although not remarkably high earnings, they are still fairly steady, with no dramatic drop.⁵⁵ Could it be that, in her sentimental and righteous tone, Miss Churchill is condemning the play and trying herself to dictate nonattendance at the theater? If so, is her poem really, then, extempore? In all events, the establishment embrace indicated in the performance of the play by the Queen's Royal Regiment in the following year appears somewhat paradoxical in this context, for it attests to the relative success of *The Deserted Daughter* in spite of the notoriety of its author, notwithstanding the "half-empty theatre," despite the damning. This degree of success is further evinced when compared to the fraught reception of *The Man of Ten Thousand* and *Knave, or Not?* which would soon follow.

One additional afterlife of *The Deserted Daughter* is worth mentioning. In October 1819 *The Steward, or Fashion and Feeling*, by Samuel Beazley, appeared on the London stage. This play openly presents itself as "founded upon *The Deserted Daughter*,"⁵⁶ and Beazley devotes a substantial introduction in the published text to explaining his motivation for writing and his practice of revision. While acknowledging the power of Holcroft's play and its "merit" (S, v), he concurrently expresses his strong objection to the idea of a parent "sacrificing his own child to infamy" (S, v); the idea of Mordent encountering Joanna in a house of prostitution, with the accompanying whiff of potential incest, fills him with "terror and disgust" (S, vi). He further explains that he has "soften[ed]" (S, vii) both the characters of Mordent and Joanna, omitting the latter's references to Lavater that had troubled some observers during the original run. The result is that Joanna, who in *The Steward* is lodged merely in the house of one of Item's dependents rather than in a house of prostitution, is a less vigorous character than she had been in Holcroft's play, lacking also the dramatic tension of the brothel situation as a context in which to display her resourcefulness. Mordent is relieved of much of the burden of guilt, as Item becomes not only the financial tormentor of Mordent but the sexual predator of his daughter. Another significant change appears in the character of Lady Anne, who is now presented as an extravagant woman of fashion, a portrayal which, Beazley explains, further "relieve[s] the character of Mordent," (S, vii).

It is clear that the tormented Mordent in Holcroft's original play had so successfully engaged Beazley's sympathy that in his own version of events he devoted serious efforts to lessening his culpability. Not surprisingly, Mordent's speech on the evils of systems—"laws make villains"—is deleted in this text. He becomes merely a victim of financial ineptitude. This adaptation thus removes many of the tensions that had unsettled Holcroft's first audiences, but in doing so, it strips the play of the affective hold that had emerged from the depiction of the overlapping power structures of class, gender, and institutions. Beazley returns *The Deserted Daughter* safely to the confines of sentimental comedy and to that strain of that genre devoid of political awareness and social critique.

* * *

Miss Churchill's poem in the *Whitehall Evening Post* had called attention to the political tensions that accompanied the reception of *The Deserted Daughter*, and we can view it, by extension, as relevant for all of Holcroft's work for the stage in the second half of the revolutionary decade. It is not known whether he saw this poem, with its linkage between the revelation of his authorship and the emptying of the theater, a result that would have pained but not surprised him. Still, he decided to present his next play, *The Man of Ten Thousand*, under his own name. His return to more overt social criticism, together with the open acknowledgement of his authorship, ensured that this play met with a very different reception. *The Man of Ten Thousand* (DL, 1796) is the most similar of these later plays to *Love's Frailties* in its critique of a decadent moneyed class. Roughly echoing Shakespeare's *Timon of Athens*, the play tells the story of the wealthy Mr. Dorington, whose benevolence and energy of action is misdirected into seemingly limitless financial support of a cohort of socially prominent but morally worthless hangers-on. When Dorington's finances are reported to have been ruined by a storm that destroys his West Indian plantations, these "friends" immediately desert him. By the time the reports of the destruction are discovered to have been false, Dorington has learned the limits of his indiscriminate beneficence and the difference between true and false friends. Accompanying these events is the secondary plot, which tells of the courtship between Dorington and Olivia, a young woman who threatens to break off their relationship not because of the supposed collapse of his fortune but because of the questionable nature of his social circle. Besides Olivia, the only ones who remain loyal after the supposed financial collapse are Herbert and Annabel, his laboring-class protégés, and a flighty young man aptly named Hairbrain, who *does* offer to help him after winning the lottery. Leaving aside for the moment the troubling nature of wealth derived from colonial holdings, it is clear that Holcroft seeks to critique the ruling classes of society, casting a wider net than in *Love's Frailties* to include not only members of the nobility but also City financiers and, controversially, the military, with the portrayal of the foolish Major Rampart. In what must have been an uncomfortable moment for many in the audience, Major Rampart cannot complete the singing of "Rule Britannia,"[57] as he blusters his way through the action. Alongside its critique of the hypocrisy and self-interestedness of the ruling classes, Holcroft's message in this play is the need to exert fortitude in a world defined by hypocrisy, arbitrariness, and betrayal, just as he questions the possibilities for, and limitations of, true sociability.

The Man of Ten Thousand ran for seven nights. It received a mixed reception in the daily newspapers and in the periodicals that later reviewed the published edition of the text. *Lloyd's Evening Post* wrote that "the plan is instructive and moral. The conduct of the fable is managed with considerable dramatic dexterity."[58] *The Monthly Review* asserted that "[t]he play has beautiful sentiments, and inculcates an excellent lesson."[59] As might be expected, the *True Briton* and the *Tomahawk, or Censor General* condemned the play, with the latter newspaper writing that "Holcroft's invectives against the high ranks, and the army, in his *republican* comedy, ought to be rewarded by damnation!"[60] This latter publication returned to comment upon the play five days later, with a brief poem which extends its criticism to John Philip Kemble, the manager of Drury Lane, who also acted the role of Dorington: "Mr. Kemble's the Man of Ten Thousand, they say, / To bring out at *Drury* a *democrat's* play," adding that the piece is "terrible stuff."[61]

Informing most if not all of these reviews is the acknowledgement of the political relevance of the play, along with the topicality that emerged from Holcroft's presence as its author. This recognition is foregrounded in the *Tomahawk's* observations, but also in the comments of sympathetic and neutral critics. Regarding Holcroft's authorship, *The Star* wrote, "A sort of mystery prevailed about the Author; and we lamented to see that so splenetic is the spirit of party, that the supposition of its being written by Mr. Holcroft set on a few mean individuals, to catch at every opportunity of displeasure. The genuine sense of the audience, however, triumphed over this pitiful attempt."[62] Specific representations and allusions within the play elicited a similarly pointed response in publications far less biased than the *Tomahawk*, first among these, not surprisingly, in the depiction of the military. Indicative of the reception of Holcroft's bumbling soldier is the later commentary of the *Monthly Review*: "The portraiture of Major Rampart . . . we can by no means admire; nor are we to wonder that it was not tolerated in the representation."[63]

Gillian Russell has shown us how "theatricality was integral to [war's] practice" during the 1790s: "the whole enterprise of the theatre . . . was dedicated to the commemoration of war and the enhancement of patriotic values."[64] Its resonances were apparent in displays of pageantry and spectacle, theatricals performed by military units (such as that which we saw with *The Deserted Daughter*), earlier historical dramas whose displacement acknowledged the contemporary conflicts and the often-conspicuous presence of officers and soldiers in theater audiences. It is not surprising, then, that Holcroft's introduction of the foolish Major Rampart on the Drury Lane stage upset prevailing sensibilities and provoked the censure of the critics. In the advertisement to the printed edition of the play, Holcroft devotes the entirety of his remarks to this character. He offers, however, no apology, instead elaborating on the major as a certain kind of contemptible but humorous character type, whose status as a military figure he pointedly disregards. Holcroft explains that the major is

> one of those persons who imagine they have uttered volumes, without having said a word: whose eager looks inform us how important they suppose their own conceptions to be; but, being too mighty for utterance, language sinks under them, and they expect the assent and applause of their companions to their Humphs? Hays? and expletives (MT, "Advertisement").

Whereas this portrayal of a nonheroic military figure aroused the ire of spectators and reviewers, another contemporary allusion in the play elicited a more sympathetic response. When Hudson, Dorington's agent in Barbados, later informs him that his property has escaped the brunt of the storm's damage, and that his "crops, which were great, are doubled in value," Dorrington responds: "Doubled? No! Let me perish indeed, rather than batten on the general distress!" (MT, 72). This interchange, as the *Universal Magazine* reported, "was received with a burst of applause by the house, and should bring a blush in the face of some of our gentlemen farmers, who monopolize grain at the moment of public scarcity."[65] The reference is to the general food scarcity of 1795–1796, in which those "gentlemen farmers" were generally seen as, if not the cause, then the abettors of a situation in which food, when available, was exorbitantly priced; farmers and suppliers were perceived as hoarders and manipulators of the market and widely "castigated for their greed."[66] Responses to rises in the price of bread and other basic foods included, as Roger Wells notes, "riots, strikes and politicization"; the scarcity was the single most cause of popular mobilization and protest during this period.[67] The critique of the public management of the crisis, in eliciting the sympathy of Holcroft's London audience, exhibited them as socially engaged and presented Dorington himself as enlightened and progressive.

It is difficult if not impossible, however, for a modern observer, as it must have been for some of Holcroft's original audiences and readers, to reconcile this "enlightened" position with the actual fact of Dorington's status as plantation owner. His wealth as a "man of ten thousand" derives from a slave economy. Dorington makes a point of expressing his concern for those enslaved people who had been left behind: "'Tis the poor wretches whom the afflicting heavens have left shelterless that demand our pity" (MT, 45), he exclaims when first hearing the news of the destruction, and later he instructs his agent to return to the island and provide relief for those persons in need. Yet there is no relinquishing of his plantations and there is nothing in the text to imply that his future philanthropy will continue to be based on anything other than the revenues from that same colonial project. The presence of a plantation and its enslaved people in Holcroft's play was just one of many such representations in the second half of the eighteenth century in which productions very often featured West Indian and African char-acters. In Jeffrey Cox's words, a "regular London theatergoer would have seen depictions of African characters or of slavery during perhaps every season of the eighteenth and early nineteenth century."[68] Yet Dorington's enslaved workers are absent from the stage; they are voiceless; and their suffering is mediated through the sympathy of the ostensibly "benevolent" plantation owner. One would be hard put to find in *The Man of Ten Thousand* those traces of an inevitable reciprocity between exploiting and exploited cultures that Joseph Roach's study of the circum-Atlantic exchange brilliantly articulates; the idea that "the unspeakable cannot be rendered forever inexpressible."[69] The grim reality acknowledged here exhibits, quite complacently, the way many men of ten thousand supported a lifestyle financed by slave exploitation. There are no mitigating factors to extricate Hol-croft from his complicity in seamlessly including the nefarious practice in his play.[70]

As any observer knew well, accompanying the already horrific conditions on the plantations was also the prevalence of hurricanes, which were a major fact of life in the Caribbean, one that exacted a high cost in human lives as of course they still do today. Matthew Mulcahy observes that in the eighteenth century, hur-ricanes "occupied a special place atop the planter's hierarchy of risk."[71] Knowing the risks, and their cost in human lives, was a chance that colonial planters were willing to take in their "quest for wealth."[72] Yet what interests Holcroft in this play is not a meditation on the institution of slavery or the possibility of its abolish-ment, nor a critique of planter economy in its wider dimensions. He remains conspicuously, troublingly, silent on those issues. He presents instead a localized critique of a moneyed class (with its military-class extension) in which social hypoc-risy is ubiquitous and where chance and arbitrariness prevail. The hurricane func-tions in *The Man of Ten Thousand* as a representation of the possibilities of risk and chance and as a plot device through which to foreground the need of the indi-vidual to exert fortitude when faced with false reports and their consequences. The specific geographical position of Dorington's estate, which ensured that his property remained intact in the aftermath of the hurricane, leads to the fortuitous outcome of his participation in the often-precarious West Indian plantation econ-omy. He has taken his chances and remained prosperous; indeed, he has emerged more prosperous than ever.

Another reflection upon the theme of chance occurs in Dorington's deal-ings with his flighty young friend, Hairbrain. Presented at the beginning of the play as another one of those parasitical hangers-on who aim to benefit from Dorington's money (he asks for 500 pounds to invest in a quack-medicine scheme), Hairbrain emerges at the conclusion as a truly caring and compassionate friend. Having won 20,000 pounds in the lottery, he insists on giving Dorington the money, unaware that the latter's plantation had escaped the damage of the storm. Hairbrain's generosity, resulting from well-timed luck, and his behavior in general emerge from a spiritual, even mystical, state of being. As he puts it, his estate is in his mind; it *is* the mind itself. Striking his forehead, he proclaims, "It is portable! Go where I will, I carry it about me! Thieves cannot steal! Confiscation cannot take it away!" (MT, 62). While Hairbrain's presence ostensibly offers audiences and readers moments of quirky comedy,[73] this character might also bear traces of Holcroft's own biography and thus have a more serious dimension. The action of the play as a whole resonates with Holcroft's personal experience, for instance in its depiction of abandonment by friends and acquaintances in a time of distress and the need for courage and resolution when faced with adversity. Reading the character of Hairbrain in the light of Iain MacCalman's research into radical enthusiasm in Newgate Prison at a time cotemporaneous with *The Man of Ten Thousand* can locate the play as a reflection upon 1790s Newgate culture more generally. This description underscores Holcroft's acknowledgement of that political and social milieu and his own experience within it.

In his essay "Newgate in Revolution: Radical Enthusiasm and Romantic Counterculture," MacCalman brings to life the world of Newgate Prison in the 1790s, showing it to be "complex, enduring and revolutionary" in which a "British radical-romantic enthusiasm" generated an alternative discourse of "subversive religio-scientific ideas" along with an alternative spiritual culture.[74] Thomas Holcroft was part of this culture. During his incarceration in the prison in 1794 in the lead-up to the Treason Trials, he made contact with other political detainees, some of whom espoused those counterculture epistemologies of religion, medicine, and the natural world. These included radicals Dr. William Hodgson, Dr. James Parkinson (who later identified the disease which carries his name), and Dr. Sampson Perry, men who shared, as MacCalman puts it, "animosities to medical/scientific orthodoxy."[75] On one hand, *The Man of Ten Thousand* critiques the "enthusiastic quackery"[76] associated with this Newgate milieu, implied in the play when Hairbrain asks, early on in the action, for money to invest in the dubious medicine scheme. Dorington denies the request by asserting that "to become a "vendor of poison by proxy [is] not much to a man's honour" (MT, 13). Yet as the play progresses, Hairbrain is taken more seriously, as he likewise moves from an involvement with quack medicines to a preoccupation with the essence of the mind. To be sure, Holcroft's focus on the mind has its basis in deep-seated beliefs that accompanied him throughout his adult life. Even before his prison experience, he had promoted the ascendancy of the human mind, claiming that "mind produces all the diseases of the body, and will cure them all: physic and drugs are only covers for ignorance . . . the mind of one person in health shall cure a whole nation of sick."[77] The exposure to the wide range of ideas circulating in Newgate must have intensified this already-present receptiveness to alternative understandings of the mind-body connection. Hairbrain's assertion that his "estate . . . is his mind" coincides with Holcroft's own long-standing beliefs, but also bears signs of his recent

Figure 3.1 Richard Newton, *Soulagement en Prison,* courtesy of the Lewis Walpole Library, Yale University

experience in Newgate and the nontraditional spiritualities with which he came into contact.

This Newgate sociability was visually portrayed in two watercolors (and subsequent prints) produced by the seventeen-year-old engraver Richard Newton, *Soulagement en Prison* (see figure 3.1) and *Promenade in the State Side of Newgate* (both of 1793). Depicting Newgate prisoners, including, among many others, Joseph Gerrald, John Horne Tooke, Daniel Isaac Eaton, and Henry Symonds, grouped together in convivial social circles, they exhibit, in MacCalman's words, "Jacobin sociability in action,"[78] while Jon Mee has argued that these pictures depict "the enlightened civility of radical associations being sustained even under duress."[79]

In *Unbounded Attachment,* her study of women's political engagement in the 1790s, Harriet Guest has examined the same prints while attuned to the mostly male sociability that they record, and which, by extension, call attention to women's vulnerability within radical social circles or exclusion from them.[80] The note from Holcroft to Godwin that announces Holcroft's excitement over the publication of Paine's *Rights of Man* (discussed in Chapter One) serves for Guest as an example of "the verbal and material exchanges of politics in the early 1790s, in which men such as Holcroft and Godwin were immersed" but from which women were removed or excluded.[81] The Godwin-Holcroft friendship exhibited in its shared political activist dimension an openness, a transparency, and at times an urgency, which was more difficult, if not impossible, for women to partake of. In *The Man of Ten Thousand*, conversely, Holcroft seems to be criticizing aspects of that sociability that was available to men. Dorington's remarks, "I have no view in the company I keep, and the dinners I give, except conviviality" (MT, 21), reveal by the end of the play that that conviviality has been ultimately false and empty. The self-reflexivity in *The Man of Ten Thousand* that references Holcroft's personal experience includes, then, besides the notion of fair-weather friends and false reports and a gesture towards nontraditional spirituality, a wider critique of social interactions by showing true friendship as a limited, precarious, and vulnerable ideal. In this sense *The Man of Ten Thousand* is among Holcroft's most pessimistic plays, as it omits any acknowledgement of the availability of reform for the corrupt elites who had been at the center of Dorington's circle, or any vision of improved communities of sociability. In his next major play, *Knave, or Not?*, this self-reflexive criticism of the central tenets of his life will also encompass his most prominent philosophical belief—that of truth itself.

* * *

In *Knave, or Not?* (DL, 1798) Holcroft continues to deliver a critique of British society, now at the close of the revolutionary decade. The contemporary awareness that infuses the play is manifested in different dimensions: generically, in the movement between comedy and melodrama; thematically, in Holcroft's relation to his own earlier conceptions of perfectibility and truth as essential components in the project of creating a better and more just society in the aftermath of the French Revolution; and textually, in the transition from manuscript to stage and then to page. Through these textual transactions Holcroft is continually testing the limits of what can be expressed; desiring to remain faithful to his original social criticism, but wishing to see his play remain onstage for the longest possible run. *Knave, or Not?* exhibits most forcefully among Holcroft's plays his ongoing negotiation of a reformist ideological position (and the pressures surrounding its performance) at the very moment when the triumph of the reaction was imminent.

Knave, or Not?, first performed on 25 January 1798 at Drury Lane, tells the story of Harry Monrose, a young man of obscure origins who infiltrates upper-class London society and, through his own deception, exposes a series of intrigues, betrayals, and crimes within the social circle of which he is now ostensibly a part. Disguised as a foreign count, Monrose has obtained the position of tutor in the home of Sir Job and Lady Ferment. He soon learns of a dark family secret: Aurelia, Lady Ferment's companion, is actually a rich heiress who has been cheated out of her inheritance by her uncle, Mr. Taunton, with the help of his friend Sir Job. Monrose has fallen in love with Aurelia, but she is in love with Oliver, Sir Job's son from a previous marriage. Susan, Monrose's sister, is aware of his schemes, and plays a crucial role in foiling her brother's invidious plan to take Aurelia for himself by force. The play concludes with Aurelia restored to her rights and united with Oliver. Monrose, notwithstanding his overly aggressive behavior toward the young woman, is welcomed by Oliver and Aurelia into their social circle, forgiven for his transgressions, and applauded for his exposure of the financial fraud.

Knave, or Not? is considered to be the Holcroft play with the most explicit political agenda and was, as such, the one in which the censor most heavily intervened. The play, drawing on themes presented in Carlo Goldoni's *La Serva Amorosa* and *Il Padre de Famiglia*, was originally submitted to the examiner on 8 January 1798. From evidence in the Larpent copy (LA 1192), we learn that the manuscript was submitted twice; the revised version was accompanied by a note from Richard Wroughton, actor and manager at Drury Lane, who wrote that "the suggested alteration is made and I trust will meet Approbation."[82] Wroughton may be referring to a long passage that is now crossed out, a speech by Monrose at the close of the second act, in which he contemplates his desired future with Aurelia, but also feels the qualms of conscience over the disguise that he has assumed. Trying to justify his actions, he asks, "Who are not impostors?" He then continues with the passage that would later be omitted:

> If I am not a lord, it seems I ought to have been. I find no difficulty in being as extravagant as a lord, as proud as a lord and as idle as a Lord. Let Lords look to it then[.] Let them be as superior to the poor in virtue as they are in power, and I will blush for being an impostor.[83]

Tellingly, this speech was restored in the published edition of the play (1798). Just as he had done in *Love's Frailties* and *The Man of Ten Thousand*, Holcroft makes a point in his prefatory remarks of responding to various criticisms of the play after it had been performed on stage. Here he calls his readers' attention to various passages, represented (as was his custom) by inverted commas, which had either given offense in the first performance of the play and were later removed, or had never been spoken onstage at all. In the published version of *Knave, or Not?* we can see both the reinstatement of this original censored passage as well as a later addition. Monrose now includes "impudence" in his catalog of lordly traits, and adds the following: "I could game like a lord, be duped like a lord, run in debt like a lord, and never pay, as naturally as if I had been born a lord. Let lords look to it, then, and reform."[84]

Altogether, the print edition of *Knave, or Not?* contains fourteen uses of inverted commas to inform the reader of passages that have been restored or added to the text. Significantly, among them are lines that *do* appear in the Larpent manuscript—thus showing Larpent had approved them—but which were deleted after the opening night performance, evidence once more for how the theater audience was often more rigid in its political censorship than was the censor himself. We recall the virulent audience reaction to other Holcroft plays as well: the contentious response to the speech on the uselessness of gentlemen in *Love's Frailties* and to the portrayal of Major Rampart in *The Man of Ten Thousand*, to name two examples. Yet the fact of actual revisions made *during* the play's run and the awareness of them by the public is what is noteworthy here, as it conclusively affirms the work of "the massed juries of Drury Lane and Covent Garden theatres," and of Holcroft's recognition of their power.[85]

Let us look at one further example of Holcroft's textual changes in *Knave, or Not?*, an additional speech that appears in inverted commas in the published version. Here Monrose rebukes a lawyer who has been complicit in the theft of Aurelia's fortune, then asks:

> What is a blockhead? A blockhead is a poor devil. Who are men of understanding? Every one who has five thousand a year. *What is a knave? He that is hanged for cheating. And what is an honest man? He that gets an estate by the same means.* Who are most courted? Men of wit. And who are they? Those that give good dinners, make their friends drunk with the best wines, and then pick their pockets at hazard and faro. Who are the most imitated? Men of fashion. And he is a man of the first fashion who associates with stable-boys in the morning, with opera dancers and demireps after dinner, and with a Babel mixture of bullies, bubbles, and pickpockets from midnight to sunrise (KN, 63).

This speech appears, unmarked, in the Larpent manuscript; Larpent had approved it, but the opening night audience at Drury Lane clearly had not. The four sentences beginning with "What is a knave?" that appear here in italics are, however, a new addition to the printed text. They provide further evidence of how Holcroft would not only reinstate in the published text what his original audience had disapproved, but also, as in the case of the "impudent lord" speech mentioned earlier, even further sharpen and expand his social criticism in that relatively safer realm. Monrose's dynamic and coherent articulation of political awareness, as it appears in print, conceals a prehistory mediated by the patchwork of omission, inclusion, and revision.

The cultural resonances in Monrose's speech appear not only in his representation of the decadence and hypocrisy of aristocratic society but also in the stylistic register in which the critique is expressed. The successive questions, "What is a knave?"; "What is an honest man?"; and so on, followed by the repeated definition of the term in politically freighted language, echo Charles Pigott's *Political Dictionary*, published three years previously in 1795. The *Dictionary* takes as its subject matter the exposure of the corrupt foundations of British society; Pigott's subtitle, "Explaining the True Meaning of Words," points to his aim of elucidating, in the spirit of radical reform, the vocabulary that anchors the political and social order. Described as "a Jacobin primer for radical artisans and labourers on the threshold of political literacy,"[86] the *Dictionary* is also a text that illustrates for its readers of all classes the power of language itself. Let us briefly look at one term noted in both the *Political Dictionary* and *Knave, or Not?* to view the similarity between the two texts. Under the entry for "fashion," Pigott writes that it is "to be lamented, that those to whom we look up to as our *betters*, should so seldom set up VIRTUE as a *fashion*; but that, instead thereof, they should only afford us an example of the most extravagant follies, of the rankest debaucheries."[87] Monrose / Holcroft, as we saw earlier, likewise defines "men of the first fashion" as those who associate with, among others, "stable-boys," "demireps," "bullies," and "pick-pockets." "Fashion" therefore becomes shorthand for decadent social power, and its appearance in both texts exemplifies their common view of the specious structures—cultural, political, and linguistic—on which that power is based.

Knave, or Not? received a mixed reception in the daily newspapers the morning after its premiere. The reviews of the play acknowledge its potent political message as well as the heightened response of the audience, in which "unfair interruptions," "hiss[ing]," and "whispers that the piece was from a Jacobin pen" echoed throughout the theater.[88] Subordinating his own opinion to that of the audience (whose "judgment . . . renders it unnecessary for us to enter into the particulars of the plot"), the reviewer for the *Sun* added that the play was "*Mitching Malicho*', and meant mischief."[89] Such must have been the reception of the radical elements in the play that even those newspapers sympathetic to Holcroft, the *Morning Chronicle* and the *Morning Post*, concurred to a certain extent with the judgment of the opening night audience and advised him to "expunge"[90] certain passages in succeeding performances, advice with which, as his inverted commas remind us, he complied. The reviewers returned to remark upon the successive performances of the play, providing an ongoing commentary on Holcroft's revisions. Thus, the *London Chronicle* stated following the second performance that "several judicious alterations and necessary omissions have taken place." At the same time, this reviewer asserted that "the *cloven foot* has not yet been amputated, and the *Knave* continues to strut about in monstrous pace . . . some of his most forbidding features have assumed a more mild and conciliating appearance; but the mask which has been thrown over his hateful nature, only serves to cover the exterior blemishes of his character, not to hide the hideous colours of his heart."[91] The newspaper returned to the play once again following the third performance to announce that it had been "so much purged of its offensive and pernicious qualities."[92] The ongoing mutability of the dramatic text becomes a dramatic text in itself, signaling the disciplining of Holcroft and his radical voice. Or at least the attempt to do so: the knave "continues to strut."

Common to these original reviews is also the way they downplay the play's comic elements and in doing so underscore the seriousness of Holcroft's message. Thus, the *Morning Post* writes that its "chief excellence is in the vigour of its passion and sentiments."[93] *The True Briton* points to the "melancholy impression" conveyed in the production. Referring ostensibly to the accumulative effect of repeatedly hearing of the "situation of the poor, and the oppressions of the rich," this newspaper's hostile reviewer insightfully, although probably unwittingly, calls attention to the affective potential of Holcroft's dramatic production.[94] What had been noteworthy and memorable to the original audience, along with Holcroft's radical expressions, had not been the comedy at all.

The same acknowledgement of a strong emotional pull that had accompanied *The Deserted Daughter* is once more evident in the reception of *Knave, or Not?*, signaling the exhaustion of traditional sentimental comedy and with it, an incipient melodramatic modality. As in *The Deserted Daughter*, melodrama is anticipated in *Knave, or Not?* in the struggle between power and powerlessness; Aurelia's disenfranchisement here echoes that of Joanna in the earlier play. Furthermore, it appears in the way in which, as Jane Moody has argued, "melodrama helps to make possible a more dynamic and nuanced view of human nature." This nuancing appears in particular in the portrayal of the villain as a figure that evokes pity.[95] Although referring to *A Tale of Mystery*, Moody's insight is also relevant for *Knave, or Not?* and is apparent in the climactic moment of confrontation between Monrose, who has just tried to seduce Aurelia, and Oliver, Aurelia's acknowledged lover, who arrives fortuitously on the scene. Although Monrose's sister, Susan, has already intervened to forestall the attack, it is Oliver who ultimately foils both the original plan as well as Monrose's subsequent insistence on a duel:

> MONROSE: Damnation! Coward! Fire!
>
> OLIVER: Fire you, madman!
>
> MONROSE: Hell!
>
> OLIVER: Think you I am to be bullied into what you call courage? If you are so wound up to murder, begin! Here is your mark! Take your level! A shot through the heart, or a bullet through the brain. Then vaunt of your dexterity; and again reiterate your epithet, gentleman.
>
> MONROSE: (*Gnashing*) To be thus baffled!
>
> OLIVER: Abandon your purpose, or dispatch: for not all the arguments of hell, nor all its fiends, shall drive me to shed the blood of human being.
>
> MONROSE: To be thus tamed! Oh! Idiot! I the master of accident? Fool! Fool! I am the very slave of prejudice.
>
> OLIVER: What! Is antipathy to crime, prejudice?
>
> MONROSE: (*Peremptorily*) Leave me, Sir—to my own contempt. I am what I despise—a braggart.
>
> OLIVER: Thank heaven! There are many braggarts in vice. You are a better man than you supposed (KN, 79–80).

This exchange marks the moment when our indignation over an act of villainy is transformed into potential compassion. The reader (or spectator) cannot but feel pity towards Monrose, a moment earlier a violent aggressor and now confronted with, and repenting, the egregiousness of his behavior. Although there are other, far less complex, villains in the play—most notably the scheming Sir Job and Mr. Taunton, the deceivers of Aurelia—it is Monrose whose actions are consistently under scrutiny and debate. The indeterminacy with which he is presented is echoed in the title *Knave, or Not?*, which foregrounds Monrose as the main protagonist and which, with its interrogative formulation, calls attention to a capaciousness in the portrayal of this character that encourages the reader or spectator to resist moral judgments.[96] And Monrose's earlier, troubling, actions towards Aurelia, along with his fraudulent behavior in general *are* ultimately forgotten; it is sympathy instead that he evokes at the end of the play. As Aurelia herself tells him, "You have proved the dignity of your mind. You have gained friends that will never forsake you" (KN, 87).

Monrose's reformation is also significant as it suggests the powers of the human mind and its capability for improvement and in doing so emphasizes the idea of perfectibility, which, of course, was one of the main ideological and philosophical issues that preoccupied Holcroft in his writing and according to which he tried to live his life. In *The Man of Ten Thousand* too, the preeminence of the human mind was foregrounded. For Holcroft more generally, it was "all important . . . mind could conquer anything" (*Life* 1: xvii), including the real or perceived errors that accompany human endeavor. As we saw earlier in this book, in his *Narrative of Facts*, published soon after his release from Newgate, he had addressed the subject of error and perfectibility, writing to Chief Justice Eyre, who had presided over the trial, that "the man and the mistake . . . ought everlastingly to be kept distinct: for the mistake is past recal [*sic*], but the man may amend. The error should never be spared; the person ought never to be attacked" (NF, 80). In *Knave, or Not?* Holcroft's understanding of the principle of perfectibility is applied in this same way. Monrose's aggressive behavior towards Aurelia is condemned while he himself is reintegrated into a forgiving social community. At the same time, this move towards perfectibility does not carry with it a rejection of the social criticism which had accompanied Monrose's actions throughout the play. *That* aspect of his worldview is not included in his professions of repentance and, it is implied, does not need to be expiated in his progress towards eventual reform.

The centrality of the political awareness expressed by Holcroft's protagonist and the efficacy of the radical critique, so memorable for many of the play's original audiences, continued to be acknowledged after its short stage run had ended. The *Anti-Jacobin Review*, for example, in its commentary on the published version of the play, notes that the character of Monrose "seems to have been framed for the purpose of expressing certain opinions and sentiments inimical to the present orders and gradations of this country" and that his opinions "occupy so much of the work . . . that it was evidently the desire of the author to render them peculiarly impressive. . . . As a vehicle of pernicious principles, [the play] is an object of rigid animadversion."[97] Holcroft must have anticipated the reception he would receive in the daily newspapers and, even more certainly, in a reactionary journal such as the *Anti-Jacobin* which, although a new journal at the time of this review, was a continuation in periodical form of the *Anti-Jacobin, or Weekly Examiner* that had been published in the previous year and which Holcroft would have known well. There is a self-reflexivity to *Knave, or Not?* that acknowledges the risks that accompany the presentation of a radical political agenda and which appears in the many instances of silencing and indiscreet speech, secrets and disclosures, and references to the power of words themselves. For example, Aurelia asks if she must be "bribed to be silent when I ought to speak, and to speak when I ought to be silent?" (KN, 55), and Susan, likewise, fears that she "shall neither know when to speak nor when to hold [her] tongue" (KN, 36–37). A remark made by Mrs. Clack, the servant in the house where Monrose works, is pertinent here: "I have put a lock upon my lips. I don't know how I came to make so free with you!" (KN, 9). So she speaks to Monrose, in lines that reverberate with the consciousness of the limits of free speech in a repressive society.[98]

Holcroft himself also placed a "lock upon [his] lips" to a certain degree. Not only did he take the advice of his first reviewers and cut the more provocative speeches from subsequent performances of *Knave, or Not?*, but, additionally, on the second night of performance he had Richard Wroughton appear on stage with an announcement to the audience. As the actor John Bannister later recalled, "Mr. Wroughton read a paper, drawn up by the author, in which he disclaimed having had any party views, and solicited a patient hearing. This request was granted, and the play went on without interruption."[99] We can only speculate as to Holcroft's feelings on this occasion. He must have been satisfied, on one hand, that his work would get another "hearing" and that he would receive additional remuneration, welcome relief for his hard-pressed financial situation. Yet it is safe to assume that he was also probably mortified at the need to so conspicuously compromise the ideological engagement of author and text; to submit to the disciplinary powers of the prevailing political consensus as manifested in the theater and in society at large.[100] Holcroft's actions within the Drury Lane theater underscore John Bugg's account of the pervasiveness of censorship and self-censorship that followed the legislation of the Two Acts—what Bugg calls a "poetics of gagging"[101]—within the field of literary production, which was saturated with silencing, fear, and the breakdown in communication.

This moment in the Drury Lane theater is especially significant as it encapsulates the issue of truth under duress, both by way of Wroughton's address to the audience (with its suggestion of a possible lack of transparency in Holcroft's own actions) as well as in reference to the function of "truth" itself as a thematic concern in *Knave, or Not?*. We know, to be sure, of the power of truth for Holcroft as a crucial marker in his conception of a just, perfectible society. In the *Narrative of Facts*, he would harness it to his defense at one of the most crucial and critical moments of his life. "Truth," he wrote there, as he recalled his speech at the doomed Committee of Conference (with its delegates from the Society of Constitutional Information and the London Corresponding Society and its plan for a British Convention) "is all-powerful" (NF, 90). Five years before writing *Knave, or Not?* he had addressed the issue of truth in the *Monthly Review*, in his review of the play *Every One Has His Fault* (1793), written by his close friend Elizabeth Inchbald. That play tells the story of a discordant group of friends and of how Mr. Harmony, Inchbald's protagonist, enables their reconciliation through a series of well-meaning falsehoods. Similarly to *Knave, or Not?*, Inchbald's play exhibits a strong political awareness; as a result, it had received a harsh reception upon its premiere from *The True Briton*, which had condemned Inchbald's representation of high prices and food shortages and her overall critique of contemporary society.[102] While Holcroft most certainly approved of Inchbald's portrayal of social ills, he chose in his review to focus instead on Mr. Harmony's propensity to lie:

> Of Mr. Harmony, we cannot help saying that we are out of patience with his benevolent lies; that is, we feel a very sincere concern that the deeply-rooted prejudice of mankind 'that falsehood may be beneficial' is thus so forcibly inculcated. The very merit of the writing increases the sin; and the auditors will go home well satisfied that the lies, which they may have ever told, were all for some good purpose or other, and therefore that they, like Mr. Harmony, are all very good people.[103]

Five years later, in *Knave, or Not?* Holcroft too would relate the story of a teller of "benevolent lies"—benevolent in the sense that Monrose's role as an impostor helps lead to the recovery of Aurelia's fortune and to the exposure of corruption at the highest levels of society. Could Holcroft, like Inchbald, have come to the conclusion that social harmony and justice can only be achieved through deception? He would claim in his journal entry of 14 November 1798, nine months after the appearance of his play, that he (still) "supposed his principles to be founded on truth" (*Life*, 2:195), but some of his earlier actions, such as the concealed authorship of *The Deserted Daughter* and the plot resolution of *Knave, or Not?*, seem to indicate a more nuanced view of its power. In 1798, with the anti-radical legislation firmly entrenched and with the consciousness of the price he had personally paid in the promotion of truth indelibly before him, how could it be otherwise? The understanding that truth itself had proved inefficacious in promoting reform and in bringing about a better and more just society may in fact be the true melodrama unfolding before us. This is melodrama because Holcroft's grappling with the notion of truth indicates the key process that the genre explicates, as Peter Brooks has argued, the process of reaching the "fundamental drama of the moral life."[104] *Knave, or Not?* May also be seen then as Holcroft's personal drama of recognition—"Who are not impostors?"—as it exhibits the vulnerability of transparency and truth, and the limitations of his political vision.

* * *

That Holcroft experienced the fraught reception of his plays and his public, cultural presence more generally as a kind of defeat is evident in the fact that he left Britain in 1799 for a self-imposed exile on the Continent. Before his departure he continued his attempts for the theater, and even had a marked success among them. This was the production of *He's Much to Blame*, adapted from Antoine de Ferriol Pont de Veyle's *Le Complaisant* and Goethe's *Clavigo*, and first performed on 13 February 1798 at Covent Garden, one week after the final performance of *Knave, or Not?* The play, which tells the story of two young couples who struggle against parental authority, pressures of class and status, and a series of both comical and sentimental misunderstandings, was presented to the public as the work of John Fenwick, another member of the "Godwin circle" and an activist for reform in his own right. *His* politics did not hinder the play's success, which extended to twenty-two nights. Philip Cox has traced the play's reception, noting the "extremely positive" responses of original reviewers, quite unlike those of its immediate predecessor, *Knave, or Not?*, and wonders how this reception would have differed had Holcroft's identity as the true author of the play been known.[105] Holcroft was delighted with his triumph. In his diary entry of 1 August 1798, he wrote of a conversation on *He's Much to Blame*, and the response of a friend who had "testified great satisfaction at the shame its success brought upon [Holcroft's] persecutors," for the king, not knowing its author, "had commanded it twice" (*Life*: 2:170). Yet regarding the same subject, William Hazlitt remarks upon Holcroft's unease at the need for less than sincere action in the concealment of his authorship, an "artifice to which . . . [he] was obliged to resort more than once" (*Life*: 2:105).

Philip Cox traces the Godwinian thought that permeates *He's Much to Blame* and argues that the play's clear message for sincerity and "steadfast adherence" to one's beliefs clearly reference Holcroft's commitment to, and belief in, "social (and political) justice."[106] At the same time, the submission of this play under Fenwick's name, as well as the reliance on chance and disguise (as in all of Holcroft's plays post–Treason Trials) also denotes, I believe, something other than sincerity. In spite of his ongoing belief in "truth," it appears that Holcroft had come to the conclusion that justice—social, domestic, legal—could only be achieved through deception, or luck, or both. *Love's Frailties*, written and produced before the Treason

Trials, is excluded from this sequence—indeed, stands apart from the later plays—in its more confident and optimistic portrayal of the availability of reform, unencumbered by the need for concealment or for a resolution that is contingent to arbitrariness: a misplaced ledger, a false report, a winning lottery ticket.

The preeminence of chance, along with the practice of deception motivated by a climate of hostility, rejection, and suspicion, provides a brief glimpse into the tense political climate at the close of the eighteenth century as it resonated in the day-to-day workings of the London stage. With Holcroft's firm belief in the power of truth, the resort to artifice and dissembling must have come feelingly. This effort resonates, for example, in Dorington in *The Man of Ten Thousand*, who had been deserted by his friends in time of distress—but it also emerges in the larger drama that was Holcroft's life, in the struggle to have his views heard in a time when he was repeatedly condemned by the public. His stories of perfectibility and sincerity during the second half of the revolutionary decade are thus not only shaped by the ideals of truth and reform but also now qualified by his recognition of the necessity of equivocation and the ineluctable self-referentiality of his own experience.

On 22 JUNE 1798 THOMAS HOLCROFT began to keep a diary. In a brief preface to the work, he wrote that he had "long felt a desire to keep memorandums of the common occurrences of life" and predicted that his determination to adhere to the journal would "not easily be shaken" (*Life*, 2:122). Yet this resolution was not sustained: the diary abruptly concludes in March 1799, less than a year after its commencement, with no explanation, comment, or concluding salutation. The observations recorded in the roughly ten months of the journal that Holcroft did keep provide a fascinating account of his life leading up to his decision to depart from Britain for exile on the Continent, as we view his daily routines, conversations, and thoughts. Through Holcroft's depiction of his involvement in the business of the theater, his interactions with politicians, intellectuals, and others at Debrett's bookshop, his encounters on the streets of London and his social evenings at home, including his close friendship with William Godwin, we are presented with a vivid canvas of life in the metropolis at the close of the eighteenth century.

This chapter focuses on Holcroft's experience recorded in his diary from June 1798 until March 1799, as he navigates what is often a hostile cultural environment but also partakes in the opportunities for sociability that it offers. The diary was included by Hazlitt in the *Memoirs of the Late Thomas Holcroft* and, together with the larger memoir in which it was published, exhibits in a different dimension many of the key issues and concepts that I examine in this book. Let us take, for example, the subject of performance. Holcroft had already performed a kind of Godwinian radicalism through self-consciously assertive personal actions during the time of the Treason Trials, as well as presenting it through anxious yet exuberant characters such as Monrose in *Knave, or Not?*. The paratextual elements that accompany the plays, moreover—his prologues, and in particular, the advertisements to the printed editions—provide an ongoing account of Holcroft's tenacity as he persists in announcing and maintaining a committed ideological position, while showing a defensiveness dictated by, and responding to, prevailing popular opinion.

In this chapter the aftermath of the Treason Trials, evoked in Holcroft's daily life as recorded in the diary, will be portrayed as it accompanies and influences the quotidian experience of a writer and onetime political activist coping with and forestalling defeat. A subdued revolutionary drama of its own, it was a quiet epilogue to his former activism. In exhibiting his life as such, Holcroft assumes an implied reader to whom he holds up his actions for scrutiny and, perhaps, judgment. More generally, the diary is a performance because, as Dan Doll and Jessica Munns assert, the "'narrator' of a diary is always a self-dramatizing persona . . . the subject of the private/personal diary is always the self in one way or another, the construction of that self is inevitably the product of shaping and selection, in short, of art."[1] Holcroft's deployment of anecdote (and there are many in his diary) underlines an additional dimension of the literariness of this journal, presenting what Mary Chamberlain and Paul Thompson have argued are the element "in most life stories . . . most immediately recognizable as having formal literary qualities."[2]

At the same time, Holcroft's diary also evinces moments of tension between this recognizably public, performative dimension and the text's status as an archive of private, personal experience. A conspicuous example of this tension appears in Holcroft's response to a report, which he had heard from Eliza Fenwick, of his amanuensis relating information from the diary about town. (The very fact of employing an amanuensis to transcribe a diary calls its private nature into question.) Acknowledging the report, Holcroft angrily claims that the journal's "contents" are "sacred" (*Life*, 2:206).[3] Yet in the same passage he writes of his desire that the "memorandum" (as he calls it there) be available in the future as a "depository of facts," so as to exhibit his "conduct, opinions, and intercourse," some aspects of which "may turn to use" (*Life*, 2:207). This duality is an ongoing feature of the work. When, we wonder, is Holcroft consciously writing to an audience? How transparent is he? What information does he withhold? In contrast, what is thought to be of "use"? This tension is further reinforced by the fact that at least some private matters never found their way into his diary. A case in point is his courtship of Louisa Mercier. Their marriage takes the reader by surprise, and we have little, if any, preparation for it, illustrating his ability to keep a secret, even, it seems, from his amanuensis. The above issues underscore Rachel Cottam's claim for diary writing in general: "as a text, the diary comes to stand as an embodiment of the paradoxical and elusive self, revealed, yet always remaining hidden, simultaneously public and private."[4]

Attempts to resolve these questions are further complicated by the fact that the diary was revised by William Godwin before its publication as part of the *Memoirs*.[5] Evidence for this intervention—and for Godwin's censorship—appears in Godwin's diary entries for January 1810, in the annotation "Ht revise."[6] Godwin was appalled at what he saw in the diary and, in a letter to Holcroft's widow Louisa, claimed that Holcroft "would never have consented" for the diary to be published.[7] Godwin had previously known of the journal's existence, but not that Hazlitt had included it in his book. In strongly objecting to its inclusion, Godwin worried of its effects on Holcroft's reputation, on Hazlitt's, and on his own.[8] Material lost following Godwin's interventions includes, from the evidence of his letter to Louisa, what appear to have been rude or tactless comments made or reported by Holcroft regarding Dr. Samuel Parr, the actress Sarah Siddons, as well as, what would have been intensely personal for Godwin, "the private transactions and affairs of [Mary] Wollstonecraft and Mr. Imlay." "Many parts," he warns Louisa, "are actionable."[9] Henry Crabb Robinson, a diarist himself, had also seen Holcroft's original unrevised diary and had been of the same opinion as Godwin, writing in his own journal of "conversations . . . anecdotes and opinions possibly painful to the feelings of many [that] were asserted with[ou]t scruple."[10] Materially, Godwin's revisions held up publication of the *Memoirs* for a number of years, from 1810 until 1816. This delay led Mary Lamb to famously call it the "Life Everlasting," an epithet to which the atheist Holcroft would probably have smiled.[11]

The uncertain factual precision of Holcroft's diary emerges in another dimension of the text as well. Within the diary many individuals are identified only by the first initial of their surname, a fact that led one of the original reviewers of the *Memoirs* to complain that "the initials are now and then so multiplied, that it renders the reading troublesome to all, except intimate acquaintances."[12] The first edition was later amended by an unknown hand to fill in most of these names. Elbridge Colby corroborated these annotations for his edition of the *Memoirs*, while occasionally suggesting possible alternatives. (In quoting from the diary, I silently accept Colby's identifications.) The presence of the original "troublesome" initials baffled, for the diary's first readers, attempts at easy identification and, despite the later identifying revisions, once more calls our attention to the text's equivocal transparency as it traverses public and private spheres of friendship, ideology, and selfhood, authenticity and studied performance, in an unsettled cultural and political world.[13]

In exploring Holcroft's personal experience, shaped, as it certainly was, by his ideological commitment and its aftereffects, I begin this chapter by briefly examining the larger work, the *Memoirs*, in which the diary is embedded, including its place within a tradition of working-class autobiography. From there, I move to a discussion of the diary itself, first briefly acknowledging the reactionary backlash at the close of the eighteenth century, a context which profoundly informs it. I pay close attention to his accounts of a dense experience of sociability and conversation, for example, in his meetings with friends and colleagues at Debrett's bookshop and the political discussions that he took part in there. I also explore the diary as a record of Holcroft's literary activity, through his management of his career and his dealings with actors, theater managers, and publishers and in which we can observe some of his methods of working. I conclude the chapter with a discussion of Holcroft's Continental exile. Letters he wrote to William Godwin during this period exhibit a different dimension of life writing as they tell the story of Holcroft's experience abroad. In doing so, they reference and expand upon many of the same concerns—literary business, economic survival, political vulnerability—that appeared during the times of their close, sociable proximity in London. As we will see, the more abstract drama of a radical life informs all the above proceedings and illustrates Holcroft's experience as a victim of the reaction at a time when the reaction was especially pervasive.

*   *   *

Thomas Holcroft began to write his memoirs with the knowledge that he was dying and managed to dictate the first seventeen chapters before finally succumbing to his illness. Godwin and other friends gave the task of preparing the book for publication to William Hazlitt, who continued Holcroft's first person account with a third person narration.[14] In these first seventeen chapters Holcroft chronicles his life story up until the age of fifteen and provides a stirring portrait of a childhood which commenced with working-class stability and later declined to the abject poverty that characterized his family's life as itinerant peddlers. Along with recollections of indigence, of being "pressed by fatigue, hunger, cold, and nakedness" (*Life*, 1: 34), Holcroft includes appealing childhood adventures and an especially entertaining retelling of his apprenticeship in the Newmarket stables. (The energy that marked his experience with the horse-minding life surely influenced his later portrayal of Goldfinch in *The Road to Ruin*.) Holcroft's narration, which ends with his decision to leave Newmarket for London, is followed by Hazlitt's account of Holcroft's path to professional success, which includes extended discussions of Holcroft's literary works along with remarks on his political activity, including his involvement in the Treason Trials in 1794. The diary is inserted toward the end of Volume II of this three-volume work; it continues into Volume III, which concludes with Holcroft's exile on the Continent and a number of his personal letters.[15]

Just as the diary exhibits tension between a private record of life and a gesture to a reading public—this is a text which "may turn to use"—the *Memoirs* as a whole reveals generic pressures of its own, bringing together an initial section of autobiography and a continuation in a third person account which then returns at one point to include the first person diary. Autobiography was a new genre, emerging in the Romantic era and as yet without established protocols or conventions.[16] Stephen Behrendt has noted the "theatrical and performative" nature of early autobiography,[17] and this aspect may be seen in Holcroft's *Narrative of Facts* and the *Letter* to Windham, also examples of his first person writing, with their assertive ideological and performative self-fashioning in the portrayal of his Treason Trials ordeal and its aftermath. It is more difficult to apply this insight to the *Memoirs*, for the first person narration is so brief and relates to a very limited period, although as it is, it forcefully displays the precocity, persistence, and achievements of Holcroft's youth with brisk cheer and energetic didactics. Had he been able to continue, it is quite possible he would have shaped it accordingly, as the self-fashioning thrust was certainly a part of his authorial repertoire. In *Memoirs of Bryan Perdue*, written a few years earlier in 1805, he has his protagonist commence that fictional autobiography by stating: "Where is the man, who, in the act of writing memoirs of himself does not find his attention drawn, or rather, fixed, on the bright and amiable part of the portrait? He proposes to write honestly, but has he the power?"[18] However, any adaptation or reframing in his own *Memoirs* surrounding his adult years—besides in the diary and maybe there too, depending on what was excised— would ultimately have to be shaped by another hand than his.

In any case, it was the story of childhood survival, of self-education, and of emergence from poverty that supplied the drama in Holcroft's *Memoirs* and which was especially memorable to readers. The *Critical Review* commended this "early portion" as "so full of curious and entertaining incidents—told in so lively and humorous a manner, that none will lay it down with dissatisfaction, and few without gratification."[19] The *Gentleman's Magazine* acknowledged the emotive power of Holcroft's childhood struggles—its reviewer was "deeply affected by . . . the misery and wretchedness" of the early years, and then "rejoiced" to see him comfortably settled at Newmarket.[20] Mary Russell Mitford commented on the strength of character that Holcroft's early experiences evinced and the fact that, although dying, he is able to tell a story that is "lucid," "lively," and "vigorous."[21] The vibrancy of this childhood narrative lays the groundwork for the continuation of the biography. Feeling the contrast between the suffering of the indigent child and the later fame that the adult Holcroft achieved, the reader recognizes the power of individual effort and the didactic value lodged in his story of overcoming obstacles of penury and neglect.

Holcroft himself had foreseen the utility of that story when he declared that "the chief intention [of his memoirs was] . . . to excite an ardent emulation in the breasts of the youthful readers" (*Life*, 1:38). In a later justification of Holcroft's beliefs (and, interestingly, using his own favorite terminology), reviewers valorized the powers of the mind. As the *Theatrical Inquisitor and Monthly Mirror* put it, the *Memoirs* "affords a most impressive and pleasing proof of the impossibility of utterly subduing the energies of a mind naturally strong and aspiring, and of the unconquerable perseverance with which such a mind will work its way to eminence and distinction, though originally placed in the most discouraging situation."[22] In 1830, an excerpt of Holcroft's memoirs appeared in the *Pursuit of Knowledge Under Difficulties*, a compilation which aimed to "shew how the most unpropitious circumstances have been unable to conquer an ardent desire for the acquisition of knowledge."[23] Dickens was influenced by the *Memoirs*, and John Harrison Stonehouse noted the way the story of Holcroft's early years resonates in *David Copperfield*.[24] Dickens himself wrote to his close friend John Forster in 1846, "Shall I leave you my life in MS. when I die? There are some things in it that would touch you very much, and that might go on the same shelf with the first volume of Holcroft's."[25] In 1852, six years after Dickens wrote that letter, the *Memoirs* was republished as Volume 17 of the *Travellers Library*. This was a series of reprinted and original nonfiction writing, in what would become 102 volumes, published by Longman at the price of 2*s* 3*d* for each volume. It was part of a wider initiative, which included Routledge, Murray, and other publishers, to cater to the reading needs of railway travelers by offering books of "valuable information and acknowledged merit" and "in a form adapted for reading while travelling, and also of a character that will render them worthy of preservation."[26] Aileen Fyfe argues that the "key distinguishing feature of the various series for travelers produced by Longman and Murray was their claim to contain works of superior literary merit." Longman's series thus included works of history, biography, travel, and a number of works on natural and social science.[27]

The writer of the preface to the *Travellers Library* edition of the *Memoirs*, like the previous reviewers of the original 1816 text, calls attention to Holcroft's "rise," implicitly emphasizing the worthiness of his story for inclusion in the Longman series: "The difficulties with which genius has frequently to contend in the varied trials of life have rarely been so strikingly exemplified as in the life of Thomas Holcroft. Cradled in poverty, with no education save what he could pick up for himself, amid incessant struggles for bare existence . . . he yet contrived to surmount the most untoward circumstances, and at last took his place, among the most distinguished writers of his age[.]"[28] Although Dickens's comment to Forster six years earlier had assumed familiarity with Holcroft's work (he had no need to elaborate on the particulars), the editor of the *Travellers Library* edition states that Holcroft's *Memoirs* had "long been a scarce book";[29] this edition not only would make it available to a new generation of readers but to a wider public by virtue of its affordable pricing.

It is difficult to overemphasize the power the story of Holcroft's upward mobility would have had on these, as well as on the *Memoirs*' original readers, even when, as they continued reading, they would encounter his political principles and the account of his arrest on charges of treason. A hint of the ambivalence his political efforts may have aroused appears in the comments of the reviewer for the *Gentleman's Magazine* in 1816: "without undertaking either to defend or blame his principles, we think it extremely interesting and beneficial to future generations, to peruse with attention these Memoirs." This reviewer later reveals his own position when he states that Hazlitt's account may convince readers "of the absurdity of that prosecution [for treason] having been attempted."[30] The writer of the prefatory remarks for the *Travellers Library* ignores this major crisis in Holcroft's life, although in reading the text itself the reader would have encountered that charged dimension of what was called "an entertaining biography of a remarkable man."[31]

To be sure, any working-class autobiography is political, in the sense that, as Jonathan Rose has argued, these autobiographies "represent an effort by working people to write their own history"; in educating themselves, working-class autodidacts challenged traditional hierarchies and "demolished justifications of privilege."[32] But can Holcroft's memoir really be counted as "working class"? David Vincent defines working-class autobiography as one in which the "autobiographer should have been the child of a working man and should have remained a member of the working class until the composition of his memoirs," although he also admits that this distinction is difficult to maintain.[33] The compelling element in Holcroft's story was surely in the way he overcame the socioeconomic reality of his early years. His "rise" was what made that story memorable, the fact that he was, as Mitford wrote, an author "sprung from the people."[34] Notwithstanding this upward mobility, he continued to be associated in some quarters with his working-class origin—either with the admiration of various reviewers or with the condescension shown, for example, by Lord Mountcashell, who, meeting him in Paris, scorned him not only for his political activities but for his "lowly class position."[35] Holcroft did not avoid the subject. The writer for the *Critical Review* who reviewed his *Memoirs* in 1816 had passed an evening with him years earlier in which, he recalled, Holcroft had "stated with perfect openness, that he himself had begged bread for the temporary sustenance of his parents."[36] The remarks of Lord Mountcashell, as well as of this critic, reinforce the irreducible awareness of class origin, whether through the disparagement of the peer or the approbation of the writer for the *Critical Review*, who nonetheless seems surprised at Holcroft's "openness" and perhaps a bit taken aback by the way his childhood poverty had been so forthrightly announced.

Recent scholarship on Holcroft has extended David Vincent's definition of working-class autobiography to decisively include Holcroft's *Memoirs* and in doing so to foreground an additional political dimension of the book. The privations of Holcroft's early years depicted in the first person narrative thus can also serve as a comment on British society as a whole, on "things as they are" in a bleak material sense, while Hazlitt's continuation suggests the means of overcoming them. As A. A. Markley puts it, Holcroft offers an enactment of the way that "specific experiences in a childhood of abject poverty could be translated into effective critiques of contemporary life as a means of improving the social and political condition of his fellow Britons."[37] This performance of social mobility, Wil Verhoeven explains, "make[s] available to the disprivileged masses some of his hard-won insights into the workings of society."[38] Markley's and Verhoeven's discussions, as well as other critical commentary on the *Memoirs*—nineteenth-century and present-day—devote, however, far less commentary to the diary than to other parts of the book (although Markley acknowledges it as the main reason for the delay in publication).[39] Among its original reviewers, The *Gentleman's Magazine* just briefly remarks that the diary "rivets our attention" while also, as we saw earlier, noting its frustration with Holcroft's use of initials to conceal the identity of some individuals.[40] The *Critical Review* states that it "contains a simple and interesting display of the thoughts, feelings, and habits of the writer, besides many amusing anecdotes."[41] In what follows, I redress this lack of critical attention by recovering Holcroft's diary as an important cultural document; the first person voice returns once more to his text to supplement the portrayal of a penurious childhood with the depiction of an anxious existence in a reactionary society, the memory of the Treason Trials keen in many minds. This narrative is far less buoyant than the earlier portrayal of his childhood and not at all "simple," as it evinces a different kind of outsiderness against which he struggled to overcome.

* * *

Holcroft's diary, written between 22 June 1798 and 12 March 1799, traverses the period in which he, along with other reformers, was continually attacked in the press as well as in countless novels, poems, satires, and squibs, at the time when these attacks were the most repeated and unremitting. Those localized attacks on his plays, such as the fraught and fractious responses to *The Man of Ten Thousand* and *Knave, or Not?*, were part of the wider barrage of hostilities directed against the 1790s activists who persisted in maintaining a critical, antigovernment and proreform position. Before turning to Holcroft's own experience amidst this onslaught as recorded in his diary, let me first briefly acknowledge some broader contexts. Heavy as the legislative and judicial repression was throughout the early-to-mid 1790s—marked by the Royal Proclamation in 1792, the Scottish treason trials in 1793, and the London trials of 1794 and intensified by the contemporaneous actions of loyalist groups, such as John Reeve's Association for the Preservation of Liberty and Property against Republicans and Levellers—the latter half of the decade, dating from the passing of the Two Acts of 1795, was even more harsh. Government paranoia was exacerbated by the close, palpable, violence that emerged with the naval mutinies in 1797, the Irish Rebellion of 1798, and the fear of a concurrent invasion of Ireland by a powerful Napoleon-led French army. There was at the same period a final, decisive clampdown on the radical societies, and habeas corpus was once again suspended in May 1798.[42] Many of those who had originally supported reform abandoned their earlier beliefs. Others who remained faithful to the cause preferred to stay silent. Peter H. Marshall succinctly sums up the prevailing atmosphere and attitudes: "The excesses of the Terror in France, the wave of patriotism which followed Britain's declaration of war on the new Republic, and

the persecution of the opposition at home, had all contributed to the want of revolutionary hopes. By 1797, the L.C.S. [London Corresponding Society] had all but
disbanded and even the resolute [John] Thelwall was driven into retirement. The
Jacobins, their fellow-travellers, and anyone else expressing opposition to Church
and King were hounded by a virulent campaign of counter-propaganda."[43] This
description appears in Marshall's biography of William Godwin, following which
he records Godwin's own acknowledgement of this course of events as expressed
in *Thoughts: Occasioned by the Perusal of Dr. Parr's Spital Sermon* (1801), Godwin's
published response to a blistering public assault on him by a man who had been a
former friend: "I was at length attacked from every side, and in a style which defied
all moderation and decency. No vehicle was too mean, no language too coarse and
insulting, by which to convey the venom of my adversaries."[44]

Holcroft had experienced similar attacks. This wave of unrelenting criticism
in the late 1790s often included him and Godwin (along with other reform activists)
as the targets of what Kenneth R. Johnston calls "extra-legal, hegemonic punishment."[45] Thomas J. Mathias had marked Holcroft and Godwin in precisely that
way in his *Pursuits of Literature* (1794), with especially long notes devoted particularly to Godwin in the expanded 1798 edition.[46] In that same year Mathias singled out Godwin and Holcroft together in his satire *The Grove*, where he calls
them "two democrats . . . with faces evil," "hypocrites . . . glaring thro' their rags."[47]
A few pages later, he elaborates:

> So Godwin mark in words of wond'rous feature
> But seem in truth, a weakly little creature.
> Holcroft in his type by slavish passions furl'd,
> A peevish insect wriggling through the world.[48]

Earlier in *The Grove*, Mathias had called Holcroft "one of those plebeii philoso-
phi";[49] he too thus recalled with disdain Holcroft's laboring-class roots. Mathias's
phrase here, "in his type," further presses this awareness of social class on his readers. Certainly the "rags" through which Godwin and Holcroft "glare" acknowledge the financial loss incurred by those who dared to so conspicuously criticize
the government. Mathias's comments clearly seek not only to represent their financial hardships but also to promote them.

Holcroft's diary, written during the very time when Mathias's works and
others like them were published, makes specific mention of various attacks aimed
at his past radical activity and present political beliefs. Thus, after reading an issue
of Benjamin Flower's newspaper, *The Cambridge Intelligencer*, and praising the cou-
rageousness and integrity of Flower (whose newspaper stood out as an enlightened beacon of journalism in the late 1790s), he adds that Godwin had "been
several times attacked there, and probably myself" (*Life*, 2:170).[50] Holcroft may be

referring in part to criticism presented earlier in the decade, not by Flower, but by a correspondent to the newspaper, who had criticized the "outrageous" ideas of *Political Justice*, an attack that a young Henry Crabb Robinson later responded to as "Philo-Godwin."[51] Holcroft's comment appears in the diary entry dated 1 August 1798. He might not yet have known that on that very day the inaugural issue of the *Anti-Jacobin Review* (successor to the *Anti-Jacobin, or Weekly Examiner*) was published. Both the *Weekly* and the *Review* sought, energetically and scathingly, to root out "Jacobinism" wherever they found it; the publications were important players in maintaining through the print media a climate of suspicion, surveillance, and pursuit at the close of the revolutionary decade. Setting the stage for its present and future concerns, this first issue of the *Anti-Jacobin Review* included James Gillray's print *The New Morality* (see figure 4.1), with its panorama of radical figures and texts. The print's companion poem of that same name, by George Canning, had been published in the *Weekly* on 9 July; an excerpt from the poem, that part which directly attacked Godwin and Holcroft, along with Thomas Paine and the deist and political theorist, David Williams, was reprinted in the new periodical: "All creeping creatures, venomous and low / Paine, W-lli-ms, G-dw-n, H-lc-ft praise Lepaux."[52] Canning's description of them as "creatures, venomous and low" is visualized in Gillray's representation. As opposed to Mathias's *The Grove*, where Holcroft was portrayed as an "insect," in the print it is now Godwin who is anthropomorphized, appearing as a diminutive donkey reading *Political Justice*. Holcroft, similarly miniaturized, is in prison shackles, holding the fictitious "Letter from an Acquitted Felon." (Godwin is not the only radical figure depicted as an animal in the print. Among others, we find Thomas Paine as a crocodile in stays, Coleridge and Southey with asses' heads, and Charles Lamb and Charles Lloyd as frogs.)

Holcroft admired Gillray's work, calling him a "man of talents . . . and uncommonly apt at sketching a hasty likeness" (*Life*, 2:160). This comment appears in his diary entry written on 25 July, a week before the publication of *The New Morality*. He does not record his response when later he would have encountered Gillray's talents in capturing his own likeness. Holcroft was a less prominent target than Godwin for the venom of the *Anti-Jacobin Review* and for writers such as Thomas J. Mathias, or for intellectual figures such as Dr. Samuel Parr. At the same time, as a survivor of the Treason Trials and as a prominent playwright, his conspicuous cultural presence in the playhouse gave his politics an immediate and unmediated exposure in a different dimension, one which was particularly visible and audible. This was the case with a frequently boisterous audience response, such as we saw in the previous chapter regarding *Love's Frailties*, *Man of Ten Thousand*, and *Knave, or Not?*, but was also apparent outside of the theater, with Holcroft's political past becoming a seamless part of his identity in his social encounters. He acknowledges that past political activity as the rumbles of reaction accompany

Figure 4.1 James Gillray, *The New Morality*, courtesy of the Lewis Walpole Library, Yale University

him in conversation and in general social interaction; the quotidian exchanges with their frequent political dimension were part and parcel of daily life.

In the section that follows, I will expand on some of those encounters— noting the location in which many took place, some individuals with whom Holcroft conversed on tense subjects, and the historical events that formed the subject of much of this sociable discourse, with the idea of free or unrestrained speech— or, more precisely, the lack of it—always present in the background. Along with conversations Holcroft had at social gatherings with friends or in chance meetings on the street, many others took place at Debrett's bookshop on Piccadilly Street, which was a popular meeting place for political and literary talk. (It was there that he had read the *Cambridge Intelligencer* on 1 August.) *The Picture of London, for 1802* describes Debrett's, as well as similar bookseller establishments, as "furnished with all the daily newspapers, [and] which are much frequented about the middle of the day by fashionable people, and are used as lounging-places for political and literary conversation."[53] Holcroft might have smiled to have been characterized as a man of fashion (we recall Monrose's invective against "men of fashion" in *Knave, or Not?*),[54] but he did often make a stop at Debrett's a part of his daily routine, and it is mentioned by name eighty-one times in the diary as a port of call. Other times it is clear that he stopped there, although the bookshop was not named specifically.[55] Located not too far from Holcroft's home on Newman Street, Debrett's was an establishment whose clientele, as David Fallon describes it, "reflects the unusual cooperation between radicals and Whigs in this period." Not socially exclusive, it counted MPs, radicals, journalists, and military personnel among its regular patrons.[56] The visitors would have included persons holding varying and diverse opinions regarding Holcroft's past political activities. Thus, for example, on 3 January 1799 Holcroft relates of a conversation he had had there with Richard Weld, who seems to have been a fixture at Debrett's, and who at this meeting conferred on him a kind of celebrity notoriety when he "reminded" him of the trouble he (Holcroft) had taken "to have himself hanged . . . when indicted for high-treason," (*Life*, 2:228).[57] Weld had addressed Holcroft "jocularly"—although he himself was a member of the reformist Society of the Friends of the People, those far from danger can allow themselves jocularity. We have no indication as to how Holcroft felt as he laconically reports this exchange. Here, as mostly elsewhere in the diary—even though it is a diary—he keeps his feelings private, with little, if any, space given to introspection.

Almost two months earlier at Debrett's, on 14 November, Holcroft had encountered Dr. Towers, whose "democracy still maintains its violence" (*Life*, 2:195 and passim). Joseph Lomas Towers was a Unitarian minister, writer, and librarian at Dr. Williams's Library.[58] He and Holcroft had both been members of the Society for Constitutional Information and would certainly have known each other from their participation in that body.[59] Their conversation, as Holcroft recorded it, turned on what Towers had called "the universal defection." Towers asked whether Holcroft himself had turned "aristocrat"; in responding to the allegation, Holcroft emphasized his continuing adherence to perfectibility and truth. The only change in his opinions, he asserted, was his understanding that "political revolutions are not so well calculated to better man's condition, as during a certain period [he], with almost all the thinking men in Europe had been led to suppose." In his reply, Towers doubted the idea of perfectibility, calling man a "radical sinner" and Holcroft, a Necessarian. The latter part of Towers's remark was true. Holcroft, like Godwin, believed in the doctrine of necessity—that human actions are predetermined by antecedent; that the "characters of men originate in their original circumstances," as Godwin had written in the third edition of the *Enquiry Concerning Political Justice*.[60] Holcroft presented a similar observation at the beginning of his *Narrative of Facts*, published following the Treason Trials (NF, 3–4), and elsewhere he summed up the doctrine quite pessimistically: "Men do not become what by nature they are meant to be, but what society makes them. The generous feelings and higher propensities of the soul are, as it were shrunk up, scared, violently wrenched, and amputated, to fit us for our intercourse in the world, something in the manner that beggars maim and mutilate their children to make them fit for their future situation in life."[61]

The political interchanges with Weld and Towers are indicative of the notoriety that accompanied Holcroft at Debrett's and in the wider social arena. Whereas with Weld he was remembered for his part in the 1794 Treason Trials, for Towers he appeared as a potential candidate for inclusion in the ranks of apostasy. One of the recurring subjects appearing in Holcroft's interactions with the Debrett's milieu (at least as he records them) is the abandonment of the reformist cause or, to use Towers's words, of "the universal defection." Discussing the issue in general terms in the bookshop, the leading attorney Thomas Erskine had remarked to Holcroft that "it was wrong to give up agitating the cause of reform without doors, i.e., [Holcroft clarifies] out of the House of Commons," adding that "the people had lost all spirit." Holcroft counters this assertion, responding that "the leaders of the people had abandoned them in a cowardly manner, and then had called the people cowards" (*Life*, 2:220). Both men were speaking as those who had earned their reformist credentials—Erskine as the chief defense lawyer in the 1794 Treason Trials (as well as in other prominent political trials, including the trial in the defense of Thomas Paine) and Holcroft as one who had been indicted in those Trials. While Erskine criticizes what he perceives as a lack of active oppositional political engagement, referencing the aftermath of the Two Acts and the government "success" in limiting public protest, Holcroft references the issue in more abstract terms, and distinguishes between the believers in reform and their leaders, implying a familiarity or at least an identification with grass-roots sentiments upon which he does not elaborate. Nonetheless, both men acknowledge the sea change that had occurred in the reform camp, which by 21 December 1798, the date of this conversation, had been profound enough, visible enough, to be asserted as a fact of reality.[62]

While Erskine and Holcroft grieve this situation in its general configuration, Holcroft elsewhere mentions specific apostates, as well as victims of the backlash, by name. One individual singled out from the former category is Dr. John Gillies, a historian and classical scholar. On 18 November 1798, Holcroft's friend John Pinkerton[63] related to Holcroft of how "in 1792, it was [Gillies's] custom to declaim vehemently at the Stratford coffee-house, in favor of republicanism; and finding the alarm that was raised, and the tide turning, he soon after wrote in praise of the King, of mixed monarchy, and of the peculiar happiness derived from it by the English" (*Life*, 2:199–200). After then remarking that Gillies was given the post of historiographer of Scotland, Holcroft sums up the matter: "the doctor's loyalty and royalty [were] confirmed (*Life*, 2: 200)"[64] A more prominent volte-face mentioned by Holcroft was that of James Mackintosh. Mackintosh, whose *Vindiciae Gallicae* (1791) had been one of the most notable responses to Burke's *Reflections on the Revolution in France* (he had also served as a Member of the French National Assembly) had turned against the French Revolution, calling it the "mother of all evil."[65] In earlier times, Mackintosh had been quite friendly with Godwin and had met Holcroft socially as well.[66] It was thus surprising to many that in a series of lectures he gave between February and June 1799, he viciously attacked Godwin to audiences which included many of the most notable figures of the time.[67] Holcroft had recorded on 20 January his knowledge of the upcoming lectures, had probably seen, as had Godwin (27 Jan. 1799 [GD]), the prospectus to the series, and appears to have had a premonition of what was to come, although perhaps not in relation to Godwin specifically. As an illustration of the disbelief felt in real time by reformists towards former like-minded friends, Holcroft's comments in the diary are worth quoting in full:

> I learn Mackintosh intends to read lectures on law; in which political government is to be introduced, and the established systems of this country highly praised. Expressed the pain I felt, that a man of such superior powers should act so false a part, and so contrary to his convictions, of which I must, in all human probability, be able to form a tolerably accurate opinion, from the many conversations I have had with him. His judgment was (and, doubtless, still is, for his faculties are in their full vigour) so clear, his perceptions so penetrating, and his opinions so decided, that I can conceive no possibility of their being so totally changed (*Life*, 2:236).

This is indignation at Mackintosh's turnaround: wonder, but not total surprise. Holcroft was well aware of the reality of the situation: the shifting tides of public opinion, the benefits of "loyalty and royalty," and the price paid by those who continued to adhere to an oppositional agenda in an anxious political climate. Among those who felt the repercussions of the backlash, were, as he writes on 23 October 1798, "the Walkers, of Manchester, ruined by the war and ministerial persecutions" (*Life*, 2:189). This brief comment calls attention to the plight of Thomas Walker, a successful cotton merchant who had been brought to trial on the charge of treason in April 1794. He was acquitted, but his business collapsed in the aftermath.[68] A little over three weeks later, on 15 November, Holcroft just as briefly records the imprisonment of the publisher Joseph Johnson for having sold Gilbert Wakefield's *Reply to Some Parts of the Bishop of Llandaff's Address*: "Johnson the bookseller sent to the King's Bench Prison for selling Wakefield's pamphlet" (*Life*, 2:196). The trial of Wakefield for publishing a highly critical response to the bishop's forceful support of the government was a pivotal moment in the struggle for the freedom of the press at the end of the eighteenth century. His conviction was, in Kenneth R. Johnston's words, "the last nail in the coffin of the 1790s reform movement."[69] Wakefield's fate (he died a few months after his release from prison, his deteriorated health resulting from his incarceration) was a sobering reminder of the consequences for those who continued to so openly criticize the government. The aftermath of the publication of his pamphlet was likewise a warning to publishers and booksellers, who were much more cautious in what they agreed to publish or sell in light of Joseph Johnson's conviction. Holcroft had known Johnson personally, and had hosted him for supper, along with Godwin and others, on 20 June 1795 (GD). The brief, even laconic, reference to Johnson's imprisonment surely conceals not only sympathy for an acquaintance so conclusively circumstanced (Holcroft, of course, had known prison life as well) but also an increasing recognition regarding the limitations of the freedom of speech in its wider manifestations. Holcroft registered his awareness of the increasing pressures on free speech in many of his writings, including the prefaces to his plays and in the plays themselves. He acknowledged the issue at Debrett's bookshop and elsewhere in relation to reaction and apostasy, but also when discussing or listening to conversations on pressing contemporary political concerns. In Holcroft's response to political and military developments as well, we can perceive the tension between public and private writing and, perhaps, a voluntary act of repressing his own speech. The text's ambiguous nature—a private diary but also possibly aimed for future scrutiny—includes rare moments of introspection which provide a glimpse into his assessment of events but, more markedly, wide swaths of information and events that lack a personal perspective, context or elaboration.

It is not surprising that as a text written between June 1798 and March 1799, the political event that appeared most frequently in the diary, especially in the early part, was the Irish Rebellion of 1798. The rebellion began after years of discontent with the overwhelming social, political, and religious inequalities in Irish society. It was influenced by the success of the revolutions in America and France and fueled by the nonsectarian vision of liberty and equality that those revolutions inspired in the United Irishmen activists and their leaders. Following an aborted attempt at French intervention in 1796, mainly orchestrated by one of the leaders of the United Irishmen, Theobald Wolfe Tone, Britain strengthened its hold on Irish political activity and aimed to crush the rebel organizations. The uprising began in May 1798, and on 30 May, the rebels had what was their most important success in occupying the town of Wexford, creating there their own version of a revolutionary republic.[70] Three weeks later, Wexford was retaken by the British at the Battle of Vinegar Hill. After months of bloody fighting, including a brief French invasion at Connaught in August, Britain reasserted its authority over Ireland. The result of this defeat was the Act of Union of 1801, which placed Ireland conclusively under British rule and made the Parliament in London the sole legislative authority over the country.

Thomas Pakenham, a historian of the Irish Rebellion, asserts that news of the war in Ireland was of little interest to the general British public: "the current disturbances [in Ireland] were no more alarming than a rebellion in some distant part of Africa."[71] Holcroft's journal tells a different story, showing that the ongoing reports of the rebellion were a prominent subject of conversation both at Debrett's and in his wider circle. For example, on 26 June Holcroft reports that the defeat of the Irish at Wexford (the battle of Vinegar Hill had taken place on 21 June) were "chief topics" of conversation at the bookshop. Some of those present were complacent: the "Irish, it was supposed . . . [were] quelled" (*Life*, 2: 131). This was certainly, as it turned out, not the case, as the French invasion of Mayo County, Connaught, aimed to support the rebels, took place at the end of the summer. The following day Holcroft read at Debrett's "the three gazettes relative to Irish affairs," including a report of the response of General Gerard Lake, the British commander, to the terms of the rebels' surrender, a response Holcroft describes as "haughty" (*Life*, 2: 131, 132).[72] As events unfolded throughout that summer, Holcroft continued to acknowledge the conversations on Ireland at Debrett's, including various rumors and accounts of captures, executions, and betrayals, as well as the "sanguinary measures" that were pursued against the rebels (*Life*, 2:163–164).[73] Months later, in January 1799, he records that the "union of Ireland [was still] the whole subject of political discourse" (*Life*, 2:236).

Holcroft was mostly a passive auditor to these conversations at Debrett's. His remarks on the "haughty" General Lake and his "sanguinary" actions were not openly verbalized but recorded in the diary as private comments. The one dimension of the Irish situation with which Holcroft more openly engaged concerned the fate of the Reverend James Coigley. His representation of the events surrounding Coigley's trial and execution exhibits caution and anxiety, originating, in this case, from his acquaintance with some of those persons directly involved. Coigley (whose name is variously rendered as Quigley, O'Quigley, O'Coigley, or

Coigly)[74] was an Irish activist who was apprehended at Margate on the southeastern English coast, along with Arthur O'Connor, a leading aristocratic member of Irish revolutionary circles, and others. They had been attempting to cross over to France when seditious, incriminating documents were found among Coigley's possessions. Coigley and O'Connor were brought to trial, and prominent Whig notables, including Charles James Fox, Thomas Erskine, and Richard Brinsley Sheridan, stepped up to testify on O'Connor's behalf. O'Connor dissociated himself from Coigley. Helped by his prominent supporters, he was acquitted, whereas Coigley, with no powerful friends to take up his defense, was convicted. He was hanged on 7 June 1798.[75]

Holcroft was acquainted with Arthur O'Connor and had a deep interest in his and Coigley's case. Over two years earlier, in the spring of 1796, he had met O'Connor three times with Godwin[76] and arguably had met him on other occasions as well. Later he calls him a "noble-minded man" (*Life*, 2:170). On 29 June he records a conversation, not at Debrett's, in which the trial was discussed, including mention of the suspected perjury of Richard Ford, the chief of police at Bow Street, and of the publication of "Fenwick's pamphlet," a reference to *A Plain Narrative of Facts Respecting the Trial of James Coigley*, written by John Fenwick. In recounting these events, Holcroft refers to O'Connor in the diary with a tone of familiarity, as "Arthur," while at the same time stating that he knows "nothing of these matters" (*Life*, 2:134).

This concluding comment is a curious one. Would Holcroft really have had no knowledge of these events, in light of his acquaintance with O'Connor and his close friendship with Fenwick?[77] It is understandable that he would want to be silent about a treason trial in a chance conversation on the street, but why does he feel the need to qualify any information he *might have had* about O'Connor and Coigley in what is ostensibly a private journal? Significantly, over a month later, on 3 August, Holcroft discusses Fenwick's pamphlet with Godwin. Here he is more forthcoming in his diary, writing that he "gave a favourable account of Fenwick's pamphlet on Coigley" (*Life*, 2:174). Fenwick's publication, which includes Coigley's address to the court, an account of his execution, as well as a letter concerning the event from one of the "patizans [*sic*] of Loyalty"[78] was certainly worthy of Holcroft's later praise, as it presents a sympathetic and moving record of Coigley's quiet heroism under duress and in facing death. The inclusion of the loyalist letter serves concurrently as yet another reminder of the insidious and ubiquitous forces of reaction as its writer looks back to the 1794 Treason Trials, declaring that "the acquittal of [Thomas] Hardy, &c. laid the foundation of the present conspiracy."[79]

Holcroft's friendship with O'Connor and Fenwick and the mention of Hardy and the Treason Trials in the loyalist appendix are indicative of a response to a pressing political event—the Irish situation—that is distanced yet with a personal dimension. This was not the case when it came to his observation of the progress of Napoleon, the second major political topic that emerges in his discussions at Debrett's and which then made its way into his diary. Napoleon only executed the coup d'état of Brumaire, becoming First Consul, in November 1799, by which time Holcroft was living in Hamburg, but his earlier leadership of the French army in the Italian and Egyptian campaigns already insured that his had become a household name; "his "personality," as Stuart Semmel puts it, "had . . . begun to fascinate."[80] The first of the many caricatures in which Napoleon appeared was published in March 1797; these caricatures exhibit the way in which his actions resonated within Britain's internal affairs, as well as its foreign ones, as he became a "mascot of opposition and radical groups in their continued support of France."[81] Napoleon's willingness to intercede on behalf of the Irish Rebellion contributed to the uneasiness and fear or, conversely, the admiration, with which he was perceived. Fascination with Napoleon is apparent in the conversations Holcroft encountered at Debrett's. At this stage (1798–1799), the information of those who congregated at the bookshop regarding Napoleon's distant military conquests was fueled and promoted by rumor rather than by hard facts and tangible knowledge. Holcroft thus records speculation, in late June, that Napoleon had "gone to the East Indies" (*Life*, 2:133), in July, that his "whole fleet [had been] taken" (*Life*, 2:163), and in December, arguments for and against rumors of his assassination (*Life*, 2:215). In his discussion of this early period of Napoleon's military leadership, Simon Bainbridge notes in passing that "in November 1798 . . . Thomas Holcroft was unaware that Napoleon was in Cairo, five months after the event."[82] In the one mention of Napoleon in the diary's entries for November, however, Holcroft merely reports what he had heard, without reflecting on the extent of his own knowledge of the course of events. Rather, there seems to have been a general uncertainty, as evinced in the ongoing speculations on assassination, defeats, and expansionist endeavors, and Bainbridge probably references Holcroft as indicative of this common opinion.

Although he does not offer his own views of these supposed military developments to the Debrett's crowd, Holcroft nonetheless occasionally interjects a personal commentary in his journal. For instance, following the reports of Napoleon's "capture" on 26 July, he adds, "An officer of note had arrived from Lord St. Vincent [an admiral in the Royal Navy]; conjecture immediately know his business: Lords were the first to believe what conjecture affirmed, and men shouted and rejoiced at the imaginary destruction of their fellow beings" (*Life*, 2:163). His remark on the illumination night following Nelson's victory over France in the Battle of the Nile in August 1798 is just as quietly critical, although much briefer. After riding in a carriage through the "mean streets leading to the Seven Dials," he wrote, "the poor did not illuminate" (*Life*, 2:180).

Considering the consensus of fear and uncertainty surrounding both Napoleon and Ireland, it is clear that any criticism Holcroft would have had—any attempt to dent the patriotic alignment of opinion he encountered—could only appear in a private text. Even then his thoughts are sparsely rendered, when given at all, in those brief asides conveying an oppositional outlook—the haughty General Lake, Lords rejoicing over the bloodshed of war, the nonalliance of the destitute residents of Seven Dials with the civic celebration. At moments when he *does* acknowledge a personal interest, such as in the case of Coigley and O'Connor, his comments are still generally spare and devoid of emotion, with little reflection or elaboration. In observing this subdued presentation, we must not forget that Godwin had edited the diary; perhaps what had been a more reflective or extended response by Holcroft has been lost as a result of that editorial work.

On 20 February 1799, Holcroft called on his friend, the engraver William Sharp (1749–1824) and "paid him for his print of the *Siege of Gibraltar*" (*Life*, 2:245). This was Sharp's engraving of the American artist John Trumbull's *Sortie Made by Garrison of Gibraltar on the Morning of the 27th November 1781* (1789), produced in 1799. Sharp was a close friend of Holcroft's, and they had both been members of the Society for Constitutional Information in 1792–1793, with Sharp a more active participant than Holcroft. Sharp had been summoned in June 1794 to testify before the Privy Council, in which he reported various statements Holcroft had made at meetings of the SCI. As we saw in Chapter One, Sharp did not incriminate his friend but rather emphasized in his testimony Holcroft's opposition to violence and his promotion of truth. The two men remained friends following the Treason Trials, even after Sharp abandoned his political activity and became an adherent to the beliefs of the religious enthusiast Richard Brothers;[83] their common interest in art—Sharp's engraving work and Holcroft's occasional picture dealing—served as one of their shared bonds. After receiving the payment for the *Sortie*, Sharp told Holcroft that the print "would become of great value, for it was the last on such a subject, meaning the destruction of war that would ever be published" (*Life*, 2:245). The print shows the death of a valiant Spanish officer, Don Jose de Barboza, at the moment of the great British victory at Gibraltar in 1783. The dying officer, a member of the defeated enemy forces abandoned by his own troops, is placed at the center of the composition as the focus of the viewer's gaze and sympathy, exposing the horrors of war and the human price it exacted regardless of national affiliation or allegiance.[84] Whether Sharp had in fact intended to imply that one would soon no longer be free to criticize the destructiveness of war cannot be determined. Holcroft, in writing of the conversation, connects the comment instead to his friend's affiliation with enthusiastic millenarianism, as if war itself, rather than the criticism of it, would cease to exist in light of Brothers's prophecies.

Holcroft enjoyed this conversation with Sharp, listening to, while privately dismissing, his friend's religious beliefs as he directs Sharp's elaboration of his thought to a religious expostulation rather than to the wider implications of free speech. It seems fitting to conclude my discussion of the political references in Holcroft's diary with this interchange, which succinctly sums up the anxious presence-yet-absence of the clampdown of freedom of expression, such as Holcroft had himself experienced, and which is noted tersely and anxiously throughout the diary, and in this case, hinted at, only to be circumvented.

*　*　*

While the topical references to current events and politics illuminate the routine existence of a suspect radical—a veteran of the 1794 Treason Trials—Holcroft's diary also presents a vibrant depiction of the daily life of a literary professional in London. The ten months in which Holcroft wrote his diary were not a successful time for him in terms of his work for the theater, a period wedged between the earlier triumphs of *The Road to Ruin*, of *The Deserted Daughter*, and, to an extent, of *He's Much to Blame*, and of his later popular and influential work with the genre of melodrama. The plays written during these ten months received far less attention than the controversial, failed comedies, *The Man of Ten Thousand* and *Knave, or Not?*. Between June 1798 and March 1799, Holcroft was involved in the production and writing of three plays, *The Inquisitor*, performed just as the diary commenced, "The Old Cloathsman," a comic opera produced as an afterpiece, the composition of which is detailed in the diary, and "The Lawyer." Holcroft's work on this latter play is frequently referenced and his efforts detailed, although it would only be performed in 1803 as *Hear Both Sides*. Likewise, the diary briefly records Holcroft's later thoughts regarding the failure of *Knave, or Not?*, which had appeared on the Drury Lane stage six months previously, and the success of the more recent *He's Much to Blame* which, with his authorship unknown, had been commanded for performance by the royal family (*Life*, 2:170).

The diary's record of Holcroft's literary engagement and his contacts with theater managers, publishers, and actors sheds light on metropolitan networks of sociability and cultural production at the close of the eighteenth century. Throughout this book I have been addressing the implications of Holcroft's political notoriety for his theatrical career and the way that political references within the plays, as well as his own reputation, dictated to a great extent the reception of those plays. I similarly noted in this current chapter Holcroft's more general deportment as it reverberates (also politically) in his daily social interactions. In what follows, I focus upon the more routine aspects of Holcroft's literary business—as we view his practice of writing, revising, and submitting his work, and his response to the criticism of professional reviewers and of his friends. It is important to remember in this context that despite the many obstacles he had to overcome in light of his past political activity and his insistence on continuing to include a proreform commentary in his plays, Holcroft always retained access to the powerful theater managers Thomas Harris (Covent Garden), John Philip Kemble (Drury

Lane), and George Colman, Jr. (Haymarket). These managers were not only willing to produce his work but were also ready to invest in new props, scenery, and costumes when staging them.[85] In spite of its disastrous reception, George Robinson published *The Inquisitor* as he had Holcroft's other unsuccessful dramatic works. (Some shorter pieces, though, were not published—"The Force of Ridicule" (1796), "The Old Cloathsman" (1798), and later, "The Escapes" [1801].) And yet the hoped-for re-creation of the enormous success of *The Road to Ruin* by both Holcroft and the theater managers would not be achieved in this period. The constant scramble to offer up yet another play, the all-too-hasty manner of writing, motivated by constant economic necessity, were crucial in denying Holcroft at this particular time a return to his earlier theatrical triumphs.

Holcroft's diary commences with the failure of *The Inquisitor*. The play, in part a translation of Johann Christoph Unzer's *Diego und Leonor* (1775), premiered on 23 June 1798 at the Haymarket and ran for three nights. It was a departure from his previous work: rather than yet another energetic drawing room comedy exposing the inequality and corruption that underpin existing social structures, the play presents a "Romeo and Juliet" drama of forbidden love, in this case resulting from religious intolerance, set in Inquisition-ruled Portugal. Despite his weighty theme—the abuse of "religion's sacred name"[86]—Holcroft described the play as a "trifling effort" (*Life*, 2:152). Nonetheless he felt deeply its lack of success and the laughter and ridicule it met with from the audience. While the word "trifling" suggests his lack of sustained commitment to the composition of the work, he nonetheless puts the blame on others: the actors "who played vilely the first night" (*Life*, 2:130) and the audience. The theaters, he remarks, are "half-filled with prostitutes and their paramours: they disturb the rest of the audience; and the author, and common sense, are the sport of their caprice and profligacy" (*Life*, 2:127). The reviewer for the *Monthly Mirror* concurred with Holcroft to a certain extent in likewise faulting the actors with a poor first night performance and the audience for being "unreasonably captious."[87] Later, Holcroft reported that the cast had performed better on the second night and that the piece was well-received (*Life*, 2:130).[88]

Notwithstanding its failure, *The Inquisitor* is indicative of larger changes occurring in drama at the close of the eighteenth century and exemplifies Holcroft's own response to these developments. We have already seen how *The Deserted Daughter* and *Knave, or Not?* prefigure melodrama, a genre which Holcroft would later so influentially shape. In this play as well, we can discern an incipient melodramatic awareness, for example in the rescue of the lovers just as they are about to commit double suicide while locked in a cell in the Inquisition prison. Holcroft's geographically and temporally distanced theocratic police state under the control of a villainous priest also recalls Matthew Lewis's *The Monk* and Ann Radcliffe's *The Italian* in its depiction of the confrontation between power and powerlessness. The play thus anticipates how, in Jacky Bratton's words, "gothic as a semiotic with instantly recognizable signs [would extend] its life in British melodrama."[89] Despite Holcroft's stated lack of serious commitment to *The Inquisitor*—a "trifling effort"—the play nonetheless represents another stepping-stone in his eventual reworking of the Georgian drama. His subtitle, "a play," reinforces Paula Backscheider's claim that the frequent use of that neutral generic marker was indicative of the "splintering" of the theater at this particular moment, as, amidst political turmoil, the gothic drama began to give way to a wider heterogeneity of forms, including melodrama.[90]

Despite his disappointment with the failure of *The Inquisitor*, Holcroft briskly moved on. The play had premiered on a Saturday night (23 June), and he began the following week with discussions and meetings in which he took in the commentary of friends, acquaintances, and the press while hoping to maximize any possible financial remuneration he might receive from the piece. At Debrett's on Monday, 25 June he read the newspaper reviews, which "were uniform in decrying" *The Inquisitor* (*Life*, 2:129), saw his acquaintance John Stoddart,[91] who "thought but indifferently" of the play (*Life*, 2:130), and went to George Colman at the Haymarket to discuss its future. Colman agreed to a third night performance, but he decided to wait upon attendance figures to determine whether it would continue for a fourth performance. (It didn't.) The following day, 26 June, Holcroft visited his publisher, George Robinson, to discuss its publication. At this meeting, Robinson promised to consider an offer made by Holcroft, apparently at an earlier time, to transfer "the whole of [his] copyrights" to the publisher (*Life*, 2:130). It is not clear whether Robinson's decision to publish *The Inquisitor* was contingent upon this more general transfer of the right to own Holcroft's other writings; in all events, Holcroft returned later that day to complete the transaction, and *The Inquisitor* went off to press. (It was published without Holcroft's name on the title page or the "advertisement.") Later that day Holcroft went to a book sale, continued on to Debrett's, and met his friend James Perry, editor of the *Morning Chronicle*. In discussing the *Inquisitor*, Perry blamed Holcroft for "writing too fast" (*Life*, 2:131).[92] Holcroft concluded the day with a social visit to the home of his friend, the painter John Opie. Over four months later, on 6 November, Holcroft finally made over his copyrights for various plays and two novels to Robinson in exchange for his debt of £340 to the publisher, along with a promissory note of Robinson to pay him £150 if the sales of these works realized earnings of £504 (*Life*, 2:193).[93]

Holcroft's activities over these two days—his negotiations with the theater manager and with his publisher, his reading and conversations at the bookshop, and, possibly, literary talk at the book sale, his chat with the newspaper publisher, and his evening conversation with Opie—illustrate a daily routine centering on literature, business, most certainly also current events and politics, and sociability, interlinked through his affiliation with, or contingency to, social networks that included the most prominent cultural figures of the time. Yet this ready access to elite networks did not translate into financial prosperity, or even stability. Holcroft's political notoriety was, to be sure, the source of his economic vulnerability, which then led, in a kind of unbreakable circle, to an urgent imperative to write yet another play and to hope for success, but also to write "too fast," as James Perry had noted, what Holcroft himself had called a "trifling effort." His attempt, in the aftermath, to salvage some kind of monetary gain from his work on *The Inquisitor*, as evident in his transaction with George Robinson, provides one specific example of the complex configuration of authorship, anonymity, ownership of literary property, and politics at a particular historical moment. *The Inquisitor*, published anonymously, might have shielded Holcroft from the direct attacks of hostile reviewers, while its role in possibly leading to the wider sale of copyright, and the settlement of Holcroft's outstanding debt to Robinson, at the same time provided a measure of financial relief.[94]

In an interesting coda to the play's stage life, the *Oracle* announced on 11 July that "Holcroft appears to have been the literary manufacturer of the unsuccessful *Inquisitor*." In returning the defeated play to public attention, the *Oracle*'s announcement underscores David Worrall's understanding of theater as a multilayered and complex social assemblage, one whose reach goes beyond specific audience attendance figures for a particular play.[95] Publicity in the newspaper advertisements and playbills, subsequent reviews, and, later, print copies to be read and discussed ensured an afterlife, even if a minimal one, which persisted in spite of any play's short-lived stage presence. The *Oracle*'s decision to announce the fact of Holcroft's authorship of *The Inquisitor* two weeks after the conclusion of its unsuccessful run posits this subject as worthy of its readers' attention and assumes a memory of the play and an interest in its fortunes that still existed; a much larger recognition factor and awareness of this particular work than implied by the actual number of nights staged or tickets sold.

While Holcroft makes many references to *The Inquisitor*, the fact that his diary was commenced just as the play reached the stage reduces any knowledge of the actual process of writing to that phrase, "a trifling effort." The diary provides more specific details regarding the composition of "The Old Cloathsman" and "The Lawyer; *(Hear Both Sides)*." In fact, the morning of the same night in which *The Inquisitor* premiered, Holcroft was already at work on "The Old Cloathsman," a comic opera. Altogether, he records twenty-five different occasions in which he worked on the piece, finally submitting it to Thomas Harris at Covent Garden on 7 August. In referencing the opera, Holcroft supplies suggestive details of his writing process. For instance, the idea for one scene came to him by "seeing a man and woman wrangle" (*Life*, 2:150). Lyrics for two of the songs were written in Green Park; the idea of composing in a busy park challenges the romanticized (and

Romanticized) notion of an author toiling in solitude at his or her desk. Holcroft devoted much effort to the opera. He mentions numerous occasions in which he sketched out a scene and then returned to revise it. In one instance he records making notes for one of the main characters before going to bed. He also sent the first act to Godwin for perusal. Godwin was not overly impressed: he returned the manuscript with "remarks, dictated evidently by the fear, that ill success will attend [Holcroft] in the future, as it has in some late attempts" (*Life*, 2:151).[96]

Holcroft's efforts for "The Old Cloathsman" were further challenged when Thomas Harris decided to stage the play as an afterpiece rather than a main piece. Holcroft, "the slave of [his] circumstances" (*Life*, 2:176) was obliged to concur. He revised accordingly, eventually presenting a two-act musical play which centers on an unscrupulous businessman and the love story that develops between his daughter and his clerk, the son of the eponymous "old cloathsman." As such, Holcroft returns in this work from the prisons of the Portuguese inquisition to the familiar drawing rooms of London to once again address the major themes that feature throughout his oeuvre—financial speculation and risk taking in an unsettled economy, along with the tensions exhibited in interstatus relations and cross-class courtship. The play displays these concerns not through tense polemics but rather with good humor; the lack of overt political rhetoric is evinced in the fact that the censor had made no markings in the manuscript text (LA 1242). The play's action is punctuated by seventeen songs, composed by Thomas Attwood, the house composer at Covent Garden for the 1798–1799 and 1799–1800 seasons. The diary reveals, however, that one of the songs was, in fact, composed by Holcroft himself, and "corrected" by his close friend, the composer William Shield (*Life*, 2:180).[97]

"The Old Cloathsman" ran for only two nights, on 2 and 3 April 1799. The newspaper reviewers detested the piece, describing it, variously, as "contemptible in the extreme," "poorly contrived," and with "insipid" dialogue. The music was viewed more favorably, and generally perceived as "better than the play deserved."[98] Holcroft was no longer keeping his diary when the play was performed (April), so we have no access to his thoughts on this hostile reception. If he felt the same hurt and surprise as at the reception of the *Inquisitor*, we can assume that the surprise was now shared by Thomas Harris. Back in August, when Holcroft had submitted the first draft of the play to the theater manager, he had agreed to give Holcroft £200 for the piece and to raise the sum to £300 if it were to run for twenty (!) nights (*Life*, 2:176). Harris had also, according to the preperformance publicity, invested in new scenery and costumes.

In this, the latest installment in Holcroft's string of failures, two additional dimensions of "The Old Cloathsman" are worth noting. In terms of plot, Dewberry, the "old cloathsman," prefigures a character type that would increasingly interest Holcroft—the working-class hero who intervenes to restore justice among his discordant social superiors. This type would be sketched out more fully, and more honestly, in "The Escapes" (1801) and *The Lady of the Rock* (1805), when anticipating or enacting melodrama. In the present case I will just comment that Dewberry is revealed at the end of the play to be in possession of a substantial fortune. He is thus able to secure the marriage of his son to the daughter of the unscrupulous Morgan, the younger Dewberry's employer, by relieving Morgan of his financial distress. This plot device—the appearance of sudden, unexpected riches that ensure the triumph of the virtuous—had featured in Holcroft's novel *Hugh Trevor* as well, and had continued to provoke comment and criticism. In fact, on 28 January 1799, as "The Old Cloathsman" was about to begin rehearsal, Holcroft writes of having read a review of *Hugh Trevor* in a French journal. Among the faults listed by the reviewer was "mak[ing] Trevor so suddenly a wealthy man . . . entirely in the novel style." Holcroft adds, in parentheses, "true; blamable" (*Life*, 2:238).[99] Although agreeing with this criticism, it was too late to apply it—if Holcroft had considered the option—to "The Old Cloathsman," which was already in the hands of theater management. In all events, the nuanced social awareness—class tensions but also contrived prosperity—that feature in this comic opera went completely unacknowledged in its public reception.

Another element in the reception of "The Old Cloathsman" involves a more realized, and noticed, political dimension, one occurring outside of the text. The review of the play published in *The True Briton* on 3 April concludes its commentary with a challenge to the playwright Thomas Dibdin to "announce it was his."[100] Dibdin, not having written it, of course refused, even though Thomas Brandon, box keeper at Covent Garden, urged him not to contradict the report.[101] Holcroft had chanced to meet Dibdin on 26 January 1799 (*Life*, 2:237–238). Dibdin acknowledged the meeting as well in his own autobiography, where he elaborated on Holcroft's kindness to him. Skirting around their differing political and religious beliefs, Holcroft had told him that "if ever [they] disputed, it ought to be," not about politics, but rather as to "who could (as brother dramatists) best serve the other."[102] Both Holcroft and Dibdin pointed out (in their diary and memoir, respectively) that it was the actor Thomas Knight who had introduced them on that January day, following which Knight had immediately departed. This action was later "attributed to a dislike [Knight] had to be publicly seen with any known political character," as Dibdin recalled.[103] Ironically, Knight would have a role in "The Old Cloathsman" and was already scheduled for the part at the time of this encounter. Knight's opportunism and hypocrisy (retreating from a meeting with Holcroft but taking a part in his play), along with the effort to conceal Holcroft's authorship of what is an innocuous, forgettable musical comedy, are indicative of the political tensions that continued to surround Holcroft during this time. His repeated success in having his work staged despite the public clamor against him (carried along in this case by Harris's optimism that "The Old Cloathsman" would reach twenty performances) but also the rumors and attempts at disinformation regarding the authorship of the piece signal a secure position in the theatre world vis-à-vis theater managers, but also the ongoing tenuousness of that position apparent in the response of those on the lower rungs of the theater hierarchy—the box keeper Brandon and the actor Knight—and more generally once his works entered the public sphere.[104]

The third play Holcroft wrote during this period, *Hear Both Sides*, was more of a success. When it was eventually produced in 1803, it ran for eleven performances. The printed text went through four editions and was also published in Philadelphia. The play presents the story of two young men, both of whom are flighty and impetuous, but also deeply compassionate, and their struggles to overcome the injustice meted out by authority figures who attempt to deny them of, variously, an inheritance and a wife. It was criticized, as Holcroft wrote in his preface, as a "somber sermonizing drama."[105] While Holcroft defends the play as a comedy, this recognition by the critics reflects, as with the *Inquisitor*, a move towards a more layered and complex sense of genre. Regarding its composition, the diary once more indicates his alacrity in completing one play ("The Old Cloathsman") and then immediately beginning another, and in doing so to move deftly between genres—in this case from a musical opera to what he perceived to be a serious comedy. The day after submitting "The Old Cloathsman" to Harris, Holcroft began work anew, conceiving characters and scenes for what was initially titled "The Lawyer." Three days later, he was obliged to put this new piece temporarily aside, so as to begin revision of the opera, after Harris had determined that it would be performed as an afterpiece. Concurrently, he was prodded by the theater manager to proceed apace with the comedy.

The relative success of *Hear Both Sides* was the result of prolonged labor and much effort over a number of years. Unlike *The Inquisitor*, it was by no means a trifling effort. In recording the process of its composition, the diary continues to reveal Holcroft's ongoing work habits and his practice of revision, as he grappled with the comments of those with whom he had shared the draft manuscript. For example, James Perry of the *Morning Chronicle* thought highly of "The Lawyer," but he advised Holcroft to remove a scene where a bailiff comes to arrest the protagonist (*Life*, 2:234). (The bailiff ultimately remained.) Two days later, Holcroft read the last three acts to his daughter Fanny and Louisa Mercier, who two months later would become his wife: "their feelings were strong, yet from their variations I could discover some defects" (*Life*, 2:234). Holcroft's phrasing suggests that the two women, daughter and future wife, were hesitant about openly expressing their criticism. Holcroft also read three acts of the play to John Stoddart. The latter's opinion is not directly noted, although implied, when Holcroft adds that the play is still "in want of further improvements" (*Life*, 2:242). Thomas Harris was a keen and critical yet supportive reader, making suggestions for revision yet "promis[ing] to put no other comedy in rehearsal" till he had Holcroft's response to his comments (*Life*, 2:234). Two weeks later, on 4 February 1799, Holcroft and Harris mutually decided in favor of more revision rather than submitting the play in its current form (*Life*, 2:242).

The most incisive criticism Holcroft received for "The Lawyer" came from William Godwin, who had read the manuscript twice. Following the return of the draft play the second time, Holcroft notes that Godwin's remarks were "of the same temper and complexion as his first" (*Life*, 2:231). The earlier instance, not recorded in real time, is, however, substantially commented upon at this later occasion. The conversation between Holcroft and Godwin is remarkable, not for its focus on any specific comments Godwin had made on the new play, which were in fact stringent—"absolutely contemptible," "must be damned" (*Life*, 2:231 and passim)— but in providing a firsthand account of how the two friends read and critiqued each other's work more generally. In this instance their belief in truth, candor, transparency, and sincerity was severely put to the test. Holcroft tells Godwin of his pain and surprise at the latter's criticism; Godwin replies that his remarks lack what he perceived as the "triumphing banter" which characterized Holcroft's comments on the manuscript of Godwin's own play, *Antonio*, which would eventually be performed on 13 December 1800, with disastrous results, when Holcroft was living in Hamburg. Godwin later revealingly adds, as Holcroft reports it: "There is another difference between us. Though I certainly give myself credit for intellectual powers, yet I have a failing which I have never been able to overcome. I am so cowed and cast down by rude and unqualified assault, that for a time I am unable to recover. You, on the contrary, I consider as a man of iron" (*Life*, 2:232). Holcroft replies by admitting that he has indeed been "hardened in sufferance," although he confesses that Godwin's remarks had kept him "wakeful and ruminating full three hours" (*Life*, 2:232–233). This interchange carries with it broader resonances beyond the response to frank literary criticism. The allusion to "sufferance" and vulnerability points to Godwin's and Holcroft's public position as targets of reactionary attack and the general suspicion that accompanied them as they attempted to make their livings in the literary world, as they were constantly confronted with the onslaught of criticism, in the *Anti-Jacobin Review*, the *True Briton*, and elsewhere, that made no attempt to distinguish between the literary and the political quality of their work. This ongoing sense of vulnerability was exacerbated, unintentionally, in the conversation that Holcroft reports in his diary, when candor and sincerity were unreservedly recruited in the cause of truth—in the most sensitive of contexts, within the closest of friendships.

Hear Both Sides was eventually performed, in spite of Harris's earlier support, at Drury Lane rather than Covent Garden. By that time—1803—Holcroft had returned from his three-year self-imposed exile in Hamburg and Paris. Back in 1799, as both the play's fate, as well as its final form, were still unclear, Holcroft was also preoccupied with the pressing matter of his departure from Britain in

July of that year. Although he does not elaborate within the diary about his future plans—to travel with Louisa and Fanny to join his elder daughter, Sophy Cole, and her husband in Hamburg—they had been formed long before he abandoned the journal in March. In his first letter to Godwin written from Hamburg, Holcroft reminds his friend: "It is full two years I believe indeed much more since I first conceived the project[.] I spoke of it frequently and I think I dare affirm oftener to you than to any other person." (This is in response to Godwin's complaint that he had not been consulted about Holcroft's plans.)[106] Evidence for Holcroft's intentions appears in the diary, however, as the date of his departure approached, most prominently in his entry for 26 February 1799. There he announces his plans, quoting from his statement to the Commissioners for the Income Bill: "My income has always been the produce of my labour; and that produce has been so reduced, by the animosity of party spirit, that I find myself obliged to sell my effects for the payment of my debts, that I may leave the kingdom till party spirit shall subside" (*Life*, 2:248). This recognition of the "animosity of party spirit" and its outcomes, a reduced income and then exile, is a clear manifestation of the fate of radical writers in the 1790s. While Holcroft's diary, which had abruptly ended more than three months before his departure, gives no specific details, a careful reader of the text, exposed to repeated accounts of failures in the theater, outstanding debts, hostility within the playhouse and without (with the actor Thomas Knight's refusal to be seen with Holcroft as just one example) will not be surprised at his decision. At the same time, reading of Holcroft's energetic social activity, political discussions at Debrett's, chance encounters and lively conversation with a large circle of acquaintance both in the bookshop and while briskly walking along the streets of London, as well as in social evenings with Godwin, Opie, and others, there is also a sense of regret at what Holcroft was forced to leave behind—those close circles of convivial friendship and the well-worn radical sociability which his diary so vividly records.

* * *

Thomas Holcroft was resilient. He continued his various literary pursuits while abroad, and from his correspondence with Godwin emerges information showing his energetic activity as a writer, an editor, a translator, and (misguidedly) a dealer in paintings. He assisted Godwin by inquiring into opportunities for translation of Godwin's works, especially the newly published *St. Leon* (1799), as well as trying to help their friend James Marshall by commissioning to him various translation projects. The period of Holcroft's exile includes some of his most telling failures—his aim to export artwork from the Continent to Britain at a high resale value ended in disaster as did his editorship of a periodical, the *European Repertory*, a journal for which he had high hopes that in the end were not grounded in the reality of the literary marketplace. Yet his years abroad also laid the foundation for the period of his later major success in melodrama, with his translation and adaptation of J. N. Bouilly's *L'Abbé De L'Épée* as *Deaf and Dumb* (1801) and René Charles Guilbert de Pixérécourt's *Coelina* as *A Tale of Mystery* (1802). During his time in Hamburg, he was also in contact, in varying degrees, with such prominent literary figures as the poet Friedrich Gottlieb Klopstock, the poet and classicist Johann Heinrich Voss, and Goethe, who sent him his poem *Hermann und Dorothea* (1801) for translation and who later commented directly to Holcroft on translation practices.[107]

The written correspondence between Holcroft and Godwin that survives from this period does not elaborate, and barely mentions, Holcroft's German literary connections. Rather, it displays a pragmatic, businesslike interaction between the two friends, but also moments in which they give expression to their close friendship and articulate their regret at the distance between them.[108] To be sure, personal letters present a variety of activities and feelings, recording both the quotidian aspects of daily life along with the reflection and emotional engagement that cumulatively make up the life story. As Bernard Bray asserts, personal letters "undoubtedly form a part of 'autobiographical' literature," but distinctively, because they are directed to one or more specific addressees.[109] Pamela Clemit has shown how the boundaries between letter writing and journal writing "were fluid in the Romantic era," with both genres exhibiting the intimacy of shared experience and the desire for reciprocal exchange.[110] To conclude this chapter I will now examine some of Holcroft's letters to that most specific of his addressees, his primary correspondent, Godwin. I focus on two specific moments, first, the cluster of letters written during the spring of 1800, in which Holcroft's economic vulnerability and his literary activity are particularly intense. I then examine his letter of 17 February 1802 and its aftermath, in which he reacts to the claims of the *Times*, which had announced him to be a French spy. In these letters, as in Holcroft's diary, we are presented with further examples of Holcroft's own voice as he reflects on his writing and on his life and now also on exilic experience.

Holcroft and Godwin corresponded regularly between July 1799 and May 1802. Five of Godwin's letters and thirty-two of Holcroft's from this period are extant; mention is made within these letters to others which are now considered lost.[111] That Holcroft was the more active correspondent of the two derives from the fact that his correspondence mainly had an instrumental purpose: at a great distance from those publishers, art dealers, and theater managers with whom he conducted business, he relied on Godwin to convey to them the material he sent over, to state his terms for publication/sale/performance, and to follow up with later negotiations. Godwin executed these tasks, and evidence from the letters and from his diary shows him in dedicated service to his friend. We can see Godwin in action in the spring of 1800, when Holcroft, in dire financial straits, repeatedly requested his service in errands and negotiations. Holcroft's letter of 1 April is a good example of this exchange. He admits to Godwin, "It is many years since I have felt the distress for money in which this winter has been passed. I am under obligations where indeed there ought to be none but where they are unhappily become intollerably [*sic*] odious."[112] Information included in this letter suggests the cause of Holcroft's destitution as he mentions both the ill-fated *European Repertory*—selling 100 copies when he had anticipated 1,000—and his picture-dealing business. Regarding that latter venture, Holcroft had anticipated that "the result cannot but be advantageous"[113] but unfortunately that was not the case. On 18 April, he wrote again to Godwin, informing him that "My Picture Sale is incomprehensible" but also announcing that he had purchased even more pictures. On 2 May, Godwin responded: "Stop! Think how much anguish, how many sleepless nights you are preparing for yourself."[114]

Holcroft's misdirected efforts originated in his need to provide for a growing family with his new wife Louisa and also in the aspiration for creative as well as domestic tranquility—to be given the conditions to write without the specter of destitution hanging over him. Envisioning the success of his journal, he had written to Godwin on 11 February that, "should it succeed it may afford me the means of writing a work very different indeed from anything I have hitherto written on which I have many years been meditating and from which I had hoped Society would derive lasting benefits."[115] As this financial boon was not realized, he instead attempted to market an eclectic variety of materials—a "secret history" including anecdotes from Russian society, an idea for a German-English dictionary, the translation of a French farce directed to George Colman at the Haymarket, and a German travel narrative.[116] None of these plans came to fruition; the farce was rejected by Colman, and *Mémoires Secrets* and *Reise von Amsterdam* were eventually translated by other hands.[117] At the same time, this was also the period when Holcroft was working, more thoughtfully, on Nicholas Bouilly's *L'Abbé de L'Épée*, which, as *Deaf and Dumb*, would become a major triumph on the London stage. Toward the end of that year, he translated and adapted Bouilly's *Le Porteur d'eau* (The Water Carrier), which also had a successful run in London. It is important to note that these adaptations, discussed in the following chapter, emerge from the same scene of frantic activity that characterized Holcroft's life in exile in the spring of 1800, that flurry of literary endeavor emerging amid the cacophony of languages and genres and with the heterogeneity of different registers of artistic production that characterizes the cultural endeavor in general. This activity acknowledges Hamburg specifically as a dynamic cultural center, which many other British writers of the period visited, including Mary Wollstonecraft, Coleridge, and William and Dorothy Wordsworth.[118]

Deaf and Dumb was performed when Holcroft was still abroad. He was proud of his work, writing to Godwin on 24 October, "I . . . had performed or had endeavoured to perform, the office of a Poet not of a translator."[119] Nonetheless, he was aware of the burden of his name and reputation, adding, "My real fear is that, should the Piece meet any strong marks of public approbation, interested and despicable motives will occasion my name to be industriously circulated; and for this I know no remedy."[120] Holcroft's recognition of the destructive potential of "despicable motives" was grounded in a reality he knew well. His name *was* "industriously circulated," not in the aftermath of the success of *Deaf and Dumb*, but much more sinisterly, in an account appearing in the *Times* a little over a year later, when he was living in Paris. The item had appeared on 26 January 1802, and Holcroft wrote of it to Godwin on 17 February. The newspaper's remarks are worth quoting at length:

> The vigilant Fouché, as it appears, is dexterous enough to avail himself of the talents and information of men of all countries. His system of police and *espionage* has lately acquired a powerful supporter in the person of one of the *soi-disant* twelve Apostles of Liberty. Our countrymen, there-fore, who resort to Paris will do well to be extremely guarded in their conduct if they wish to be secure against the arts of this Informer; who, though, once in the *road to ruin* it now seems is in the high way to fortune.[121]

The mention of one of the "Twelve Apostles" (a name that refers to the twelve men indicted for high treason in the autumn of 1794) already suggests Holcroft as the person in question, while the reference to the "road to ruin" conclusively seals the identification, showing us the strength of that play in cultural memory. Holcroft understood, and was appalled at, the reference. This event came at a period of rela-tive calm for him. He had received a check for £266.6 from Godwin for "The Escapes" a short time earlier, promising a period of financial stability,[122] and he had developed new social connections in Paris, such as with the family of Lord and Lady Mountcashell, to whom he had received a letter of introduction from Godwin. Lady Mountcashell was the former Margaret King, to whom Mary Wollstonecraft had been governess in 1786–1787. Now, in 1802, she invited Fanny Holcroft to live with the family as governess to her children. Holcroft was unsure whether his daughter should accept the offer, writing to Godwin, "we sincerely wish you were here to help us consider the question and to decide."[123] In the end, Fanny took the position, only to be released the following month, following the appearance of the *Times* report. As Holcroft relates it to Godwin,

> A few days ago, being at Lord Mountcashel's on one of his public nights, Lady Mountcashel, after great civility and placing my daughter at the Piano—forte to play and sing, with praises, compliments, and every apparent satisfaction, put a letter in my hand at going away to inform me that Lord Mountcashel having been so repeatedly warned against me as

a Democrat tried for high treason, domestic peace required her to part with my daughter.[124]

Holcroft furiously demanded that Godwin publish his account in the press, and considered taking legal action. Godwin did not acquiesce to this demand. A different account of Fanny's life with the Mountcashells survives in the journal of Claire Clairmont, with an ungenerous view of her behavior, including her various supposed eccentricities along with the news that she had briefly eloped.[125]

In spite of his anger, Holcroft took no action; Fanny quietly returned home. The *Times* report, ridding the Mountcashells of an apparently unsuitable governess, also enables an understanding of the entrenched powers by which Holcroft's name was "industriously circulated" and its seemingly inevitable outcome. This incident clearly exhibits the interplay between politics and the theater that I address throughout this book—in this case, in a basic identification achieved when the political "apostle" meets the "road to ruin"—and which then had social and economic implications in Fanny Holcroft's dismissal from her position. Holcroft had attempted to live in Paris a socially eclectic life, as indicated in his evening meetings with the Mountcashells and the young British intellectuals Thomas Manning and George Tuthill, but also in his contact with men such as John Ashley, former secretary of the London Corresponding Society and now himself an exile in Paris.[126] He also met with such French Revolution veterans as Jean-Lambert Tallien, Merlin de Thionville, and Antoine-Joseph Santerre (who had led Louis XVI to the guillotine), meeting them at a breakfast hosted by the English expatriate Lewis Goldsmith.[127] All the while he visited local theaters in search of pieces to translate. The pressures on Fanny Holcroft's integrity, and thus on her father's, shows, however, that his position still faced challenges; as the *Times* report indicates, any tranquility would ultimately be proved as specious.

Holcroft's visits to the theaters (in Paris but also in Germany) eventually yielded important results with the success of his adaptations of *Deaf and Dumb* and "The Escapes" and the groundbreaking triumph of *A Tale of Mystery*, which, in introducing melodrama to the British stage, helped shape the theatrical landscape for many years to come. His return to England in the fall of 1802, with the premiere of his melodrama soon to follow, can be seen, then, as a victorious reemergence on the London theater scene. The success of this play was unhindered by his political notoriety, and he basked in his triumph. But until that moment, he experienced many setbacks, obstacles, and persecutions, the report in *The Times* being only the last of a long series. Holcroft's life writing records much of this experience—from his diary entries with their documentation of a dense and at times anxious urban sociability, to the acknowledgment of the vicissitudes of playwriting under the shadow of a radical reputation, and finally to the exile which he documents in his letters to Godwin. While not always forthcoming, or truly trans-parent, the first person writing of this crucial period nonetheless affords us the chance to share with Holcroft, even if imperfectly, a political and literary life defined by vulnerability and humiliation but also an intense social experience and close friendships and an exile that also laid the groundwork for later professional success.

THE PREVIOUS CHAPTER EXAMINED HOLCROFT'S exile in Hamburg and Paris, as he actively wrote and translated, continually observing new continental publications and performances, always with the aim of assessing the chances for success of those works back at home. Despite his physical absence from Britain, his career as a playwright was not in abeyance, as indicated in the brisk trans-Channel traffic of correspondence with William Godwin, which included plays sent over with instructions to Godwin for negotiating terms of performance with theater manager Thomas Harris of Covent Garden and others. Among these plays were *Deaf and Dumb* and the musical entertainment, "The Escapes" (also called "The Water Carrier"), which were both performed on the London stage in 1801. Earlier works were also revived in London during these years, for example, *The Road to Ruin* (Covent Garden, October 1799, October 1801) and *The Deserted Daughter* (Covent Garden, May 1800, June 1801). During the time of his exile, *The Road to Ruin* was also produced further afield, for instance in Dublin (Crow Street Theatre, 1801) and in New York (Park Theatre, 1801). Not only was Holcroft able to maintain during these years a substantial presence on the English-speaking stage through these revivals, but also, in contrast to his unsuccessful appraisal of art for the British market, to shrewdly identify and cater to popular taste in the theater with the new dramatic pieces that he sent over from the Continent.[1] The most successful outcome of Holcroft's experience abroad was realized two months after his return to London in September 1802, when his translation and adaptation of René Charles Guilbert de Pixérécourt's *Coelina, ou L'Enfant du Mystère* as *A Tale of Mystery* appeared on the Covent Garden stage.[2] With this work he helped usher in, in Britain, what would become the most prevalent dramatic and literary form, the "key modality"[3] of the nineteenth century, the melodrama, a genre that combined pantomime, spectacle, special effects, and continuous music to explore extreme states of being, ethical polarities, power, and powerlessness.

Throughout the nineteenth century and till the present time, Holcroft is identified as the "father" of British melodrama, a position granted him mainly through his work on *A Tale of Mystery*. The play was an immediate sensation and was remembered throughout the nineteenth century as such in later accounts and retrospectives. John Genest, that insightful chronicler of the theater, and a commentator always sympathetic to Holcroft, wrote that the *Tale of Mystery* "was the first of those Melo-drames, with which the stage was afterwards inundated . . . it was the first and best" (Genest 7:579). Genest's *Account of the English Stage* was published in 1832, the same year of the Great Reform Bill and the year of the parliamentary hearings of the Select Committee on Dramatic Literature, set up to investigate the current state of the theaters and propose suggestions for their reform. The actor and theater manager George Bartley, appearing before the committee, likewise recalled that the *Tale of Mystery* was "the first drama . . . to have been so called," that is, named as melodrama.[4] Looking back on its first performance many years later, in 1878, the writer for the periodical *All the Year Round* recalled both the fascination but also confusion with which Holcroft's play was received: "The production of . . . A Tale of Mystery at Covent-Garden Theatre in 1802, was the occasion of very considerable excitement. The new work, avowedly borrowed from the French stage by Mr. Holcroft, the author of The Road to Ruin, was described in the playbills as a 'melodrama.' To the British playgoer of the period, the term was very strange; doubt prevailed, indeed, as to its precise signification."[5] This writer later adds that "many have dated the fall of the patent theatres from the production of A Tale of Mystery and the first appearance of the word 'melodrama' in their playbills."[6] The implication that Holcroft's play had caused the "fall," that is, the undoing of the Drury Lane/Covent Garden monopoly, acknowledges the prominent role that melodrama more generally had played in its demise, a fact that has been reiterated in modern critical assessments.[7] Holcroft appears in these accounts as a revolutionary in another dimension; his play leading the way for the overhaul of the outdated theater patent system, although, ironically, the patent theaters had been the regular homes of all of his plays and the venues where he had experienced glittering success as well as painful humiliation and failure and where he had always had regular access to theater managers. Holcroft died in 1809, many years before the legal reform of the theaters was finally implemented in 1843. Could he have anticipated that his adaptation of Pixérécourt's *Coelina* might lead to such wide-ranging changes? Would he have seen his work in this respect as revolutionary? Is melodrama, as introduced and shaped by Holcroft, radical only insofar as it changed the theater system so significantly, or are the themes that he introduced in his melodramas radical in themselves and as such an extension of his earlier dramatic works?

In engaging with these questions, I begin this chapter with a short discussion of melodrama in a more general context before moving on to examine those two Holcroft's plays that immediately preceded *A Tale of Mystery*—*Deaf and Dumb* and "The Escapes." Not specifically categorized or remembered as melodrama (although some observers note how *Deaf and Dumb* anticipates it), these plays lay the foundation for Holcroft's work in the genre, through his deployment of various themes and dramatic strategies. I then discuss *A Tale of Mystery* which had such a crucial role in the development of melodrama. I conclude with *The Lady of the Rock* (1805), Holcroft's second melodrama, briefly comparing it to Joanna Baillie's *The Family Legend* (1810) in order to examine differences and divergences which illuminate Holcroft's thematic concerns as they appear in the new genre. In engaging with these plays I will be attentive to the differences that emerge in relation to Holcroft's source material as well as revisions made from manuscript texts to print editions. These variants expose his ongoing efforts to shape the genre of melodrama in a way that illuminates his social and political concerns as well as, especially in *The Lady of the Rock*, his increasing compliance with his audience's wishes. Yet before I proceed, it is important to recall that occasional references to melodrama have already appeared in earlier chapters of this book—in my discussions of the later performances of *The Road to Ruin* (Chapter Two), of the incipient melodramatic aesthetic that appeared in *The Deserted Daughter* and *Knave, or Not?* (Chapter Three), and in a brief allusion that was noted in my comments on *The Inquisitor* (Chapter Four). Thus, while this chapter presents a more detailed analysis of Holcroft's engagement with melodrama, it is also clear that the subjects with which it deals and the expansiveness of its modality are pervasive throughout his work more broadly.

* * *

David Mayer writes that there is "no such thing as a last word about melodrama,"[8] and any first word on the subject is likewise not easy to establish. Melodrama gained much of its grip on the public imagination by tapping into the long-held "predilection" of theatergoers for nonspoken performance[9] and drew upon the thriving illegitimate theatrical culture that proliferated at the end of the eighteenth century, which included opera, dance, pantomime, burletta, equestrian displays, and grand spectacles. It is connected to the popularity of imported German plays by writers such as Schiller and Kotzebue, and of both German and homegrown gothic drama, as melodrama later filled the void that emerged with gothic's decline.[10] The strictly literal account of melodrama's origins in the British context begins, however, in August 1802, when Thomas Holcroft and Henry Harris, son of Covent Garden proprietor Thomas Harris, were both in Paris, the former translating *Coelina* and the latter keeping an eye out for new plays to import to the British stage. Harris wrote to his friend, the playwright Frederick Reynolds, of an "entirely novel species of entertainment . . . called melodrama" that was being performed at the Théâtre de la Porte Saint-Martin and mentioned Holcroft's translation, as he knew of it, as emerging from "one of [those] pieces."[11] The success of Holcroft's efforts when his translated play reached the London stage has already been noted, and it led to the dominance of the genre that would continue throughout the nineteenth century.

What underlying concerns did melodrama speak to? Why did it so quickly ignite the stage in 1802 and afterward? Twentieth-century and twenty-first-century critics have explained that this popularity emanated from, and spoke to, existing cultural uncertainties in a changing world. Peter Brooks argued in his influential study *The Melodramatic Imagination* that melodrama drew upon these anxieties by offering new moral values for the society that emerged with the French Revolution and a way of understanding a world in which traditional Christian beliefs had been destabilized. This new dramatic form arose to articulate in their stead the "location, expression and imposition of basic ethical and psychic truths" that have now been secularized.[12] Almost three decades earlier, Wylie Sypher had asserted that melodrama became a "modality of the 19th-century mind" as it emerged in a society grappling with dialectical polarities in contention: "the good . . . and the bad, the proud and the humble, the hard and the soft, the simple and the devious, the rich and the poor."[13] While these studies importantly exhibit melodrama as a crucial cultural force, they make little mention of Holcroft, or of any of the other early British writers who so effectively shaped it, and, without whom, it would not have been recognized as a modality.[14] Other critics have explored melodrama by paying close attention to the specific contexts of its earliest Anglophone development—textual, authorial, theatrical, performative, and political—while concurrently acknowledging its wider cultural and aesthetic purview. Louis James has argued that melodrama was (also) "a style, located in speech, gesture, mental and emotional attitudes, which can be recognized also in fiction, painting, early film, journalism, or a Chartist sermon."[15] Elaine Hadley likewise stresses its pervasiveness: "a version of the 'melodramatic' seems to have served as a behavioral and expressive model" throughout British society in the nineteenth century.[16] "Taking melodrama seriously," to use James's words,[17] critics have continued to view its affiliation with the spiritual, ethical, and existential uncertainty that Sypher and Brooks identified. Aligned to ongoing apprehensions regarding relevant social and political issues such as increasing urbanization, changes in class, status, bureaucratic and market structures, as well as imperial and domestic political crises, melodrama offered theater audiences a way to try to understand a changing world.[18] As David Mayer puts it, melodrama, through all these different dimensions, is a "theatrical or literary response to a world where things are, or seem to go wrong, where ideas of secular and divine justice and recompense are not always met, where suffering is not always acknowledged, and where the explanations of why there is pain and chaos and discord are flawed or deeply and logically inconsistent."[19]

Mayer's lyric definition persuasively assigns melodrama its wide-ranging cultural reach, while his emphasis on a "theatrical or literary response" importantly insists upon the centrality of texts and performances in shaping it. Mayer and other influential critics observe the increasing dramatic and thematic sophistication of melodrama as the genre developed throughout the nineteenth century, suggesting a trajectory whereby subjects such as guilt and innocence become psychologically internalized.[20] Yet it is necessary to recognize that complex dramas of psychological exploration, such as Leopold Lewis's *The Bells* (1871) or the trenchant political awareness emerging from plays like John Walker's *The Factory Lad* (1832) have their basis in the earliest productions of dramatic works identified as melodrama. An event where "a dress-suited Lyceum audience" thronged to watch *The Bells*[21] must also acknowledge its indebtedness to, and continuity with, the genre's very beginnings, when its popularity aroused anxiety and was widely perceived as a threat to "legitimate" culture; when its ubiquitous presence then destabilized the monopoly of the patent theater system (making the legitimacy of the Lyceum Theatre possible); when it played a major role in bringing about theater reform.

The confusion, suspicion, and hostility that accompanied the earliest appearance of melodrama was articulated by prominent voices in literary culture. Coleridge famously regarded it, and contemporary theater more generally, as a "modern jacobinal drama . . . [whose] popularity consists in the confusion and subversion of the natural order of things."[22] Leigh Hunt and Charles Lamb were equally uncharitable, regarding melodrama as a cultural threat.[23] Walter Scott was of the same mind, utilizing the same political allusion as Coleridge to record the way that, for him, melodrama undermined social order: "The most obvious fault of this species of composition is the demoralizing falsehood of the pictures it offers us. The vicious are frequently presented as objects less of censure than of sympathy; sometimes they are selected as objects of imitation and praise . . . the higher and better educated classes [are shown] as uniformly deficient in those feelings of liberality, generosity, and honour . . . [Melodrama is] . . . the groundwork of a sort of moral Jacobinism."[24] Scott's novels were adapted as melodramas by Thomas Dibdin and others and were extremely popular. Dibdin's adaptations, such as *The Lady of the Lake* (1811) and *The Heart of Midlothian* (1819), do not exhibit what Scott had identified as a "demoralizing" repertoire of values, nor do they indicate any kind of "moral Jacobinism," focusing instead on song and spectacle and minimizing the complexities of Scott's own politics, such as in the portrayal of the Porteus Riots in *Midlothian* and the nuances of the Highlands Rebellion in *The Lady of the Lake*.

Prior to these assessments, the anxiety regarding melodrama was conveyed in a visual representation. *The Monster Melodrama*, by Samuel De Wilde, which was published in *The Satirist* on 4 December 1807, is a good example (see figure 5.1). The print portrayed a three-headed creature positioned against the backdrop of

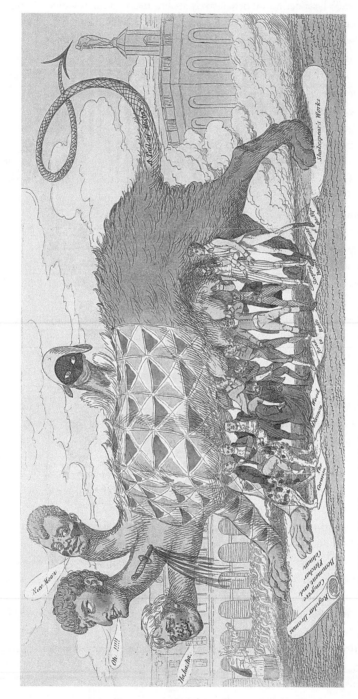

Figure 5.1 Samuel De Wilde, *The Monster Melodrama*, © The Trustees of the British Museum

Covent Garden and Drury Lane theaters. The heads are of theater managers Richard Brinsley Sheridan, John Philip Kemble, and the great comedian, clown, and pantomime actor, Joseph Grimaldi, while the figure of Harlequin, the popular pantomime figure, emerges from the middle of its back. Supporting it from below are prominent well-known contemporary writers, including Frederick Reynolds, Matthew Lewis, and Holcroft himself; his founding melodrama is acknowledged in the monster's posterior—a "Tail of Mystery." Texts also play a prominent role in this print. In addition to the allusion referenced in the "tail" of mystery, each playwright stands upon one of his own texts, thus Reynolds upon his play, *The Caravan* (1803), Lewis, upon *The Wood Demon* (1807), William Dimond on *The Hunter of the Alps* (1804), and Holcroft, on *The Road to Ruin*. These plays are contrasted with the legitimate drama located under the creature's fore and hind paws, the works of Congreve, Fletcher and Beaumont, Colman, and Shakespeare.[25]

The nervousness and uncertainty with which De Wilde regards melodrama and the current state of theater more broadly as, in Jane Moody's words, a "dangerous irrationality of mass, sensuous gratification"[26] is clearly evident in the monstrosity foregrounded in the print. At the same time, he seems to have confused Holcroft's contributions to contemporary dramatic production entirely. Why in fact is Holcroft standing on *The Road to Ruin?* The play had never before been identified with illegitimacy. Its only home in the metropolis had been at this point—1807—in the Theatre Royal Covent Garden. It had been first performed a decade before the other plays scattered on the ground in *The Monster Melodrama* and had not gained its fame through extravagant special effects or scenery. (Reynolds's play, also known as *The Driver and His Dog*, had achieved much of its renown from a scene in which a trained dog saved a drowning child by jumping into real water.) It had survived the period of Holcroft's incarceration in 1794, and had emerged unscathed when he was censured for *Love's Frailties*, *The Man of Ten Thousand*, and *Knave, or Not?* and when he had been excoriated in the *Anti-Jacobin Review*. It would later be identified nostalgically with the beloved "old English comedies" of the premelodrama past, although the later revivals drew on melodramatic style. True, *The Road to Ruin* had been referenced by the *Times* in its pursuit of Holcroft in Paris, but that was a political maneuver and not connected to the play's status within a generic repertoire. The misidentification of *The Road to Ruin* as affiliated with melodrama in this print signals the anxiety surrounding the emergence of that genre in these early years, as the illustrator decisively yet mistakenly conflates Holcroft's oeuvre rather than recognizing his more nuanced position as a writer of comedies in the traditional eighteenth-century style but also, now, as the innovator of a new dramatic form. That said, there are other continuities between Holcroft's melodrama and his earlier work, which the illustrator of *The Monster Melodrama* does not address. These continuities are thematic—the representation of silencing, the emergence of the working-class hero, the criticism of social inequality, and the ideal of perfectibility. These themes will be examined in the section that follows, as they are exhibited in the two Holcroft plays, *Deaf and Dumb* and "The Escapes," which were performed the year before *A Tale of Mystery* appeared on the stage.

* * *

Deaf and Dumb opened at Drury Lane on 24 February 1801, after being submitted to the censor two weeks earlier on 9 February by theater manager John Philip Kemble. Holcroft's play was translated and adapted from Jean-Nicholas Bouilly's *L'Abbé de L'Épée* (1799), which had been highly successful on the Paris stage. Holcroft's adaptation was also a major success. It ran throughout the rest of the season, and it would be performed regularly throughout Britain and worldwide for many years to come.[27] Holcroft had originally intended the play for Covent Garden, and Thomas Harris would surely have regretted his decision to reject it in light of its triumph at the rival house.[28] William Godwin had noted the play's popularity in a letter to Holcroft in Hamburg; he saw it two times during the early weeks of its run.[29] It received positive reviews, with critics praising the acting as well as its novelty. As the *Morning Chronicle* wrote, "Nothing of the kind was ever attempted before." Holcroft was not identified in this review as the playwright, although the newspaper, in mistakenly announcing August von Kotzebue as the author of the original text, felt the need to reassure its readers that "those who see [the play] performed will not only leave the Theatre with their principles undebauched, but with a greater love of virtue, and a deeper abhorrence of guilt."[30] Bouilly's play had been written to commemorate the work of the Abbé Charles Michel de L'Épée, who had developed a sign language system and founded the first free school for the deaf in France in 1755. The establishment of a national government-supported institution for the deaf in 1799 and the erection of a monument to the memory of De L'Épée was the occasion for the appearance of Bouilly's play, which dramatizes a real-life event in which De L'Épée worked to have an abandoned deaf-mute recognized as the Comte de Solar and restored to his rightful position.[31] *L'Abbé de L'Épée* also includes a subplot involving a pair of young lovers who overcome the obstacle of parental intransigence; the exposure of the crime against the young count also enables the fulfillment of their love.

Holcroft's *Deaf and Dumb*, appearing two years after Bouilly's play, has a similar plot while foregrounding Holcroft's ongoing concern with the injustices inherent in, and emerging from, prevailing class hierarchies and patriarchal tyranny but also indicating, as throughout his work, the possibility of reform. Holcroft's play tells the story of Darlemont, who years before had taken his deaf-mute nephew, Julio, the heir to the family estate, from their home in Toulouse to Paris and, with the help of his servant, had him dressed in rags and then abandoned in the metropolis. Now, with his usurped status as head of the estate, Darlemont plans the marriage of his son and heir, St. Alme, to the daughter of the president of the district, although St. Alme is in love with Marianne, the sister of his friend, Franval, a young lawyer.[32] The portrait of the young count hanging on the wall of the palace serves as a constant reminder of their guilt to Darlemont, and Dupré, the servant who had assisted him in the scheme. The abandoned Julio had been brought to the Abbé de L'Épée and renamed Theodore, had been taught sign language, and, once able to communicate, had related to Abbé de L'Épée the basic facts of his story. Now, years later, they arrive in Toulouse in search of justice (Julio/Theodore had remembered his birthplace generally as in the south of France). They are aided by Franval, Marianne, and St. Alme, as well as by various servants who remember the young count and others who recognize him from the portrait. Justice is eventually restored: Darlemont signs a written confession of his crime and Julio/Theodore is recognized as the heir, but also insists on giving half of his fortune to St. Alme, who had been unaware of his father's actions. The play concludes with Abbé de L'Épée vigorously urging the marriage of St. Alme and Marianne. We can assume that this marriage will take place, although Darlemont does not reappear on stage to give it his blessing.

There are no very remarkable differences in terms of plot between Bouilly's play and Holcroft's adaptation, although Holcroft had written to Godwin that he had "given a new catastrophe to the fable" and that his play "was no translation." He also complained of the "laborious alterations" that Kemble was undertaking.[33] The result of Kemble's editorial work was that ultimately no changes appear in the play's resolution to differentiate it from its French source. (With no evidence for a new "catastrophe," it is intriguing to consider what Holcroft had originally had in mind.) Those differences that appear elsewhere in the play are suggestive of Holcroft's ongoing ideological concerns. As Jane Moody has pointed out, the more prominent role given to Julio/Theodore's portrait in Holcroft's play acknowledges a heightened political awareness: "the Palace [is] a place of oppressive secrecy, suspicion and deceitful signs . . . [and] the picture comes to represent the impossibility of buying silence."[34] Bouilly's text, in contrast, gives a more prominent role to Abbé de L'Épée, to his methods of teaching the deaf but also to his devoutness and to his recognition of divine assistance in enabling the successful outcome of Julio's story. Holcroft, in contrast, places more emphasis on the psychological complexity of the characters Dupré and Darlemont, as the exposure of their deception becomes imminent.[35] Darlemont has six soliloquies in Holcroft's play as opposed to one in Bouilly's, and his guilt is more tempered with remorse, as is evident in the following example, when the exposure of his crime approaches:

> I know not what to think, nor what course to take. Is this fellow's account true, or false? Am I betray'd, or not? Nor dare I tax him too closely! That would excite suspicion. Horrible uncertainty!

> O, let no man ever trust himself into the path of guilt! It is a labyrinth beset with dismay and remorse, and not to be retrod without a miracle![36]

Although Darlemont does not reappear on stage after his written confession to the crime, Holcroft suggests his eventual reform and a more universal triumph of justice, as de L'Épée proclaims a "father's return to virtue" and posits the example of Julio's story as one which "may terrify the unjust man from the abuse of trust, and confirm the benevolent in the discharge of all the gentle duties of humanity" (DD, 81). Abbé de L'Épée likewise has the final word in Bouilly's play, but there he simply thanks Providence and declares that his work is done. Holcroft's conclusion is consistent with his wider ideological agenda through the idea of perfectibility—Darlemont *can* and *will* reform—linked to the emergence of truth and justice. Moreover, the servant Dupré's remorse is also highlighted by Holcroft. Dupré explains his complicity in the abandonment of Julio through the opportunity that the deed had supposedly offered of an equivalency of status with his master, "the wild vanity of sharing your [Darlemont's] confidence—your familiarity—and becoming—instead of him you call your slave—your friend" (DD, 36–37). This misguided hope for a social equality that would be achieved by committing a criminal act, in corrupting the servant, also shows more generally the degeneration of a society on the basis of class hierarchies.

Accompanying this idealistic Holcroftian worldview is also the recognition of the grim realities that underpin society, appearing in the prominent role given to silencing and muteness as key themes in the play. The figure of the mute is an absolutely central feature of melodrama, which becomes, as Peter Brooks puts it, "symbolic of the defenselessness of innocence."[37] *Deaf and Dumb*, as well as Bouilly's original play, are part of a wide repertoire of representations of this figure on the eighteenth-century stage. *L'Abbé de L'Épée* emerges from the French theater, where the mute had been ubiquitous. The figure was popular as well across the Channel, drawing on British theatergoers' love of pantomime. Holcroft's importing of the work of Bouilly (and later of Pixérécourt) gave the mute an additional, influential presence, decisively introducing the "aesthetics of muteness"[38] as a central feature whereby nonverbal movements are no longer simply pantomimic entertainment. Instead, Julio's gestures are a holistic element in the play's web of communications. His signs, movements, and utterances further along and politicize the narrative and the revelation of Darlemont's crimes. Julio's inarticulate cries when identifying evidence of his disenfranchisement, such as the "shriek" (DD, 12) uttered when recognizing the place of his birth, anticipate what would later become an equally prominent feature in *A Tale of Mystery* and then a touchstone of British melodrama. Silenced and defenseless characters articulate their victimization in haunting, expressive sounds, unintelligible yet decipherable at the same time.[39]

There is an additional alteration that Holcroft made to Bouilly's play that is worth noting. In Act III, scene ii, Holcroft's version has Marianne sing a song. The lyrics were written by Matthew Lewis while the music was composed by the Irish vocalist and composer Michael Kelly, a prominent figure in the theater world, who had composed the music to Lewis's *The Castle Spectre* (1797) and Sheridan's *Pizarro* (1799), among many other plays.[40] The song was published separately and called the "favourite song in the new historical drama of 'Deaf and Dumb, or, The Orphan Protected.'"[41] The song does not further the plot of *Deaf and Dumb* in any way, appearing rather as a brief interlude in which Marianne expresses to the audience her love for St. Alme. Its presence may nonetheless signal various continuities and developments, pointing, first, to Kemble's recruitment of Lewis and Kelly, an intervention indicating his understanding that music was an increasingly important feature to be integrated into the drama more widely. Holcroft would himself develop a musical dimension more fully in "The Escapes," and a musical score would later function as an integral, defining element in *A Tale of Mystery* and then in melodrama more generally.

* * *

"The Escapes" was first performed on 14 October 1801 at Covent Garden. Like *Deaf and Dumb*, it was a translation of a work by Jean-Nicholas Bouilly, in this case, Bouilly's libretto for Luigi Cherubini's opera, *Les Deux Journées, ou le Porteur d'eau* (1800). The music for Holcroft's adaptation was composed by Thomas Attwood (with whom he had collaborated on "The Old Cloathsman") and included some of Cherubini's original score.[42] The English text was not published; the Larpent copy called it "a musical entertainment" (LA 1332). Attwood's musical score was published separately.[43] The Huntington Library catalogue attributes "The Escapes" to "Thomas John Dibdin or Thomas Holcroft," and I must be precise here in claiming Holcroft's authorship of the piece. "The Escapes" was recognized as Holcroft's work by Hazlitt in the *Memoirs* (*Life*, 2:299) and in other sources that discuss the play.[44] Holcroft himself notes, in a letter to Godwin from Paris that "the music of The Escapes is admired more perhaps than I can make you believe," while thanking Godwin and their friend James Marshall for their "care for the Opera."[45] Holcroft's authorship of the play is decisively confirmed by the Covent Garden account books held at the British Library, where his earnings for the play are recorded.[46]

On the other side of the issue, Dibdin includes in his *Reminiscences* a letter written to him by Attwood: "I am in great want of certain songs and duetts for the 'Escapes' if you will oblige me by writing them, I shall esteem it a great favour, and be happy to pay whatever is your accustomed remuneration . . . the fact is, I shall get nothing for the 'Escapes' without some additional songs &c, and shall be extremely benefited, if you will undertake them."[47] Earlier in his book, Dibdin had clearly written of his work with Attwood on the musical entertainment, asserting that "Mr. Attwood was the first composer I had written with at Covent Garden when we produced . . . 'The Escapes' [among other plays]."[48]

In reconciling these claims for authorship, what emerges is the possibility that Dibdin contributed *some* songs to the piece, as suggested by C. B. Oldman.[49] It is not clear why Dibdin gave the impression that he alone had written the libretto for "The Escapes" or why Holcroft had made no mention of Dibdin's contributions. The two men had an amicable relationship, putting aside their political differences in the spirit of the collegiality of "brother dramatists . . . best serv[ing] each other."[50] The evidence in Dibdin's autobiography, leading as it presumably had, to the partial misidentification for the authorship of "The Escapes" in the Huntington's Larpent catalogue, echoes, if briefly, that other occurrence, in 1799, in which Dibdin had been asked to falsely acknowledge his authorship of "The Old Cloathsman." Then it had been the result of the hostile political climate, whereas in this case what emerges is most probably an unacknowledged, perhaps unwitting, collaboration from two writers circulating in many of the same theater milieux. Thomas Harris at Covent Garden, desiring more music for the piece, must have contacted Dibdin to supply it since Holcroft was at a distance, in Hamburg.

The text of "The Escapes" recognizably aligns itself with Holcroft's earlier work as it reverberates with his ongoing promotion of liberty, truth, and the energy of benevolent action, resilience, and resourcefulness. Following Bouilly, Holcroft tells the story of Michelli, a water carrier living in Paris in 1647, and his rescue of Armand, the president of the Parlement of Paris and his wife Constantia, as they attempt to flee the city and the persecutions of the vindictive Cardinal Mazarin. Michelli contrives to have Armand and Constantia smuggled out of Paris by his son Antonio in his little water cart. Armand and Constantia, in working-class disguise, undergo many searches and interrogations before finally making their way to the town of Gonesse, where Antonio is to be married. After further altercations with the authorities (the military plays a prominent role in this play), Armand inadvertently exposes his true identity to a group of soldiers in Gonesse who attempt to accost his wife. Michelli the water carrier then suddenly appears with a pardon from the queen. (It is not explained why he, and not higher dignitaries, executes this crucial errand, although it decisively situates his importance as a working-class savior.) The play concludes as Armand and Constantia take part in Antonio's wedding, singing, "And may we all forever be/ Humane and gentle, just and free."[51]

Bouilly's story of a heroic rescue was said to have been based on a real-life event occurring during the upheavals of the French Revolution. He transposed the action to 1647 so as to avoid trouble with the revolutionary authorities.[52] (Cardinal Mazarin is a historical figure from that time; the domestic strife between King Louis XIV and the nobility, known as the Fronde, would actually begin in 1648.) Holcroft's translation, which retains the 1647 setting, cuts the narrative substantially while remaining faithful to the main plot of the story. Suggestively, he included some brief reformist additions. Thus, the nobly born Constantia declares that "the proudest boast of birth, the brightest honor ancestry can bestow is affinity to benevolence and virtue" (E, 5), a claim that recalls Holcroft's earlier reformed noblewoman, Lady Fancourt, who had asserted, in *Love's Frailties*, that "riches, rank and power are feeble arms, as opposed to the energies of mind and virtue."[53] Likewise, Armand, entering the water carrier's house and explaining the reason for his escape from Paris, declares that "laws are the people's property" (E, 4). This comment, unmarked and perhaps overlooked by Larpent, gives a wider political inflection to Armand's criticism of his persecutor, a tyrannical cleric. One passage, at least, was excised by the censor.[54] It appears at the beginning of the second act, which opens with a chorus of singing soldiers. Whereas in Bouilly's original text, the soldiers sing of the greatest vigilance that directs their steps ("que la plus grande vigilance dirige tous vos pas"),[55] Holcroft had them sing of "the Culprit seize where e'er he wanderest/ For soldiers must obey" (E, 9). Larpent must have been anxious about giving these common soldiers a greater agency and a more reluctant spirit in enforcing tyrannical directives—they too have the potential to be working-class heroes—and the song was deleted. "The Escapes" had a successful run of twelve performances; nonetheless, the text was not published, and it is barely examined, if at all, in discussions of Holcroft's theatrical career. Even the fact of his authorship, as we have seen, is disputed to a certain extent in the historical record.

Holcroft's source text, Bouilly and Cherubini's *Les Deux Journées*, was by far more successful—Beethoven very much admired it[56]—and the opera has had a robust afterlife, still being performed and recorded (albeit not frequently) in the twentieth and early twenty-first centuries.[57] The opera has been recognized as a "rescue opera," although David Charlton persuasively sub-categorizes it as an "exemplary action opera," a type of work that stresses "the role of individual action" bound up with humanity and moral purpose."[58] The place of *Les Deux Journées* in the history of opera, and at this particular cultural moment, is a fascinating subject; for my purposes in this chapter, it is important also to note the commonalities between rescue operas, with their focus on wrongful imprisonment and their depiction of incarceration, and the gothic novel.[59] To be sure, *Les Deux Journées* and "The Escapes" present incarceration and rescue in more benign terms than in the darker prisons of the gothic—*their* prisons are first the hospitable lodgings of Michelli in which they take refuge, then his little water cart, and later the guardroom of the soldiers and the pastoral country cottage in Gonesse—yet there is still the sense of a looming threat of interment as opposed to the will to individual and political freedom.[60] Anthony Arblaster perceptively recognizes the "democratic vein" of Cherubini's score—the music is sung mainly in ensembles rather than as solo arias; moreover, the opera exhibits a "quite striking use of melodrama: spoken dialogue against musical background or interjections."[61] Holcroft and Attwood retained these elements in their adaptation as well. The gothic ambience, as it slips into melodrama, provides a crucial link between Holcroft's adaptation of this libretto and his own later success with *A Tale of Mystery*.[62]

*   *   *

A Tale of Mystery, translated by Holcroft from Pixérécourt's *Coelina, ou L'Enfant du Mystère* was first performed at Covent Garden on 13 November 1802. The play tells the story of Bonamo, his son Stephano, his ward Selina (heiress to a substantial fortune, whom all believe to be his niece), and the mute Francisco, who had been given shelter at the family home in Savoy the week before. Selina and Stephano are in love, but their prospects are threatened when the Count Romaldi seeks to press her marriage with his son. Bonamo refuses the offer, recognizing the fear that Romaldi arouses in all who encounter him, including Francisco. Infuriated by the decision, Romaldi returns the following day during the celebration of Selina and Stephano's engagement to reveal that Selina is the natural daughter of Francisco. Bonamo immediately disowns and banishes her, along with her father, but not long afterwards, he receives information from a former associate of Romaldi revealing the true nature of events: Francisco is Romaldi's brother, and he and Selina's mother had been privately married. Romaldi, discovering the event, sold Francisco to pirates. When Francisco escaped, Romaldi had attempted to have him assassinated, an action in which Francisco's tongue had been cut out. Bonamo had received earlier hints of this from his housekeeper Fiametta, but they had been ignored or disparaged. Recognizing the injustice done to Francisco and the fact that Selina is not a "natural" daughter, the party sets out to find them. The story reaches its climax when the father and daughter take shelter at the home of the miller Michelli—interestingly, the same name as the heroic water carrier in Holcroft's earlier play—who had also witnessed the earlier events surrounding the attack on Francisco eight years earlier. Romaldi, now a wanted man, has likewise come to Michelli's residence. As the archers who have been sent to apprehend him arrive, Selina and Francisco step in to protect him from their violence, and the play concludes with a general plea for mercy.

Like *Deaf and Dumb*, *A Tale of Mystery* showcases the mute, disenfranchised victim of corrupt power and greed and in doing so establishes this character type as central to the melodramatic repertoire. Once again, Holcroft's play was not simply a translation, but rather an adaptation that clearly nuances the negotiation between crime and retribution to endow the work with his particular vision of moral reform and perfectibility rather than with a triumph aided by divine assistance or with the anticipation of punitive justice. Thus, in Pixérécourt's play, as Romaldi (called Trugelin in this version) is apprehended by the police, the peasants' desire for revenge on the villain is forestalled by both Dufour (Bonamo) and Michaud (Michelli) who reiterate the supremacy of the law but also the notion that the virtuous man punishes, but does not kill.[63] Holcroft, conversely, has archers (rather than "paysans")[64] attempt to neutralize the villain. As Moody notes, the archers "represent a form of political obfuscation, deliberately rendering as vague as possible the state's moral role in the punishment of individuals."[65] There are no aggressive peasants on the scene in *A Tale of Mystery*, and the working-class awareness, if we may call it that, is entirely benevolent, exhibited through Michelli's active yet nonviolent efforts in apprehending Romaldi and in the moral voice of the servant Fiametta, who fearlessly stands up to her master at Selina's banishment: "You are a hard hearted uncle, an unfeeling father, and an unjust master! Every body will shun you! You will dwindle out a life of misery, and no body will pity you; because you don't deserve pity."[66] In this speech, as Diane Long Hoeveler has argued, "for the first time on the popular British stage a female housekeeper, a servant, issues orders to, and offers words of condemnation to her aristocratic employer."[67] Crucially, moreover, Holcroft's play concludes with a rejection of any punishment. In its place appears the forceful representation of the wronged Selina and Francisco and their active interventions on Romaldi's behalf. Their "entreaties and efforts" (TM, 50), Selina's call to let her father's "virtues plead for my uncle's errors" (TM, 50), along with Bonamo's plea for general mercy, comprise the final actions of the play. Pixérécourt's play, conversely, concludes with a vague sense of retribution but also a more celebratory closure, emphasizing the lovers' happiness with a festive song and dance.

Holcroft not only altered Pixérécourt's play; he also significantly revised his own work, as is evident when viewing the Larpent copy of the play.[68] The manuscript concludes, like the French play, with a song, but, notwithstanding this "merriment" (LA 1361, 20), it exhibits, as Jeffrey Cox has shown, a more "somber" tone in the events leading up to the finale. Bonamo invokes his plea for mercy but adds that "the prince must be obey'd."[69] In the printed text, the prince is not acknowledged at this moment, and his role as the arbiter of institutional power is omitted; the call for justice is not contingent on obedience to the state. In his detailed discussion of *A Tale of Mystery*, Cox notes the innovative features of this melodrama, the sophisticated stage design (especially in the final scene with the pursuit of Romaldi), the inclusion of a ballet number in Selina and Stephano's engagement party as an example of its generic hybridity, and, especially, in the prominent use of nonverbal communication. This includes pantomime, which is Francisco's means of communication, and, especially, the music of composer Dr. Thomas Busby. The musical score is, in Cox's words, the "key to understanding the emotions that rise and fall in the play," expressing, variously, joy, dejection, solemnity, contention, threat, pain, disorder, discontent, and alarm. The extensive stage directions that appear in the text call attention to the way the thrust of the play is carried along by means other than spoken dialogue.[70] The sheer novelty of this hybrid form revolutionized British drama. The genre took over the stage and was a key factor in the movement for the dismantling of the monopoly of the patent theaters and for theater reform.

But was *A Tale of Mystery* revolutionary in other ways? Was Holcroft imbuing his text with another more urgent *political* reform? Cox suggests that he was not, arguing that, especially when viewing the print edition together with the manuscript, we can discern the "essentially reactionary nature of melodrama." Noting that "as a man of the left [Holcroft] is clearly not offering some simple conservative vision," he nonetheless claims that Holcroft's groundbreaking play concludes with a "return to a strong sense of conventional order." As evidence he cites the reaffirmation of the master-servant relationship (although Fiametta articulates the moral indictment in the play, her words are not really heeded, and she is silent at its close) and hence the more expansive reassertion of the noble patriarchal regime along with, in the manuscript version, the authority of the police and the rule of the law.[71] I want to suggest, conversely, that to view the conclusion of *A Tale of Mystery* with its upholding of the societal and hierarchical status quo as equivalent to a reactionary thematics is to overlook the depth of Holcroft's investment in Godwinian philosophical politics in this play and throughout his writings. As we have been seeing in this book, Holcroft's radicalism was always situated within Godwin's distinctive political philosophy, a nonviolent worldview that promoted political justice through the pursuit of the common good—"first-order impartiality"—and the rejection of the primacy of one's own personal concerns.[72] Godwin addressed the subjects of crime, punishment, and perfectibility (among many others) within the argument for his ideal community of reason. Regarding criminals specifically, he stressed that universal moral censure rather than punishment or coercion is sufficient to ensure their amendment. "No individual," Godwin writes, "would be hardy enough in the cause of vice, to defy the general consent of sober justice that would surround him. . . . He would be obliged, by a force not less irresistible than whips and chains, to reform his conduct."[73]

These were Holcroft's principles as well. He upholds them, consistently, in his personal experience and his imaginative writing. His *Narrative of Facts* (1795), written shortly after his release from prison, articulates his beliefs on crime, punishment, condemnation, censure, and retribution and the promotion of reform and perfectibility in their place. Relevant for all of Holcroft's works, including *A Tale of Mystery*, the comments from the *Narrative of Facts* are worth quoting again: "the mistake is past recal, but the man may amend. The error should never be spared, the person ought never to be attacked" (NF, 80). In Holcroft's plays and melodramas the idea of reform through individual perfectibility is foregrounded through denouements that stress nonviolent, nonpunitive redemption, and a sense of regret for the offenses committed that is clearly verbalized or announced on stage and in the stage directions. Presented in the characters Monrose (*Knave, or Not?*), Mordent (*The Deserted Daughter*) Darlemont (*Deaf and Dumb*), Romaldi (*A Tale of Mystery*), and, as we shall shortly see, Maclean in *The Lady of the Rock*, these representations indicate not only the centrality of a villain who evokes pity[74] but also the approved position which stresses that that pity should be given. This idea is promoted in *A Tale of Mystery* through Selina and Francisco's efforts for a nonviolent reconciliation rather than through vengeful retribution—the "man" and the "mistake" are kept distinct by those who have suffered from him the most. Romaldi's deeds are excoriated, but charity for him is urged.

The manuscript version of "A Tale of Mystery" further expands upon this issue. Whereas the published play simply articulates Bonamo's general call for mercy and Selina's entreaty to let her "father's virtues plead for [her] uncle's errors," LA 1361 includes Grimaldi's (as Romaldi was called in the manuscript) voiced acknowledgement of his "deep remorse" and Bonamo's rejoinder that "if repentance be indeed sincere, mercy, we hope, will not be denied," (LA 1361, 20). While this conditionality—"we hope"—references the role of the state in ultimately meting out punishment or mercy, and thus ostensibly reinforces Cox's view of a more somber, conservative conclusion, the elaborated sentiments at the same time forcibly emphasize that impetus toward perfectibility that is so central to Holcroft's thinking. This is perfectibility which will be effected first on a personal, individual level and will then result not in a chaotic overthrow of government or the immediate disbanding of hierarchies. Fiametta will remain a servant and the prince will rule, but the society in which they live will become a better place through gradual, nonviolent reform, brought together in the communion of like-minded people. We have seen this gradualism throughout Holcroft's work, in the "villains" listed above and also in the social structures they inhabit. *Love's Frailties*, with its much-censured line that "the most useless and often the most worthless of all professions [is] that of a gentleman" also keeps the present social structure intact. Lady Fancourt will reform by recognizing that true nobility is in the "energies of mind and virtue," but she will not lose her noble title.[75] Monrose exhorts for the reform of lords in *Knave, or Not?*[76] but while his own reform is noted at the conclusion of the play, the members of the decadent and corrupt society in which he lives do not relinquish their status. In these plays, then, as in *A Tale of Mystery*, Holcroft's politics are evinced, as always, in the idea of perfectibility attained through private judgment and nonviolent individual effort and examined through the crises, struggles, and, ultimately, moral triumphs of lived experience. This is a movement leading forward, as Holcroft and Godwin so sincerely believed, to a just society whose time will undoubtedly, gradually, arrive, rather than backwards to reaction. "What magic is there in the pronoun 'my?'" Godwin had memorably asked in *Political Justice*,[77] and in *A Tale of Mystery* this question is definitively answered. There is no magic; rather, the underlying idea of first-order impartiality that the question rhetorically promotes is shown through the actions of Selina and Francisco, who energetically abandon their personal concerns, and a desire (if there had been one) for the punishment of their persecutor and carry forward a project of a more universal and all-encompassing benevolence which is, in its wider context, the project of political reform.

Another kind of optimism, more firmly located in time and place, appears in Holcroft's introductory remarks to the published version of *A Tale of Mystery*. As opposed to many of his other prefaces, the glow of success radiates from his "advertisement" to this play, which is itself prefaced by a dedication to Muzio Clementi. Musician, composer, piano builder, pedagogue, and music publisher, Clementi (1752–1832), was a close friend of Holcroft's, and they had often met socially in the time leading up to Holcroft's exile. Clementi had loaned him £100 in January 1799 (*Life*, 2:228), an act Holcroft remembered gratefully.[78] Basking in the triumph of *A Tale of Mystery*, Holcroft celebrates their friendship while remembering the "proofs so indubitable" of Clementi's generosity (TM, front matter). He likewise allows himself a view of the future: "Should my name be fortunate enough to reach posterity . . . may we [Holcroft and Clementi] . . . stand recorded friends, in still more enlightened and therefore still more happy ages" (TM, front matter). Attention to posterity also informs the advertisement that follows this dedication when, after praising the "performers, composer of the music, the scenery and the dances," as well as the "applause" bestowed by the public, Holcroft records his own reflections on the innovative drama that he has produced and the emerging theatrical moment of which he is a part:

> I should be tempted to say something of the nature, powers,
> and scenic effects of the Melo-Drame; but that my thoughts
> must necessarily be given with too much brevity and haste. Other
> Dramatic writers will certainly produce these effects in a much more
> mature and perfected state; and of the pleasures they yield I shall be
> happy to partake (TM, front matter).

Anticipating the durability of melodrama, Holcroft is convinced that the genre will evolve and will be "perfected." There is no evidence—how could there have been?—that he foresaw that the dramatic genre would expand to become a "modality" through which the whole range of human experience could be articulated. Although he envisioned in his dedication to Clementi a future "still more" enlightened and happy, the sense is that, at the moment of his success, he views the world as (fairly) enlightened and happy at the present time. In doing so, he presents us with an appealing view of his moment of triumph along with the anticipation of his future place in the annals of British drama.

* * *

Although very much pleased with the success of *A Tale of Mystery*, Holcroft did not immediately return to writing melodrama. His second and final work in the genre, *The Lady of the Rock*, was first performed at Drury Lane on 12 February 1805, almost three years after *A Tale of Mystery*. In the interim, the much revised *Hear Both Sides*, on which he had been working intermittently since 1799, was performed, also at Drury Lane, in January 1803, and ran for eleven nights. The proximity of the staging of *A Tale of Mystery* in November 1802 and *Hear Both Sides* three months later exhibits Holcroft's work almost simultaneously in the more traditional dramatic form as well as in the emerging melodramatic one. And yet, instead of building on the triumph of the former play and the more modest success of the latter, he spent the following years writing nondramatic texts, completing his *Travels from Hamburg, through Westphalia, Holland, and the Netherlands to Paris* (1804) and publishing his novel *The Memoirs of Bryan Perdue* (1805). When he eventually returned to the drama, it was to melodrama. This time it was not with an adaptation from the French, but rather with a piece modeled on a Scottish legend. Holcroft had encountered the story in Arthur Aiken's *Annual Review* of January 1803, in a review of *A Companion and Useful Guide to the Beauties in the Western Highlands of Scotland and the Hebrides* (1799), written by Sarah Murray ("Mrs. Murray of Kensington") and accompanied, as was customary, by lengthy extracts from the book. One of the extracts relates Mrs. Murray's account of the legend of the "Lady's Rock," which centers on the Maclean and Campbell clans of the Scottish Highlands in the sixteenth century. Lord Maclean, furious over the barrenness of his wife, Ellen, who is a Campbell, has her conveyed to a rock out at sea and abandoned there, with the intent that she will perish when the rock is submerged in the high tide. She is rescued when her cries are heard by a fishing vessel that happens to pass by. Unaware of her survival, Maclean decides to hold an elaborate funeral for her and relates to his brother-in-law, Campbell, his grief at her death. Campbell sends for his sister, very much alive, to the astonishment of her "bereaved" husband. Many years later, Mrs. Murray concludes, Campbell's brother Donald took his revenge on Maclean, stabbing him on a street in Edinburgh.[79]

In his prefatory comments to the published version of *The Lady of the Rock*, Holcroft quotes the *Annual Review*, which had observed that "this tale might be dramatized with very powerful effect, by a skillful writer."[80] He then records his own deliberations: "At first, I thought otherwise . . . this opinion I afterwards changed, and produced the Piece which is now before the public" (LR, iv–v). In perhaps implying that he had dramatized the tale with "powerful effect," Holcroft was at odds with his reviewers, for the play had a tepid reception. The "effect" was not seen as powerful but rather as "not fully equal" to Holcroft's other plays, as the *European Magazine* remarked.[81] The memory of *A Tale of Mystery* led even the *Anti-Jacobin Review*, so adversarial to Holcroft in the more distant past, to comment that *The Lady of the Rock* was "altogether unworthy the talents of such a writer."[82]

Holcroft's adaptation of the Scots legend revises Mrs. Murray's account in significant ways. The cause for Maclean's anger at his wife is no longer barrenness, a situation to which, as Holcroft stated in his introduction, a present-day audience would not be receptive (LR, iv), but instead, a supposed infidelity on her part, a suspicion planted in his mind by his brother Dugald. (Dugald's motives here are his own love for Ellen and his sense that he had been robbed of it, as well as anger at his status as a younger brother.) In fact, in Holcroft's version the Macleans do have a child (unnamed in the play) who plays an important role. Her father asks her to report to him the presence of men who come to visit her mother. The man who visits is Lady Maclean's brother, Campbell, who, because in disguise, is suspected mistakenly to be her lover. Maclean's demand of his daughter, "Don't cry, and I will kiss you whenever you come and tell me who is here" (LR, 6) is indicative of what Holcroft saw to be the child's instrumental purpose in the story: as he puts it, he had "intended to convey a public moral, and teach parents the vice of encouraging their children to be spies" (LR, vi). This representation, which was more detailed in the manuscript version and in the first night performance on stage (a point to which I will return) aroused indignation amongst the audience. As a result, Holcroft writes in his preface, "I curtailed the part of the child: for dramatic writers must not reason, but comply with the public feeling" (LR, vi).[83] This is a Holcroft attentive to public judgment, and willing to excise what was offensive to his audience with some slight self-justification but seemingly no deep regret or resentment, unlike the defiant stance which had appeared in the prefaces to many of his earlier plays.

Elsewhere in *The Lady of the Rock*, however, he persists in promoting his social agenda—"a public moral," as he calls it—as he further revises Mrs. Murray's version of the legend of the Lady's Rock. Appearing as a continuity with his earlier works, Holcroft once again examines the subject of repentance and perfectibility, and, particularly in this play, the role of the working-class hero in enabling reconciliation and reform. Thus, the villainy of Dugald, the traitorous and vengeful brother (not present in Mrs. Murray's account) who accidentally poisons himself but who has a chance to confess his culpability before the poison takes effect, deflects part of the guilt of the attempted murder from Maclean. It likewise enables Ellen to forgive her husband: "my dear lord was miserably deceived" (LR, 30). Earlier, before knowing of his brother's actions, Maclean had already felt qualms of conscience—"Insidious villainy . . . detested act! Infernal jealousy!" he cries (LR,

22), although he ultimately carries out the plan and still insists on combating the Campbells, members of Ellen's clan, before she reappears. Notwithstanding this brief moment of reflection, there is little real deliberation on the lord's part: his smooth reintegration into favor exhibits an all-too-neat closure. The presentation of a more detailed moral and psychological struggle on the part of the perpetrator of evil is missing in this play, and there is little nuancing in the portrayal of the villain who evokes pity and the victim who grants it. (The other major villain, Dugald, is a flat character with no nuancing.)

The political valence of *The Lady of the Rock* is more clearly evident in a different dimension of the work, that of the depiction of the fisherman, the true hero of the play. Mrs. Murray's story only briefly mentions "people in a vessel"[84] who rescue the Lady of the Rock, but in Holcroft's play the fisherman assumes a major role, first saving Ellen Maclean's brother, Campbell, from a shipwreck, then delivering Ellen from the rock and bringing her to his cottage, and later confronting Lord Maclean himself with the insinuation of the crime just as the clans prepare for battle. Despite this challenge, at first glance it can be supposed that the fisherman conforms rather to a conservative position. He exhibits profound loyalty and deference to those above him in the social hierarchy. He admonishes his son to "always think and speak well of [his] betters" (LR, 11) and later commands his wife to "hold [her] tongue" (LR, 26) after she condemns the attempted murder of Ellen Maclean. He elsewhere claims that he will serve his lord "as long as [he has] a breath of life" (LR, 18). He seems content in accepting his position as a simple cottage dweller with one of his thirteen children in service to the nobility. At the same time, he refuses Dugald's command given together with his brother the Lord to convey Ellen to the rock: "I hope to go to heaven. I'll not have murder on my head!" (LR, 20). While his refusal might be attributed to this wish to later "go to heaven," and thus the fear of an even higher—religious—authority, the fisherman goes against orders by actively venturing out to save Ellen while also stepping up at the moment before the crucial confrontation between the Maclean and Campbell clans to verbally confront the lord who is complicit in the crime. Clearly, he is not here "thinking and speaking well of his betters," as he had earlier directed his son to do.

At the close of the play, the fisherman is recognized as the true hero of the action by Lord and Lady Maclean and her brother, Campbell, and is invited to move with his family into the castle.[85] As the lord proclaims, "Nobler than noble, thou art indeed my saviour" (LR, 31). (Earlier, after being rescued Lady Maclean also calls the fisherman her "noble saviour" (LR, 26).) The fisherman's rejoinder to these closing encomiums, "I can't speak" (LR, 31), accompanied by a stage direction signaling his brushing off tears, indicates, quite conventionally, his emotion in being recognized and rewarded by those at the top of the social ladder. On another level, however, his actions here and throughout the play suggest the way he represents the true moral leadership of the community and thus an alternative nobility—of conscience, values, and individual action—that is introduced as an ideal. (Significantly, he will be living at the castle.) In this reading, his speechlessness at the close of the play implies, rather than deference, his criticism of what has passed. Within the existing framework of power all that remains for him to do at this point is to adhere to the directives that he had been offering to his family throughout the play—to indeed "hold his tongue" and not to relate his own opinion of the treacherous events that he had witnessed throughout the play. His earlier criticism of the lord's culpability is suppressed in the glow of the final reconciliation but exhibits at the same time an idealized alternative moral leadership. In this sense, the fisherman follows Fiametta in *A Tale of Mystery*, Michelli in "The Escapes," and to an extent the eponymous "old cloathsman" whom we saw in the previous chapter, as voices of working-class moral authority. Cognizant of the existing power structures, their vision is never fully articulated or substantiated, yet present and memorable nonetheless.

In viewing the manuscript version of "The Lady of the Rock" (LA 1423), it is clear that Holcroft, eager for the success of his play and influenced by the criticism of the first night performance, also "held his tongue" while devising the revisions that would appear in later performances on stage and then in print. These changes occlude the more energetic melodramatic aesthetic he had originally envisioned. Among the themes that had been originally elaborated upon and then omitted or condensed are both the role of the child and the more extensive coverage given to working-class assertiveness. The manuscript reveals that the depiction of the child-as-spy, which had upset the first night audience, had been expansive, including a dialogue between the girl and Andrew, the fisherman's son, who works as a servant in the castle. The conversation is curious (and unsettling) as the fifteen-year-old Andrew and the young girl contend over who loves their mother the most. One wonders why two youngsters of such different ages and classes would argue about such a matter. At the same time, Andrew also has the opportunity in this dialogue to include some oblique class criticism. When acknowledging the lord's crossness, Andrew exclaims that he can't understand it: "he's nothing at all to do, and can eat wine and cake all day long" (LA 1423, 10), another iteration of the "uselessness of a gentleman." In the manuscript it is Andrew who announces Lady Maclean's "death," giving an opportunity for the ever-cautious fisherman to warn him to "hold his tongue between his teeth" (LA 1423, 31).

The manuscript version of the play exhibits other changes as well. Besides minor elements such as revisions of songs and those characters who sing them (the music had been selected and also composed by Holcroft's daughter, Fanny) and the moving of some of the action, Lord Maclean's repentance and regret had originally been more fully developed. He expands upon his uneasiness when the plot to kill his wife is finalized, and laments his daughter's betrayal of her mother, although it is he who had initiated it when he provoked her to spy. Later he says, "what a monster have I been!" (LA 1423, 40). His confrontation with the fisherman is more robust, and the latter, too, abandons his caution in expressing more fully his contempt for the lord. Accumulatively, these changes reveal the manuscript to be a more complex, more substantially articulated, and thus a bleaker story than the revised version of the play. I have dwelled on these changes because the play that Holcroft had originally conceived might signal the direction in which melodrama *might have gone*; the direction in which he wanted it to go, before compromising the vision to comply with audience approbation. The manuscript play reveals a world fomenting with domestic and class tension; the more developed understanding that one's speech must always be policed; a child betraying and betrayed, whose inner torment after succumbing to her father's emotional blackmail is signaled in her argument with the servant boy in a pitiful competition over maternal love. Significantly, in both versions the girl never reappears to greet her rescued mother. The grim horror of the averted drowning is neatly erased in the emotional reconciliation, but might also survive unarticulated, in the words that the fisherman "can't speak," just as the original manuscript of "The Lady of the Rock" as a whole suggests more complex possibilities for the melodrama itself at this early stage of its development that are likewise silenced.

Following *The Lady of the Rock*, Holcroft never returned to melodrama, and in his final play, *The Vindictive Man* (1806), he returns to more traditional playwriting. *The Lady of the Rock* was far less commented upon than *A Tale of Mystery*, in its own time, through the nineteenth century, and in current critical assessments, both *as* melodrama and for its place within Holcroft's dramatic oeuvre as a whole. I want to conclude my discussion of this play, and this chapter, by briefly looking at another dramatization of the Scots legend of the lady of the rock, Joanna Baillie's *The Family Legend* (1810). While not connected to Holcroft's play (Baillie seems to have been unaware of his melodrama), her tragedy, in exhibiting a different way to approach the famous story also, by the comparison, illuminates Holcroft's play and his concerns as a dramatist at this particular time.[86] *The Family Legend* retells the story of the lady of the rock with a more detailed treatment, in stately blank verse, of both the tense clan rivalry and the psychological torment of the Maclean chief, torn between his love for his wife and his wish to prevent insurrection in his clan, whose members reject the alliance. Lady Maclean (called Helen in this version) is also more fully developed as a character. She is given a romantic backstory with the English Sir Hubert de Grey, whom she forswears in order to marry Maclean and thus to support her clan's political interests. Maclean's death, at the hands of her brother John of Lorne, enables her to later marry this suitor, allowing, as Mieke O'Halloran has argued, both Scottish and British identities to be celebrated within the context of a unified Britain.[87]

John Genest, in writing of Holcroft's *The Lady of the Rock*, had remarked that in *The Family Legend*, Baillie had "dramatized the story in a much better manner," and when discussing the latter play when it was performed at Drury Lane in 1815, his comments were mostly favorable (Genest 7: 647; 8: 459–460). Baillie's drama is more psychologically nuanced, and the spectator or reader receives a more expanded sense of Highland cultural tensions. There is a clearer exposition of the long-standing clan rivalry that dictates both Helen's marriage to Maclean and then her attempted murder. Although there is a former lover in the vicinity, there is no suspected infidelity, such as had appeared in Holcroft's account. Baillie, like Holcroft, discards the barrenness that had been the motive in the original legend. In her play the Macleans' newborn baby's future status as a mixed-clan heir infuriates the Macleans, but his identity as such signals a future Highland unity in which events are finally resolved. Holcroft's *The Lady of the Rock*, in contrast, treats both Scottish-English and intra-Scottish tensions superficially, if at all. His revision of the Scots legend grounds its political emphasis in the depiction of a certain kind of working-class heroism, albeit one which in the end willingly, or at least pretending to be so, subordinates itself to class and status hierarchies. He does not engage with a wider context of Scottish nationhood, and the strife between the warring clans—with its potential threat to national unity—is not elaborated. (His source text, Mrs. Murray's *Travels*, had likewise averted the political aspects of the subject.) His play concludes with a seamless, nonviolent reconciliation between the Campbells and the Macleans: after massing for battle, the clans not only "sheath their swords" but "cordially shake hands, like friends and brothers" (LR, 30) after a messenger arrives with Ellen, who also calls for peace.

Yet it is the rescue of Ellen/Helen from the rock that presents what is perhaps the most telling contrast between Holcroft's and Baillie's plays, and best exemplifies the difference between their divergent concerns in their respective adaptations of the Lady's Rock legend. In Holcroft's play the fisherman has a central, active role in tracing and rescuing the betrayed woman. In *The Family Legend*, Baillie depicts a group of fishermen, Sir Hubert de Grey's companions in sport, who, in going to meet him, happen to pass the rock, hear Helen's faint cries, but continue on, unwilling to break their engagement with the nobleman: "Were it not your honour is impatient/ Main-land to make, we had not come so soon."[88] Although these fishermen believe that the faint cries they have heard must have come from a wounded bird or dog, their instinctive generosity and eagerness to rescue the sufferer is subordinated to their unquestioning obedience to the nobleman's orders. Their role in Helen's rescue becomes simply one in which they execute commands, having no active, independent agency of their own.

Other tensions in *The Family Legend* replace the class-based anxieties that informed Holcroft's melodrama, and Baillie's interrogation of British national unity and Scots history was what certainly caused Walter Scott to tremble so nervously in the Edinburgh theater at the opening-night performance of the play.[89] If that Edinburgh audience had gasped at the plight of Helen Maclean clinging to

the treacherous rock, it would have emerged also from the profound consciousness of nation, history, and heritage. Holcroft's audience at Drury Lane in 1805
might likewise have been moved by the scene of the lady on the rock, but more
likely their response exhibited their admiration for the technical prowess of the
theater's "machinist," Mr. Johnson. Holcroft had praised Johnson in his prefatory
remarks for how he had devised the "agitation and terror excited by the elements"
in the central scene in which Ellen is stranded on the rock (LR, vi). This "agitation" would not have been underscored for the Drury Lane audience by any kind
of more substantial, psychologized, terror that could have emerged from a dense
exposition of a family drama of ruthless betrayal and a complex account of an
unforgiving historical animosity. For in the end, Holcroft had no project regarding Scottish or Anglo-Scottish identity. By his own account, he had read a story
in a literary review and taken up the challenge of dramatizing it. In doing so, he
emphasized the concerns which continued to interest him—individual reform and
perfectibility, working-class agency and incremental change that would lead, as
he so profoundly hoped, to a more just society. Significantly, it is only in his version of the tale that Maclean does not die.

It would remain for James Hogg to combine the elements that had variously
appeared in Holcroft's, Baillie's, and Mrs. Murray's accounts of the legend of the
lady's rock. In "A Horrible Instance of the Effects of Clanship," which appeared
in *Blackwood's Magazine* in 1830, he retells the legend, setting it in a bleak, deso-
late, and frozen Highlands landscape. The true savior in this story is the servant
woman Ecky who, together with a miller, heroically brings about the rescue of the
betrayed lady and the exposure of the villains who attempt to kill her.[90] Surely
Holcroft would have appreciated this story, with its emphasis on working-class
compassion, resilience, and energy. Staying in the conjectural mode, we can also
wonder what he would have thought of other later developments in the genre of
melodrama which he had so influentially brought to England with *A Tale of Mystery* and which then came to dominate the British stage. He would have seen of
course increasing technical prowess. The ingenuity he had praised in Johnson's
stagecraft in *The Lady of the Rock* would later expand to include technologies that
produced sophisticated aquatic scenes with rivers, dams, and ships at sea; horses
galloping, trains traveling and wrecked. He would have also viewed many enact-
ments of disability—for instance, the unjustly accused mute in Barnabas Rayner's
The Dumb Man of Manchester (1837) or the blind victim of noble treachery in
James Kenney's *The Blind Boy of Bohemia* (1807). (Kenney would later marry Holcroft's widow, Louisa.) To be sure, he would have encountered instances of working-
class assertiveness, perhaps most notably in John Walker's *The Factory Lad* (1832).
A grim account of politically aware workers disenfranchised by a factory owner
and replaced by automation, the play's central character kills the owner and sets
the factory afire. Holcroft would have forcefully rejected the act of violence,

although he surely would have felt sympathy for the economic vulnerability that precipitated it.

Triumphant in the success of *A Tale of Mystery*, Holcroft had written in his preface to that play that "other dramatic writers will certainly produce . . . melodrama in a much more mature and perfect state" (TM, viii). Together with the thematic and technical innovations that were developed, melodrama would emerge beyond the theater to become a central modality of nineteenth-century culture. Along the way it would be manifested not only in a more "mature and perfect state," as Holcroft envisioned, but also in many bad plays with embarrassing excesses. These excesses helped shape the word "melodrama" as a pejorative "value judgment . . . a technical term for bad drama or bad acting that exists till today."[91] Yet the genre's very survival also testifies to its capaciousness as a mode of representation that, as Holcroft clearly recognized, could give expression to the universal themes that interested him so strongly—the role of truth, retribution, justice, power versus powerlessness, and as he insistently showed, the availability of reform and perfectibility as the means for enacting change in a world in need of political justice.

THE SUCCESS OF *A TALE OF MYSTERY* in 1802, the production after much delay of the more traditional *Hear Both Sides* in 1803, and the subsequent implementation of melodramatic themes and forms also in *The Lady of the Rock* in 1805 exhibit the early years of the nineteenth century as a time of creativity, productivity, and innovation for Thomas Holcroft. The fact that in histories of the theater he is acknowledged for his major role in the development of melodrama in Britain indicates the strength of his contribution and the ongoing recognition of it as such. Following *The Lady of the Rock*, however, he did not continue to engage with the genre. His final play was the more traditional drawing room drama *The Vindictive Man*, performed and then published in 1806. Following this play, Holcroft published no more dramatic writing.

This chapter concludes *Thomas Holcroft's Revolutionary Drama* by examining Holcroft's final years and some occurrences in the aftermath of his death. The literary texts I examine in this chapter represent both failure with *The Vindictive Man* and success with "Gaffer Gray." This was originally an inset poem appearing in the novel *The Adventures of Hugh Trevor* (1794–1797), which, somewhat surprisingly, took on a quite robust life of its own, in Britain and across the Atlantic. Moving beyond literary texts, I consider the last years of Holcroft's life, including his row with William Godwin, as well as what can be constructed of the lives of his children. Crucial remembrances, such as those indicated in the letters of Charles and Mary Lamb, are also examined. Like the other chapters in this book, this chapter presents its subject chronologically. As we thus proceed through the final years of Holcroft's life and examine the period following his death, we will view a writer no longer at the height of his powers; no longer prominently voicing his ardent brand of radicalism and his ideas for political reform; and, in his final years, without the comfort of conversation with his closest friend. As his death was acknowledged, however, and his life summarized, recalled, and eulogized, his political struggles and his literary oeuvre *were* widely remembered. This was the case, of course, in the immediate period following his demise, but likewise with the many revivals of *The Road to Ruin* that were to come, or the later publications of the *Memoirs* or "Gaffer Gray." His name was also softly resonant, sometimes—throughout the years—when the politics of the revolutionary decade were recollected.

*   *   *

The Vindictive Man was first produced on 20 November 1806 at Drury Lane and had a two-night run. The play weaves together stories of long-held resentments and hidden benevolent actions, of enmity and eventual reconciliation. Although we cannot ascertain if Holcroft knew this would be his final play, the course of events presented there exhibit a reckoning or reconsideration, as he engages with ideas and characters that had featured in his earlier work. The play's plot centers on the head of a banking house (Anson, the eponymous vindictive man) whose intransigence toward his brother is challenged by an enlightened daughter, Emily. His story includes his unlikely friendship with Goldfinch, the quirky horsing character who had memorably featured in *The Road to Ruin*. The second plotline tells of a provincial father and his daughter, Rose, who come to London after Rose inherits the money of her late aunt, who had been the mistress of a wealthy man. Both young women attempt to achieve social and economic justice in unjust situations (Emily speaks out against Anson's refusal to help or to recognize his brother, and Rose insists upon returning an inheritance which was not earned by virtuous means.) Their moral victories conclude the play: the Anson brothers are reconciled, and Rose falls in love with, and is set to marry, the rightful heir to the fortune and thus to share her received wealth through a union which combines emotional and financial equity.

The Vindictive Man, with its economic narratives linked together in an intergenerational domestic structure, and most prominently in the reappearance of Goldfinch, announces a continuity with *The Road to Ruin*, which was still being revived in the patent theaters at the beginning of the nineteenth century. There was a performance of *The Road to Ruin*, to cite just one example, at the Haymarket on 13 June 1805, about five months before the appearance of *The Vindictive Man* (Genest 7:673). Among the similarities between the two plays, we can also count the appearance of a Jewish moneylender / pawnbroker. In contrast to the stereotypically caricaturized Silky in the earlier play, Abrahams in *The Vindictive Man* is not the object of criticism or derision but is portrayed in a more nuanced manner, and his actions are mostly innocuous. As Jeremy Webster notes, Abrahams appears as "humble, helpful and discreet"; he is treated "humanely" by Holcroft, and his comic function emerges from his jargon and accent.[1] It is hard to say, however, whether this character truly represents a volte-face from Holcroft's earlier anti-Semitic articulations. Two years before *The Vindictive Man*, in his *Trav-*

els from Hamburg, through Westphalia, Holland and the Netherlands to Paris, he had given a harsh, stereotypical, description of the Jews he had met during his journey, while at the same time adding, "Far be it from me to depress the depressed."[2]

Nonetheless, the portrayal of Abrahams is conciliatory, and that tone extends to other elements in this play, as they exhibit fleeting reflections upon major events in Holcroft's life. What is possibly an oblique reference to his most critical period appears, suggestively, in an approved character's, Maitland's, stoic sojourn in Newgate Prison. "I must patiently suffer injurious words," he says in his jail cell, incarcerated for a debt resulting from his efforts to help Anson's brother. "Time only can defend me . . . the day will come at last that shall restore my honor."[3] The most prominent reconciliation—that of the Anson brothers—with its felicitous resolution to a long-standing feud may also acknowledge Holcroft's row with William Godwin, now almost two years in continuance, and his hopes for a renewal of their friendship. The final lines of the play, a general call for "love, harmony, and happiness to all" (VM, 82), would in this sense articulate Holcroft's desire for a personal rapprochement with his closest friend, one that would only be achieved on his deathbed. Godwin saw the play on 20 November, the first night of the two-night run, with his wife, Mary Jane, and James Marshall, among others (GD). One wonders if Godwin, in viewing the feuding characters, considered the referentiality to his and Holcroft's situation.

The most obvious retrospective echo in *The Vindictive Man* appears in the revival of Goldfinch, that character who became the talk of the town upon his original appearance in *The Road to Ruin* and whose catchphrase, "that's your sort," had "resounded in all the drawing rooms of London" (*Life*, 1: xvii–xviii). In *The Vindictive Man*, the phrase "that's your sort" is once again repeatedly uttered, but this time it falls flat, lacking the exuberance of the original. Indeed, there is nothing appealing about this later Goldfinch. His attempt to abduct Emily Anson by force precludes any sympathy for the character from the spectator or reader as does his friendship with the conniving Harriet, the friend of Rose's beneficiary, who, it is implied, works in prostitution. It is almost needless to say that this portrayal did not lead to a similar success as with the Goldfinch of *The Road to Ruin*. Ironically, some of the audience did not know that Holcroft was the author of *The Vindictive Man*. As Charles Lamb related the matter to his friend Thomas Manning, the theater spectators, on seeing Goldfinch revived, "were displeased at [the supposed author] stealing from the Road to Ruin."[4]

The anger at what turned out to be Holcroft's "theft" of his own creation underscores his inability to re-create the recognizable energy of the original character. Lamb's insightful description to Manning of this first performance further elaborates on the fact that there were other reasons, too, behind the play's failure: "[B]e sorry for Holcroft, whose new play, called the Vindictive Man was damned about a fortnight since. It died in part of its own weakness, & in part for being choked up with bad actors" (Lamb, 2:244). Focusing mainly on this bad acting, Lamb explains to Manning that the actors who were originally cast, Drury Lane stars John Bannister and Dorothy Jordan, did not in the end appear in the production. Lamb details the weakness of those who did perform, singling out for particular censure Vincent de Camp, who played Goldfinch. His performance, in Lamb's words, exhibited the "idea stript of its manner" and caused the actor to be "hooted & bellow'd off the stage, before the second act was finished, so that the remainder of his part was forced to be with some violence to the play omitted" (Lamb, 2:245).[5] The audience also took offense at the presence of a prostitute on the stage. This rowdy reception at the first night performance had immediate implications. Although the play had earned a fairly respectable £218.17s.2d at the premiere, the box office receipts fell to a meagre 95.18s.6d on the second and final night.[6]

Lamb writes of being "sorry for Holcroft." Holcroft, unrealistically, as it turned out, had entertained some hopes for the play, promising financial aid to Eliza Fenwick if it succeeded.[7] In his introductory material for the published version of *The Vindictive Man*, he instead had to acknowledge its failure. He dedicates the play to his daughter Fanny, who had approved of the work, and she certainly would have commended the affectionate father-daughter relationships that make up a major part of the play. Fanny, Holcroft wrote, "was partial enough to admire the scenes as they were written, and the Play, when it became a whole" (VM, introductory matter). He writes of the "patient resignation" that accompanies every writer, noting also Fanny's own literary vocation in this context.

The general "advertisement" that follows uses the appearance of the published text as an opportunity to reconsider the "oblivion"(VM, introductory matter) to which the play was consigned by the audience at Drury Lane. Holcroft is far less argumentative in detailing its defeat than was the case regarding some of his earlier dramatic works. In a resigned tone and matter-of-fact language, he expresses none of the frustration toward the theater personnel such as he had shown in another of his failed plays, *The Inquisitor* (1798), where he put the blame on the actors "who played vilely the first night" (*Life*, 2:130). (In *The Vindictive Man* the case for bad acting is acknowledged instead by Lamb.) He displays none of the political anger that appeared in the introductions to *Love's Frailties* (1794) and *Knave, or Not?* (1798). True, *The Vindictive Man* lacks the trenchant social criticism and political currency which had featured in those plays as well as his others from the 1790s, and which had motivated their condemnation. It also puts aside the vision of working-class heroism which had appeared in his recent melodramas, *A Tale of Mystery* and *The Lady of the Rock*. The political climate was less charged, or charged in a different way, in 1806, and a response by Holcroft to his critics in that same earlier besieged tone would have been irrelevant if not anachronistic. To be clear, this was *not* a time of political complacency. Jon Mee notes that "especially after the threat of invasion receded from 1805, radicalism revived, and with its revival came a new wave of prosecutions in an attempt to control the pressure for change."[8] Holcroft's activist moment, however, had passed.

* * *

Alongside the calamitous afterlife of Goldfinch and the general failure of *The Vindictive Man*, there also appeared during these same years the recognition and revival of one of Holcroft's major successes in terms of the wide resonance and later popularity of his work, a text with a strong and dynamic, widespread, later reception. This was the poem "Gaffer Gray," which had originally appeared as an inset text in Holcroft's *The Adventures of Hugh Trevor*, a novel which itself was widely noticed upon its publication and then in later years. *Hugh Trevor* follows the story of the eponymous hero who overcomes childhood poverty and later the tensions and intrigues of London society as he attempts to choose a vocation and find his place in the world. Holcroft, not surprisingly, sees this quest for self and place as profoundly political, and the novel presents a detailed, all-encompassing survey of the wrongs of society as exhibited in those established and interlinked enterprises of power—land, law, religion, education, government. This portrayal, by virtue of the capaciousness of the novel genre and the lack of the institutionalized censorship that hovered over the drama, is broader and more detailed than those criticisms Holcroft included in his plays. If in *Love's Frailties*, to cite one example, a character exhorts on the "uselessness of gentlemen,"[9] then *Hugh Trevor* devotes much narrative space to delineating in detail that very uselessness, and the inefficaciousness of that status, through the fictional Earl of Idford—silly, parasitical, and worthless.

Hugh Trevor's publishing history provides insights into the political resolutions that Holcroft offers in the novel while also ultimately shuffling our expectations. The first three volumes appeared in 1794 and the latter three in 1797; the book's publication is thus punctuated by Holcroft's experience in the Treason Trials and by the general clampdown and suppression of speech of the Two Acts that followed in 1795. Surely the latter three volumes of Holcroft's novel were written under a less optimistic horizon, both general and personal, than in 1793, when he was writing the earlier volumes. (Godwin notes reading the manuscript of the first part of *Hugh Trevor* on 13 June 1793 [GD].) Holcroft regularly participated in the meetings of the Society for Constitutional Information throughout 1793, arguing there for the value and availability of truth. The year 1797, conversely, would have been colored by his experience in the Treason Trials as well as in their aftermath, when the epithet "acquitted felon" was repeatedly flung at him. The hostility was such that in offering his dramatic work to the public, he concealed his authorship or submitted it through a third party. It is puzzling therefore to note the contrived conclusion to *Hugh Trevor* in which, by sheer coincidence, Hugh encounters and rescues his long-lost uncle and, following the reunion, this man of means makes Hugh his wealthy heir. The novel ends with a sense of specious optimism—nothing in society has changed—and the implication that the struggle for survival can be resolved and the means to finding one's place in the world can be achieved through chance, good luck, and kindness to strangers. (Hugh had assisted his uncle, not knowing his identity, after the latter had been wounded.) Hugh describes himself at the conclusion as a "man of great wealth,"[10] making sure to note that he still contributes to the social good. As noted in Chapter Four, Holcroft wrote in his diary in January 1799 of encountering a review of the French translation of *Hugh Trevor*, in which the reviewer praised the novel but criticized the improbability of the ending, to which Holcroft had admitted, "true, blamable" (*Life* 2:238). The magical bequeathing of unexpected wealth upon the long-suffering protagonist seems to contradict everything that came before and is especially notable when we consider that this conclusion was written following Holcroft's life-altering experience in the Treason Trials. His life and the lives of his fellow defendants had been spared, but the horizon was bleak. He would have known that there was to be no real-life felicitous coincidence awaiting him.

Holcroft's retrospective recognition—"true, blamable"—underscores this incongruity, which emerged most probably from his acquiescence to the rudiments of the "novel style." Until this conclusion, however, the novel devotes great energy to portraying the seemingly futile social and vocational aspirations of its protagonist and the lack of any kind of privileged benevolence that is receptive to the struggle. Before I turn to "Gaffer Gray," a poem which illustrates this lack, I wish to remain for another moment with *Hugh Trevor* as a whole and to briefly note that it left a strong impression on various readers, among them Stendhal, whose novel *The Red and the Black* was published in 1830. Brian Rigby argues for Holcroft's influence upon Stendhal and compares *Hugh Trevor* and *The Red and the Black*'s similar depictions of "poor autodidacts who make good" alongside the portrayal of educational and clerical corruption accompanied by the "conscious politicization of the picaresque."[11] *The Red and the Black* illustrates more incisively than *Hugh Trevor* the psychological cost of the struggle against social intransigence as depicted in Stendhal's protagonist Julien Sorel. Stendhal also integrates more seamlessly into his narrative Godwin's and Holcroft's belief that "characters of men originate in their original circumstances"; that "man is happy . . . [or ignorant as a] result of the circumstances under which he exists."[12] He brilliantly applies this understanding—the inescapability of Julien's original circumstances in dictating how he lives his life and later as it leads to his eventual destruction. Rather than *Hugh Trevor*, it was *Memoirs of Bryan Perdue* which anticipated that psychological complexity, through Holcroft's more nuanced portrayal of his eponymous protagonist's ethical struggle and the relation between his early circumstances and his later actions and feelings.

The poem "Gaffer Gray" appears in the earlier part of *Hugh Trevor*, in Volume III, chapter 8, and, along with the narrative sequence in which it appears, shows the rigidity of social and political hierarchies and the outsider solidarity that forms a generous resistance to them. The poem is introduced as a received manuscript, ostensibly written by Hugh's friend and former school tutor, Wilmot, now a struggling dramatist in London who had gone missing and, unbeknownst to Hugh at this moment, had attempted suicide. Leafing through Wilmot's papers at the house of the man's sister, he discovers "Gaffer Gray." The poem is an anapestic ballad, whose six stanzas tell the story of a poor old man in search of warmth and a glass of ale. Because of its centrality to my discussion, I include the poem in its entirety:

I
Ho! Why dost thou shiver and shake,
  Gaffer Gray!
And why doth thy nose look so blue?
  "Tis the weather that's cold;
  Tis I'm grown very old,
And my doublet is not very new,
  Well-a-day!"

II
Then line thy worn doublet with ale,
  Gaffer Gray;
And warm thy old heart with a glass.
  "Nay but credit I've none;
  And my money's all gone;
Then say how may that come to pass?
  Well-a-day!"

III
Hie away to the house on the brow,
  Gaffer Gray;
And knock at the jolly priest's door.
  "The priest often preaches
  Against worldly riches;
But never gives a mite to the poor,
  Well-a-day!"

IV
The lawyer lives under the hill,
  Gaffer Gray;
Warmly fenc'd both in back and in front.
  "He will fasten his locks,
  And will threaten the stocks,
Should he ever more find me in want,
  Well-a-day!"

V
The squire has fat beeves and brown ale,
 Gaffer Gray;
And the season will welcome you there.
 "His fat beeves and his beer,
 And his merry new year
Are all for the flush and the fair,
 Well-a-day!"

VI
My keg is but low I confess,
 Gaffer Gray;
What then? While it lasts man we'll live.
 The poor man alone,
 When he hears the poor moan,
Of his morsel a morsel will give,
  Well-a-day! (HT, 225–6)

The social criticism in the poem, directed towards the interconnected power of Church, law, and land, echoes Hugh's experiences with institutional authority, although the full confrontation with the bishop, lawyer, and squire of his own acquaintance are yet to come. The generosity shown by the narrator of the poem towards Gaffer Gray is re-created in the sense of fellowship among Hugh, Wilmot, and their friend Turl, who is modeled on Holcroft's close friend, the engraver William Sharp (*Life*, 2:64n), and the "shabby genteel" sociability that unites them throughout the narrative.[13]

 Anne Chandler, in wondering why Holcroft chose to have the poem written by Wilmot and not by the protagonist, suggests that perhaps Holcroft wanted to satirize "Hugh's awe towards cultural authority . . . through his misguided enthusiasm for Wilmot's poem."[14] Yet whatever the degree of Hugh's response to cultural authority at this point, whether he locates that authority in his former tutor, and if his response is in fact satirized, the claim for a misguided enthusiasm towards the poem is not borne out by the reception of "Gaffer Gray" in the world outside the book. The poem is, with *The Road to Ruin*, almost certainly Holcroft's most reprinted and disseminated work; real-life readers, along with Hugh, loved it from its initial appearance. William Hazlitt's response is indicative: "Gaffer Gray" "is distinguished by . . . [a] fulness of feeling, and the same simple, forcible, and perfect expression of it. There is nothing wanting, and nothing superfluous. The author has produced exactly the impression he intended" (*Life*, 2:23). The poem was already included in July 1794 in the poetry section of *The Gentleman's Magazine*, along with another inset poem from *Hugh Trevor*, "The Perjured Lover." It also appeared in the *Town and Country Magazine* that same month and in the *Annual Register* and the *Scots Magazine* later that year.[15] The inclusion of "Gaffer

Gray" in July 1794 in prominent publications thus brought approved attention to Holcroft and his writing at the time when the warrant for his arrest in the Treason Trials was yet unserved; this was that "summer of the memorable 1794," when, he stressed, "the timid shunned me, the moderate regarded me with an evil eye, and the violent never mentioned me but with virulence and odium" (NF, 17, 62). Such was the popularity of "Gaffer Gray" that it served as a bulwark for Holcroft during this tense time. Together with the ongoing fame of *The Road to Ruin*, it created a kind of parallel status for him concurrent to that of a political radical, in which he was acknowledged as an accepted man of letters. This "approved" literary status, as we have seen throughout this book, was often tenuous, overshadowed by and vulnerable to political developments, but was still maintained throughout the turbulent 1790s and amidst the onslaught of hostility that engulfed him.

Reprinted, then, very soon after its initial appearance, "Gaffer Gray" appears never to have been out of print in the decades that followed. Mary Russell Mitford, in a chapter in her *Recollections of a Literary Life* (1852) that lauded Holcroft's accomplishments as an autodidact and in particular his achievement with *The Road to Ruin*, likewise praises "Gaffer Gray," albeit somewhat ambivalently in relation to its perceived political message. The poem, she writes, has "the great fault of setting class against class, a fault which generally involves a want of truth; but it does its work admirably, and produces exactly the effect intended in the fewest possible words."[16] Chandler notes that the "catchy 'Well-a-day' refrain indicates that Holcroft intended it to be set to music,"[17] and indeed it almost immediately was. In that context of reception, the poem's "great [political] fault," as Mitford had had it, seems either to have been unnoticed or ignored. We find multiple editions of the ballad accompanied by musical scores appearing already in 1794 and 1795, soon after the first volumes of *Hugh Trevor* were published, perhaps at the same time as the reprint in the *Gentleman's Magazine*.[18] It was soon anthologized, and included in collections such as *Five Excellent New Songs*, published in 1795, and *The Yorkshire Musical Miscellany* (1800). In the preface to the *Miscellany* the editor writes that this selection includes "among the most admired and approved songs, and pathetic airs, taken from the latest works, with accuracy, belonging to the best esteemed Men."[19] That same year another musical adaptation was published in London under the title, "Ho, why dost thou shiver. Gaffer Gray. A favorite ballad sung at all the principal concerts."[20] In his essay "On Song Writing" (1822), John Thelwall recognized the poem's suitability for music but was unaware of these adaptations. He wrote that "Gaffer Gray" is a song of "unrivalled beauty; and if it hath never been set to music (which we believe it hath not) we are sure it is well worthy of being so: still more worthy of being read and conned by every heir of ease and affluence: by every friend of humanity."[21] Different adaptations also appeared in the United States throughout the nineteenth century, one in 1856 with the following title: "'An Old English Ballad by Holcroft', Arranged for the Piano Forte and respectfully dedicated to the Masonic Fraternity of New Haven Connecticut by Frank C. Smith."[22] This indicative American publication is in addition to the British musical scores and anthologies that made their way across the Atlantic.[23]

As well as being set to music, "Gaffer Gray" was also rebranded as a text for children and then included in general educational compilations and readers. It was first published as a children's text by William and Mary Jane Godwin for the Juvenile Library in 1806 as *Gaffer Gray: or, the Misfortunes of Poverty, A Christmas Ditty very fit to be chanted at Whitsuntide*. The epigraph from James Thomson's *The Seasons* (added by the Godwins) locates the poem within a wide tradition of sympathetic identification with the poor, while the reference to Christmas reinforces the poem's theme of charity.[24] The publication is accompanied by beautiful copperplate illustrations by the artist William Mulready (see figure 6.1). Mulready had worked with Godwin during this period on *Fables Ancient and Modern* that Godwin published in 1805 under the pseudonym "Edward Baldwin, Esq." and which included seventy-three of his copperplate illustrations.[25] Godwin, under the pseudonym Theophilius Marcliffe, also wrote a biographical account of Mulready's early life.[26]

The Juvenile Library's *Gaffer Gray* appeared in two subsequent reprints, in 1816 and 1823. Holcroft's name appears in none of these editions. The poem's political inflection and its critique of power structures through a representative lawyer, churchman, and landowner (what Mitford had reductively called "setting class against class") could serve as evidence for the politicization of children's literature in the aftermath of the French Revolution and the emergence of a rights discourse in that context. Fearing that outcome, self-appointed watchdogs such as the educator and children's writer Sarah Trimmer scoured publications looking for radical or subversive content.[27] In a time of such dense contemporary awareness and commentary, a political referentiality could indeed seem to be inescapable. For William Godwin the willingness to extend the French Revolution debate to include younger readers was in fact desired. Pamela Clemit argues that "Godwin turned to children's books as a continuation of his radical program of the 1790s . . . yet the Juvenile Library was not solely a money-making venture. Godwin inherited from the Rational Dissenters a lasting faith in the printed book as an agent of reform . . . [and so] he later turned to children's books to enfranchise a new generation of middle-class readers and their parents."[28] Robert Anderson recognizes a political awareness that informs the publications of the Juvenile Library, even as its texts do not refer specifically to current events: these works address "liberty, tyranny, autonomy, nationality, obedience, communality, hierarchy, equality, the distribution of property."[29] Although he does not mention "Gaffer Gray" specifically, Anderson's list aptly describes Holcroft's range of concerns and Godwin's awareness of it as such when publishing the poem.

Figure 6.1 William Mulready, *Gaffer Gray* (Salutation), courtesy of the
Carl H. Pforzheimer Collection of Shelley and His Circle, The New York Public
Library, Astor, Lenox, and Tilden Foundations

From a stand-alone publication published by the Juvenile Library, "Gaffer Gray" moved to other pedagogical platforms. The poem appeared in W. F. Mylius's *Poetical Class Book*, published in 1819 also by the Juvenile Library and then reprinted in multiple editions through 1825. Designed for older learners, the *Class Book* is a thoughtful and wide-ranging compilation of canonical and contemporary poems; Mylius, as a good educator, does not underestimate the abilities of his students. He includes staples such as Shakespeare, Milton, the eighteenth-century favorites Pope, Thomson, and the Wartons, as well as the near-recent or contemporary Cowper, Wordsworth, Coleridge, Byron, Walter Scott, Charlotte Smith, Mary Robinson, Anna Barbauld, Robert Burns, and even Matthew ("Monk") Lewis, in addition to Holcroft and many others. These selections would have introduced young people to the "necessary part of a just education"[30]—the act of reading and reciting poetry. Mylius's inclusion of "Gaffer Gray," along with poems such as Cowper's "The Negro's Complaint" (1788), Burns's "Lament of Mary, Queen of Scots" (1791), and Mary Robinson's "The Fugitive" (1800) would also have familiarized pupils with the rhetoric, the vocabulary, as well as, of course, the thematics of social justice and political awareness.

"Gaffer Gray" appeared in another school anthology, the *Literary Reader, for Academies and High Schools, consisting of selections in prose and verse*, compiled by the American educator Arethusa Hall and published in 1850. This collection featured British, American, and Continental writers including Shakespeare and Milton, Coleridge and Wordsworth, Charles Lamb, Carlyle, and Dickens, as well as American writers such as Franklin, Hamilton, Emerson, Longfellow, and, interestingly, the radical Joel Barlow, whose pamphlet had been discussed many years earlier at one of the meetings of the Society for Constitutional Information in which Holcroft had been in attendance. The Continental selection included, among others, Goethe, Schiller, and Madame de Staël. In her preface, Hall states her aim of presenting texts that collectively introduce a cultural and intellectual history, rather than a political survey of "the intrigues of rulers [and] wars."[31] Each selection is accompanied by a brief biographical sketch of the author; that of Holcroft presents the familiar narrative of his rise as a self-made man of letters. The same year as Hall's book was published, "Gaffer Gray" was also included in Robert Chambers's *Cyclopedia of English Literature*, where Chambers writes, "The song . . . has a forcible simplicity and truth in particular cases, which made it a favourite with the public."[32]

Chambers's acknowledgement of public favor assumes a wide readership of the poem, emerging, perhaps, from a familiarity with the *Adventures of Hugh Trevor*, with some of the musical arrangements, or with the Juvenile Library edition and Mylius's subsequent reprinting. Of these editions, it is only the Godwins' publications (1806, 1816, 1823) that omit Holcroft's name. While it is difficult to state with certainty the reason for this omission, it is important to note that the volume was first published on 26 May 1806,[33] by which time Godwin and Holcroft were no longer speaking; an intense, deeply felt friendship had unraveled. We cannot know, moreover, if Holcroft had seen the new edition of his poem produced by the Juvenile Library. If he had, what were his feelings? Would the sumptuously illustrated stand-alone volume have touched a chord in this strong, resilient, stubborn, austere, and sometimes impulsive man? In the following section I will discuss the Holcroft-Godwin row and with it, Holcroft's final years, as well as the friends' rapprochement, occurring at Holcroft's bedside in the final days of his life.

* * *

"I wish I could laugh oftener," wrote Holcroft in his *Travels from Hamburg, through Westphalia, Holland, and the Netherlands to Paris.*[34] Published in 1804, the *Travels* documents the journey of Holcroft and his family as they made their way from Germany, through the Netherlands, and on to their destination in Paris, a journey and residence that began in 1801 and concluded with the Holcrofts' return to Britain in September 1802. Throughout his narrative Holcroft offers glimpses and impressions of landscapes, cities, and people, commentary on historical and current events, as well as social, political, and cultural reflections. This comment appears toward the beginning of the text and references Holcroft's difficult period of exile in Germany and the aftereffects of his sojourn, when money was a constant concern and various literary and artistic endeavors disappointed him, such as his misguided attempt at picture dealing and his failure in publishing a literary journal. This sense of disappointment and defeat leaves its mark in this brief comment—"I wish I could laugh oftener"—even as he writes his travelogue with an ever-curious eye and with the attention to whimsical detail that feature also in his diary and letters.

Upon his return to Britain Holcroft would have been encouraged by the success of his plays *Deaf and Dumb* (1801), *A Tale of Mystery* (1802), and to a lesser extent, *Hear Both Sides* (1803). His *Travels*, published in 1804, was also generally well received.[35] He settled back into the routine of life in London, now with a growing family; besides his adult daughters from previous marriages, Sophy Cole, Ann Harwood, and Fanny, he would eventually have six children with his wife, Louisa.[36] His friendship with Godwin continued, while the new wives of both men certainly added a different dimension to their relationship. Upon hearing of Godwin's second marriage while still in France, Holcroft had sent his good wishes, writing on 1 January 1802: "I would say something that should convey my feelings: but what are common place expressions, of wishing you joy, hoping you may be happy. . . . I know you deserve the love and friendship of the whole earth."[37] In his letters written throughout the remainder of his stay, he repeatedly expressed his desire for friendship with the new Mrs. Godwin. Fanny too wrote an addendum to one of her father's letters to Godwin to convey her congratulations and to express her own desire to befriend Mary Jane Godwin: "And do you think, my dear Mr Godwin, tho' I have not yet written to congratulate you on your marriage, that I do not as well as your faithful friend Louisa, most sincerely and warmly participate in your happiness? No: you do us justice: you judge our hearts to your own and I hope you make interest in Mrs Godwin's for two candidates to her friendship will endeavour to deserve it."[38] Fanny wrote her congratulations on 1 March 1802; she had not written in the January letter probably because she was experiencing at that time a particularly distressing turn of events in her personal life, the marriage engagement that had been cancelled and then the disastrous employment with the Mountcashell family.[39]

Fanny, along with her father and Louisa, frequently saw the Godwins upon their return to Britain. In this first year after the Holcrofts' return, it is clear from evidence in Godwin's diary that these meetings proceeded on a regular basis, with reciprocal visits which included different members of the two families on various occasions. Not only close proximity but also, most probably, the tranquil progression of these sociable associations during this period rendered letter writing unnecessary. After about a year, however, things changed. Three clusters of correspondence emerge to indicate instances of argument and misunderstanding, with the written word serving as a means of exploring and elucidating the matters at hand, further aiming to resolve the tension or, in the final case, to terminate the friendship.

The first argument occurred in September 1803 and revolved around the fact that Holcroft clearly did not like Mary Jane Godwin and had apparently, as Godwin wrote, "something like insulted [her;] the partner of his life."[40] Pamela Clemit explains that the row may have already begun in mid-August, at a dinner engagement at Holcroft's home, with either both Godwins present or only Mary Jane.[41] Godwin's accusation that Holcroft "persist[s]" in acting in a certain, unacceptable manner towards his wife (Clemit, 2:281, 2:281n) suggests an ongoing behavior on the part of his friend, the knowledge of which he—Godwin—had contained, possibly for some time, within himself. After a heated correspondence over a number of days, the friends were supposedly reconciled. "I can now return to my habitual feelings towards you, which are those of kindness & sympathy in the extreme," Godwin wrote on 11 September (Clemit, 2:285). Yet despite these warm words, the promise of reconciliation remained only on paper. Two months later, on 16 November, Godwin was still struggling to comprehend the situation, once again reflecting on Holcroft's stubbornness regarding Mary Jane. Perhaps forced by this accusation into action, Holcroft wrote to her on 24 November denying any resentment on his part. Godwin, tired of arguing, finally relented, writing on that same day, "Let us be at peace" (Clemit, 2:296). The fact that that day—24 November—Mary Jane Godwin called on Louisa Holcroft may suggest either a face-to-face visit to cement the rapprochement or, as the editors of the Godwin Diary speculate, a business visit regarding a translation venture in which Mary

Jane and Louisa were involved, possibly connected to William Lane's Minerva Press.[42] The personal friendship was enmeshed, as throughout the years of their acquaintance, in a web of interconnected social ties and literary and business interests.

The next flare-up between Godwin and Holcroft was in fact connected to literary endeavor. Nearly a year had gone by following the first altercation before there was need to write again, at least insofar as the extant letters indicate. The next letter appears from Holcroft to Godwin on 23 September 1804. In it, Holcroft provided his critique of Godwin's work-in-progress, the play *Faulkener,* eventually staged in 1807 and published the following year. Godwin and Holcroft repeatedly read and criticized each other's work, proceeding according to the dictates of stern sincerity and truth accompanied by what was often a bracing candor. In Chapter Four we saw Holcroft on the receiving end of this process, responding to Godwin's commentary on his play "The Lawyer (*Hear Both Sides*)." Holcroft had recorded in his diary his pain and surprise at the severity of Godwin's remarks, which had kept him up half the night (*Life*: 2:232–3). This time it was Godwin who was taken aback. Acknowledging at first with gratitude the special care that Holcroft had taken with the manuscript, the engagement with the criticism and revision of the play dissolved through late September and October into tension and hurt feelings. Holcroft had specified that Godwin "adopt the piece" as he had sent it, or reject it entirely (Clemit, 2:317), a request that strained Godwin, anxious and vulnerable in writing for the theater and aware, as Julie Carlson has observed, that drama was "the compositional arena in which Holcroft [had] a clear upper hand."[43] In the end, Godwin revised his own material, nonetheless admitting to Holcroft on 4 December 1804 that he had included "a very few words from your copy," despite Holcroft's "prohibition" (Clemit, 2:328). The argument was over for now.

The title of Carlson's essay, "On Literary Fractures," foregrounds the prominent role of writing itself in the demise of the friends' relationship. This element is certainly evident in the *Faulkener* episode and even more pertinently in what became the final blow to the friendship, Holcroft's perception of the minor character, Scarborough, in Godwin's novel *Fleetwood* (1805) as a representation of himself.[44] Yet whereas in earlier instances the "literary fractures" of Godwin and Holcroft were healed through conversation or simply yielding, the break following *Fleetwood* was decisive. The portrayal in that novel of Scarborough as a stern father and strict disciplinarian and his son's early death as an outcome of that parental behavior most certainly touched a raw nerve. Just before William Holcroft committed suicide in November 1789, Godwin had traveled with the boy's worried father to Deal in an attempt to find him. Now, in 1805, Godwin denied in a letter to James Marshall that William Holcroft had been his model, but Thomas Holcroft saw it otherwise.[45] In Carlson's words, "the passage hits so close to home that . . . [Holcroft's] survival necessitate[d] severing contact with his best friend."[46] Finding him intractable, Godwin, in one final letter to Holcroft written on 2 March, laments the loss of their twenty-year friendship: "I will never think of you, but as of a dear friend, who died on the 28th of February last . . . I will always think & speak of you with the tenderness due to a deceased friend who, after twenty years of an attachment difficult to be paralleled, has expired" (Clemit, 2: 340).

Such must have been the anger at the implied representation in *Fleetwood*— in addition to the accumulated frustration over various altercations with the God- win household—that at this crucial moment Holcroft forgot, or laid aside, the major precept according to which he had tried to live his life, the separation of persons and their errors, a splitting which enabled the gradual movement towards perfectibility: "the mistake is past recal, but the man may amend," In this book I have repeatedly quoted the phrase to show Holcroft's application of Godwinian philosophy in his imaginative texts and in his life experience, specifically in the conclusions to many of his plays, where punishment is never an option, and in looking back at his Treason Trials ordeal. Persuasive and heartfelt as it was in other contexts, in 1805, in his own life and in relation to Godwin, the principle was unable to support him.

Although no longer in voluntary contact, Godwin's diary indicates that the two men, having many mutual friends, encountered each other from time to time in the following years—at the homes of the Irish activist Archibald Rowan (23 October 1805) and the Lambs (18 April 1806), as well as meeting at an unspec- ified location on 14 October 1805 (GD). Godwin also went to see *The Vindictive Man* on 20 November 1806. In an account written a few years before the breakup with Godwin, we receive a view of Holcroft as a man at this time still energetic and forceful. William Austin, a young American pursuing legal studies at Lin- coln's Inn, describes him: "Mr. Holcroft, though nearly sixty, has suffered noth- ing, either from years, laborious mental exertion, or persecution. He has all the activity and vivacity of youth."[47]

Holcroft still maintained at this time a social circle with a small group of literary and artistic friends. Additional glimpses of him in later years are provided by some of these friends, including in the letters of Charles and Mary Lamb. The Lambs write of many social visits throughout the years, among them the first visit of Holcroft, Louisa, and Fanny to their house on 19 February 1805 (Lamb: 2:208) and an invitation to tea at the Holcrofts' home on 10 May 1806 (Lamb: 2:226). In the same letter to Thomas Manning in which he describes the failure of *The Vin- dictive Man*, Lamb conveys a knowledge of Holcroft's residence, writing with familiarity of the interior decorations—"his lo[ng] neck'd Guido that hangs oppo- site as you enter"—and describes the painter George Dawe, as he "sits & stands about at Holcroft's & says nothing" (Lamb: 2:245, 2: 247). Manning, Lamb's main correspondent, as well as George Tuthill (later Sir George), were mutual friends of

Holcroft and Lamb. Both had been residing in Paris while Holcroft was living there, and both had visited him at his home, Manning having met Holcroft through Tuthill. Tuthill had supported him in his desire to counteract the assault against him in the *Times* of 26 January 1802, and the accusation that he was a spy.[48] Both Tuthill and Manning were briefly detained by the French government, along with many other young British men residing in France in the period following the collapse of the Amiens peace treaty, by which time Holcroft was back in England.

Brief accounts of Holcroft's life in these final years appear also in other sources. We saw in Chapter Four, in a review of Holcroft's *Memoirs* in the *Critical Review*, how the reviewer (perhaps Lamb himself) had remarked on passing an evening with Holcroft in which Holcroft had told stories of his impoverished childhood.[49] It is appealing to imagine the old radical, surrounded by family and friends, interested listeners, as he recounted those childhood memories accompanied most certainly by a sense of achievement in his rise from humble beginnings and satisfaction in a life meaningfully lived. Further information about these final years appears in the letters of Eliza Fenwick, who was in fairly regular contact with Holcroft at this time. Holcroft had been close to John Fenwick, her estranged husband, who was struggling with alcoholism, debt, and poverty. He had been on the run since 1799 and in 1806 was imprisoned in the Rules of the Fleet. In that year Holcroft was giving acting lessons to the Fenwicks' daughter, also named Eliza, and had promised to give the family financial support if *The Vindictive Man* were successful. In a letter written to Mary Hays on 25 October 1806, Mrs. Fenwick noted that she rarely went out; "when she did, it was to Mr. Holcroft's & then I did not go to tea but went at 8 o' Clock."[50] That visit took place, and the letter written, a month before the unsuccessful run of *The Vindictive Man*. Holcroft had been sanguine about the success of his play, and Eliza Fenwick had been hopeful for the promised aid, but they were disappointed once more. Like other instances previously mentioned in this book, the Fenwicks' story illustrates how life was a continual struggle for the 1790s radicals, through the ongoing resonances of the cultural backlash, of Pitt's oppression, and then its aftermath.[51] Some years later, looking back on her social connection with Holcroft, Eliza Fenwick remembered another aspect of the Holcroft family's life. In December 1811, again writing to Hays, and mentioning her children's attitude toward religion, she remarks that she "used to be so disgusted & shocked at the blind, coarse, ignorant infidelity of Holcroft's children that I should almost have preferred making sectaries of mine."[52] In the same vein Joseph Cottle writes of Samuel Taylor Coleridge's horror when he recalled encountering Holcroft's eight-year-old son who "came up to him and said, 'There is no God!'"[53] In all events, Eliza Fenwick would go on, in 1807, to manage the Godwins' Juvenile Library, working under challenging conditions.[54] She would have known that Godwin and Holcroft were not on speaking terms at that time.

Holcroft and Godwin would be reunited only in March 1809, during Holcroft's final illness. As Hazlitt relates it, Holcroft had been increasingly troubled with respiratory problems in the last year of his life and had difficulty walking. He was "confined to his house . . . about half a year before his death" and to his bed in his final two months. It was during these two months that he dictated his *Memoirs* (*Life*, 2: 308). Apparently he retained his optimism till almost the very end and believed in his eventual recovery (*Life*, 2:309). When finally accepting that death was near, he sent word to Godwin to come to his bedside. The meeting, on 19 March, was sentimentalized by Hazlitt in the *Memoirs:* "On Sunday, he expressed a wish to see Mr. Godwin, but when he came, his feelings were overpowered. He could not converse, and only pressed his hand to his bosom, and said, 'My dear, dear friend'" (*Life*, 2:310). Godwin returned in the following days, meeting other friends who participated in the deathbed vigil, including the painter George Dawe, George Tuthill, Thelwall, Henry Crabb Robinson, the Lambs, Mrs. Nicholson (wife of William), and Hazlitt (GD, 20 March, 21 March, 23 March).[55] Holcroft died on Thursday, 23 March 1809.

Hazlitt observes that Holcroft was "in complete possession of himself" as he approached death (*Life*, 2: 309). The emphasis on the sharpness of Holcroft's faculties, along with the fact that he was confined to his bed in the final two months of his life, suggests that along with, and surely because of, the dictation of his auto-biography, there was ample time for thinking. We can imagine some of his musings as he looked back on his life, remembering fame, disappointment, fear, triumph, regret, and surely a present anxiety for what awaited his wife and six young children, penniless as they were, and Fanny, too, vulnerable in her perceived singularity. Emerging from this period of incessant reflection and reckoning is a surprising notation appearing in the parish records of St. Marylebone's Church, London, which reveals that the six young Holcroft children were baptized on 1 March 1809, a little over three weeks before their father died.[56] Did Holcroft have reason to reconsider, and to embrace a renewed belief in God and of a divine judgment? Did he ultimately decide to "repair" what Eliza Fenwick had called the "blind, coarse, ignorant infidelity" which had been clearly apparent to her in his children's behavior? Did Louisa Holcroft, herself professing atheism,[57] express an opinion on the subject of her children's religious identity? I have found no record to indicate Holcroft's deliberations on the question of baptism, but, weak and unable to write, barely able to speak, it is almost impossible that he would have announced the subject, or written about it, in any case. It seems more likely that Holcroft and his wife were instead motivated by pragmatism, drawn from their knowledge of the world and anxiety over their children's future and their ability to receive an education, job opportunities, and parish relief in the future.

Holcroft's death was recorded in the "Church of England baptisms, marriages and burials" register for St. Marylebone, London, 1786–1812.[58] The funeral took place on 1 April 1809 and would have adhered to Church of England practices.[59] In attendance were Godwin, Holcroft's dear friend the composer William Shield, his son-in-law Colonel Harwood, his physician Dr. A. Buchan, who attended him at his death, and other friends—Nicholson, Lamb, Thelwall, Dawe, and Ralph (GD). "Ralph" is unidentified by the editors of the Godwin Diary. The reference is most likely to the "Mr. Ralph" mentioned in *Life*, 2:292 and identified there as Holcroft's amanuensis. Thomas Laqueur has examined the way funerals in this period "became the occasion for a final accounting, a stocktaking of worldly success," a "rite of passage" that spoke of the "history of the deceased."[60] Laqueur focuses on the presence of material trappings and status-generated resources to examine changing funeral practices in the eighteenth and nineteenth centuries, but his insight is also applicable in Holcroft's case for illustrating a different kind of stocktaking, or summative history, with his funeral appearing as a snapshot of 1790s political activism in its aftermath. This funeral entourage exhibits Holcroft's place within a notable intellectual circle, which, if not a cohesive or intact group, still came together for the occasion. In doing so they mourned the loss of their friend but also raised through their collective attendance the memory of their cultural endeavors and political engagement and of a once-vigorous public presence.

Holcroft's life and achievements were noted in the days and weeks after his decease. We saw in Chapter Two the obituary in the *Morning Post* that linked together his radical past and his career as a dramatist, singling out *The Road to Ruin* as his notable literary achievement.[61] Godwin's obituary essay in the *Monthly Magazine* for May 1809 likewise foregrounds Holcroft's politics along with the recognition of his most famous play.[62] Adding a bit of trivia, he notes that, within the play, Holcroft had originally intended to make his politically aware tradesman a shoemaker. "At the request of the writer of this article," Godwin reveals, "he is now a hosier," a reminiscence that exhibits a lighter side to his and Holcroft's mutual literary critiquing.[63] On a more serious note, he mentions the events of 1794, calling Holcroft's involvement in the Treason Trials the "great action of [his] life," adding that "if Pitt's administration had succeeded" in its efforts and the twelve defendants had been executed, "the constitution and liberties of England would have been destroyed."[64] Godwin calls to mind once more the work of the reformers, and also, subtly, his own intervention. His "Cursory Strictures on the Charge Delivered by Lord Chief Justice Eyre to the Grand Jury," first appearing in the *Morning Chronicle* on 21 October 1794 and later published separately, is often credited with destroying the government's case;[65] he implies here that it helped to save the nation fifteen years earlier. The obituary concludes with an appeal for financial aid that would enable Louisa and Fanny Holcroft to open a school.[66] This mention of monetary relief underscores once more the aftereffects of oppositional political action and the financial vulnerability that was its outcome during the revolutionary decade and beyond. Three of Holcroft's friends mentioned in this chapter—Eliza Fenwick, Archibald Rowan, and John Thelwall—in addition to Godwin and Holcroft are included by Kenneth R. Johnston in his book *Unusual Suspects*, in the list of the victims of Pitt's backlash, which included financial depletion as a likely outcome. The number of victims, Johnston adds, could easily be doubled; among Holcroft's friends it could include Charles Lamb, whom Johnston acknowledges elsewhere in his book, and William Nicholson, whom he does not.[67]

It is not surprising, then, that the public was called upon to help finance Louisa and Fanny's proposed school. Yet even before the publication of Godwin's obituary, Holcroft's friends sought to provide immediate aid for his family, establishing an ad hoc committee for that purpose. Godwin's diary shows that he met some of these friends in the days before the funeral—Lamb, Nicholson, George Tuthill, and the son-in-law Colonel Harwood (GD, 24, 26 March). On 5 April these men gathered at the Crown and Anchor, now joined by Thelwall, George Dawe, Henry Crabb Robinson, John Stoddart, Thomas Hardy, the journalist John Collier, and the radical Paul Thomas Le Maitre (GD). Robinson wrote in his *Reminiscences* that he had "exerted [himself] zealously" there, contributing £20, which was beyond his means at the time, and that about £450 was raised altogether. Regarding the participants he adds that "a large proportion of [them] were more likely to become objects of beneficence than to contribute to relieve the wants of others," a poignant illustration of the philanthropic practices of the Godwin circle, mostly impoverished themselves but giving generously to others, also on this occasion.[68] Perhaps the idea for Godwin's call for donations in the *Monthly Magazine* was planned here, or the appeal for relief to the Royal Literary Fund; most probably they came up there with the idea to write his biography with the goal of collecting additional money from its publication.[69] In May Robinson wrote to his brother Thomas that they had expected more from the subscription—to reach £1000—due to "Holcroft's distinction."[70]

The Royal Literary Fund (RLF) was applied to a little over a month later, on 20 May, shortly after the publication of Godwin's obituary. The RLF had been set up in 1790 by the minister, deist, and political activist David Williams to assist financially distressed writers or their families. Its founding was predicated, as Jon Mee explains, "on a sense of the influence of men of letters on political affairs."[71] The application to the RLF on behalf of the Holcroft family was eventually submitted not by one of the group who had met at the Crown and Anchor, but rather by the playwright Thomas Dibdin with whom Holcroft had had a fine working relationship; Holcroft's remark ten years earlier as to how he and Dibdin should not think of their political differences but rather how each "could . . . best serve the other" received its ultimate expression in this final service.[72] Dibdin's letter, addressed to David Williams, includes a typed page which briefly states Holcroft's rise from obscurity, his six young children "wholly unprovided for," and the idea of opening the school.[73] It is accompanied by a handwritten text in which Dibdin, referring to the fact that the relief is requested for surviving dependents of a deceased author and not for the author himself, acknowledges that the children of Robert Burns ("the late Scottish bard") had received aid from the RLF as well as there being "other precedents of a similar nature." In the end, the committee granted thirty guineas to the Holcroft family, a significant amount to a widow when the usual payment was between £10 and £20 and at a time when some applications were refused.[74]

* * *

Much of the information concerning the Holcroft family in the years following Thomas's death can be retrieved from Godwin's diary, the letters of Charles and Mary Lamb, and the *Reminiscences* of Henry Crabb Robinson. From Robinson we learn that Louisa and Fanny's school was established in Camden Town and that it existed on shaky footing; he noted in 1812 that Louisa had made a "bad business of it."[75] That year Louisa married the dramatist James Kenney, who, Robinson recalls, took upon himself the care for the school as well. There is little information about Fanny in the period immediately following Holcroft's death, although Lamb had reported to Manning just after the event (28–29 March) that she bore her father's death "much better than [he] could have supposed" (Lamb, 3:3). Whereas following Holcroft's death Louisa appears not infrequently in Godwin's diary, not only as a correspondent to Godwin about the matter of her late husband's journal but also visiting him at his home, Fanny disappears entirely from the diary in these same years. A fleeting glimpse of her appears elsewhere, when Lamb writes to Manning at the beginning of 1810 that she, is well (Lamb: 3:37). Little, if anything else, can be traced from this two-year period, and it is not known how long she remained with the Kenneys, if she did so, following their marriage.

Fanny and Louisa's careers as schoolmistresses were short-lived. Louisa remarried, and Fanny continued to earn her living by writing and translating, as she had been educated to do by her father, and by teaching elsewhere. Fanny Holcroft had been publishing already as a very young woman, with a number of her poems appearing in the *Monthly Magazine* in the years 1797–1803. "The Negro," published there in October 1797, is the most well known of these poems and engages with an urgent contemporary concern. It formed part of a wider antislavery discourse and a poetic effort in which many eighteenth-century women writers took part. The condemnation of Christian hypocrisy and its complicity with the practice of slavery gave the poem a particular Holcroftian touch, while also appearing in opposition to her father's disturbing complacency over enslavement exhibited in *The Man of Ten Thousand* and *Bryan Perdue*: "Yes, let me teach this Christian crew, / the dying Negro can forgive."[76] Fanny's life has been summarized and her work anthologized in Andrew Ashfield's *Romantic Women Poets*,

Volume 2, where Ashfield includes a number of poems and a short biography,[77] and in *Orlando: Women's Writing in the British Isles from the Beginnings to the Present*, an electronic resource.

Fanny was proficient in music, studying under Holcroft's friend, the musician and pedagogue Muzio Clementi, and playing Haydn and Mozart in the evenings (*Life*, 2: 135, 188). She had composed the score to Holcroft's melodrama *The Lady of the Rock* and in 1818 published "Sweet Friendship," a "canzonet," "affectionately inscribed to Mr. and Mrs. Kenney," which indicates the cordial relations that seem to have still existed with her late father's wife.[78] As a young woman she had translated plays from Spanish, German, and Italian for Holcroft's short-lived publication the *Theatrical Recorder*, published in two volumes in 1805–1806.[79] Although superseded today by other English translations of these plays, this translation project is important for its own time, indicative of how, in Frederick Burwick's words, "the Holcrofts, father and daughter, contributed to an expansive movement to import the literature of the Continent, especially France, Germany and Italy."[80] Additionally, Fanny wrote original novels, *The Wife and the Lover* (1813) and *Fortitude and Frailty*, "inscribed to the revered memory of her lamented father" (1817), and a play, "The Goldsmith" (1827). The play, performed at the Haymarket in August-September 1827 and later revived there, tells the story of a goldsmith, Cardillac, who is also a diamond thief, his daughter, Isabella, her lover, Oliver, and the discovery and exposure of her father's crimes. Fanny Holcroft employs melodramatic themes and techniques in the play—of course melodrama was the dominant theatrical mode at this time—with her stage directions, including detailed calls for music at critical moments in the action and a supposedly "supernatural" statue, which is the secret cache for the stolen diamonds. Oliver's dilemma, how to expose Cardillac's crime but at the same time to shield the virtuous Isabella from the knowledge of it, is accompanied by her love and obedience to her father, and at the end of the play, it is declared that she will never learn of his wrongdoings. In this work, as well as in her novels, Fanny never moves beyond conventional themes, behaviors, and tropes. The play was never printed, which is surprising given its very respectable run at the Haymarket, with twenty-six performances in 1827, twelve in 1828, and a scattering of others through 1835.[81] This may be explained by the fact that Fanny, especially at this time, years after Thomas Holcroft's death, most certainly did not have the easy access to publishers that her father had.

Despite her literary output, Fanny relied mostly on teaching to earn her living. In a letter she wrote to Henry Colburn, the publisher of her novel *The Wife and the Lover*, she gave her address as "Mrs. Jackson's School" in the Somers Town neighborhood of London.[82] She also traveled to various private homes to give music lessons. One of her pupils was Georgiana Gordon, later to become the prominent Australian artist, Georgiana McCrae. Georgiana was the natural daughter of the

Marquis of Huntly and Jane Graham and lived with her mother in Somers Town. Fanny had a number of pupils, and McCrae recalls her "tired from the long walks" as she went from "one pupil's house to the next."[83] Fanny made a strong impression on the young girl, and years later the adult Georgiana McCrae would leave a moving account: "Of all the right-minded, clean-spirited and clever women I have met with none excelled poor Fanny Holcroft. Her conversation, precepts & general information were most valuable to me, a very Quixote was she in Honour and Truth."[84] Importantly, McCrae's biographer states that through Fanny Holcroft, Georgiana met the painter John Varley, who would become her art teacher and thus influence her career as a painter.[85] Varley, a close friend of William Blake, was the brother-in-law of Muzio Clementi. The link to Varley suggests that Fanny maintained some contact with Clementi following her father's death.

Little is known of Fanny's life in her later years. Described by her father as "gentle [and] courageous"[86] and by McCrae as having "intelligence and integrity,"[87] she was perceived by others as singular, perhaps eccentric. The story of her experience as a governess at Lord and Lady Mountcashell's home in 1802 in Paris and her prompt dismissal was disseminated in various accounts that emphasized her peculiarity, such as the one related by Claire Clairmont, where Fanny is described as "luckless" and with "affections [that] excited . . . ridicule."[88] Fanny remained in contact with Godwin and with Charles and Mary Lamb following her father's death. Henry Crabb Robinson recalled seeing her many years later, in 1824, at the home of the Lambs. He wrote, "There I had a melancholy impression produced by seeing Fanny Holcroft—old & poor—plain & silly, but with a kind heart—I recollected hearing her praised by M[rs] Clarkson about thirty years ago & longing for her acquaint[an]ce, which I should then have thought an honour."[89] The mention of the famous abolitionist Clarkson family, as well as the remembrance of Fanny in better days, was in stark contrast to the present picture. A keen reader of Jane Austen, Robinson may have been recalling Austen's *Emma* (1816) and the famous description of Miss Bates presented toward the end of the novel, in Mr. Knightley's rebuke to the heroine: "She is poor; she has sunk from the comforts she was born to; and if she live to old age, must probably sink more . . . from a period when her notice was an honour."[90] It is more difficult to find traces of Fanny Holcroft in the twenty years from this remembrance (1824) and till her death. Her presence is noted, albeit infrequently, at the homes of the Godwins and the Kenneys (GD, 11 April 1828, 9 May 1829). Her final mention in the Godwin Diary is in 1830. Her death, in 1844, was noted in the newspapers.[91] She died alone, save for the company of an illiterate servant, in what was called a "mania,"[92] circumstances that substantiate in a haunting way Austen's prognosis of what awaited the economically vulnerable single woman.

The six younger Holcroft children went their separate ways. Villiers, the eldest of Holcroft's children with Louisa, went to India and died there either in

1835 or 1836.[93] Henry went to France (GD 22 July 1820), where his mother and Kenney and the youngest Holcroft child, Ellen, had preceded him, and he remained there long after the Kenneys had returned to England; his presence was noted there in 1834.[94]. Harwood emigrated to America, arriving in New York in 1832.[95] Henry and Harwood had initially stayed behind in England after their mother had left for France, although they were boys aged only thirteen and fifteen. They visited Godwin during this time, with Henry sleeping at Godwin's house for four nights during the Christmas period in 1819 (GD 25 December 1819). Ellen died age seventeen at Versailles in 1825.[96]

More is known of the namesakes. The younger Louisa and Thomas were linked to artistic and intellectual circles, and both were connected to the writer and thinker Thomas Carlyle. In 1828 Louisa Holcroft had married John Badams, a scientist and manufacturer and a very close friend of Carlyle, who described him as "among the men I loved most in the world."[97] Carlyle mentions Louisa Badams frequently in his letters, the negative aspects he perceived in her intensifying as the acquaintance progressed. Thus, he describes Louisa as "loving, resolute [but] too girlish" in a letter to his wife, Jane Welsh Carlyle (CLO, 17 August 1831). (During this visit to London he met Godwin, describing him as the "bald, bushy-browed, thick, hoary, hale little figure with spectacles: taciturn enough.") Two years later he would describe Louisa as having an "artificial inconstant vehement nature. . . . Why did they ever wed?" (CLO, to John Carlyle, 29 March 1833). Badams died in 1834, and Carlyle did not remain in contact with his widow; Jane Welsh Carlyle wrote to her mother-in-law over a year later of Louisa's remarriage to the son of her (Louisa's) half-sister Sophy from Sophy's own second marriage (CLO, 1 May 1835). This was Barham Cole Mergez, whose father, Georges, had been a general in Napoleon's army and who was a cousin of Danton (GD). Louisa, like her mother and siblings, met the Lambs socially and was a frequent visitor at Godwin's, last visiting him on 1 July 1835, less than a year before his death. She died in 1869.

Whereas Thomas and Jane Carlyle describe Louisa Badams in increasingly harsh terms, with Jane referring to her after the marriage to Mergez as part of a "rabble of mongrel French who have neither common sense nor common decency" (CLO, To Margaret A. Carlyle, 1 May 1835), Thomas Carlyle's relationship with her brother, Thomas Holcroft, whom he had met initially as Badams's brother-in-law, was based on a more cautious footing of give-and-take and mutual benefit. Tom Holcroft was a journalist who worked for the *Morning Herald*. He would regularly send Carlyle newspapers, especially the *Examiner*, a paper Carlyle would later write for (see, for example, CLO, Thomas Carlyle to John Carlyle, 1 October 1833). Carlyle provided Holcroft with a letter of introduction before he went to Paris as his newspaper's correspondent (CLO, Carlyle to John Stuart Mill 18 August 1834). The younger Holcroft also spent some years in India and was later the secretary of the Royal Asiatic Society.[98] On 4 November 1847, following the publication of a new edition of Joseph Cottle's *Reminiscences* of Coleridge and now back in England, he wrote an indignant letter to the *Times*. As we saw earlier in this chapter, Cottle had written of Coleridge's horror at the atheism of the young Holcroft children. Now denying the charge, Tom Holcroft promised to publish "correspondence and other manuscript records" to refute the claim.[99] The story was picked up by *Punch*, which presented a more energetic defense of the late dramatist—"a man of iron independence of character . . . a political reformer."[100] His son, in contrast, was more concerned with the charge itself than with vindicating his father in a historical view. Yet despite his promise, nothing further was submitted by him on the subject. Being the namesake of a famous (or notorious) person would have defined his own life to a great extent. His death, in 1852, following a second visit to India, was noted in the newspapers, and indeed the obituaries identified him as "the son of the well-known writer and political character of that name."[101] It could not have been an easy burden for the younger Holcroft, with the attendant pressures of money, career, and status to be navigated and with a Victorian mind-set he may have adopted. He treaded cautiously.

Like his siblings, the younger Thomas Holcroft maintained contact with Godwin and with the Lambs. It is moving to see the evidence for these lifelong friendships as they unfolded throughout the years and to recall the final deathbed reconciliation of Godwin and Holcroft in 1809 which enabled this later, ongoing sociable contact with Godwin as it was now renewed. I want to conclude this chapter and this book with a brief mention of one such sociable gathering, a dinner party which took place at the home of Charles and Mary Lamb on 2 August 1824. In attendance, besides the Lambs, were James and Louisa Kenney, Louisa's son Tom, Fanny Holcroft, Mary Wollstonecraft Shelley, and Godwin (GD). The Kenneys were back from France (and at supper without her daughter Ellen, who would die the following year). What kind of relationship did Thomas have with his half-sister Fanny? To what degree did the Kenneys maintain contact with her? Did those in attendance speak with Mary Shelley of Percy Shelley's death two years earlier, or of her success with *Frankenstein*, adapted for the stage by Richard Brinsley Peake as *Presumption!* a year before? Did they speak of politics? Of the theater? Of Holcroft himself? Did they laugh? Charles Lamb had experienced a different kind of sociability, famously, seven years previously at the "immortal dinner" given by the artist Benjamin Haydon, which he had attended along with Wordsworth, Keats, and others. There, in an event later widely recognized, commemorated, and restaged, Lamb had taken part, through conversation and sociable connections, in cultural work which was also, in Gillian Russell and Clara Tuite's words, a "fundamental part of [the] self-definition [of] Romantic writers."[102] Although very different from Haydon's dinner, and, in contrast, almost negligible in terms of the intersections and resonances of cultural power that it emitted, this gathering on 2 August 1824 still exhibits a dimension, an enactment, of Romantic-era concerns, a continuity of sorts that acknowledges through community and sociability the life and times of Thomas Holcroft and of the next generation. As we saw throughout this book, recognition of his life and work appeared and reappeared in print, on stage, on film in 1913, on radio in 1949, and in the usual but also unexpected places. This recognition persevered in the collective cultural memory—albeit inconsistently, at times echoing defeat but elsewhere conspicuous and triumphant—for many years that followed.

* * *

I wish to stay with this dinner gathering for one more minute. Holcroft's story is told, and his family—wife, children, and friends—have appeared in a final portrayal, in the dinner table tableau I have just described. This is for me an appealing picture: the persons represented include writers and a philosopher, and some—like Godwin, Mary Shelley, and the Lambs—remain well known till the present day. All, in their own time, were friends, sharing an evening of sociability on that August evening which was, I hope, convivial.

In trying to bring the story of Thomas Holcroft and his family back to view, I have often had the opportunity in the years of writing this book to consider its relevance to our own here and now, a relevance that stood out to me at many a moment. What would Holcroft have thought had he been able to see our present time? And what can present-day readers learn from Holcroft? On one hand, he might have been taken aback by the change in the way we perceive his beloved Truth. The belief in truth as articulating ideas of equality, freedom, and social justice is still relevant, but its rational unequivocalness as Holcroft saw it has been replaced in a large degree by a valorizing subjectivity. Today it is common and accepted and encouraged for all to "speak their own truth." What would Holcroft have made of this relativism? And what can we in the twenty-first century learn about our own relativizing through viewing his embrace of the monolithic idea of Truth? The struggle against intransigent government and social systems in our own time would also have been familiar, as well as the sway of popular acceptance—those apostasies that exist today and reflect that same characteristic of bending before the storm and of appeasing the hegemony that had in his own time so appalled him.

Other ideas in which Holcroft believed are still relevant, as they hold out a promise for a better world: the power of education to alleviate poverty and to improve society; the need for alternatives to carceral repression and punitive force; the imperative of nonviolent political activism; the importance of conversation; the power of the printed (and now electronic) word to map out philosophies of acceptance or rebellion and, with it, the urgency still of "print magic"—the ability of writing to repair society and to change the world.

INTRODUCTION

1. Michael Billington, "The Road to Ruin," *The Guardian*, 10 September 2002. See also Emma Dunford, *ReviewsGate*, 11 September 2002; Charles Spencer, *The Telegraph*, 10 September 2002, Benedict Nightingale, *The Times* 10 September 2002, and, somewhat less favorably, Rhoda Koenig, *The Independent*, 18 September 2002.

2. The 1937 production of *The Road to Ruin*, the last production of the play in London until 2002, occurred at the Ambassadors Theatre. It was noted for the wrong reasons: the actor who played Goldfinch, Hay Petrie, forgot his lines, a fact that was reported even in *The New York Times*, 12 February 1937. There was a revival in the Theatre Royal Bristol in 1954 and a BBC radio adaptation starring Maurice Denham in 1949.

3. See, for example, L. W. Conolly, *The Censorship of English Drama 1737–1824* (San Marino, CA: Huntington Library Press, 1976); Gillian Russell, *The Theatres of War: Performance, Politics and Society, 1793–1815* (Oxford: Clarendon Press, 1995); Jane Moody, *Illegitimate Theatre in London, 1770–1840* (Cambridge: Cambridge University Press, 2000); David Karr, "'Thoughts That Flash Like Lightning': Thomas Holcroft, Radical Theater, and the Production of Meaning in 1790s London," *The Journal of British Studies* 40, no. 3 (July 2001): 324–356; and David Worrall, *Theatric Revolution: Drama, Censorship, and Romantic Period Subcultures, 1773–1832* (Oxford: Oxford University Press, 2006).

4. An exception was the performance of *Venice Preserved*, which somehow managed to receive a license for Drury Lane in 1794 but was discontinued after two nights of contention. Recognizing the Examiner's authority in this context, Elizabeth Inchbald wrote in 1808 regarding *Venice Preserved*: "it is played repeatedly every year; except when an order from the Lord Chamberlain forbids its representation, lest some of the speeches . . . should be applied, by the ignorant part of the audience, to certain men or assemblies in the English state," *Remarks for The British Theatre* (1806–1809); (Delmar, NY: Scholars Facsimiles and Reprints, 1990), "Venice Preserved," 1.

5. Conolly, 84–85.

6. Thomas Holcroft, *Love's Frailties* (London: 1794), 66.

7. James Epstein and David Karr, "Playing at Revolution: British 'Jacobin' Performance," *The Journal of Modern History*, 79:3 (September 2007), 495–530, 496.

8. *The European Magazine* 1 (1782), 48.

9. Elbridge Colby, "Thomas Holcroft, Radical," *The Mid-west Quarterly* 5:1 (October 1917), 44–60, 56.

10. Elizabeth Inchbald, *The Artist*, 1:14 (August 1807), 9–19, 16. Further references will be cited in the text.

11. There are many studies that focus on novel writing and its specific function as a genre of response; see for example, Gary Kelly, *The English Jacobin Novel, 1780–1805* (Oxford: Clarendon Press, 1976); Miriam Wallace, *Revolutionary Subjects in the English "Jacobin" Novel, 1790–1805* (Lewisburg: Bucknell University Press, 2009); and, much earlier, Allene Gregory, *The French Revolution and the English Novel* (New York and London: The Knickerbocker Press, 1915), all of which afford Holcroft a prominent place. It is important to note that despite Inchbald's acknowledgment of the novelist's free agency and my

own distinctions, the pressures of reception and politics can be found, of course, in novels of the period as well. William Godwin wrote in the preface to the second edition of *Caleb Williams* (1795) how he had withheld his preface in the first edition of the novel "in compliance with the alarms of the booksellers." The book had appeared in the same month, May 1794, when the arrests on the charge of treason had begun. See William Godwin, *Caleb Williams*, ed. Pamela Clemit (Oxford: Oxford University Press, 2009), 312.

12. Jon Mee, *Print, Publicity, and Popular Radicalism in the 1790s: The Laurel of Liberty* (Cambridge: Cambridge University Press, 2016), 8.

13. John Barrell, "Divided We Grow: When Pitt Panicked" *London Review of Books*, 5 June 2003.

14. Mark Philp, "Introduction," William Godwin, *An Enquiry Concerning Political Justice* (1793), ed. Mark Philp (Oxford: Oxford University Press, 2013), xvi.

15. Charles Kegan Paul, *William Godwin: His Friends and Contemporaries*, 2 vols. (London: S. King, 1876), 1:17.

16. Mark Philp, *Godwin's Political Justice* (London: Duckworth, 1986), 169, 171.

17. Philp, *Godwin's Political Justice*, 171–172.

18. Gillian Russell and Clara Tuite, "Introduction," *Romantic Sociability: Social Networks and Literary Culture in Britain 1770–1840*, ed. Gillian Russell and Clara Tuite (Cambridge: Cambridge University Press, 2002), 4.

19. Russell and Tuite, "Introduction," 4.

20. For the case of Frost, see James Epstein, "'Equality and No King': Sociability and Sedition: The Case of John Frost," in *Romantic Sociability*, 43–61. For the case of Merry, see Jon Mee, "'Reciprocal Expressions of Kindness": Robert Merry, Della Cruscanism, and the Limits of Sociability," in *Romantic Sociability*, 104–122.

21. Kenneth R. Johnston, *Unusual Suspects: Pitt's Reign of Alarm and the Lost Generation of the 1790s* (Oxford: Oxford University Press, 2013), 16.

22. Johnston, 12.

23. This work of recovery includes, among many others, the scholarship of Jon Mee, who examines sociability and community; John Barrell's magisterial account of the Treason Trials; John Bugg's book on silencing and self-censorship in the period following the Two Acts; Pamela Clemit's work on letters and life writing; Gillian Russell's, Jane Moody's, David Worrall's, and Jeffrey Cox's work on Romantic theater. For Mee, see, in addition to his essay "Reciprocal Expressions" and his book *Print, Publicity, and Popular Radicalism* cited above, *Conversable Worlds: Literature, Contention and Community 1762 to 1830* (Oxford: Oxford University Press, 2011); John Barrell, *Imagining the King's Death* (Oxford: Oxford University Press, 2000); John Bugg, *Five Long Winters: The Trials of British Romanticism* (Stanford: Stanford University Press, 2014); Pamela Clemit, ed., *The Letters of William Godwin*, 6 vols. projected. (Oxford: Oxford University Press, Vol. 1, 2011, Vol. II, 2014); Gillian Russell, *The Theatres of War: Performance, Politics and Society, 1793–1815* (Oxford: Clarendon Press, 1995); Jane Moody, *Illegitimate Theatre in London, 1770–1840* (Cambridge: Cambridge University Press, 2000); David Worrall, *Theatric Revolution: Drama, Censorship, and Romantic Period Subcultures, 1773–1832* (Oxford: Oxford University Press, 2006); David Worrall, *Celebrity, Performance, Reception: British Georgian Theatre as Social Assemblage*, (Cambridge: Cambridge University Press, 2013); Jeffrey N. Cox, *Romanticism in the Shadow of War: Literary Culture in the Napoleonic War Years* (Cambridge: Cambridge University Press, 2014). For the role of women specifically in this engagement, see Harriet Guest, *Unbounded Attachment: Sentiment and Politics in the Age of the French Revolution* (Oxford: Oxford University Press, 2013) and my *Revolutionary Imaginings in the 1790s: Charlotte Smith, Mary Robinson, Elizabeth Inchbald* (Basingstoke: Palgrave, 2009), among many others.

24. Jon Mee, review essay, "William Godwin's Moment," *Huntington Library Quarterly* 75:1 (March 2012), 123–129, 123.

25. See, for example, David O'Shaughnessy, *William Godwin and the Theatre* (London: Routledge, 2015) and Robert M. Maniquis and Victoria Myers, ed. *Godwinian Moments: From Enlightenment to Romanticism* (Toronto: University of Toronto Press, 2011).

26. Peter Marshall, *William Godwin* (New Haven and London: Yale University Press, 1984), esp. 390–391.

27. Roy Hattersley, *The Edwardians* (London: Hachette, 2004), 1.

28. Hattersley, 65. Masterman's title acknowledges Thomas Carlyle's influential use of the phrase "condition of England question" in his essay "Chartism" (1839). Two years earlier he had written *The French Revolution* (1837) with its narrative, generic, and political complexities. For a discussion of the Edwardians in this general context, see Hattersley, Chapter One and Patrick Parrinder, "Historical Imagination and Political Reality: A Study in Edwardian Attitudes," *Clio*, 4:1 (October 1974), 5–25, 12–13. Carlyle's friendship with Holcroft's son Thomas Jr. will be discussed in Chapter Six.

29. G. S. Veitch, *The Genesis of Parliamentary Reform* (London: Constable & Co., 1913); Philip A. Brown, *The French Revolution in English History* (London: C. Lockwood, 1918).

30. H. N. Brailsford, *Shelley, Godwin, and Their Circle* (1913), rpt. (Hampden, CT: Archon Books, 1969), 44–45.

31. *Tragical Consequences or A Disaster at Deal*, ed. Edmund Blunden (London: 1931), n.p.

32. In her chapter on Holcroft, Gregory focuses on his novels while also presenting a forceful, enthusiastic, and original account of his life. In another chapter of her book, she mentions the drama of the Revolutionary decade, singling out, interestingly, *The School for Arrogance* as Holcroft's most doctrinaire play, 285–286.

33. Gregory, 49–50.

34. Elbridge Colby, "Justice in Georgia," *The Nation* 123 (1926), 32–33; John Prados, *Lost Crusader: The Secret Wars of CIA Director William Colby* (Oxford: Oxford University Press, 2003), 20–21. As this reference makes clear, Elbridge Colby was the father of one-time CIA director William Colby.

35. Colby quotes the "sometimes so strange and sometimes so good" comment as the remark of a contemporary of Holcroft's without additional information as to his or her identity.

36. Thomas Holcroft, *A Letter to the Right Honourable William Windham on the Intemperance and Dangerous Tendency of His Public Conduct* (London, 1795), 14.

37. For mounted fan-leaf, with six scenes from the play *The Road to Ruin*, with quotations on the body of the fan. c.1792, see URL https://www.britishmuseum.org/collection/search?keyword=road&keyword=ruin&keyword=mounted&keyword=leaf&keyword=fan

38. Louisa Thomas, "The Art of Biography, 4," interview with Hermione Lee, *The Paris Review* 205 (Summer 2013), 135–165, 139.

39. Hermione Lee, "Virginia Woolf and Offence," in *The Art of Literary Biography*, ed. John Batchelor (Oxford: Clarendon Press, 1995), 129–150, 136.

CHAPTER 1 — THOMAS HOLCROFT AND THE TREASON TRIALS

1. [Thomas Holcroft,] [1792?] [The Abinger Papers, Oxford, Bodleian Libraries, MS Abinger, c.1, fol.100, cited in Harriet Guest, *Unbounded Attachment*, 1. The note first appeared in print in Kegan Paul, *William Godwin*, 1:69. Although most scholars believe that the note refers to *Rights of Man* Part I, Mark Philp has argued that "Holcroft's cryptic little message" actually refers to the publication of Part II of the famous treatise. Holcroft's laudatory, "Hail for the new Jerusalem! The Millennium!" Philp writes, would signal the more "deserving" text of Part II in terms of its true revolutionary content. Mark Philp, "Godwin, Holcroft and the Rights of Man," *Enlightenment and Dissent* 1 (1982), 37–42, quote at 42.

2. Guest, 2. In citing the passage, Guest is particularly concerned to contrast the vibrant Holcroft-Godwin exchange with the absence of women from the energetic sphere of

political engagement and sociability that appeared in Britain at the time of the French Revolution.

3. The anecdote of Holcroft's membership in a publication committee appears in *Life* (1: xli), as well as in various studies of Thomas Paine, for example, Ronald F. King and Elsie Begler, *Thomas Paine: Common Sense for the Modern Era* (San Diego: San Diego State University Press, 2007), 156.

4. Barrell and Mee note the prosecution of publishers, such as James Ridgeway, H. D. Symonds, and Daniel Eaton in 1793, and that most radical publishers had spent time in Newgate Prison during this period, "Introduction," xx–xxi. Kenneth R. Johnston examines Jordan and Johnson's arrest over the publication of Gilbert Wakefield's *Reply* to the Bishop of Llandaff's *Address to the People of Great Britain* (1798), *Unusual Suspects*. See especially chapter 10.

5. Gillian Russell, "Burke's Dagger: Theatricality, Politics, and Print Culture in the 1790s," *British Journal for Eighteenth-Century Studies* 20 (March1997), 1–16, 2. For a comprehensive study of the place of theater in late eighteenth and early nineteenth-century culture, see her seminal *The Theatres of War*.

6. In addition to Russell's work, see James Epstein and David Karr, "Playing at Revolution"; David Karr, "Thoughts That Flash like Lightning"; and David O'Shaughnessy, *William Godwin and the Theatre*. Although he does not mention theater and theatricality per se, James T. Boulton's pioneering book, *The Language of Politics in the Age of Wilkes and Burke* (London: Routledge and Kegan Paul, 1963), laid the groundwork for these later studies and countless others, by examining key texts of the Revolution debate—those of Burke, Paine, Godwin, and James Mackintosh—using literary tools and arguing for the literariness of the writing.

7. Epstein and Karr, 509–511.

8. *The History of Two Acts* (London: 1796), 578. The speaker was George Hardinge. I thank Jon Mee for bringing this material to my attention.

9. The publication of *Rights of Man, Part I* and its place as a central event in relation to the wider issues of reform activism is acknowledged by John Barrell and Jon Mee in their "Introduction" to *Trials for Treason and Sedition*, ed. John Barrell and Jon Mee, 8 vols. (London: Pickering and Chatto, 2006–2007), 1:ix–li, esp. xi–xiii.

10. John Keane, *Tom Paine: A Political Life* (Boston: Little, Brown and Co., 1995), 329.

11. As Marilyn Butler observed, *Rights of Man* "being placed in the hands of the masses made it a political tool; the cheapness was an essential part of the offense." Marilyn Butler, ed. *Burke, Paine, Godwin, and the Revolutionary Controversy* (Cambridge: Cambridge University Press, 1984), 8.

12. O'Shaughnessy, 41.

13. Edmund Burke, *Reflections on the Revolution in France*, ed. J.G.A. Pocock (Indianapolis and Cambridge: Hackett Publishing Company, 1987), 57.

14. Burke, 60.

15. Burke, 70, 71.

16. Steven Blakemore, *Intertextual War: Edmund Burke and the French Revolution in the Writings of Mary Wollstonecraft, Thomas Paine, and James Mackintosh* (Madison, NJ: Farleigh Dickinson University Press, 1997), 96.

17. Burke, 78–79.

18. Thomas Paine, *Rights of Man, Common Sense, and Other Political Writings*, ed. Mark Philp. (Oxford: Oxford University Press, 1995), 112. Paine's text is shot through with numerous dramatic allusions and associations.

19. *Rights of Man*, 234.

20. Joseph M. Butwin, "Seditious Laughter," *Radical History Review* 18 (Fall 1978), 17–34, 22.

21. *Rights of Man*, 235.

22. Russell, *Theatres of War*, 24.

23. E. P. Thompson, *The Making of the English Working Class*, rev. ed. (Harmondsworth: Penguin, 1968), 173; quoted in Mee, *Print, Publicity, and Popular Radicalism*, 62.
24. Epstein and Karr, 496.
25. Russell, "Burke's Dagger." In a speech in support of the Alien Bill, Burke had taken a dagger from his pocket and proclaimed that it was his intention to "to keep the French infection from this country; their principles from our minds, and their daggers from our hearts," 2.
26. Epstein and Karr, 508.
27. William Godwin, "Of Choice in Reading," *The Enquirer: Reflections on Education, Manners, and Literature in a Series of Essays* (London: 1797), 137. For a discussion of Godwin's idea of moral and tendency in relation to his own writing, see Miriam Wallace, *Revolutionary Subjects*, Chapter One, esp. 44–45. See also Jon Mee, "Treason, Seditious Libel and Literature in the Romantic Period," *Oxford Handbooks Online* (2016). As Mee notes, Godwin's thinking on the subject of moral and tendency was surely influenced by the many trials he had attended in the previous years, 10. https://www.oxfordhandbooks.com/view/10.1093/oxfordhb/9780199935338.001.0001/oxfordhb-9780199935338-e-113. Accessed December 30, 2021.
28. Holcroft mentions "the first remarkable era in my life," setting the sequence for other subsequent notable "eras."
29. Markers of a comfortable life are exhibited in the fact that during this early period, Holcroft had received some schooling, some access to horseback riding, and instruction on the violin. See *Life*1:1.
30. [Thomas Holcroft] *A Plain and Succinct Narrative of the Late Riots and Disturbances in the Cities of London and Westminster* (London: 1780); "On the death of Samuel Foote, Esq." was published together with another poem, "On Age," in 1777. Holcroft identifies himself there as "Thomas Holcroft, of the Theatre Royal, Drury Lane."
31. For texts produced in the early years of Holcroft's professional life, see, in addition to the *Memoirs* and to Colby's useful supplementary introduction, the chronology of Holcroft's life and works in *Re-Viewing Thomas Holcroft, 1745–1809*, ed. Miriam L. Wallace and A. A. Markley (Burlington, VT: Ashgate, 2012), xvii–xx, and their Introduction, especially 6–7.
32. Holcroft's translation of *The Follies of a Day* has received much attention. Hearing of its success in Paris, he traveled to that city with the express purpose of translating it into English. Together with his friend Nicholas Bonneville, he attended the play every evening, committing it to memory and transcribing it together with Bonneville once back at home (*Life*: 1:272–273). Holcroft had lived in Paris for a short period in the previous year as a correspondent for the *Morning Herald*.
33. *The Life of William Nicholson 1753–1815 by His Son William Nicholson Junior*, ed. Sue Durrell (London and Chicago: Peter Owen Publishers, 2018), 42, 44. The original manuscript is at the Bodleian Library.
34. Mark Philp, "Introduction," William Godwin, *An Enquiry Concerning Political Justice*, xxxi.
35. Godwin, *Enquiry*, 54.
36. Philp, "Introduction," xxxii.
37. Godwin, *Enquiry*, 389.
38. John Barrell and Jon Mee argue that the LCS and the Sheffield Society for Constitutional Information were the most important of the societies. John Barrell and Jon Mee, "Introduction," *Trials for Treason and Sedition*, 1: xii. Mary Thale makes the important distinction between the reform societies and the numerous public debating societies active in the capital. In these debating societies, there was no need for approval of a new member by a committee or by the veteran membership; one simply paid an entrance fee and attended. Mary Thale, "London Debating Societies in the 1790s," *The Historical Journal* 32:1 (June 1989), 57–86.

39. Quoted in Mee, *Print, Publicity, and Popular Radicalism*, 74. Among the professions cited for various LCS members later detained in 1794, we find a silversmith, a wax chandler, a hair dresser, a tailor, and a hatter. Barrell, *Imagining the King's Death*, 191.

40. Eugene Charlton Black, *The Association: British Extraparliamentary Political Organization, 1769–1793* (Cambridge, MA: Harvard University Press, 1963), 178.

41. For Parkinson, see Iain MacCalman, "Newgate in Revolution: Radical Enthusiasm and Romantic Counterculture," *Eighteenth-Century Life* 22:1 (February 1998), 95–110, 101.

42. We will see later in this book examples of the reaction to Holcroft's class origins, such as in the deprecating comments of Thomas Mathias and the writers of the *Anti-Jacobin Review*, of Lord Mountcashell, and, much more appreciatively, in various accounts of Holcroft's life, especially in the reviews of his *Memoirs*.

43. *The True Briton*, 27 February 1799. The newspaper wrote this account of Merry's life following his death in December 1798. For more on Merry's life, his radical engagement with the French Revolution, and his position as a déclassé radical, see Jon Mee, "Reciprocal Expressions of Kindness" and "'The Magician No Conjuror': Robert Merry and the Political Alchemy of the 1790s," in *Unrespectable Radicals? Popular Politics in the Age of Reform*, ed. Michael T. Davis and Paul Pickering (Burlington, VT: Ashgate, 2008), 41–55.

44. Mee, *Print, Publicity, and Popular Radicalism*, 14.

45. Burke, 69.

46. *Pig's Meat* was a periodical published by Thomas Spence; *Hog's Wash* was the subtitle of a pamphlet, *Politics for the People*, written by Daniel Eaton.

47. Albert Goodwin notes more generally the influx of new recruits to the SCI in the spring of 1792 as "men of humble origins, who had achieved a 'respectability' by their professional skills or ability." Albert Goodwin, *The Friends of Liberty: The English Democratic Movement in the Age of the French Revolution* (London: Hutchinson, 1979), 215. Goodwin mentions Holcroft, of course, as one of this group, 216.

48. Goodwin, 215. A writ was issued for Paine's arrest on 21 May 1792. His trial took place in December of that year.

49. Barrell, *Imagining the King's Death*, 183.

50. Mee, *Print, Publicity, and Popular Radicalism*, 75.

51. Mee, *Print, Publicity, and Popular Radicalism*, 8.

52. Thomas Holcroft, *Knave, or Not?* (London: 1798), iii; *The Lady of the Rock* (London: 1805), vi. These examples are indicative of a pervasive and self-reflexive didactic thrust that appears in Holcroft's writing, especially in the paratexts where he introduces his material. The status of his diary as both a public and private text will be discussed in Chapter Four.

53. As Marilyn Butler notes, the twelve-month period beginning in February 1792 was the "*annus mirabilis* of eighteenth-century radicalism"; generally, Butler, *Burke, Paine, Godwin*, 7. Not surprisingly, then, Holcroft's imaginative writing was widely supported during this time, giving him a miracle year of his own.

54. The novel was discussed positively in the *Monthly Review* and in the *Analytical Review*, with the latter writing that it was "calculated to strengthen despairing virtue [and to add] fresh energy to the cause of humanity." The *Critical Review*, however, faulted the way "a philosophical leveller becomes the hero of a novel." (The *Critical Review* is referring to the co-protagonist of *Anna St. Ives*, Frank Henley, who, along with the eponymous Anna, expounds on Godwinian principles throughout the book.) The *Analytical Review* 13 (1792), 74; *The Critical Review* 4 (1792), 460. The *Monthly Review*'s measured discussion of *Anna St. Ives* appeared in Vol. 8 (1792), 151–155.

55. Miriam Wallace, "Constructing Treason, Narrating Truth: The 1794 Treason Trial of Thomas Holcroft and the Fate of English Jacobinism," *Romanticism on the Net*, 45 (February 2007) para. 7. https://www.erudit.org/en/journals/ron/2007. Accessed December 30, 2021.

56. See, for instance, *Enquiry Concerning Political Justice*, 114–118.

57. Quoted in Goodwin, 215. Goodwin sees the Whig Friends of the People Association, who were viewed with suspicion over their support of Paine, as one of the main targets of the Proclamation. Another motive of the promoters of the bill was the desire to split the Whig party and draw the more conservative faction into a coalition government, 207.

58. Goodwin, 215, 233.

59. In this observation, Hazlitt borrows from Holcroft's own account, in the *Narrative of Facts*, of the SCI as an association that was the "focus of . . . opprobrium." Hazlitt's description of the surveillance of the waiters is taken directly from the *Narrative*, 14.

60. Cecilia Lucy Brightwell, *Memorials of the Life of Amelia Opie* (London and Norwich: 1854), 52.

61. In the Introduction to the *Memoirs*, we read of Holcroft's "stern and irascible" nature (*Life*: 1: xxxix); the playwright Frederick Reynolds is quoted as mentioning his "frank, blunt manner" (*Life*: 1: xlvii), and we learn of altercations with Coleridge and Horne Tooke (*Life:* 1: xli–xlii).

62. Thomas J. Howell, ed. *A Complete Collection of State Trials and Proceedings for High Treason and Other Crimes and Misdemeanors*, 33 vols. (London: 1818), 24: 510.

63. John Barrell, *Imagining the King's Death*, 187.

64. For a discussion of the arms gathered by the societies, particularly the London Corresponding Society and their part in leading to the arrest and trial of the members of the societies, see Barrell, Ch. 7, "The Arming of the LCS."

65. Barrell, *Imagining the King's Death*, 188.

66. This quotation appears in a letter addressed to Scott that Holcroft appended to the *Narrative*.

67. Barrell, *Imagining the King's Death*, 191.

68. Barrell, *Imagining the King's Death*, 191; Goodwin, 332–333.

69. This altercation had occurred on a visit to William Sharp, who was under house arrest during the time of the May 1794 arrests; this was a more comfortable option to prison and was afforded him in return for giving evidence. Godwin had accompanied Holcroft on this visit to Sharp, as noted in his Diary: "Call on Sharp with Holcroft" (GD, 25 May 1794).

70. Barrell, *Imagining the King's Death*, 316.

71. Holcroft elaborates in the *Narrative* as to the cause for this hostile reception: "The nation through the ministerial prints was taught to consider me as something worse than a suspected person" (NF, 62).

72. For a discussion of the paranoia that pervaded society at this time, see Bugg, *Five Long Winters*.

73. Godwin's diary notes, for example, suppers with Holcroft and Merry at Holcroft's home on 11 June, 15 June, and 17 August. Godwin visited Newgate on 16 July, dining there with Gerrald and others. He visited the Tower, where Thelwall and others were incarcerated, on 16 August. He also mentions six visits to Mrs. Thelwall between May and November 1794 (GD).

74. Holcroft had been arrested on 7 October. The *Morning Chronicle* reported on it the following day, 8 October, and Godwin read of the event when he received the newspaper on 9 October.

75. *Morning Chronicle*, 8 October 1794.

76. Barrell, *Imagining the King's Death*, 315.

77. *St. James Chronicle*, 7 October 1794; partially quoted in Barrell, 316.

78. The letter is dated 10 October 1794. Godwin had written to Holcroft's daughter, Ann, upon hearing the news of his arrest, asking her to inform him if Holcroft is in need of "consolation." Godwin to Ann Holcroft, 9 October 1794, Clemit, 1: 106. Holcroft, in his reply, had rejected the idea of consolation and, as this quotation from his letter shows, had chosen his favorite emphasis on utility and promotion of his political and philosophical views.

79. MacCalman, 96.

80. Judith Pascoe, *Romantic Theatricality: Gender, Poetry and Spectatorship*: (Ithaca and London: Cornell University Press, 1997), 3. Pascoe devotes Chapter 2 of her book to the Trials.
81. Bugg, 60.
82. Barrell and Mee, "Introduction," xxxvi, xxxviii
83. Brightwell, 52.
84. Pascoe, 48–52. Quotations at 48, 51.
85. Pascoe, 48.
86. Barrell and Mee, xxxiv.
87. Barrell and Mee, xxxiv.
88. *Morning Post*, 2 December, 1794. Italics here and throughout the passage are the *Morning Post*'s. The idiosyncratic punctuation such as in use of quotation marks and dashes in this extract is as it appears in the original.
89. *Morning Post*, 2 December, 1794.
90. *Morning Post*, 2 December, 1794.
91. See, for example, the *St. James Chronicle*, 29 November–2 December 1794 and the *London Chronicle*, 29 November–2 December 1794.
92. *St. James Chronicle*, 29 November–2 December 1794.
93. William St. Clair, *The Godwins and the Shelleys: A Biography of a Family*. (Baltimore: Johns Hopkins University Press, 1989), 132.
94. Pascoe, 36–37, 38.
95. Thelwall and Holcroft of course knew each other and often met socially, especially between the years 1793 and 1797, when Thelwall was still living in London. William Godwin's diary notes thirty-three meetings in which Godwin, too, took part. Thelwall contributed the Prologue to Holcroft's 1794 play, *Love's Frailties*, another indication of the close contact between the two men, especially in that turbulent year.
96. Walsh himself achieved a bit part in literary history when he was featured (although not mentioned by name) in Coleridge's *Biographia Literaria* (1817). He was the spy sent to investigate Coleridge and Wordsworth, neighbors in Somerset, who, Coleridge relates, initially aroused Walsh's suspicion when he eavesdropped on them discussing "Spy Nozy"—actually the philosopher Spinoza. For a detailed discussion of the event and its wider implications, see Johnston, *Unusual Suspects*, Ch.12.
97. John Thelwall, *The Tribune* 4 (4 April 1795), 87.
98. This dialogue appears in Steve Poole, "Preface," *John Thelwall: Radical Romantic and Acquitted Felon*, ed. Steve Poole (London: Routledge, 2015), xiii.
99. Mee, *Print, Publicity, and Popular Radicalism*, 168.
100. George Eliot, *Middlemarch* (1871–1872), ed. W. J. Harvey, (Harmondsworth: 1965), 274. The reference appears as a comment on the relationship between Fred Vincy and Mary Garth. The issue of performance and self-fashioning is a key one in the novel, reflecting both personal relationships, as here, and also in the way the characters function in the wider public sphere, in the provincial town at the moment before the passage of the Reform Bill.

CHAPTER 2 — *THE ROAD TO RUIN* AND ITS AFTERLIVES

1. A. M. Williams, "A Group of Revolutionaries," *Saint George: A National Review Dealing with Literature, Art, and Social Questions in a Broad and Progressive Spirit*, 8:32 (October 1905), 296–312, 296.
2. Williams, 296.
3. Williams, 307.
4. Jacky Bratton, *New Readings in Theatre History* (New York: Cambridge University Press, 2003), 37–38.
5. A discussion of this aspect of intertheatricality appears in Frederick Burwick, *Romantic Drama: Acting and Reacting* (New York: Cambridge University Press, 2009). Burwick

notes that in Siddons's farewell to the stage, the performance of *Macbeth*, "the curtain was dropped at the close of her mad scene (v.i.). This was the finale that the audience had come to see, and they refused to allow the play to continue," 4.

6. Charles Lamb, "On the Acting of Munden," *Essays of Elia, To Which Are Added Letters, and Rosamund, A Tale* (Paris: Baudry's European Library, 1835), 162–163.

7. *The Academy*, 4:86 (December 1873), 468.

8. Susan Branson, *These Fiery Frenchified Dames: Women and Political Culture in Early National Philadelphia* (Philadelphia: University of Pennsylvania Press, 2001), 182, n.43; Russell, *The Theatres of War*, 112.

9. Lucyle Werkmeister, in *A Newspaper History of England, 1792–1793* (Lincoln: University of Nebraska Press, 1967), 27, notes that Harris, in addition to his duties in the theater, also served as paymaster for the Treasury. A detailed account of Harris's life, as well as of his Treasury associations, appears in Warren Oakley, *Thomas (Jupiter) Harris: Spinning dark Intrigue at Covent Garden Theatre, 1767–1820* (Manchester: Manchester University Press, 2018). Oakley goes into impressive detail regarding Harris's government connections and allegiances, but he doesn't account for the paradoxical relation of his staunch Royalism to his continued professional support of Holcroft, even after the latter's release from prison.

10. The performance of *The Road to Ruin* on 8 January 1795 and the box office earnings are noted in the Covent Garden account books, held in the British Library. British Library Add MS 29949 (Covent Garden Account Books).

11. Judith Milhous, "Reading Theatre History from Account Books," in *Players, Playwrights, Playhouses*, ed. Michael Cordner and Peter Holland (Basingstoke: Palgrave Macmillan), 2007, 101–131, 113.

12. The four prints in the series are *Twelve at Noon, Twelve at Night, Five in the Afternoon*, and *Five in the Morning*, and they show various examples of the degenerate lifestyle of the young dandy. Interestingly, *Twelve at Night* features a line from *The Road to Ruin*, Goldfinch's famous catchphrase, "That's your sort."

13. London Guided Walks, "A Road to Ruin Walk," accessed December 30, 2021, https://www.londonguidedwalks.co.uk/road-to-ruin-walk.php.

14. *The Times*, 26 January 1802.

15. An interesting twist to this political identification appears in a playbill announcing the performance of *The Road to Ruin* at the Theatre Royal, York, on 16 March 1805. There the performance took place "by desire of the high Sheriff, and Gentlemen of the Grand Jury," in town for the Lent session of the assizes. This would have been a very different Grand Jury "directive" than the one Holcroft faced with his indictment in 1794. Playbills from Theatres in York, England, Folio 767 P69B Y82, quoted courtesy of the Lewis Walpole Library.

16. *The Morning Post*, 27 March 1809.

17. Inchbald, *Remarks*, "The Road to Ruin," 1.

18. *The London Recorder, or Sunday Gazette*, 26 February 1792.

19. *Saturday Review of Politics, Literature, Science, and Art* 56 (December 22, 1883), 798.

20. Barbara J. Todd, "The Remarrying Widow: A Stereotype Reconsidered," in *Women in English Society, 1500–1800*, ed. Mary Prior (New York: Routledge, 1985), 25–53, 25–26. Well-known examples of this character type include Widow Blackacre in William Wycherley's *The Plain Dealer* and Lady Wishfort in William Congreve's *The Way of the World*.

21. Devoney Looser, *Women Writers and Old Age in Britain, 1750–1850* (Baltimore: Johns Hopkins University Press, 2008), 107.

22. In the review in the *General Evening Post* of 18 February 1792, Mrs. Merry was singled out for "particular mention."

23. Michael Ragussis, *Theatrical Nation: Jews and Other Outlandish Englishmen in Georgian Britain* (Philadelphia: University of Pennsylvania Press, 2010), 89–92. Ragussis suggests that the representation of the Jew became more sympathetic through the years. These

more positive portrayals influenced, and were influenced by, the legislation for Jewish emancipation that began in 1830.

24. Ragussis, 92–93.

25. Ragussis, 45.

26. Ragussis, 45.

27. See, for example, the sympathetic portrayal of Jews as implied in the analogy between Caleb's plight and his disguise as a Jew in Godwin's *Caleb Williams* (1794). In her *Remarks for the British Theatre*, in discussing Richard Cumberland's *The Jew* (1794), Inchbald writes that "when a zealous Christian writes in favour of a Jew, it is a proof of the truest Christianity . . . Mr. Cumberland has . . . rescued [Jews] from the stigma" from which they suffered. *Remarks*, "The Jew," 3–4. For a different view of Holcroft's relation to the Jews, see Jeremy W. Webster, "Re-Writing Shylock: Thomas Holcroft, Semitic Discourse, and anti-Semitism on the English Stage," in *Re-Viewing Thomas Holcroft*, 71–85. Webster argues that rather than exhibiting anti-Semitism, Holcroft "deconstruct[s] the binary of 'Jew' and 'Christian'" to critique both Christianity and his culture's treatment of Jews, 85. This argument is an appealing one. However, it does not reflect Holcroft's regular practice of direct, blunt articulation of his moral positions.

28. "The Road to Ruin" typescript, BBC Third Programme, 29 May 1949, 22. Quoted by permission of the BBC Written Archives. The introduction was listed as spoken by Compton Mackenzie, the son of actor and director Edward Compton of the Compton Comedy Company and a prolific writer himself. The introduction has not survived, nor has the actual broadcast. The play was adapted by Ronald Simpson, who played the part of Sulky.

29. Todd Endelman, "The Checkered Career of 'Jew' King: A Study in Anglo-Jewish Social History," *AJS Review* 7/8 (1982–83), 69–100, 75. John King, the subject of Endelman's essay, was a very prominent figure who was also slightly connected to the Godwin circle. For a time he supported reformist causes. He frequently met Godwin for meals and social visits; Holcroft was present at seven of these meetings, for dinner, supper, or tea. He in fact hosted King, along with others, twice, for tea, on 21 April 1795 and 5 May 1795 (GD). Holcroft's diary records that he had met, and briefly spoke with, King, on 24 November 1798, *Life*, 2:202–203. We can assume that there were other, nonrecorded encounters as well.

30. This account appears in Chapter 17, the last one narrated by Holcroft himself.

31. Marilyn Morris, "Princely Debt, Public Credit, and Commercial Values in Late Georgian Britain," *Journal of British Studies* 43 (July 2004), 339–365, 340.

32. Morris, 359.

33. See, for example, *The Public Advertiser* (20 February 1792), whose reviewer wrote that "[a]t a time, when dissipation is carried to so extravagant a height by every class of mankind, we hope, the Comedy may prove a salutary check to it." *The Morning Chronicle* wrote that "[g] aming is truly and morally set up as the road to ruin," (20 February 1792).

34. Morris, 359.

35. *St. James Chronicle*, 21 February 1792.

36. LA 935. These erasures were later returned to the published text of the play and appear with inverted commas (quotation marks) to signify to the reader that they had been "omitted in representation," Thomas Holcroft, *The Road to Ruin* (London: 1792), front matter. Further references will be taken from this edition and cited as RR and the page number parenthetically in the text. We will see more examples of Holcroft's practice with inverted commas in the following chapter.

37. [William Godwin,] "An Account of the Late Mr. Thomas Holcroft, Author of *The Road to Ruin*, etc . . ." *Monthly Magazine* 27 (1809), 358. Holcroft's father had been a shoemaker. A few years later, following the first production of *The Road to Ruin*, the profession would acquire a political significance: Thomas Hardy, the leader of the London

Corresponding Society and a defendant in the 1794 Treason Trials, was a shoemaker, a fact that was often mentioned in political discussions and criticisms.

38. Allardyce Nicoll, *A History of Late Eighteenth-Century Drama, 1750–1800* (Cambridge: Cambridge University Press, 1927), 55.

39. *The Morning Chronicle*, 20 February 1792.

40. Russell, *Theatres of War*, 145.

41. *The London Stage, 1660–1800*, ed. Charles Beecher Hogan, 5 vols. (Carbondale: Southern Illinois University Press) 5:1428. See also Karr, "Thoughts That Flash like Lightning,"350. Karr suggests that with the increasing radical activity in London in the early months of 1792, the authorities might have had something to do with the prologue's removal.

42. *The London Chronicle*, 1 March 1792; *The Diary, or Woodfall's Register*, 3 March 1792.

43. Mary Russell Mitford, *Recollections of a Literary Life: or Books, Places, and People*, 3 vols. (London: 1852), 1: 131. See also Hazlitt's remarks about the "Road to Ruin," in *Lacy's Acting Edition of Plays*, vol. 42 (London: 1823).

44. Lamb, "On the Acting of Munden," 163.

45. Notices appeared, for example, in the *Whitehall Evening Post* on 28 November 1789 and in the *London Chronicle* in the issue of 1–3 December 1789.

46. Benedict Nightingale, *The Times*, 10 September 2002.

47. *Morning Chronicle*, 20 February 1792; *Life*, 1:294–295.

48. *Morning Post*, 3 November 1819.

49. See the *Oriental Observer and Literary Chronicle* (Calcutta), 7 October 1837, the *Geelong Advertiser and Intelligencer*, 26 October 1853, the *Birmingham Daily Post*, 26 May 1871, and *The Era*, 25 August 1872. For the Norwegian American production, see Napier Wilt and Henriette C. Koren Naeseth, "Two Early Norwegian Dramatic Societies in Chicago," *Norwegian-American Studies* 10 (1930), 44–75, 67.

50. This comment appears in a clipping, under the heading "The Calendar" for 23 March, with no newspaper title or year noted. It is signed A.B.L. Apparently this column noted important events that took place in past years on a certain date, in a version of "on this day in history." 23 March 1809 was the date of Holcroft's death. The clipping, with no further identification, is held in the Gabrielle Enthoven Collection of the Theatre and Performance Archives at the Victoria and Albert Museum in London.

51. *The Illustrated Weekly News* 30 November 1889; *The Boy's Halfpenny Journal* 11.10 (1879), 150.

52. Moody, *Illegitimate Theatre in London*; David Worrall, *Theatric Revolution*.

53. For the "Tom and Jerry" productions, see Bratton, 155–168.

54. For detailed discussions of the 1831–1832 campaign, see Bratton, especially chapter 3, and Katherine Newey, "Reform on the London stage," in *Rethinking the Age of Reform, Britain 1780–1850*, ed. Arthur Burns and Joanna Innes (Cambridge: Cambridge University Press, 2003), 238–253.

55. Newey, 244.

56. John Barrell expresses this idea in relation to the radical movements of the 1790s more generally in "The Reptile Oculist," *London Review of Books* 26:7, 1 April 2004, 23.

57. *The Times*, 11 February 1867.

58. The *School for Scandal* had been performed for 404 nights at the Vaudeville, *The Era*, 2 November 1873. According to *The Sunday Times* of 21 November 1880, reviewing the revival of *The Road to Ruin* at Sadler's Wells, that play had been performed between "100 to 200 nights" at the Vaudeville in its 1873 run.

59. *The Era*, 2 November 1873.

60. *Pall Mall Gazette*, 18 November 1880.

61. *Pall Mall Gazette*, 18 November 1880.

62. *The Times,* 21 November 1880.

63. *The Leader,* 24 March 1888.

64. Lou Warwick, *The Mackenzies Called Compton: The Story of the Compton Comedy Company, Incorporated in the History of Northampton Theatre Royal and Opera House, 1884–1927* (Blackburn: Warwick, 1977), 182.

65. Warwick, 185.

66. *The Saturday Review*, 22 December 1883.

67. See, for example, the comments of the critic for *The Academy*, 19 February 1887. In reviewing a production of *The Road to Ruin* in which Compton played the "double," the critic wrote that "[h]owever well an actor may disguise himself, and however versatile may be his powers of impersonation, something of his own individuality will perforce peep through, reminding us, by however so little, of that which we knew from the playbill to be the fact—that the two characters are played by one and the same actor."

68. Warwick, 179.

69. Nina Auerbach, "Before the Curtain," *The Cambridge Companion to Victorian and Edwardian Theatre*, ed. Kerry Powell (Cambridge: Cambridge University Press, 2004), 3–14, 3.

70. Amy Cruse, *The Englishman and His Books* (London: Harrap, 1930), 167–177.

71. Evidence for the play's September and December performances (and the absence of an October one) appears in Ransom. October 1802 is known, in terms of Holcroft's literary output, for the premiere of *A Tale of Mystery*.

72. Godwin saw the play three times in February 1792, as well as in October 1795, September 1798, September 1813, November 1819, October 1822, October 1825, and October 1832 (GD).

73. This production made headlines in February 2013, when a copy of the script used by Olivier was discovered among old theater memorabilia. The discovery was reported in the *Birmingham Mail* online, accessed December 30, 2021, http://www.birminghammail.co.uk/whats-on/theatre-news/rare-1926-olivier-script-uncovered-1313480. Olivier remembered his performance in *The Road to Ruin* as "the hopelessly unsuccessful second lead," Laurence Olivier, *Confessions of an Actor* (New York: Simon and Schuster, 1982), 66.

74. For the announcement of the BBC radio play, see *BBC Radio Times*, 27 May 1949. For the 1937 production at the Ambassadors Theatre, see. J. P. Wearing, *The London Stage, 1930–1939: A Calendar of Productions, Performances, and Personnel* (Lanham, MD: Rowman and Littlefield, 2014), 582. For Petrie forgetting his lines, see my Introduction, n.2.

75. British Film Institute, accessed December 30, 2021, http://www.bfi.org.uk/films-tv-people/4ce2b6b47507b.

76. Lincoln's *Road to Ruin* was advertised in *The Argus* on 11 October 1913 and two years later in the *Morning Bulletin* of Rockhampton, Queensland on 22 July 1915. See also Graham Shirley and Brian Adams, *Australian Cinema, The First Eighty Years* (Canberra: National Library of Australia, 1983), 41; Ray Edmondson and Andrew Pike, *Australia's Lost Films: The Loss and Rescue of Australia's Silent Cinema* (Canberra: National Library of Australia, 1982), 65–70. These films are not to be confused with the 1928 *The Road to Ruin*, which tells the story of a young woman whose life is ruined by promiscuousness and drugs. It was the top-earning film of 1928, and was made into a talkie in 1934. Its title reflects a usage of the phrase "road to ruin" as connected to a more amorphous representation of moral decline.

77. Peter Brooks, *The Melodramatic Imagination: Balzac, Henry James, Melodrama, and the Mode of Excess* (New Haven: Yale University Press, 1976); David Mayer, "Encountering Melodrama," *The Cambridge Companion to Victorian and Edwardian Theatre*, 145–163.

78. *The Argus*, 11 October 1913.

CHAPTER 3 — RADICALISM, AUTHORSHIP, AND SINCERITY IN HOLCROFT'S LATER PLAYS

1. These included "The Rival Queens" (1794), *Love's Frailties* (1794), *The Deserted Daughter* (1795), *The Man of Ten Thousand* (1796), "The Force of Ridicule" (1796),

Knave, or Not? (1798), *He's Much to Blame* (1798), *The Inquisitor* (1798), and the after-piece "The Old Cloathsman" (1799). "The Rival Queens," "The Force of Ridicule," and "The Old Cloathsman" were not published. *Heigh-ho for a Husband* (1794) is attributed, variously, to Holcroft or, more frequently, to Francis Waldron. The evidence seems to go against the attribution to Holcroft. William Hazlitt makes no mention of the play in his biography of Holcroft. Furthermore, William Godwin's diary shows that Godwin had consistently attended the first night performances of Holcroft's plays. However, he only saw *Heigh-ho for a Husband* at its 1802 revival (CG, 5 Feb 1802). However, the British Library catalogues *Heigh-ho*'s Irish edition as written by Holcroft, and A. A. Markley includes it in his chronology of Holcroft's life and works, *Re-Viewing Thomas Holcroft*, xix.

2. Mitford, *Recollections of a Literary Life*, 1: 136.
3. David Worrall, *Celebrity, Performance, Reception*, 1, 24. See Worrall's introduction for a detailed description of assemblage theory in general.
4. Worrall, *Celebrity, Performance, Reception*, 103–104.
5. Review of *Love's Frailties*, *The Monthly Review* 13 April 1794, 446.
6. Bugg, *Five Long Winters*.
7. For a discussion of the Gagging Acts, see also Goodwin, *The Friends of Liberty*, especially 387–388.
8. Bugg, 6.
9. Johnston, Chapter 1. See especially 12–16.
10. Johnston, 12.
11. Johnston, 162.
12. It is important to note that interventions occurred on both sides of the political spectrum. The most notable instance of radical intervention may be the events accompanying the production of Otway's *Venice Preserved* at Drury Lane in October 1794. There, speeches from the play promoting republican virtue, or criticizing government corruption, were appropriated by the audience in the pit and gallery from a Roman to a contemporary context, and were enthusiastically applauded. Recall also, as mentioned in Chapter Two, the events at Drury Lane in February 1792 (on the night of the premiere of *The Road to Ruin* at Covent Garden), when audience members called for the singing of the French revolutionary song "Ça Ira" at a performance of *Macbeth*. For a detailed discussion of the events surrounding the *Venice Preserved* production, see Barrell, *Imagining the King's Death*, 567–569.
13. E. P. Thompson, *The Romantics: England in a Revolutionary* Age, ed. Dorothy Thompson (1997), rpt. (New York: The New Press, 1999), 86.
14. Diane Long Hoeveler, "The Temple of Morality: Thomas Holcroft and the Swerve of Melodrama," *European Romantic Review*, 14:1 (2003), 49–63.
15. The subtitle was dropped in the printed edition of the play. The play was originally called *The Amorous Cynic*. Godwin's diary reveals that Holcroft had worked on the text for many months and that Godwin had read it in manuscript (CG 21 February 1793; 28 September 1793).
16. George Taylor mistakenly dates the play as appearing "soon after [Holcroft's] being tried for treason," yet the play was performed in February 1794, whereas the warrant for Holcroft's arrest was dated 7 October 1794, and those for his colleagues in May. George Taylor, *The French Revolution and the London Stage, 1789–1805* (Cambridge: Cambridge University Press, 2000), 102. This timeline is important, as I argue in this chapter, because Holcroft's experience as a defendant shaped his later, post–Treason Trials presentation of a reformist agenda in a different way and because of the increased hostility in the public's reception of his work.
17. Thelwall's contribution to the preface has been discussed by Georgina Green, "John Thelwall Author of the Prologue to Thomas Holcroft's *Love's Frailties* (1794)?," *Notes and Queries* 55:4 (December 2008), 422–424.

18. Thomas Holcroft, *Love's Frailties* (London: 1794), vi. Further references will be cited in the text as LF.

19. The prologue was also published separately in the *Whitehall Evening Post* in the issue of 15–18 February 1794, in the *Public Advertiser or Political and Literary Diary* on 17 February 1794, and in *The World*, on 17 February 1794.

20. The similarity between the two works is most apparent in the story line presenting the love between the son of an aristocratic family and the daughter of a poor painter. Unlike in *Love's Frailties*, where the acceptance of the interclass marriage results from the (eventual) patriarchal acceptance of the virtuous romance, von Gemmingen's patriarch encourages the marriage because the young woman who is involved with his son has become pregnant. Following the marriage the couple is banished to a distant estate. For a discussion of *Der deutsche Hausvater* in the context of the German drama of the late eighteenth century, see A. Menhennet, "Drama Between Two Stools: Leisewitz's *Julius von Tarent* and von Gemmingen's *Der deutsche Hausvater*," *Oxford German Studies* 6:1 (1971), 33–49.

21. *The World*, 6 February 1794.

22. *The European Magazine*, 25 (1794), 138. The disruption continued to be mentioned many years later. See, for example, the account quoted earlier in *Life* (2:94) and in Genest, 7: 160.

23. *St. James Chronicle*, 6 February 1794.

24. *The Times*, 15 February 1794. The newspaper is referring to Holcroft's membership in the Society for Constitutional Information. In contrast, the *Public Advertiser or Political and Literary Diary* also noted the "great applause" the play received (6 February 1794).

25. John Thelwall, *The Tribune, A Periodical Publication, Consisting Chiefly of the Political Lectures of J. Thelwall. Taken in Short-hand by W. Ramsey, and Revised by the Lecturer.* 3 vols. (London: 1795–1796), 3: 310. Qtd. in Green, "John Thelwall," 423.

26. Epstein, "'Equality and No King,'" 43.

27. For the persecution of Thelwall, see Thompson, *The Romantics*, Chapter 9; Johnston, Chapter 13; and Mee, *Print, Publicity and Popular Radicalism*, especially Chapter Six.

28. Thomas Holcroft, *Love's Frailties*, LA 1008.

29. Johnston, 15.

30. Holcroft, *Letter* to Windham, 8.

31. In another change, Mordent was originally called "Honeywood."

32. The similarity to *The Fashionable Lover* appears in the way both plays tell the story of a young woman under the power of an avaricious guardian who finds herself unknowingly in a house of prostitution. *The Deserted Daughter* is much more complex in its presentation of the guardian's reform, as well as in the energy and spiritedness of the female protagonist.

33. *The Oracle and Public Advertiser*, 4 May 1795. The review incorrectly identifies Mordent as Morland.

34. *The Whitehall Evening Post*, 2–5 May 1795.

35. *The British Critic*, Vol. 6 (1795), 422; *The Analytical Review*, Vol. 22 (1796), 48–51. See also *The Monthly Review*, Vol.17 (1795), 189–191.

36. *The Pocket Magazine, or Elegant Repository of Useful and Polite Literature* (1794–1796), 336.

37. *The Analytical Review* (22), 48.

38. *The Analytical Review* (22), 48.

39. Thomas Holcroft, *The Deserted Daughter* (London: 1795), 62. Further references will be cited in the text as DD.

40. LA 1077, Act I, sc. ii

41. Adolphus William Ward and Alfred Rayney Waller, eds., *The Cambridge History of English Literature* (15 vols.) (Cambridge: Cambridge University Press, 1932), 13:2, 277–278.

42. George Taylor notes as well that "the happy outcome" of *The Deserted Daughter* was caused by "fortunate accidents of coincidence," rather than by "beneficial providence or enlightened good sense," 103.

43. *Analytical Review* (22), 48.
44. *The Monthly Review* (17), 191; *The Oracle*, 4 May 1795.
45. Hoeveler, "The Temple of Morality," 58; Taylor, 103.
46. Hoeveler, 60, 59.
47. Holcroft's translation of Lavater's *Essays on Physiognomy* in 1789 was a marked success.
48. *The Oracle*, 4 May 1795.
49. Inchbald, *Remarks*, "The Deserted Daughter," 1.
50. The play also appeared in *Dicks' Standard Plays*, along with Holcroft's *Duplicity* (1781), *The School for Arrogance* (1791), *The Road to Ruin* (1792), *He's Much to Blame* (1798), *Deaf and Dumb* (1801), and *A Tale of Mystery* (1802).
51. George O. Seilhamer, *The History of the American Theatre: New Foundations* 3 vols. (Philadelphia: 1891), 3:320–322.
52. *The Oracle*, 12 October 1796.
53. Russell, *Theatres of War*, 111. For a discussion of military theatricals in general, see, especially, 133–139. The play performed together with *The Deserted Daughter* on this occasion, Samuel Foote's *The Prize*, was, as Russell shows, a favorite in amateur military theatricals.
54. Milhous, "Reading Theatre History from Account Books," 113.
55. Account books for the Covent Garden Theatre. British Library Add MS 29949.
56. The play's full title in the first edition (London: 1819) appears as *The Steward, or Fashion and Feeling* (founded upon *The Deserted Daughter*) without Beazley's name. The Stanford University copy of the play, available on Google Books, has the name "Thomas Holcroft" penciled in. Later editions (Boston: 1856; London: 1884) include Beazley's name, as well as the fact that the play was altered from Holcroft's *Deserted Daughter*. Further references will be from the 1819 edition and cited parenthetically in the text as S.
57. Thomas Holcroft, *The Man of Ten Thousand* (London: 1796), 52. Further references will be cited in the text as MT.
58. *Lloyd's Evening Post*, 22 January 1796.
59. *The Monthly Review* (19), March 1796, 353–354. This review refers to the published edition of the play.
60. *Tomahawk, or Censor General*, 6 February 1796; *The True Briton*, 25 January 1796.
61. *The Tomahawk or Censor General*, 11 February 1796.
62. *The Star*, 26 January 1796. A negative comment on the play also appears in a letter of William Wordsworth: "I have attempted to read Holcroft's *Man of Ten Thousand*, but such stuff," George McLean Harper, *William Wordsworth: His Life, Works and Influence*, 2 vols. (New York: Russell & Russell, 1960), 1:289; qtd. in *Life*, 2:96.
63. *The Monthly Review* (19), 354. Similarly, the *Universal Magazine* (98: January 1796) wrote that this portrayal of a military man "will never be a recommendation with a London audience," 68.
64. Russell, *Theatres of War*, 51, 60.
65. *Universal Magazine* (98), 68.
66. Roger Wells, *Wretched Faces: Famine in Wartime England 1793–1801* (Gloucester: Alan Sutton, 1988), 84. Wells notes that during the crisis of the summer of 1795 (which would have been the relevant context for Holcroft's play of January 1796), the idea of "artificial scarcity" was offset to a certain extent by the "recognisably adverse weather conditions" that year, 89. See also E. P. Thompson, *The Making of the English Working Class*, 62–68. Thompson notes that 1795 was the "climactic year for such 'riots' . . . when the older popular tradition was stiffened by the Jacobin consciousness of a minority," 65.
67. Wells, 76.
68. Jeffrey Cox, "Introduction," in *Slavery, Abolition, and Emancipation*, ed. Peter J. Kitson and Debbie Lee, 8 vols. (London: Pickering and Chatto, 1999), 5: ix, qtd. in Julie Carlson, "Race and Profit in English Theatre," in *The Cambridge Companion to British Theatre 1730–1830*, eds. Jane Moody and Daniel O'Quinn (Cambridge: Cambridge University

Press, 2007), 175–188, 176. There has been much recent work on this topic. See, for example, Jeffrey Cox and Dana Van Kooy, "Melodramatic Slaves," *Modern Drama* 55:4 (Winter 2012), 459–475 and Michael Ragoussis, *Theatrical Nation*.

69. Joseph Roach, *Cities of the Dead: Circum-Atlantic Performance* (New York: Columbia University Press, 1996), 4.

70. Ten years later, in *Memoirs of Bryan Perdue* Holcroft has the eponymous Bryan travel to Jamaica and eventually become overseer to a number of plantations, thus presenting a more expanded, and even more troubling, view of complicity with slavery.

71. Matthew Mulcahy, "Weathering the Storms: Hurricanes and Risk in the British Greater Caribbean," *The Business History Review* 78:4 (Winter 2004), 635–663; 637.

72. Mulcahy, 663.

73. The role of Hairbrain was played by the comedian John Bannister. Bannister's biographer alludes to the idiosyncratic nature of the role when he writes that Bannister "had no reason to regret the discontinuance of this play, as the character he had to sustain was every way unworthy of him," John Adolphus, *Memoirs of John Bannister*, 2 vols. (London: 1839), 1: 364.

74. MacCalman, "Newgate in Revolution," 95.

75. MacCalman, 101.

76. MacCalman, 104.

77. *Life*: 1, xxxii; qtd. in MacCalman, 102.

78. Newton produced these pictures for his imprisoned radical employer, William Holland, MacCalman, 96.

79. Mee, *Conversable Worlds*, 149.

80. Guest, 50.

81. Guest, 1.

82. LA 1192, front matter.

83. LA 1192, 31.

84. Thomas Holcroft, *Knave, or Not?* (London: 1798), 43. Further references are cited in the text as KN.

85. Conolly, *The Censorship of English Drama*, 84–85. Conolly uses the metaphor of the jury specifically in relation to Holcroft.

86. Nicholas Rogers, "Pigott's Private Eye: Radicalism and Sexual Scandal in Eighteenth-Century England," *Journal of the Canadian Historical Association* 4:1 (1993): 247–263, 261. Rogers mentions the *Political Dictionary* only briefly; his main point in this essay is to discuss Pigott's more widely known works, *The Jockey Club* (1792) and *The Female Jockey Club* (1794), texts that present an ongoing critique of the upper classes through their focus on sexual scandal. Rogers meticulously documents Pigott's radicalism, noting that he had been arrested in September 1793 for "toasting the French Republic and calling the King a 'German hog butcher who had sold his Hanoverian subjects to the British for thirty pieces of silver,'" 258. Pigott's indictment was ultimately rejected by the grand jury, but not before he had spent a month in Newgate Prison.

87. Charles Pigott, *A Political Dictionary: Explaining the True Meaning of Words* (London, 1795), 31. The *Dictionary* was published posthumously, after Pigott's death in 1794.

88. *The Oracle and Public Advertiser, The True Briton, The Morning Chronicle*, all of 26 January 1798.

89. *The Sun*, 26 January 1798. This reviewer is quoting *Hamlet*, III, ii, 131. As the *OED* explains, in later use, the phrase "miching malicho" was taken to be "generally suggestive of dark deeds, mystery or intrigue".

90. *The Morning Chronicle*, 26 January 1798. *The Morning Post* writes that "this piece deserves to remain on the stage, and no doubt will do so, with success, if some of the passages . . . be pruned away," 26 January 1798.

91. *The London Chronicle*, 25–27 January 1798.

92. *The London Chronicle*, 27–30 January 1798.

93. *The Morning Post*, 26 January 1798.
94. *The True Briton*, 26 January 1798.
95. Moody, *Illegitimate Theatre in London*, 91.
96. John Genest, always an astute observer, wrote regarding the play that "it is not easy to say whether [Monrose] is a knave or not," Genest, 7: 335.
97. *The Anti-Jacobin Review* 1 (1798), 52. A similar later review appears in Robert Bisset, *The Historical, Biographical, Literary, and Scientific Magazine*. 3 vols. (London: 1800), 2: 88–89.
98. This reference to locked lips may be compared with the poem "Billy Pitt's New Bills; or Lock Jaws, a Ballad," which had appeared in the *Cambridge Intelligencer* on 21 November 1795. John Bugg discusses the poem in *Five Long Winters*, in regard to the lead-up to the passing of the Two Acts and the awareness of the silencing that would soon prevail, 92–93. Holcroft's reference to "a lock upon . . . lips" a little over two years later, although appearing ostensibly in the innocuous context of a servant's comment, may also reference the same need for silence as it was internalized in radical writing.
99. Adolphus, *Memoirs of John Bannister*, 2:19; quoted in *Life*, 2:104.
100. In the end, Holcroft was dissatisfied with the management of Drury Lane for its treatment of *Knave, or Not?*. He wrote in his diary entry of 29 October 1798 of the "very improper conduct of [the theater's] proprietors in refusing to notice the letters [he] wrote to them, when they ceased, without apparent cause, to play 'Knave, or Not?'," *Life*, 2:191.
101. Bugg, 6.
102. *The True Briton*, 30 January 1793, 1 February 1793.
103. *The Monthly Review* 10 (1793), 303–304.
104. Peter Brooks, *The Melodramatic Imagination*, 12.
105. Philip Cox, "'Perfectly Harmless and Secure'? The Political Contexts of Thomas Holcroft's *He's Much to Blame*," in Wallace and Markley, eds., *Re-Viewing Thomas Holcroft*, 87–101, 89. Cox writes that despite his radical associations, "Fenwick did not at this stage share Holcroft's extreme notoriety in the eyes of either theatre-goers or writers for periodicals," 88.
106. Cox, "'Perfectly harmless and secure'"?, 101.

CHAPTER 4 — HOLCROFT'S DIARY AND OTHER LIFE WRITING

1. Dan Doll and Jessica Munns, "Introduction," *Recording and Reordering: Essays on the Seventeenth and Eighteenth Century Diary and Journal*, ed. Dan Doll and Jessica Munns (Lewisburg, PA: Bucknell University Press, 2006), 9–21, 13.
2. Mary Chamberlain and Paul Thompson, "Introduction," *Narrative and Genre*, ed. Mary Chamberlain and Paul Thompson (London and New York: Routledge, 1998), 1–21, 11.
3. The information which Holcroft specifically objected to being made public was his opinion of "Mr.— . . . [who] was not a man of principle" (*Life*, 2:206). This name is not glossed by Elbridge Colby.
4. Rachel Cottam, "Diaries and Journals," in *Encyclopedia of Life Writing: Autobiographical and Biographical Forms*, ed. Margaretta Jolly, 2 vols. (Chicago: Fitzroy Dearborn Publishers, 2001), 1:268.
5. A. A. Markley, "Transforming Experience into Reform in Holcroft's Memoirs and Literary Works," in *Re-Viewing Thomas Holcroft*, 181–196, 183.
6. "Ht" was Godwin's regular abbreviation of Holcroft's name throughout his diary. This comment appears in Godwin's entries for 23 and 26 January 1810 (GD).
7. Kegan Paul, *William Godwin: His Friends and Contemporaries*, 2: 176.
8. As Markley puts it, "having been burned by the violent public reaction to his own frankness" regarding the relationship between Mary Wollstonecraft and Gilbert Imlay, a subject that had apparently been acknowledged in Holcroft's journal, Godwin "knew what

another published reference to this relationship would cost him and his family." "Transforming Experience," 183.

9. Kegan Paul, 2: 177. Gilbert Imlay had been Wollstonecraft's lover in the early 1790s and the father of her daughter, Fanny.

10. These comments appear in Crabb Robinson's diary entry for 8 January 1811. Quotations from Crabb Robinson's Diary, Reminiscences and Correspondence used throughout this book are presented with the permission of the Director and Trustees of Dr. Williams's Library, London, and the Crabb Robinson Project (editors Timothy Whelan and James Vigus), School of English and Drama, Queen Mary University of London. I am grateful to James Vigus for sharing this material with me before publication.

11. *The Letters of Charles and Mary Lamb*, ed. Edwin V. Marrs, 3 vols. (Ithaca, NY: Cornell University Press, 1976–1978), 2: 68.

12. *The Gentleman's Magazine* (April 1816), 342.

13. As Rachel Cottam writes, "the use of a code . . . encapsulates the paradoxical nature of the diary, for diarists simultaneously reveal themselves to, and conceal themselves from, others." 1:268.

14. The circumstances of the writing and completion of the *Memoir* are well summarized in David McCracken, "Hazlitt and a Case of Charitable Journalism," *Keats-Shelley Journal* 28 (1979), 26–27.

15. Colby's 1925 edition of the memoir was published in two volumes; the diary appears as a substantial part of the second volume.

16. Stephen Behrendt, "'I am not what I am': Staged Presence in Romantic Autobiography," *Romantic Autobiography in England*, ed. Eugene Stelzig (Burlington, VT: Ashgate, 2009), 145–160, 147.

17. Behrendt, 148.

18. Thomas Holcroft, *Memoirs of Bryan Perdue* 3 vols. (London: 1805), 1: 1. Tellingly, later in the book the narrator has an extended disquisition on the need to state the truth when writing a memoir (1:76–79).

19. *The Critical Review* (May 1816), 434–451, 435.

20. *The Gentleman's Magazine* (April 1816), 341–342, 341.

21. Mitford, *Recollections of a Literary Life*, 1:112.

22. *The Theatrical Inquisitor and Monthly Mirror* (July 1816), 38–43, 39.

23. George L. Craik, *The Pursuit of Knowledge Under Difficulties, Illustrated by Anecdotes*, 2 vols. (London: 1830), 1:1. The account of Holcroft appears in 1: 406–416. Despite his inclusion in the collection, which implies a degree of regard, the overall view of Holcroft is disparaging, and Craik calls him "an inferior man" (1:406) to William Gifford (whose story precedes that of Holcroft). Under Gifford's editorship of the *Anti-Jacobin, or Weekly Examiner*, which appeared in 1797, Holcroft was frequently criticized.

24. John Harrison Stonehouse, *Green Leaves: New Chapters in the Life of Charles Dickens* (London: Piccadilly Press, 1931), 53–54.

25. Charles Dickens to John Forster, 4 November 1846; quoted in Stonehouse, 53. Stonehouse does not mention *The Pickwick Papers* in connection to Holcroft, although the connection was noted by at least one contemporary. See Chapter Two, note 50.

26. Asa Briggs, *A History of Longmans and their Books 1724–1990: Longevity in Publishing* (London and New Castle, DE: The British Library and Oak Knoll Press, 2008), 280. Routledge had been the pioneering firm in this initiative, launching its series, the *Railway Library*, in 1848. Longman's *Travellers Library* was begun in 1851. Longman's *Travellers Library* is not to be confused with Jonathan Cape's series of the same name, which appeared in the interwar years in Britain.

27. Aileen Fyfe, *Steam Powered Knowledge: William Chambers and the Business of Publishing, 1820–1860* (Chicago and London: The University of Chicago Press, 2012), 161. The biggest selling author in the series was Thomas Babington Macaulay.

28. *The Travellers Library*, 17 (London: 1852), preface, n.p.

29. *The Travellers Library*, 17, preface.
30. *The Gentleman's Magazine* (April 1816), 341, 342.
31. *The Travellers Library*, 17, preface.
32. Jonathan Rose, *The Intellectual Life of the British Working Classes* (New Haven and London: Yale University Press, 2002), 2, 21. Holcroft is not included in Rose's magisterial study, which commences with the nineteenth century, although his experience as an autodidact reinforces Rose's insights, in particular the claim that the self-taught working-class reader was primarily influenced by the exposure to canonical literature. Although at first the young Holcroft simply read whatever came his way, including chapbooks, ballads, and sundry religious tracts (as well as the Bible), he later cited Pope, Shakespeare, Milton, and Dryden as those authors who "held the highest place in his esteem," (*Life*, 1:173).
33. David Vincent, *Bread, Knowledge and Freedom: A Study of Nineteenth-Century Working-Class Autobiography* (London: Europa Publications, 1981), 2.
34. Mitford's chapter devoted to Holcroft is called "Authors Sprung from the People," 1:111.
35. Janet Todd, *Daughters of Ireland: The Rebellious Kingsborough Sisters and the Making of a Modern Nation* (New York: Ballantine Books, 2003), 289.
36. *The Critical Review* 5th series, 3 (May 1816), 435. I have found no definitive evidence for the identity of this writer, whose review suggests a close familiarity with Holcroft. One possible candidate is Charles Lamb, who was a frequent visitor to the Holcroft home in the last years of Holcroft's life.
37. Markley, 181.
38. W. M. Verhoeven, "Politics for the People: Thomas Holcroft's Proto-Marxism," in *Re-Viewing Thomas Holcroft*, 197–217, 198.
39. Markley, 183.
40. *The Gentleman's Magazine* (April 1816), 342.
41. *The Critical Review* (May 1816), 447.
42. See Albert Goodwin, *The Friends of Liberty*, chapters 10 and 12; Mark Philp, "Introduction," in *Resisting Napoleon: The British Response to the Threat of Invasion, 1797–1815*, ed. Mark Philp (Aldershot: Ashgate, 2006); and Clive Emsley, *British Society and the French Wars, 1793–1815* (London: Macmillan, 1979).
43. Marshall, *William Godwin*, 211.
44. William Godwin, *Thoughts Occasioned by the Perusal of Dr. Parr's Spital Sermon, Preached at Christ Church, April 15, 1800: Being a Reply to the Attacks of Dr. Parr, Mr. Mackintosh, the Author of an Essay on Population, and Others* (London: 1801), quoted in Marshall, 211.
45. Kenneth R. Johnston, *Unusual Suspects*, 37. For an excellent overview of the impact of the reaction on Godwin specifically, see Pamela Clemit's introduction to *The Letters of William Godwin, Volume II* especially xxx–xxxii, as well as evidence from Godwin's letters themselves.
46. Thomas J. Mathias, *The Pursuits of Literature . . . A Satirical Poem*, 4th ed. (London: 1798). See, for example, the long note in which Mathias scathingly criticizes Godwin's *Political Justice* and his *Enquirer*, 369–376.
47. Thomas J. Mathias, *The Grove, a Satire by the Author of the Pursuits of Literature, with Notes, including Various Anecdotes of the King* (London: 1798), 16.
48. Mathias, *The Grove*, 21.
49. Mathias, *The Grove*, 17, n.
50. For a detailed discussion of Flower and the *Cambridge Intelligencer*, see Bugg, chapter 3.
51. Marshall, 214.
52. "The New Morality," *The Anti-Jacobin Weekly*, 9 July 1798; *The Anti-Jacobin Review* 1 (August 1798), 115. Louis Marie de La Révellière Le Peaux was one of the members of the French Directory in 1798 and a firm believer in theophilanthropy, the attempt, in France at the time of the French Directory, to replace Christianity with a kind of deism. The reference thus appropriately links him to David Williams, who had established a deist church

in London. For a fascinating account of Williams's activity during the 1790s, see Mee, *Print, Publicity, and Popular Radicalism*, 75–78.

53. *The Picture of London, for 1802; Being a Correct Guide to All the Curiosities, Amusements, Exhibitions, Public Establishments, and Remarkable Objects, in and near London; with a Collection of Appropriate Tables* (London: 1802), 27.

54. Thomas Holcroft, *Knave, or Not?*, 63.

55. For example, it is clear that although he doesn't write "Debrett's," Holcroft visited the bookshop on 3 July; he spoke with Weld (whom he mentions only in the context of that establishment) and read the "Reviews and Monthly Magazine." *Life*, 2:136.

56. David Fallon, "Booksellers in the Godwin Diaries," *Bodleian Library Record*, 24:1 (April 2011), 25–34, 31.

57. Holcroft frequently met Richard Weld at Debrett's and conversed with him on topical matters such as the Irish Rebellion and the campaigns of Napoleon. The editors of the Godwin diary state that Weld had met, or was mentioned by, Godwin in 1796–1797, and conclude that Weld was "fairly senior, Whiggish, and 'au courant' with London politics and people," GD, "Weld," editorial notes. David Fallon further notes that Weld had been a founder member of the Society of the Friends of the People and a member of the Friends of the Liberty of the Press, and had died of an apoplectic fit in December 1799. "Booksellers in the Godwin Diaries," 31.

58. For brief details of Towers's life, see the website *Dissenting Academies Online*, accessed January 3, 2022, http://www.english.qmul.ac.uk/drwilliams/portal.html.

59. Holcroft and Towers had been together at meetings at the Society for Constitutional Information on 7 December 1792 and 28 March 1794. Howell, *State Trials*, 24:529, 561.

60. William Godwin, *Enquiry Concerning Political Justice, and Its Influence on Morals and Happiness*, 3rd. edition, 2 vols. (London: G. G. and J. Robinson, 1798), 1:24.

61. Qtd. in H. N. Brailsford, *Shelley, Godwin, and Their Circle*, 31–32. Brailsford does not cite the source for this comment.

62. Earlier in 1798 Erskine had published a long essay in the *Monthly Magazine* on the subject of the House of Commons, acknowledging the progress achieved over the centuries, but still concluding with a warning for each citizen that "while he pays the tribute of duty and obedience to government, he may know when the reciprocal duty is paid back to the public and himself." *Monthly Magazine* 5 (April 1798), 252.

63. John Pinkerton (1758–1826) was a Scottish poet and historian. He is frequently mentioned in Holcroft's diary, and Holcroft seems to have had a very amicable relationship with him. They occasionally dined together.

64. There was a financial exchange here as well. According to this account, Dr. Gillies had offered to give up a one-hundred-pound yearly annuity from Lord Hopetour, (to whom he had formerly been tutor) if the lord would intervene with his friend Lord Henry Dundas to procure for Gillies the post.

65. James Mackintosh, *Memoirs of the Life of Sir James Mackintosh Edited [from His Letters and Journal] by His Son*, 2 vols. (London: 1835), 1:125, qtd. in Marshall, *William Godwin*, 222.

66. Godwin's diary indicates seven occasions between the years 1792 and 1796 in which Holcroft met socially with Mackintosh, for dinner, supper, or tea (GD).

67. For a discussion of Mackintosh's lectures and their wider effect, see Marshall, 222–224.

68. For an account of Walker's trial and the events leading up to it see Barrell, *Imagining the King's Death*, 170–181.

69. Johnston, 185. Holcroft was also critical of Wakefield, writing in the diary on 22 February 1799: "Argued at Debrett's against the immorality of invective, for which I consider Gilbert Wakefield as very blamable." *Life*: 2:247.

70. Thomas Pakenham, *The Year of Liberty: The Story of the Great Irish Rebellion of 1798* (1969); rpt. (London: Panther Books, 1972). For Wexford as a revolutionary republic, see especially 214–220.

71. Pakenham, 267.

72. General Lake responded with severity to the rebel forces once he had succeeded in recapturing Wexford, and he had most of their leaders executed. Pakenham, 292–294, 306–308. He later suffered a humiliating defeat during the French invasion of Connaught when he retreated with his troops at Castlebar on 29 August.

73. For example, Holcroft mentions the execution of the Sheares brothers, the respite given to the republican Oliver Bond, and the rumors that the latter, along with the O'Connor brothers, had informed against the rebellion. *Life*, 2: 152, 166, 170.

74. Coigley himself stated at his arraignment, "My real name, my Lords, is James Coigley, not James O'Coigley." [John Fenwick], *A Plain Narrative of Facts Respecting the Trial of James Coigley; Including His Letter to an Irish Gentleman, in London and A. Young's Letter to G. Lloyd* (London: 1798), 3. This pamphlet should not be confused with Fenwick's longer work, *Observations on the Trial of James Coigly, for High Treason . . . To Which Is Added an Appendix, Containing an Interesting Correspondence, Relative to the Trial . . . and Also Letters Written by Mr. Coigly, etc . . .* (London:1798).

75. Pakenham, 147–148; Dáire Keogh, "An Unfortunate Man: James Coigly, 1761–1798," *History Ireland* 6:2 (Summer 1998), 27–32.

76. These meetings took place on 2 March 1796, 10 March 1796, 22 May 1796 (GD).

77. Holcroft's diary records many meetings with John and Eliza Fenwick, who were in a distressed financial situation. He wrote on behalf of Fenwick to the publisher Robinson and advanced him £3 on one occasion. See, for example, *Life*, 2: 192, 193. Later he would help Eliza Fenwick, after her separation from her husband.

78. Fenwick, *Plain Narrative*, 4.

79. Fenwick, *Plain Narrative*, 4. The writer of this loyalist letter is identified simply as "A. Young." Fenwick, as writer and compiler of the text, must have known his identity, as implied at the conclusion of the letter, where he adds, "The Father of the Author of this Letter says that it was written as a piece of pleasantry. Good God! Is Man's life to be sported with in this manner?" 5.

80. Stuart Semmel, *Napoleon and the British* (New Haven and London: Yale University Press, 2004), 21.

81. Simon Bainbridge, *Napoleon and English Romanticism*, (Cambridge: Cambridge University Press, 1995), 35.

82. Bainbridge, 32. Although apparently relying on Holcroft's diary, Bainbridge does not give a direct source for this mention of Holcroft.

83. Barrell, *Imagining the King's Death*, 523.

84. The political implications of the focus on de Barboza were noted by Trumbull, who wrote to Thomas Jefferson that "there are people here [in London] foolish enough to be half affronted that I have paid so much compliment to the Spanish officer." John Trumbull to Thomas Jefferson, 29 May 1789. Manuscript / Mixed Material. *The Thomas Jefferson Papers*, Library of Congress, accessed January 3, 2022, http://hdl.loc.gov/loc.mss/mtj .mtjbib004305.

85. The advertisements for *The Inquisitor* boasted of "new scenes, dresses and decorations." *Morning Post*, 23 June 1798.

86. Thomas Holcroft, *The Inquisitor* (London: 1798), 74.

87. *The Monthly Mirror*, 6 (July 1798), 50.

88. Following the second performance, the *Oracle and Public Advertiser* wrote that "the reception [of the play] was more gracious than on Saturday, and with some alterations, may greatly increase its public estimation." 26 June 1798. This optimistic view was not realized, and the play ended its run with the third performance.

89. Jacky Bratton, "Romantic Melodrama," in *The Cambridge Companion to British Theatre 1730–1830*, 115–127, 121.

90. Paula Backscheider, "Reflections on the Importance of Romantic Drama," *Texas Studies in Language and Literature*, 41:4 (Winter1999), 311–329, 312. Backscheider focuses in this

essay on the 1797–1798 theater season in London; *The Inquisitor* appeared at the end of that season, in the summer repertoire of the Haymarket. In her book *The Gothic Ideology: Religious Hysteria and Anti-Catholicism in British Popular Fiction* (Cardiff: University of Wales Press, 2014), Diane Long Hoeveler uses a quotation from *The Inquisitor* as an epigraph to her chapter, "Inquisitions, Autos-de-Fé, and Bloody Tribunals," although she does not, in what then follows, discuss Holcroft's play. "Inquisitions,"147.

91. John Stoddart, a lawyer, a writer, a former disciple of Godwin, and later a brother-in-law of Hazlitt, often met Holcroft socially along with Godwin and others in the latter half of the 1790s (GD).

92. Perry's frankness with Holcroft results from the long acquaintance between the men. They had met as actors in the provincial company of Joseph Booth during the 1770s. Perry left acting, and in London, he first edited the *European Magazine* and then purchased the *Morning Chronicle*, which became identified with the Whigs. Thomas L. Ashton, "Peter Parker in Perry's Paper: Two Unpublished Byron Letters," *Keats-Shelley Journal* 18 (1969), 49–59, 53.

93. These plays were *The School for Arrogance, The Deserted Daughter, The Man of Ten Thousand,* and *Knave, or Not?*; the novels were *Anna St. Ives* and *Hugh Trevor.* The diary does not report any further financial transactions between the two men.

94. For a brilliant discussion of authorship, anonymity, publishing, and copyright in the eighteenth century, see Robert J, Griffin, "Anonymity and Authorship," *New Literary History* 30:4 (Autumn 1999), 877–895.

95. David Worrall, *Celebrity, Performance, Reception.* For Worrall's presentation of these issues as relevant to *The Inquisitor,* see especially his Introduction.

96. Godwin does not mention his reading of "The Old Cloathsman" in his diary. He saw the play on 2 April (GD).

97. This song was entitled "When Sharp Is the Frost," LA 1242, 3.

98. The first two quotations come from the *Courier and Evening Gazette,* 3 April 1799. The third and fourth come from the *Oracle and Daily Advertiser* of the same date. As if to reinforce the comments of the *Oracle,* the score of one song from the opera, "Dan Cupid They Say Is a Bold Little Boy," was published separately, with the understanding that there was a market for the song to be played and sung in private performance.

99. The journal was *La Decade Philosophique, Littéraire et Politique.* Holcroft recorded other points of criticism of *Hugh Trevor* that the journal's reviewer made and his own assessment of that criticism in parentheses: "the plan proposed is incomplete (true), that some of the conversations are too long (true), that my satire on professions is unfounded (false), that I have not put my morality sufficiently in action (false again, the law part excepted), that probability is not quite enough regarded (perhaps not)." Holcroft copied out the journal's concluding remarks, which most certainly would have pleased him: "En un mot, [*Hugh Trevor* est] l'ouvrage d'un penseur, d'un homme de talent, d'un observateur habile et exercisé, d'un ami de mœurs, et de la vertu; disons encore d'un écrivain patriote, hardi défenseur des droits sacrés du peuple." (*Life,* 2:239). The lengthy and detailed review of *Hugh Trevor* appears in *La Decade Philosophique, Littéraire et Politique* (L'An 7, Vendémiaire, Brumaire, Frimaire), 462–475.

100. *The True Briton,* 3 April 1799.

101. Thomas Dibdin, *The Reminiscences of Thomas Dibdin of the Theatres Royal, Covent Garden, Drury Lane, Haymarket &c., in Two Volumes* (London: 1827) 1:243. Brandon was a fairly important figure in Harris's theater operations. See Oakley, *Thomas (Jupiter) Harris,* especially 27–29, where Brandon's loyalty to Harris but also his general unscrupulousness are shown.

102. Dibdin, 1:248.

103. Dibdin, 1:248–249.

104. To appreciate Holcroft's relatively secure position as a playwright, it is useful to compare his career to the unfortunate experiences of William Godwin in his efforts to have his

dramatic work accepted by the patent theaters. In Pamela Clemit's edition of *The Letters of William Godwin, Volume II* (1798–1805), we can view Godwin's ongoing attempts to negotiate with the theater managers, efforts which concluded in one much-maligned performance of *Antonio* (1800) and literally years of delay before the eventual staging of *Faulkener* (1807).

105. Thomas Holcroft, *Hear Both Sides* (London: 1803), "Preface."

106. Letter from Thomas Holcroft to William Godwin, 19 July 1799, The Abinger Papers, Oxford, Bodleian Libraries, MS Abinger, c.4, f.125–126. The note from Godwin in which he had expressed this opinion does not survive. It had been included in a parcel in which Godwin had sent the manuscript for volume II of Godwin's novel *St. Leon*. The novel would be published on 2 December 1799.

107. Gregory Maertz, in *Literature and the Cult of Personality: Essays on Goethe and His Influence*, (Stuttgart: ibidem-Verlag, 2017), discusses Holcroft as a translator from German and acknowledges Holcroft's place within a wider Anglo-German exchange. Maertz suggests that the translation of *Hermann und Dorothea* served for Holcroft as an "exercise in centering himself in a foreign otherness." *Literature and the Cult of Personality*, 44.

108. Pamela Clemit notes that "letters between men rarely have the intensity or duration of binary exchanges," as does the correspondence of women. "Letters and Journals," *The Oxford Handbook of British Romanticism*, ed. David Duff (Oxford: Oxford University Press, 2018), 418–433, 424. Still, there are a few intense emotional moments in the epistolary exchange between Holcroft and Godwin such as one that Godwin writes soon after Holcroft's departure from England: "I bear you the highest regard; I think of you continually; I felt the loss of you an irreparable one." Godwin to Holcroft, 13 September 1799, Clemit, *Letters*, 2:95.

109. Bernard Bray, "Letters: General Survey," trans. Monique Lamontagne, in *Encyclopedia of Life Writing*, ed. Margaretta Jolly, 2:552.

110. Clemit, "Letters and Journals," 429.

111. These numbers refer to the letters held in the Abinger collection at the Bodleian Library. While there are Holcroft holograph letters to other recipients in other archives, such as the British Library and the New York Public Library, it is highly likely that all surviving correspondence between Holcroft and Godwin is housed in the Abinger collection.

112. Letter from Thomas Holcroft to William Godwin, 1 April 1800, The Abinger Papers, Oxford, Bodleian Libraries, MS Abinger c.4, f.100–101.

113. Letter from Thomas Holcroft to William Godwin, 1 April 1800, The Abinger Papers, Oxford, Bodleian Libraries, MS Abinger, c..4, f.100–101.

114. Letter from William Godwin to Thomas Holcroft, 2 May 1800, The Abinger Papers, Oxford, Bodleian Libraries, MS Abinger c.4, f. 104; reproduced in Clemit, 2: 137.

115. Letter from Thomas Holcroft to William Godwin, 11 February 1800, The Abinger Papers, Oxford, Bodleian Libraries, MS Abinger c.4, f. 85.

116. These were *Mémoires secrets sur la Russie* by Charles François Philibert Masson, *Le Collatéral* by Louis-Benôit Picard, and *Reise von Amsterdam über Madrid und Cadiz nach Genoa in den Jahren 1797 und 1798* by Christian August Fischer. The idea for the German-English dictionary was Holcroft's own. *The Mémoires* were first mentioned on 27 May, *Le Collatéral*, on 29 April, Fischer's *Reise*, on 1 April, and the idea for the dictionary on 3 June.

117. These appeared in English as *Secret Memoirs of the Court of St. Petersburg, Particularly towards the End of the Reign of Catherine II and the Commencement of That of Paul I* (1801), and *Travels in Spain in 1797 and 1798* (1802). The names of the respective translators do not appear.

118. For a brief survey of culture in Hamburg at the turn of the nineteenth century, see Matthew Jeffries, *Hamburg: A Cultural History* (Northampton, MA: Interlink Books, 2011), especially the Introduction and Chapter One. The Wordsworths were in the city in the autumn of 1798, a little less than a year before Holcroft. Not knowing German,

they were particularly unhappy there. Lucy Newlyn, *William and Dorothy Wordsworth: All in Each Other* (Oxford: Oxford University Press, 2013), Chapter Four.

119. Letter from Thomas Holcroft to William Godwin, 24 October 1800, The Abinger Papers, Oxford, Bodleian Libraries, MS Abinger c.6, f. 61.

120. Letter from Thomas Holcroft to William Godwin, 24 October 1800, The Abinger Papers, Oxford, Bodleian Libraries, MS Abinger c.6, f. 61.

121. *The Times*, 26 January 1802. Joseph Fouché was Napoleon's Minister of Police.

122. The £266.6 were the earnings from "The Escapes" (actually listed in the Covent Garden account books as £266.10.). British Library, MS. Egerton 2299, f 85, f.97. The play ran for twelve nights. He had also received £200 as advance payment. The relatively low earnings (even with the advance) result from the fact that afterpieces were, in Judith Milhous's words, "very scantily compensated." Milhous, "Reading Theatre History from Account Books," 125.

123. Letter from Thomas Holcroft to William Godwin, 1 January 1802, The Abinger Papers, Oxford, Bodleian Libraries, MS Abinger c.7, f. 80–81.

124. Letter from Thomas Holcroft to Godwin, 17 February 1802, The Abinger Papers, Oxford, Bodleian Libraries, MS Abinger c.7, f.91–92.

125. *The Journals of Claire Clairmont*, ed. Marion Kingston Stocking (Cambridge, MA: Harvard University Press, 1968), 125–126. For another account of this story, see Janet Todd, *Daughters of Ireland*, 288–289.

126. For Ashley, see E. P. Thompson, *The Making of the English Working Class*, 173. Holcroft had gone to Ashley to order a pair of boots, as indicated in his letter to Godwin of 27 May 1802. The Abinger Papers, Oxford, Bodleian Libraries, MS Abinger c. 7, f. 126–127. While in the shop, Ashley tells Holcroft a long and complex story that underscores some of the intrigues within the British expat community.

127. This breakfast gathering is noted by John Keane in *Tom Paine: A Political Life*, 449–450.

CHAPTER 5 — HOLCROFT'S MELODRAMA

1. Not all of Holcroft's offerings, however, were successful. In a letter of 29 April 1800 from Hamburg, he boasted to Godwin of his translation and adaptation of Louis-Benoît Picard's play *Le Collatéral*, which he aimed for the Haymarket, the play being "of that light kind which [he supposed] best calculated for that Place." The play was not accepted, and no further trace of this adaptation remains. Letter from Thomas Holcroft to William Godwin, 29 April 1800, The Abinger Papers, Oxford, Bodleian Libraries, MS Abinger c.4, f.119.

2. Holcroft's return to Britain can be dated to mid-September 1802. *A Tale of Mystery* premiered on 13 November that year. Although, as Elbridge Colby notes, Charles Lamb had written to a friend on 24 September 1802 that "Holcroft [had] not yet come to town," it appears that he actually had. He had called on Godwin on 16 September, when Godwin was out of town. They finally met on 19 September, when Godwin called on the Holcrofts in the morning, and they dined at his house later that day. *Life*, 2:298; GD.

3. Rohan McWilliam, "Melodrama and the Historians," *Radical History Review* 78 (Fall 2000), 57–84, 57.

4. *Report from the Select Committee on Dramatic Literature, with the Minutes of Evidence: Ordered, by the House of Commons, to Be Printed, 2 August 1832*, (London: 1832), 182.

5. "Melodrama," *All the Year Round* 21 (9 November 1878), 436–442, 436. The author of this piece is not named.

6. "Melodrama," 440. It was only in 1843 that Parliament implemented the proposals of the Select Committee of 1832.The reference here to playbills as key mediators in this cultural development—the "birth" of melodrama—underscores Gillian Russell's understanding of the power of playbills to record "the immediacy and significance of the theatrical event

in both social and cultural life"; of how they are "expressive of the power of print and its related information networks." Gillian Russell, *The Playbill and Its People* (Canberra: National Library of Australia, 2011), ix.

7. Jane Moody, *Illegitimate Theatre in London*; Katherine Newey, "Reform on the London Stage."

8. David Mayer, "Encountering Melodrama," 146. Mayer refers to melodrama's "vitality" and mutability; the fact that it "continues to this very day in motion pictures, indifferent to criticism and objection," 146.

9. Simon Shepherd, "Melodrama," *English Drama: A Cultural History*, ed. Simon Shepherd and Peter Womack (Oxford: Blackwell, 1996), 188–218, 190.

10. Peter Mortensen, "Robbing *the Robbers*: Schiller, Xenophobia and the Politics of British Romantic Translation," *Literature and History* 11:1 (May 2002), 41–61; Paula R. Backscheider, "Reflections on the Importance of Romantic Drama."

11. Frederick Reynolds, *The Life and Times of Frederick Reynolds*, 2 vols. (London: 1826), 2: 346. This interchange is mentioned in Shepherd, 194, 218n.

12. Peter Brooks, *The Melodramatic Imagination*, 15.

13. Wylie Sypher, "Aesthetic of Revolution: The Marxist Melodrama," *The Kenyon Review*, 10:3 (Summer 1948), 431–444, 431.

14. Brooks mentions Holcroft only in passing, when acknowledging *A Tale of Mystery* as a French import, 89. His argument regarding the birth of melodrama focuses solely on French examples of the genre. Later he does, of course, expand upon the adaptation of this modality by British authors such as Dickens and Henry James.

15. Louis James, "Taking Melodrama Seriously: Theatre, and Nineteenth-Century Studies," *History Workshop Journal* 3 (Spring 1977), 151–158, 152.

16. Elaine Hadley, *Melodramatic Tactics: Theatricalized Dissent in the English Marketplace, 1800–1885* (Stanford: Stanford University Press, 1995), 3.

17. James, "Taking Melodrama Seriously," 152.

18. Mayer, 146; Hadley, 3.

19. Mayer, 148.

20. See, for example, Louis James, "Was Jerrold's *Black Ey'd Susan* More Popular than Wordsworth's Lucy?" in *Performance and Politics in Popular Drama*, ed. David Bradby, Louis James, and Bernard Sharratt (Cambridge: Cambridge University Press, 1980), 3–15. James compares the "simple guilt and innocence of *A Tale of Mystery*" to the more sophisticated psychological treatment of the issue in Dion Boucicault's *The Corsican Brothers* (1852) and Leopold Lewis's *The Bells* (1871), 14.

21. James, "Jerrold's Black Ey'd Susan," 14.

22. Coleridge made these remarks in his discussion of Charles Maturin's melodrama, *Bertram* (1816) in the *Biographia Literaria* (1817), quoted in George Erving, "Coleridge as Playwright," in *The Oxford Handbook of Samuel Taylor Coleridge*, ed. Frederick Burwick, (Oxford: Oxford University Press, 2009), 392–411, 403.

23. Juliet Johns, *Dickens's Villains: Melodrama, Character, Popular Culture* (Oxford: Oxford University Press, 2003), 46.

24. Walter Scott, "Essay on the Drama," *Supplement to the Encyclopedia Britannica* (1819), quoted in Mayer, 154.

25. For discussions of, and identifications in, "The Monster Melodrama," see Moody, 55, and Michael Kilgarriff, *The Golden Age of Melodrama* (London: Wolfe Publishing, 1974), 12–13.

26. Moody, 55.

27. It is interesting to note that *Deaf and Dumb* has transcended its original moment and is now viewed as a resource on deafness. Copies of the play are held in dedicated collections on deaf education, in the Farrar Deaf Education Collection at Rylands Library at the University of Manchester and in the Gallaudet Deaf Rare Materials Collection at Gallaudet University in Washington DC. Just as this book was going to press, Terry F. Robinson's essay, "Deaf Education and the Rise of English Melodrama" was published

in *Essays in Romanticism* 29:1 (Spring 2022), 1–31. As her title indicates, Robinson examines the connection in depth.

28. Holcroft had written to Godwin from Hamburg on 13 May 1800: "I mean to make an attempt on Covent Garden with the Abbé de L'Epée and on Drury Lane with an alteration of the Lawyer." Letter from Thomas Holcroft to William Godwin, 13 May 1800, The Abinger Papers, Oxford, Bodleian Libraries, MS Abinger c.5, f.126–127. In the event, both of these plays ("The Lawyer" renamed as *Hear Both Sides*) were eventually performed at Drury Lane. Holcroft wrote to Godwin of Harris's rejection on 2 September 1800. The Abinger Papers, Oxford, Bodleian Libraries, MS Abinger c.6, f.40.

29. Godwin to Holcroft, 6 March, 1801. Clemit, 2:215–216. Godwin's attendance is noted in GD: 24 February 1801, 23 March 1801.

30. *The Morning Chronicle*, 25 February 1801. In the preface to the printed edition, Holcroft sets the matter straight by stating that his play is adapted from Bouilly, while noting that "it has since had the honour to be translated into German by the celebrated Kotzebue." Thomas Holcroft, *Deaf and Dumb* (London: 1801), v. Benjamin Thompson translated Kotzebue's version into English and included it in Volume 3 of his six-volume work, *The German Theatre* (London: 1801).

31. Frederick Burwick, *Romantic Drama,* 37; Patrick McDonagh, "The Mute's Voice: The Dramatic Transformations of the Mute and Deaf-Mute in Early Nineteenth-Century France," *Criticism* 55:4 (Fall 2013), 655–675, 655.

32. This young woman was called Clemence in Bouilly's play, while the name Marianne was given to a former servant.

33. Letter from Thomas Holcroft to William Godwin, 24 October 1800. The Abinger Papers, Oxford, Bodleian Libraries, MS Abinger c 6, f.60–61.

34. Moody, 89.

35. Holcroft himself had noted in his prefatory remarks that the character of Darlemont, and still more of Dupré, are "brought more forward in the canvas than they were by the original author." v.

36. Thomas Holcroft, *Deaf and Dumb, or the Orphan Protected* (London: 1801), 69. Further references will be cited in the text as DD.

37. Brooks, 60.

38. Moody, 62.

39. Shepherd presents a compelling discussion of the mute, of Julio's "shriek," and of that register of utterance in general in his "Melodrama," 199–200.

40. A discussion of Kelly and his work appears in Burwick, *Romantic Drama*, Chapter Eight.

41. This song is catalogued in the British Library as *The Favourite Song in . . . Deaf and Dumb, or the Orphan Protected. Sung by Mrs Mountain . . . Written by G. M. [sic] Lewis, with Accompaniments for the Harp or Piano Forte* (London: 1801).

42. Margaret Ross Griffel, *Operas in English: A Dictionary* (Lanham, MD: Scarecrow Press, 2012), 155.

43. The score was published as Thomas Attwood, *The Escapes, or the Water Carrier: A Favorite Musical Entertainment, as Now Performing with the Greatest Applause at the Theatre Royal Covent Garden* (London: 1801).

44. See, for example, Allardyce Nicoll, *A History of English Drama*, 2nd ed, 6 vols. (1952), 6: 142, (V.6). Theodore Fenner, *Opera in London: Views of the Press, 1785–1830* (Carbondale: Southern Illinois University Press, 1994), 642. Griffel also identifies it as such. 155. Genest writes that this play "was said to have been written by [Holcroft]." 7:549.

45. Letter from Thomas Holcroft to William Godwin, 1 January 1802. The Abinger Papers, Oxford, Bodleian Libraries, MS Abinger c. 7, f. 80–81.

46. Covent Garden Account Books, MS. Egerton 2299, f. 85, f.97. The information on Holcroft's earnings from "The Escapes" is also quoted in Patricia Sigl, "Mrs. Inchbald's *Egyptian Boy*," *Theatre Notebook*, 43:2 (1989), 57–68, 67, n.

47. Thomas Dibdin, *Reminiscences*, 1:326.

48. Dibdin, 1: 313.
49. C. B. Oldman, "Attwood's Dramatic Works," *The Musical Times*, 107 (January 1966), 23–26, 25.
50. Dibdin, 1: 248.
51. Thomas Holcroft, "The Escapes," LA 1332, 22. Further references will be cited in the text as E.
52. Edward J. Dent, *The Rise of Romantic Opera*, ed. Winton Dean (Cambridge: Cambridge University Press, 1976), 82–83.
53. Thomas Holcroft, *Love's Frailties* (London: 1794), 73.
54. Some of the marked passages are merely chunks of text that have been crossed out but then recopied on the following page.
55. J. N. Bouilly, *Les Deux Journées, Comédie Lyrique, en trios actes* (Paris: An XI [1802]), 27.
56. Dent, 85.
57. A CD recording of the opera was released as recently as 2002 by the Chorus Musicus Köln and Das Neue Orchester. Notable twentieth-century performances include a production of the opera in London with the Royal Philharmonic Orchestra in 1947 and a performance in 1950 at Carnegie Hall. The London production is available to listen to on YouTube, accessed January 6, 2022. https://www.youtube.com/watch?v=Hr9Y9xaDMnE
58. David Charlton, "On Redefinitions of 'Rescue Opera'," *Music and the French Revolution*, ed. Malcolm Boyd (Cambridge: Cambridge University Press, 1992), 169–188, 183. See also Anthony Arblaster, *Viva La Libertà!: Politics in Opera* (London: Verso, 1997). Arblaster emphasizes the "disinterested idealism" vested in the benevolent action of the rescue in Bouilly's opera. 48.
59. Stephen Meyer, "Terror and Transcendence in the Operatic Prison, 1790–1815," *Journal of the American Musicological Society* 55:3 (Fall 2002), 477–523. See especially 487–488. For the rescue opera's investment in the gothic, see also Charlton.
60. At the same time, the relations between the working-class savior and the aristocrats in *Les Deux Journées* were capacious enough to invite varying interpretations: mutual benevolence between the classes which overrides class distinctions, or, in contrast, the rescue of innocent aristocrats that would create sympathy for them by reminding the audience of the events of the Reign of Terror. Arblaster, 48–49.
61. Arblaster, 48.
62. For a detailed discussion of the links between gothic and melodrama, see Diego Saglia, "'I Almost Dread to Tell You': Gothic Melodrama and the Aesthetic of Silence in Thomas Holcroft's *A Tale of Mystery*," *Gothic Studies* 14:1 (May 2012), 93–107.
63. René Charles Guilbert de Pixérécourt, *Coelina, ou L'Enfant du Mystère* (Paris, 1800), "L'homme vertueux punit, mais il n'assassine pas." 51.
64. Pixérécourt, 51.
65. Moody, 90.
66. Thomas Holcroft, *A Tale of Mystery*, 2nd ed. (London: 1802), 35. Further references will be cited in the text as TM.
67. Diane Long Hoeveler, "The Temple of Morality," 59. Hoeveler argues that it is this positioning of Fiametta as the voice of "moral and social authority" which makes *A Tale of Mystery* truly revolutionary. We saw in Chapter Three Hoeveler's argument for female authority in *The Deserted Daughter*.
68. Thomas Holcroft, "A Tale of Mystery," LA 1361.
69. Cox, *Romanticism in the Shadow of War*, 41. There are no censorial interventions in the manuscript, unlike in many other Holcroft plays.
70. Cox, 43–45. The quotation appears at 42.
71. Cox, 47, 48.
72. Mark Philp, "Introduction," *An Enquiry Concerning Political Justice*, xxxii.
73. Godwin, *Enquiry*, 300.

74. Moody, 91.
75. Holcroft, *Love's Frailties*, 66, 73.
76. Holcroft, *Knave, or Not?*, 43.
77. Godwin, *Enquiry*, 54.
78. On 15 August 1800 Holcroft wrote to Godwin, "I have not yet told you nor can I at present tell, how nobly Clementi has behaved to me: but you and more than you shall some day hear." Letter from Thomas Holcroft to William Godwin. The Abinger Papers, Oxford, Bodleian Libraries, MS Abinger c6, f.31.
79. The full review of Mrs. Murray's book appears in *The Annual Review and History of Literature* (January 1803), 402–408. References to her text are from the extracts that appear in the *Annual Review*.
80. Thomas Holcroft, *The Lady of the Rock* (London: 1805), iv. Further references will be cited in the text as LR. The quotation appears in the *Annual Review* on 405.
81. *The European Magazine* 47 (1805), 134.
82. *The Anti-Jacobin Review* 21 (1805), 106.
83. The manuscript version of the play contains a more extended version of the child's speech. It is very likely that her speeches had appeared thus onstage in the first performance and were later curtailed following the criticism. Holcroft once again in this play uses his practice of inverted commas to indicate what had been omitted in representation, but there is no such punctuation here in reference to the child, and her words were not returned to the printed version.
84. *Annual Review* (January 1803), 405.
85. John Adolphus, the biographer of the actor John Bannister, notes that the fisherman, played by Bannister, was "the real hero" of the work. *The Memoirs of John Bannister,* 2:132.
86. The *Lady of the Rock* was briefly recalled to public attention in a biographical account of Baillie that appeared following her death in 1851 in the *Dublin University Magazine* (37). The similarities and differences between the Holcroft's play and Baillie's were not expanded upon, although it was noted that Baillie "appears to have been entirely ignorant" of Holcroft's melodrama. 531.
87. Mieke O'Halloran, "National Discourse or Discord? Transformations of *The Family Legend* by Baillie, Scott and Hogg," in *James Hogg and the Literary Marketplace: Scottish Romanticism and the Working-Class Author*, ed. Sharon-Ruth Alker and Holly Faith Nelson (Farnham: Ashgate, 2009), 43–56, 43. O'Halloran stresses Walter Scott's influential role in the production of Baillie's play. He had written the prologue which (with Henry Mackenzie's epilogue) helped further frame the drama through a vision of British unity. 47–48.
88. Joanna Baillie, *The Family Legend*, 2nd ed. (Edinburgh: 1810), 49.
89. O'Halloran, 43. Although the play was generally well received, Dorothy McMillan notes that the Mclean clan was "offended with Miss Baillie's representation of their ancestor." "Unromantic Caledon: Representing Scotland in *The Family Legend*, *Metrical Legends*, and *Witchcraft*," in *Joanna Baillie, Romantic Dramatist*, ed. Thomas C. Crochunis (London and New York: Routledge, 2004), 69–86, 78.
90. James Hogg, "A Horrible Instance of the Effects of Clanship," *Blackwood's Edinburgh Magazine* (October 1830), 680–687. Hogg changed the names of the characters. Instead of being left to die on the rock, Hogg has his heroine, Julia M'Kenzie, thrown from a high bridge.
91. Simon Shepherd, "The Unacceptable Face of the Theatre," in *English Drama: A Cultural History*, ed. Simon Shepherd and Peter Womack, 219–248, 219.

CHAPTER 6 — FINAL YEARS AND OTHER AFTERLIVES

1. Webster, "Re-Writing Shylock," 83. The use of accent as a comic device could also obviously signal entrenched prejudice. Holcroft uses this means with many ethnicities, for example with Scots dialect in *The Deserted Daughter*.

2. Thomas Holcroft, *Travels from Hamburg, through Westphalia, Holland, and the Netherlands to Paris*, 2 vols. (London: 1804) 1:70.
3. Thomas Holcroft, *The Vindictive Man*, 2nd ed. (London: 1807), 29. Further references will be cited in the text as VM.
4. Charles Lamb to Thomas Manning, 5 December 1806, *The Letters of Charles and Mary Anne Lamb*, 2: 245. All references to the Lamb letters will come from this edition unless otherwise stated and henceforth cited in the text as Lamb, with volume and page numbers.
5. If De Camp in fact did not return to the stage that evening, the audience would have missed his break with Anson (it is not clear in any case why this respectable banker would keep Goldfinch as a friend, his professed loyalty to Anson's father notwithstanding) and other important plot developments.
6. Records of Drury Lane Theatre for *The Vindictive Man*, 20–21 November 1806. Folger MS, W.b.310 Folger Shakespeare Library, Washington, DC.
7. Eliza Fenwick wrote of the matter to Mary Hays on 23 December 1806 in a section of the letter regarding her daughter's theatrical training: "Had Holcroft's play [*The Vindictive Man*] succeeded he, who entertains sanguine expectations of her success, would gladly have aided me, but now that is impossible." *The Fate of the Fenwicks, Letters to Mary Hays (1798–1828)*, ed. A. F. Wedd (London: Methuen, 1927), 19.
8. Jon Mee, "Treason, Seditious Libel, and Literature in the Romantic Period," *Oxford Handbooks Online*), 12, accessed January 7, 2022, https://www.oxfordhandbooks.com/view/10.1093/oxfordhb/9780199935338.001.0001/oxfordhb-9780199935338-e-113.
9. Holcroft, *Love's Frailties*, 66.
10. Thomas Holcroft, *The Adventures of Hugh Trevor* (1794–1797), ed. Seamus Deane (Oxford: Oxford University Press, 1978), 494. Further quotations from the novel come from this edition and cited in the text as HT.
11. Brian Rigby, "Stendhal and the English Jacobin novelist Thomas Holcroft," in *Stendhal en l'Angleterre, Proceedings of the London Colloquium, French Institute*, ed. K. G. McWatters and C. W. Thompson, (Liverpool: Liverpool University Press, 1983), 191–210, 203, 199. Rigby notes Stendhal's familiarity with late eighteenth-century British political thought, particularly regarding 1794. 203–4.
12. Godwin, *Enquiry Concerning Political Justice*, 3rd. edition, 1:24; NF, 3–4.
13. Anne Chandler, "Holcroft and the Art of Sinking in Poetry," in *Re-Viewing Thomas Holcroft*, 31–49, 40. Chandler uses the term "shabby genteel" to describe Wilmot, but it is appropriate for all three friends. In a different analysis from the one I present here, Chandler questions "Gaffer Gray's" relevance to the novel, writing that the poem "allegorizes nothing in the novel's plot, except, vaguely, the hypocrisy of privilege." 41.
14. Chandler, 41.
15. *The Gentleman's Magazine*, 64:2 (July 1794), 653; *The Annual Register* 36 (1794), 414; *The Town and Country Magazine* 26 (July 1794), 307); *The Scots Magazine* 56 (September 1794), 546. "The Perjured Lover" had appeared in *Hugh Trevor*, Volume III, Ch. 7 (a chapter before "Gaffer Gray") and was ostensibly written by Belmont, the villain of the novel, whose misdeeds are unknown to Hugh at this point.
16. Mitford, *Recollections of a Literary Life*, 1: 131.
17. Chandler, 40.
18. There were editions of the poem set to music published by J. Dale (1794), G. Goulding (1795), and one called "Gaffer Gray, a Scotch song," published by Bland & Weller (1795).
19. *Five Excellent New Songs* (London: 1795); *The Yorkshire Musical Miscellany, comprising an elegant selection of the most admired songs in the English language* (Halifax: 1800), "Preface," n.p.
20. G. Goulding (c.1795).
21. *John Thelwall: Selected Poetry and Poetics*, ed. Judith Thompson (New York: Palgrave Macmillan, 2015), 178. Thelwall's generous praise here is nonetheless accompanied by the

terse assertion that Holcroft was a "sour, cold and laborious man, misanthropic in his feelings and visionary in his notions." Writing in 1822, Thelwall makes no mention of his and Holcroft's shared status as defendants in the Treason Trials. He had attended Holcroft's funeral in 1809.

22. This score is located at the Gilmore Music Library of Yale University, MSS NO Misc. 365, Series no I, Box 1, fol. 2. It was published in both New York and Philadelphia in 1856. I am very grateful to Richard Boursy for calling my attention to this piece and for his kind assistance when I visited the Yale Music Library.

23. Many years earlier, the poem had appeared in America in the poetry section of the *Monthly Anthology and Boston Review* 4 (April 1807), where it was called a "celebrated ballad," and *The Adventures of Hugh Trevor*, a "valuable work." 196.

24. The epigraph, "And little think the gay licentious proud / Whom pleasure, power, and affluence surround, / How many pine in want!" is adapted from James Thomson, *The Seasons*, "Winter." 322–323; 332.

25. Brian Alderson notes the Godwins' use of the copperplate technique, of which "Gaffer Gray" was but one example, and its role in developing a new kind of aesthetics in the production of children's literature. The Juvenile Library's copperplate books thus exhibited "a new kind of elegant picture book," as well as a more sophisticated "interplay of picture and text" than what had come before. "'Mr. Gobwin' and His 'Interesting Little Books, Adorned with Beautiful Copper Plates,'" *Princeton University Library Chronicle*, 59:2 (Winter 1998), 159–189, 172.

26. Clemit, 2: xxxix. The following year, 1807, Mulready would illustrate one of the Juvenile Library's most notable publications, Charles and Mary Lamb's *Tales from Shakespeare*. In 1843 the pioneer industrial designer Henry Cole wrote in his diary, "In the Evg reading Nursery Rhymes and life of Mulready written by Godwin . . . also looking at his Gaffer Gray, Little Old Woman . . . He said that for the Little Old Woman and Gaffer Gray Godwin had never paid him anything though he was poor at the time." Quoted in Geoffrey Summerfield, "The Making of the Home Treasury," *Children's Literature* 8 (1980), 35–52, 39–40.

27. Matthew Grenby, "Politicizing the Nursery: British Children's Literature and the French Revolution," *The Lion and the Unicorn* 27:1 (January 2003), 1–26, 1.

28. Pamela Clemit, "Philosophical Anarchism in the Schoolroom: William Godwin's Juvenile Library, 1805–25," *Biblion: The Bulletin of the New York Public Library* 9: nos. 1–2 (Fall 2000–Spring 2001), 44–70, 48.

29. Robert Anderson, "Godwin Disguised: Politics in the Juvenile Library," *Godwinian Moments: From the Enlightenment to Romanticism*, ed. Victoria Myers and Robert Maniquis (Toronto: University of Toronto Press, 2011), 125–146, 130.

30. William Frederic Mylius, *The Poetical Class-Book: Reading Lessons for Every Day in the Year, Selected from the Most Popular English Poets, Ancient and Modern* (London: 1810), iii.

31. [Arethusa] Hall, *A Literary Reader, for Academies and High Schools consisting of selections in prose and verse, from American, English and other foreign literature, chronologically arranged* (Boston: 1850), v.

32. Robert Chambers, *Cyclopedia of English Literature: A Selection of the Choicest Productions of English Authors, from the Earliest to the Present Time*, 2 vols. (Boston: 1851), ii, 546.

33. Alderson, 172.

34. Holcroft, *Travels from Hamburg*, 1:42.

35. The *Monthly Review* writes that in the *Travels* Holcroft is "always alert, intelligent, and . . . conscientious. He strives . . . to paint with accuracy the scenes which presented themselves to his observations, and to render his narrative morally impressive as well as amusing." *Monthly Review* 45 (1804), 113–126, 113–14. Other, slightly less favorable reviews appeared in the *Edinburgh Review* 4 (1804), 84–99, and *The Critical Review*, 3rd ser. (1804) 1: 84–99, 2:153–164.

36. Sophy Cole and her husband resided in Hamburg; Holcroft was in close contact with them there. Ann was married to Captain (later Colonel) William Harwood, who, like Thomas Holcroft, had been a member of the Society for Constitutional Information. The names and birth dates of his younger children appear in the Introduction and below.

37. Letter from Thomas Holcroft to William Godwin, 1 January 1802. The Abinger Papers, Oxford, Bodleian Libraries, MS Abinger c.7, f. 80–81.

38. [Fanny Holcroft] Letter from Thomas Holcroft to William Godwin, 1 March 1802. The Abinger Papers, Oxford, Bodleian Libraries, MS Abinger c.7, f. 95–6.

39. In responding to Godwin's question on the subject of the marriage, Holcroft wrote briefly that the young man was "not what his letters appeared to paint him." Letter from Thomas Holcroft to William Godwin, 1 January 1802. The Abinger Papers, Oxford, Bodleian Libraries, c.7, f. 80–81.

40. Godwin to Holcroft, 3 September 1803. Clemit, 2: 280.

41. Clemit, 2:281, 281, n.

42. GD, note to entry of 24 November 1803. The editors base their speculation on the fact that twice—24 November and 1 December, one week later—Mary Jane had visited both Lane (presumably the reference is to William Lane, the publisher at the Minerva Press) and the Holcrofts.

43. Julie Carlson, "On Literary Fractures," *The Wordsworth Circle* 42:2 (Spring 2011), 129–138, 133.

44. There was already an ongoing tension between the two men. On 1 January 1805 Godwin had written to Holcroft, hurt that the latter had drunk to the health of three other friends the preceding Sunday at dinner and not to him. Holcroft replied the following day, denying any intentions of insult; rather the men he had toasted had saved his life through their medical attentions. Clemit, 2:331. Despite the clarification, the reciprocal visits slackened off in January and February, with only three meetings, one of which in took place in large company (GD 15 January, 20 January, 15 February 1805).

45. Godwin wrote to Marshall on 28 February, "I protest to you that, if I meant any body in the character, I meant myself . . . I was sometimes harsh to Tom Cooper & Tom Cooper fell into a decline." Clemit, 2:339. Thomas Abthorpe Cooper was a young relation of Godwin's, who lived with him for a time in the 1790s. He became an actor and later emigrated to the United States, where he had a very successful career.

46. Carlson, "On Literary Fractures," 131.

47. William Austin, *Letters from London: Written During the Years 1802 & 1803* (Boston: 1804), 204.

48. For the first meeting, see Letter from Thomas Holcroft to William Godwin, 21 January 1802. The Abinger Papers, Oxford, Bodleian Libraries, MS Abinger, c.7, f. 80–81. The reference appeared in an addendum to a letter begun on 1 January, and then continued. Holcroft mentions Tuthill's support over the *Times* affair on 17 February 1802. c.7, f. 91–92. Manning had liked and esteemed Holcroft from those initial encounters in Paris, and continued throughout the years to inquire about him, his wife, and daughter. See *The Letters of Thomas Manning to Charles Lamb*, ed. G. A. Anderson (London: Martin Secker 1925), 62, 81, 95, 101.

49. *The Critical Review* 5th series, 3 (May 1816), 435.

50. *The Fate of the Fenwicks*, 16.

51. Godwin's financial problems have been well documented. A brief overview of his situation in the first years of the nineteenth century appears in St. Clair, *The Godwins and the Shelleys*, 287–292. In spite of his distressed finances, Godwin gave money to William Nicholson, his and Holcroft's mutual friend, who was imprisoned at this time for failing to make bail and who would later die in poverty. St. Clair, 290. This same ethos of financial aid and mutual support which prevailed among this circle, even when the giver himself or herself was economically distressed, is evident in Holcroft's support—or wish to support—Eliza Fenwick, as well as in the efforts of the committee set up to aid his family after his death.

52. *Fate of the Fenwicks*, 54. This letter is dated simply December 1811, with no day stated.

53. Joseph Cottle, *Reminiscences of Samuel Taylor Coleridge and Robert Southey*, 2nd ed. (London: 1848), 331.

54. As St. Clair writes, "Mrs. Fenwick worked in Godwin's shop six days in the week . . . [and] went without food all day . . . since there was no fire in the shop, she suffered badly from the cold." 290. Fenwick eventually followed her daughter, who had gone to work for a theater in Barbados. She later moved to New York, dying there in 1840. For an excellent recent discussion of Fenwick's life, see Jamie Rosenthal, "From Radical Feminist to Caribbean Slaveowner: Eliza Fenwick's Barbados Letters," *Eighteenth-Century Studies* 52:1 (Fall 2018), 47–68.

55. On 22 March, Godwin writes, "na"—his abbreviation for "not at home"—next to the record of this visit; he probably was not permitted to see the dying man.

56. Church of England Parish Registers 1538–1812, London, England. London Metropolitan Archives. P89 / MRY1 / 012, accessed January 7, 2022, via https://www.ancestry.co.uk. These children are Villiers, Henry, Harwood, Thomas, Louisa, and Ellen.

57. Cottle mentions a social gathering in which the Holcrofts and Coleridge were present and in which religion and atheism were discussed. After Coleridge stressed the idea of early religious education, Louisa Holcroft replied that "she was quite surprised at Mr. Coleridge talking in that way before her, when he knew that herself and Mr. Holcroft were atheists." Cottle, 331. This incident is included in *Life*: 1:xliv–xlv. Cottle continues his criticism by including another comment from Coleridge about Holcroft, where he blamed his—Holcroft's—strict parenting for William Holcroft's suicide. 332.

58. London Metropolitan Archives, London, England. P89/MRY1/315, accessed January 7, 2022, via https://www.ancestry.co.uk.

59. Julie Rugg and Brian Parsons, *Funerary Practices in England and Wales* (Emerald Publishing: Bingley, UK: 2018), 6.

60. Thomas Laqueur, "Bodies, Deaths and Pauper Funerals," *Representations* 1 (February 1983), 109–131, 114, 126.

61. *Morning Post*, 27 March 1809.

62. This article, unsigned, is titled, "An Account of the Late Mr. Thomas Holcroft, Author of *The Road to Ruin*, etc . . . ," *Monthly Magazine* 27 (May 1809), 358–9. Evidence for Godwin's authorship (besides internal evidence showing a close familiarity between the subject of the article and the writer) appears in his diary notations for 6, 10, and 12 April 1809, where he wrote, "Ht," and the number of pages written.

63. *Monthly Magazine* 27 (1809), 358.

64. *Monthly Magazine* 27 (1809), 359.

65. St. Clair, 130–133.

66. *Monthly Magazine* 27 (1809), 359.

67. Johnston, *Unusual Suspects*, 13–14.

68. Henry Crabb Robinson, *Reminiscences*, entry listed for "March 1809." Robinson wrote the entry many years later, on 21 August 1848.

69. St. Clair, 305.

70. Henry Crabb Robinson, *Reminiscences*, HCR Correspondence, 1809–17, letter 15.

71. Jon Mee, *Print, Publicity, and Popular Radicalism*, 75.

72. Dibdin, *Reminiscences*, 1: 248.

73. British Library MSS, Royal Literary Fund, RLF Loan 96 1/230. With parts of the typed letter very similarly worded to the conclusion of the Godwin obituary in the *Monthly Magazine*, it is possible that this text was sent to Dibdin, with the request for it to be submitted along with his own handwritten application. There is, however, no mention of Dibdin in GD in this context.

74. I am grateful to Matthew Sangster, cataloguer of the RLF archive, for explaining to me the significance of the amount of money given to the Holcroft family.

75. Henry Crabb Robinson, *Reminiscences*, entry for 4 April 1812.

76. Moira Ferguson includes Fanny's "The Negro" in the tradition of British women's anti-slavery writing. Regarding the poem specifically, she argues that the first person narration in the poem "endows the slave protagonist with enhanced awareness," although he still remains a "non-threatening, emasculated slave." Moira Ferguson, *Subject to Others: British Women Writers and Colonial Slavery, 1670–1834* (New York: Routledge, 1992), 240.

77. Andrew Ashfield, ed. *Romantic Women Poets, 1788–1848*, Volume 2 (Manchester: Manchester University Press, 1998), 87–95.

78. The advertisement announcing publication of the canzonet appears in *The Repository of Arts, Literature, Fashions, Manufacturers, &c*, Second Series, 5:25 (January 1818), 108.

79. These include *Philip the Second* from the Italian of Vittorio Alfieri, *From Bad to Worse*, from the Spanish of Calderon de la Barca, and both *Emilia Galotti* and *Minna von Barnhelm* from the German of Gotthold Lessing.

80. Frederick Burwick, *A History of Romantic Literature* (Hoboken, NJ: Wiley-Blackwell, 2019), 205. See also Maertz, *Literature and the Cult of Personality*, Chapter One.

81. There are two manuscript copies of the play extant, slightly differing. One is held in the collection of the Lord Chamberlain's Plays at the British Library, and the other is held in the Chawton House Library. The Chawton manuscript is catalogued as C1380; the Lord Chamberlain's copy, in a different hand, is at the British Library, Add MS 42885, ff.150-182b. It was submitted to the censor on 18 August 1827. Evidence for the run at the Haymarket comes from Ransom. The play was misattributed to Louisa Holcroft, in a review of the play from 24 August 1827. The Godwin Diary also attributes the play to Louisa, in the notation of Godwin's attendance at the play on 23 August 1827. However, the name "Fanny Holcroft" appears in the manuscript from the Lord Chamberlain's Plays, as well as in the Chawton manuscript. Louisa Holcroft is not known to have written professionally.

82. Fanny Holcroft to Henry Colburn, 17 December 1814. British Library Add MS 78687 Vol. DXX, Letter 60, f. 102v. This is a collection of manuscript letters by women collected by William Upcott. Among the women whose letters appear are Elizabeth Inchbald, Mary Wollstonecraft, Mary Hays, Lady Caroline Lamb, and Felicia Hemans, to mention a few. Fanny's second, better-known novel, *Fortitude and Frailty* was published by W. Clowes, a firm that would become one of Britain's largest publishers. Henry Colburn, too, was an important publisher of the first half of the nineteenth century, publishing works by authors such as Lady Caroline Lamb, Charles Maturin, and Sydney Owenson (Lady Morgan) (ODNB).

83. Brenda Niall, *Georgiana: A Biography of Georgiana McCrae, Painter, Diarist, Pioneer* (Melbourne: Melbourne University Press at the Miegunyah Press, 1994), 18.

84. Niall, 19.

85. Niall, 19.

86. Thomas Holcroft, *Travels from Hamburg* 1:12.

87. Niall, 19.

88. Stocking, ed. *The Journals of Claire Clairmont*, 125.

89. Henry Crabb Robinson, *Reminiscences*, entry for 29 February 1824.

90. Jane Austen, *Emma*, ed. Ronald Blythe (New York: Penguin Books, 1985), 368. Robinson's reading of Austen is noted in Brian Southam, ed., *Jane Austen: The Critical Heritage*, 2 vols. Vol 1, 1811–1870 (London: Routledge, 1968), rpt. 1995, 85–86. Regarding *Emma*, Robinson noted the "silly chattering Miss Bates." 86.

91. *The Examiner*, 19 October 1844.

92. "Fanny Holcroft," in Susan Brown, Patricia Clements, and Isobel Grundy, eds., *Orlando: Women's Writing in the British Isles from the Beginnings to the Present*. Cambridge: Cambridge University Press, 2006, accessed January 7, 2022, http://orlando.cambridge.org.

93. Two possible results, both retrieved from the British Library India Office catalogue, tell somewhat different stories. One records a Villiers Holcroft, who died, a pauper, in 1835. The other notes just "V. Holcroft," who died in 1836, but states that this was the son of the author of "The Road to Ruin and other works."

94. Thomas Carlyle, a friend of John Badams, the husband of the younger Louisa Holcroft, writes in a letter of 18 May 1834 that "Mrs Badams, preparing to go to France to her Brother." Thomas Carlyle to John A. Carlyle. All quotations are taken from the website, *The Carlyle Letters Online [CLO]*. Ed. Brent E. Kinser, Duke University Press, 2007–2016, accessed January 7, 2022, https://www.carlyleletters.org. Further references will be cited in the text as CLO with the date of the letter and, if not noted earlier, the name of the recipient.

95. National Archives, USA, Microfilm #237, Rolls 13–18, accessed January 7, 2022, https://www.MyHeritage.co.il. No further information for him exists.

96. Ellen Holcroft's death was noted in *Galignani's Messenger* on 18 November 1825. This was a daily English-language newspaper published in Paris by the Italian publisher Giovanni Antonio Galignani. The Kenneys had moved back and forth between England and France during these years. They are mentioned as being in France in 1820 and 1822, appear in England (as evidenced in Godwin's diary) in 1823, and briefly in 1824 and 1825. The poet Thomas Moore noted in his diary that he saw Louisa a number of times, both while living in France (July–August 1820) and then following his return to Britain (July 1824). *Memoirs, Journal, and Correspondence of Thomas Moore*, ed. Lord John Russell, 8 vols. (London: 1853), 3: 127, 3: 136, 3: 334, 4: 221. Ellen's death in Versailles in November 1825 implies that her mother and stepfather were with her in France at that time.

97. Quoted in Kenneth J. Fielding, "John Badams," *The Carlyle Encyclopedia*, ed. Mark Cumming (Madison, NJ: Farleigh Dickinson University Press, 2004), 23.

98. Brief summaries of the life of Thomas Holcroft, Jr. appear in Edwin W. Marrs, ed., *The Letters of Charles and Mary Lamb* 2:249, n2 and in *Carlyle Letters Online*.

99. *The Times*, 4 November 1847.

100. *Punch*, vols. 12–13 (1847), 189.

101. *John Bull*, 14 February 1852; *Lloyd's Weekly Newspaper* 15 February 1852.

102. Gillian Russell and Clara Tuite, "Introduction," *Romantic Sociability*, 4.

MANUSCRIPT COLLECTIONS

The Abinger Papers. Oxford. Bodleian Libraries.
MSS Abinger.
c.1 fol.100
c.4, f. 85; f.100–101; f. 104; f.119; f.125–6
c.5, 126–7
c.6, f.31; f.40; f. 60–61;
c.7, f. 80–81; f.91–2; f. 95–6.; f. 126–7
Chawton House Library MSS.
Church of England Parish Registers 1538–1812. London. London Metropolitan Archives.
Covent Garden Account Books. British Library. Add MSS 29949.
Evelyn Papers. Vols. DXIX–DXXII. "Original Letters collected by William Upcott of the London Institution. Distinguished Women." British Library. Add MS 78687.
Gabrielle Enthoven Collection of the Theatre and Performance Archives at the Victoria and Albert Museum, London.
John Larpent's Plays. The Huntington Library. San Marino, California, USA.
LA 935 ("The Road to Ruin")
LA 1008 ("Love's Frailties")
LA 1077 ("Tis a Strange World [The Deserted Daughter]")
LA 1192 ("Knave, or Not?")
LA 1242 ("The Old Cloathsman")
LA 1332 ("The Escapes")
LA 1361 ("A Tale of Mystery")
LA 1423 ("The Lady of the Rock")
Lord Chamberlain's Plays. Vol. XXI. Add MSS 42885. British Library. (Fanny Holcroft, "The Goldsmith")
Playbills from Theaters in York, England. Lewis Walpole Library.
Records of Drury Lane Theatre. Folger Shakespeare Library. Washington, DC.
MSS Royal Literary Fund. British Library.

PRE-TWENTIETH-CENTURY NEWSPAPERS AND PERIODICALS

Newspapers (place of publication United Kingdom unless indicated otherwise)

The Anti-Jacobin Weekly
9 July 1798
The Argus (Australia)
11 October 1913
Birmingham Daily Post
26 May 1871
The Courier and Evening Gazette
3 April 1799
The Diary, or Woodfall's Register
3 March 1792

The Era
25 August 1872
2 November 1873
The Examiner
19 October 1844
Galignani's Messenger (France)
18 November 1825
Geelong Advertiser and Intelligencer (Australia)
26 October 1853

General Evening Post
18 February 1792
The Illustrated Weekly News
30 November 1889
John Bull
14 February 1852
The Leader (Australia)
24 March 1888
Lloyd's Evening Post
22 January 1796
Lloyd's Weekly Newspaper
15 February 1852
The London Chronicle
1–3 December 1789
1 March 1792
25–27 January 1798
27–30 January 1798
The London Recorder, or Sunday Gazette
26 February 1792
Morning Bulletin (Australia)
22 July 1915
The Morning Chronicle
20 February 1792
8 October 1794
26 January 1798
25 February 1801
The Morning Post
2 December 1794
26 January 1798
23 June 1798
27 March 1809
3 November 1819
Oriental Observer and Literary Chronicle
    (India)
7 October 1837
Pall Mall Gazette
18 November 1880
The Public Advertiser (from March 1794 the
    Oracle and Public Advertiser; from
    September 1798 *Oracle and Daily
    Advertiser*)
20 February 1792
17 February 1794
4 May 1795

12 October 1796
26 January 1798
26 June 1798
11 July 1798
3 April 1799
St. James Chronicle
21 February 1792
6 February 1794
7 October 1794
2 December 1794
*Saturday Review of Politics, Literature, Science
    and Art*
22 Dec 1883
The Star
26 January 1796
The Sun
26 January 1798
The Times
15 February 1794
26 January 1802
4 November 1847
11 February 1867
21 November 1880 (*Sunday Times*)
Tomahawk, or Censor General
6 February 1796
11 February 1796
The Tribune [John Thelwall]
4 April 1795
The True Briton
30 January 1793
1 February 1793
25 January 1796
26 January 1798
27 February 1799
3 April 1799
Whitehall Evening Post
28 November 1789
15–18 February 1794
2–5 May 1795
28–30 May 1795
The World
6 February 1794
17 February 1794

Periodicals
The Academy (4:1873); (31:1887)
The Analytical Review (13:1792); (22:1796)
The Annual Register (36:1794)
The Annual Review and History of Literature (2:1803)
The Anti-Jacobin Review (1:1798); (21:1805)
The British Critic (6:1795)

The Boy's Halfpenny Journal (11:1879)
The Critical Review (n. s. 4:1792); (ser. 3.1: 1804); 1 (ser.5.3:1816);
La Decade Philosophique, Littéraire et Politique (L'An 7, Vendémiaire, Brumaire, Frimaire [1798–1799]
Dublin University Magazine 37 (1851)
Edinburgh Review 4 (1804)
The European Magazine (1:1782); (25:1794); (47:1805)
The Gentleman's Magazine (64:1794); (86:1816)
Monthly Anthology and Boston Review (4:1807) (United States)
Monthly Magazine (5:1798); (27:1809)
Monthly Mirror (6:1798)
Monthly Review (8:1792); (10:1793); (13:1794); (17:1795); (19:1796); (45:1804)
The Pocket Magazine, or Elegant Repository of Useful and Polite Literature. 1794–1796
Punch (12–13:1847)
The Repository of Arts, Literature, Fashions, Manufacturers, &c. Second Series. 5:1818.
The Scots Magazine (56:1794)
The Theatrical Inquisitor and Monthly Mirror (9:1816)
The Town and Country Magazine (26:1794)
The Universal Magazine (98:1796)

WEBSITES

BBC Radio Times (Genome). https://genome.ch.bbc.co.uk/years/1949.
Birmingham Mail Online. http://www.birminghammail.co.uk.
British Film Institute. http://www.bfi.org.uk/.
Carlyle, Thomas, and Jane Welsh Carlyle. *The Carlyle Letters Online* [*CLO*]. Edited by
    Brent E. Kinser. Duke University Press. 2007–2016. www.carlyleletters.org.
The Diary of William Godwin, edited by Victoria Myers, David O'Shaughnessy, and Mark
    Philp. Oxford: Oxford Digital Library, 2010. http://godwindiary.bodleian.ox.ac.uk.
Dissenting Academies Online. http://www.english.qmul.ac.uk/drwilliams/portal.html.
London Metropolitan Archives. Church of England Parish Registers, via https://www
    .ancestry.co.uk.
London Playbills and Programs Collection. Harry Ransom Center. University of Texas at
    Austin. https://norman.hrc.utexas.edu/playbills.
London Walks. https://www.londonguidedwalks.co.uk.
National Archives, USA. Microfilm #237. Rolls 13–18. https://www.archives.gov/research
    /immigration/port/new-york.html.
Orlando: Women's Writing in the British Isles from the Beginnings to the Present. Edited by
    Susan Brown, Patricia Clements, and Isobel Grundy. http://orlando.cambridge.org/.
Thomas Jefferson Papers. Washington: Library of Congress. http://hdl.loc.gov/loc.mss/mtj
    .mtjbib004305.

PRE-TWENTIETH-CENTURY BOOKS AND ESSAYS

Adolphus, John. *Memoirs of John Bannister.* 2 vols. London: 1839.
Austen, Jane. *Emma.* (1816). Edited by Ronald Blythe. New York: Penguin Books, 1985.
Austin, William. *Letters from London: Written During the Years 1802 & 1803.* Boston: 1804.
Baillie, Joanna. *The Family Legend.* 2nd ed. Edinburgh: 1810.
Beazley, Samuel. *The Steward, or Fashion and Feeling.* London: 1819.
Bisset, Robert. *The Historical, Biographical, Literary, and Scientific Magazine.* 3 vols. London:
    1800.
Bouilly, J. N. *Les Deux Journées, Comédie Lyrique, en trios actes.* Paris: An XI [1802].
Brightwell, Cecilia Lucy. *Memorials of the Life of Amelia Opie.* London and Norwich: 1854.

Burke, Edmund. *Reflections on the Revolution in France* (1790). Edited by J.G.A. Pocock. Indianapolis and Cambridge: Hackett Publishing Company, 1987.

Chambers, Robert. *Cyclopedia of English Literature: A Selection of the Choicest Productions of English Authors, from the Earliest to the Present Time.* 2 vols. Boston: 1851.

Cottle, Joseph. *Reminiscences of Samuel Taylor Coleridge and Robert Southey.* 2nd ed. London: 1848.

Craik, George L. *The Pursuit of Knowledge Under Difficulties, Illustrated by Anecdotes.* 2 vols. London: 1830.

Dibdin, Thomas. *The Reminiscences of Thomas Dibdin of the Theatres Royal, Covent Garden, Drury Lane, Haymarket &c., in Two Volumes.* London: 1827.

Eliot, George. *Middlemarch* (1871–2). Edited by W. J. Harvey. Harmondsworth, UK: Penguin Books, 1965.

[Fenwick, John]. *A Plain Narrative of Facts Respecting the Trial of James Coigley; Including His Letter to an Irish Gentleman, in London and A. Young's Letter to G. Lloyd.* London: 1798.

Five Excellent New Songs. London: 1795.

Gaffer Gray: or, the Misfortunes of Poverty, A Christmas Ditty Very Fit to be Chanted at Whitsuntide. London: The Juvenile Library, 1806. Reprinted 1816, 1823.

Genest, John. *Some Account of the English Stage, from the Restoration in 1660 to 1830.* 10 vols. Bath: 1832.

Godwin, William. *An Enquiry Concerning Political Justice* (1793). Edited by Mark Philp. Oxford: Oxford University Press, 2013.

———. 3rd edition. 2 vols. London: G. G. and J. Robinson, 1798.

———. *Caleb Williams, or Things As They Are* (1794). Edited by Pamela Clemit. Oxford: Oxford University Press, 2009.

———. "Of Choice in Reading." *The Enquirer: Reflections on Education, Manners and Literature in a Series of Essays.* London: 1797.

———. *Thoughts Occasioned by the Perusal of Dr. Parr's Spital Sermon, Preached at Christ Church, April 15, 1800: Being a Reply to the Attacks of Dr. Parr, Mr. Mackintosh, the Author of an Essay on Population, and Others.* London: 1801.

Hall, [Arethusa]. *A Literary Reader, for Academies and High Schools Consisting of Selections in Prose and Verse, from American, English and Other Foreign Literature, Chronologically Arranged.* Boston: 1850.

The History of Two Acts. London: 1796.

"Ho, Why Dost Thou Shiver. Gaffer Gray. A Favorite Ballad Sung at All the Principal Concerts." London: 1795.

Hogg, James. "A Horrible Instance of the Effects of Clanship." *Blackwood's Edinburgh Magazine,* October 1830, 680–687.

Holcroft, Fanny. "The Negro." *Monthly Magazine,* 4 (October 1797), 286.

Holcroft, Thomas. *The Adventures of Hugh Trevor.* 6 vols. London: 1794–1797. Edited by Seamus Deane. Oxford: Oxford University Press, 1978.

———. *Deaf and Dumb.* London: 1801.

———. *The Deserted Daughter.* London: 1795.

———. *Duplicity.* London: 1782.

———. *Elegies.* I. "On the Death of Samuel Foote." II—"On Age." London: 1777.

———. *Hear Both Sides.* London: 1803.

———. *He's Much to Blame.* London: 1798.

———. *The Inquisitor.* London: 1798.

———. *Knave, or Not?* London: 1798.

———. *The Lady of the Rock.* London: 1805.

———. *A Letter to the Right Honourable William Windham on the Intemperance and Dangerous Tendency of his Public Conduct.* London: 1795.

————. *The Life of Thomas Holcroft, Written by Himself, Continued to the Time of His Death from His Diary Notes & Other papers by William Hazlitt, and Now Newly Edited with Introduction and Notes by Elbridge Colby.* In two volumes. (1925). Reprint, New York: Benjamin Blom. 1968.

————. *Love's Frailties.* London: 1794.

————. *The Man of Ten Thousand.* London: 1796.

————. *Memoirs of Bryan Perdue* 3 vols. London: 1805.

————. *Memoirs of the Late Thomas Holcroft, Written by Himself and Continued to the Time of His Death, from His diary, Notes, and Other Papers.* Edited by William Hazlitt. London: 1816.

————. Reprint, London: Travellers Library, 1852.

————. *Narrative of Facts Relating to a Prosecution for High Treason.* London: 1795.

————. *The Road to Ruin.* 1792.

————. *The Road to Ruin.* Reprint, *Lacy's Acting Edition of Plays*, 42. London: 1823.

————. *A Tale of Mystery.* London: 1802.

————. *Travels from Hamburg, through Westphalia, Holland, and the Netherlands to Paris.* 2 vols. London: 1804.

————. *The Vindictive Man.* London: 1806.

Howell, Thomas J., ed. *A Complete Collection of State Trials and Proceedings for High Treason and Other Crimes and Misdemeanors.* 33 vols. London: 1818.

Inchbald, Elizabeth. *Remarks for The British Theatre* (1806–1809). Delmar, NY: Scholars Facsimiles and Reprints, 1990.

Lamb, Charles. "On the Acting of Munden." *Essays of Elia, To Which Are Added Letters, and Rosamund, A Tale.* Paris: Baudry's European Library, 1835.

Mackintosh, James. *Memoirs of the Life of Sir James Mackintosh Edited [from His Letters and Journal] by His Son.* 2 vols. London: 1835.

Mathias, Thomas J. *The Pursuits of Literature . . . A Satirical Poem.* 4th ed. London: 1798.

————. *The Grove, a Satire by the Author of the Pursuits of Literature, with Notes, including Various Anecdotes of the King.* London: 1798.

"Melodrama." *All the Year Round* 21 (9 November 1878): 436–442.

Mitford, Mary Russell. *Recollections of a Literary Life: or Books, Places and People.* 3 vols. London: 1852.

Mylius, William Frederic. *The Poetical Class-Book: Reading Lessons for Every Day in the Year, Selected from the Most Popular English Poets, Ancient and Modern.* London: 1810.

Paine, Thomas. *Rights of Man, Common Sense and Other Political Writings.* (1791, 1792). Edited by Mark Philp. Oxford: Oxford University Press, 1995.

Paul, Charles Kegan. *William Godwin: His Friends and Contemporaries.* 2 vols. London: S. King, 1876.

The Picture of London, for 1802; Being a Correct Guide to All the Curiosities, Amusements, Exhibitions, Public Establishments, and Remarkable Objects, in and near London; with a Collection of Appropriate Tables. London: 1802.

Pigott, Charles. *A Political Dictionary: Explaining the True Meaning of Words.* London: 1795.

de Pixérécourt, René Charles Guilbert. *Coelina, ou L'Enfant du Mystère.* Paris: 1800.

Report from the Select Committee on Dramatic Literature, with the Minutes of Evidence: Ordered, by the House of Commons, to be Printed, 2 August 1832. London: 1832.

Reynolds, Frederick. *The Life and Times of Frederick Reynolds.* 2 vols. London: 1826.

Russell, Lord John, ed. *Memoirs, Journal, and Correspondence of Thomas Moore.* 8 vols. London: 1853.

Scott, Walter. "Essay on the Drama." *Supplement to the Encyclopedia Britannica.* 1819.

Seilhamer, George O. *The History of the American Theatre: New Foundations.* 3 vols. Philadelphia: 1891.

Thelwall, John. *Selected Poetry and Poetics.* Edited by Judith Thompson. New York: Springer, 2015.

Whelan, Timothy, and James Vigus, eds. *Henry Crabb Robinson's Diary, Reminiscences, and Correspondence* (forthcoming). Cited by permission of the Director and Trustees of Dr. Williams's Library, London, and the Crabb Robinson Project, School of English and Drama, Queen Mary University of London.

The Yorkshire Musical Miscellany, Comprising an Elegant Selection of the Most Admired Songs in the English language. Halifax, UK: 1800.

TWENTIETH-CENTURY AND TWENTY-FIRST-CENTURY BOOKS AND ESSAYS

Alderson, Brian. "'Mr. Gobwin' and His 'Interesting Little Books, Adorned with Beautiful Copper Plates.'" *Princeton University Library Chronicle* 59, no. 2 (Winter 1998): 159–189.

Anderson, G. A., ed. *The Letters of Thomas Manning to Charles Lamb.* London: Martin Secker, 1925.

Anderson, Robert. "Godwin Disguised: Politics in the Juvenile Library." In *Godwinian Moments: From the Enlightenment to Romanticism*, edited by Victoria Myers and Robert Maniquis, 125–146. Toronto: University of Toronto Press, 2011.

Arblaster, Anthony. *Viva La Libertà!: Politics in Opera.* London: Verso, 1997.

Ashfield, Andrew, ed. *Romantic Women Poets, 1788–1848.* 2 vols. Volume 2. Manchester: Manchester University Press, 1998.

Ashton, Thomas L. "Peter Parker in Perry's Paper: Two Unpublished Byron Letters." *Keats-Shelley Journal* 18 (1969): 49–59.

Auerbach, Nina. "Before the Curtain." In *The Cambridge Companion to Victorian and Edwardian Theatre*, edited by Kerry Powell, 3–14. Cambridge: Cambridge University Press, 2004.

Backscheider, Paula. "Reflections on the Importance of Romantic Drama." *Texas Studies in Language and Literature* 41, no. 4 (Winter 1999): 311–329.

Bainbridge, Simon. *Napoleon and English Romanticism.* Cambridge: Cambridge University Press, 1995.

Barrell, John. "Divided We Grow: When Pitt Panicked." *London Review of Books*, 5 June 2003.

———. *Imagining the King's Death.* Oxford: Oxford University Press, 2000.

———. "The Reptile Oculist." *London Review of Books*, 1 April 2004.

Barrell, John, and Jon Mee, eds. *Trials for Treason and Sedition.* 8 vols. London: Pickering and Chatto, 2006–7.

Behrendt, Stephen. "'I am not what I am': Staged Presence in Romantic Autobiography." In *Romantic Autobiography in England*, edited by Eugene Stelzig, 145–160. Burlington, VT: Ashgate, 2009.

Billington, Michael. "The Road to Ruin." *The Guardian*, 10 September 2002.

Black, Eugene Charlton. *The Association: British Extraparliamentary Political Organization, 1769–1793.* Cambridge, MA: Harvard University Press, 1963.

Blakemore, Steven. *Intertextual War: Edmund Burke and the French Revolution in the Writings of Mary Wollstonecraft, Thomas Paine, and James Mackintosh.* Madison, NJ: Farleigh Dickinson University Press, 1997.

Blunden, Edmund, ed. *Tragical Consequences or A Disaster at Deal.* London: Fytton Armstrong, 1931.

Boulton, James T. *The Language of Politics in the Age of Wilkes and Burke.* London: Routledge and Kegan Paul, 1963.

Brailsford, H. N. *Shelley, Godwin, and Their Circle.* 1913. Reprint, Hampden, CT: Archon Books, 1969.

Branson, Susan. *These Fiery Frenchified Dames: Women and Political Culture in Early National Philadelphia.* Philadelphia: University of Pennsylvania Press, 2001.

Bratton, Jacky. *New Readings in Theatre History.* Cambridge: Cambridge University Press, 2003.

———. "Romantic Melodrama." In *The Cambridge Companion to British Theatre 1730–1830*, edited by Jane Moody and Daniel O'Quinn, 115–127. Cambridge, Cambridge University Press, 2007.

Bray, Bernard. "Letters: General Survey." Translated by Monique Lamontagne. In *Encyclopedia of Life Writing: Autobiographical and Biographical Forms*, edited by Margaretta Jolly, 2: 551–553. 2 vols. Chicago: Fitzroy Dearborn Publishers, 2001.

Briggs, Asa. *A History of Longmans and Their Books 1724–1990: Longevity in Publishing*. London and New Castle, DE: The British Library and Oak Knoll Press, 2008.

Brooks, Peter. *The Melodramatic Imagination: Balzac, Henry James, Melodrama, and the Mode of Excess*. New Haven: Yale University Press, 1976.

Brown, Philip A. *The French Revolution in English History*. London: C. Lockwood, 1918.

Bugg, John. *Five Long Winters: The Trials of British Romanticism*. Stanford: Stanford University Press, 2014.

Burwick, Frederick. *A History of Romantic Literature*. (Hoboken, NJ: Wiley-Blackwell, 2019.

———. *Romantic Drama: Acting and Reacting*. Cambridge: Cambridge University Press, 2009.

Butler, Marilyn, ed. *Burke, Paine, Godwin, and the Revolutionary Controversy*. Cambridge: Cambridge University Press, 1984.

Butwin, Joseph M. "Seditious Laughter." *Radical History Review* 18 (Fall 1978): 17–34.

Carlson, Julie. "On Literary Fractures." *The Wordsworth Circle* 42, no. 2 (Spring 2011): 129–138.

———. "Race and Profit in English Theatre." In *The Cambridge Companion to British Theatre 1730–1830*, edited by Jane Moody and Daniel O'Quinn, 175–188. Cambridge: Cambridge University Press, 2007.

Chamberlain, Mary, and Paul Thompson. "Editors' Introduction." In *Narrative and Genre*, edited by Mary Chamberlain and Paul Thompson, 1–21. London and New York: Routledge, 1998.

Chandler, Anne. "Holcroft and the Art of Sinking in Poetry." In *Reviewing Thomas Holcroft, 1745–1809*, edited by Miriam L. Wallace and A. A. Markley, 31–49. Milton Park: Routledge, 2012.

Charlton, David. "On Redefinitions of 'Rescue Opera.'" In *Music and the French Revolution*, edited by Malcolm Boyd, 169–188. Cambridge: Cambridge University Press, 1992.

Clemit, Pamela. "Philosophical Anarchism in the Schoolroom: William Godwin's Juvenile Library, 1805–25." *Biblion: The Bulletin of the New York Public Library* 9, nos. 1–2 (Fall 2000–Spring 2001): 44–70.

———. Letters and Journals." In *The Oxford Handbook of British Romanticism*, edited by David Duff, 418–433. Oxford: Oxford University Press, 2018.

Clemit, Pamela, ed. *The Letters of William Godwin, Vol. I: 1778–1797* (Oxford: Oxford University Press, 2011); *The Letters of William Godwin, Vol. II: 1798–1805* (Oxford: Oxford University Press, 2014).

Colby, Elbridge. "Justice in Georgia." *The Nation*, 14 July 1926, 32–33.

———. "Thomas Holcroft, Radical." *The Mid-west Quarterly* 5, no. 1 (October 1917): 44–60.

Conolly, L. W. *The Censorship of English Drama 1737–1824*. San Marino, CA: Huntington Library Press, 1976.

Cottam, Rachel. "Diaries and Journals." In *Encyclopedia of Life Writing: Autobiographical and Biographical Forms*, edited by Margaretta Jolly, 1: 267–269. 2 vols. Chicago: Fitzroy Dearborn Publishers, 2001.

Cox, Jeffrey N. "Editor's Introduction." In vol. 5, *Slavery, Abolition, and Emancipation*, edited by Peter J. Kitson and Debbie Lee. London: Pickering and Chatto, 1999.

———. *Romanticism in the Shadow of War: Literary Culture in the Napoleonic War Years*. Cambridge: Cambridge University Press 2014.

Cox, Jeffrey, and Dana Van Kooy. "Melodramatic Slaves." *Modern Drama* 55, no. 4 (Winter 2012): 459–475.

Cox, Philip. "'Perfectly Harmless and Secure'?: The Political Contexts of Thomas Holcroft's *He's Much to Blame*." In *Re-Viewing Thomas Holcroft, 1745–1809: Essays on His Work and Life*, edited by A. A. Markley and Miriam L. Wallace, 87–101. Milton Park, Routledge, UK, 2012.

Cruse, Amy. *The Englishman and His Books*. London: Harrap, 1930.

Dent, Edward J. *The Rise of Romantic Opera*, edited by Winton Dean. Cambridge: Cambridge University Press, 1976.

Doll, Dan, and Jessica Munns. "Editors' Introduction." In *Recording and Reordering: Essays on the Seventeenth and Eighteenth Century Diary and Journal*, edited by Dan Doll and Jessica Munns, 9–21. Lewisburg: Bucknell University Press, 2006.

Dunford, Emma. "The Road to Ruin." *Reviewsgate*, 11 September 2002.

Durrell, Sue, ed. *The Life of William Nicholson 1753–1815 by His Son William Nicholson Junior*. London and Chicago: Peter Owen Publishers, 2018.

Edmondson, Ray, and Andrew Pike. *Australia's Lost Films: The Loss and Rescue of Australia's Silent Cinema*. Canberra: National Library of Australia, 1982.

Emsley, Clive. *British Society and the French Wars, 1793–1815*. London: Macmillan, 1979.

Endelman, Todd. "The Checkered Career of 'Jew' King: A Study in Anglo-Jewish Social History." *AJS Review* 7/8 (1982–83). 69–100.

Epstein, James. "'Equality and No King': Sociability and Sedition: The Case of John Frost." In *Romantic Sociability. Social Networks and Literary Culture in Britain 1770–1840*, edited by Gillian Russell and Clara Tuite, 43–61. Cambridge: Cambridge University Press, 2002.

Epstein, James, and David Karr. "Playing at Revolution: British 'Jacobin' Performance." *The Journal of Modern History* 79, no. 3 (September 2007): 495–530.

Erving, George. "Coleridge as Playwright." In *The Oxford Handbook of Samuel Taylor Coleridge*, edited by Frederick Burwick, 392–411. Oxford: Oxford University Press, 2009.

Fallon, David. "Booksellers in the Godwin Diaries." *Bodleian Library Record Journal* 24, no. 1 (April 2011): 25–34.

Fenner, Theodore. *Opera in London: Views of the Press, 1785–1830*. Carbondale: Southern Illinois University Press, 1994.

Fielding, Kenneth J. "John Badams." In *The Carlyle Encyclopedia*, edited by Mark Cumming. Madison, New Jersey: Farleigh Dickinson University Press, 2004.

Fyfe, Aileen. *Steam Powered Knowledge: William Chambers and the Business of Publishing, 1820–1860*. Chicago and London: The University of Chicago Press, 2012.

Garnai, Amy. *Revolutionary Imaginings in the 1790s: Charlotte Smith, Mary Robinson, Elizabeth Inchbald*. Basingstoke, UK: Palgrave, 2009.

Goodwin, Albert. *The Friends of Liberty: The English Democratic Movement in the Age of the French Revolution*. London: Hutchinson, 1979.

Green, Georgina. "John Thelwall Author of the Prologue to Thomas Holcroft's *Love's Frailties* (1794)?" *Notes and Queries* 55, no. 4 (December 2008); 422–24.

Gregory, Allene. *The French Revolution and the English Novel*. New York and London: The Knickerbocker Press, 1915.

Grenby, Matthew. "Politicizing the Nursery: British Children's Literature and the French Revolution." *The Lion and the Unicorn* 27, no. 1 (2003): 1–26.

Griffel, Margaret Ross. *Operas in English: A Dictionary*. Lanham, MD: Scarecrow Press, 2012.

Griffin, Robert. J. "Anonymity and Authorship." *New Literary History* 30, no. 4 (Autumn 1999): 877–895.

Guest, Harriet. *Unbounded Attachment: Sentiment and Politics in the Age of the French Revolution*. Oxford: Oxford University Press, 2013.

Hadley, Elaine. *Melodramatic Tactics: Theatricalized Dissent in the English Marketplace, 1800–1885*. Stanford: Stanford University Press, 1995.

Harper, George McLean. *William Wordsworth: His Life, Works and Influence*. 2 vols. New York: Russell & Russell, 1960.

Hattersley, Roy. *The Edwardians*. London: Hachette, 2004.

Hoeveler, Diane Long. *The Gothic Ideology: Religious Hysteria and Anti-Catholicism in British Popular Fiction*. Cardiff: University of Wales Press, 2014.

———. "The Temple of Morality: Thomas Holcroft and the Swerve of Melodrama." *European Romantic Review* 14, no. 1 (2003): 49–63.

Hogan, Charles Beecher, ed. *The London Stage, 1660–1800*. 5 vols. Carbondale: Southern Illinois University Press, 1968.

James, Louis. "Taking Melodrama Seriously: Theatre, and Nineteenth-Century Studies." *History Workshop Journal* 3 (Spring 1977): 151–158.

——— "Was Jerrold's *Black Ey'd Susan* More Popular than Wordsworth's Lucy?" In *Performance and Politics in Popular Drama*, edited by David Bradby, Louis James, and Bernard Sharratt, 3–15. Cambridge: Cambridge University Press, 1980.

Jeffries, Matthew. *Hamburg: A Cultural History*. Northampton, MA: Interlink Books, 2011.

Johns, Juliet. *Dickens's Villains: Melodrama, Character, Popular Culture*. Oxford: Oxford University Press, 2003.

Johnston, Kenneth R. *Unusual Suspects: Pitt's Reign of Alarm & the Lost Generation of the 1790s*. Oxford: Oxford University Press, 2013.

Karr, David "'Thoughts That Flash like Lightning': Thomas Holcroft, Radical Theater, and the Production of Meaning in 1790s London." *The Journal of British Studies* 40, no. 3 (July 2001): 324–56.

Keane, John. *Tom Paine: A Political Life*. Boston: Little, Brown and Co, 1995.

Keogh, Daire. "An Unfortunate Man: James Coigly, 1761–98." *History Ireland* 6, no. 2 (Summer 1998): 27–32.

Kilgarriff, Michael. *The Golden Age of Melodrama*. London: Wolfe Publishing, 1974.

King, Ronald F., and Elsie Begler. *Thomas Paine: Common Sense for the Modern Era*. San Diego: San Diego State University Press, 2007.

Koenig, Rhoda. "The Road to Ruin." *The Independent*, 18 September 2002.

Laqueur, Thomas. "Bodies, Deaths and Pauper Funerals." *Representations* 1 (February 1983): 109–131.

Lee, Hermione. "Virginia Woolf and Offence." In *The Art of Literary Biography*, edited by John Batchelor, 129–150. Oxford: Clarendon Press 1995.

Looser, Devoney. *Women Writers and Old Age in Britain, 1750–1850*. Baltimore: Johns Hopkins University Press, 2008.

MacCalman, Iain. "Newgate in Revolution: Radical Enthusiasm and Romantic Counterculture." *Eighteenth-Century Life* 22, no. 1 (February 1998): 95–110.

Maertz, Gregory. *Literature and the Cult of Personality: Essays on Goethe and His Influence*. Stuttgart: ibidem-Verlag, 2017.

Maniquis, Robert M., and Victoria Myers, eds. *Godwinian Moments: From Enlightenment to Romanticism*. Toronto: University of Toronto Press, 2011.

Markley, A. A. "Transforming Experience into Reform in Holcroft's Memoirs and Literary Works." In *Re-Viewing Thomas Holcroft, 1745–1809: Essays on His Work and Life*, edited by A. A. Markley and Miriam L. Wallace, 87–101. Routledge: Milton Park, UK, 2012.

Marrs, Edwin V., ed. *Letters of Charles and Mary Lamb*. 3 vols. Ithaca: Cornell University Press, 1976–78.

Marshall, Peter. *William Godwin*. New Haven and London: Yale University Press, 1984.

Mayer, David. "Encountering Melodrama." In *The Cambridge Companion to Victorian and Edwardian Theatre*, edited by Kerry Powell, 145–163. Cambridge: Cambridge University Press, 2004.

McCracken, David. "Hazlitt and a Case of Charitable Journalism." *Keats-Shelley Journal* 28 (1979): 26–27.

McDonagh, Patrick. "The Mute's Voice: The Dramatic Transformations of the Mute and Deaf-Mute in Early Nineteenth-Century France." *Criticism* 55, no. 4 (Fall 2013): 655–675.

McMillan, Dorothy. "Unromantic Caledon: Representing Scotland in *The Family Legend, Metrical Legends*, and *Witchcraft*." In *Joanna Baillie, Romantic Dramatist*, edited by Thomas C. Crochunis, 69–86. London and New York: Routledge, 2004.

McWilliam, Rohan. "Melodrama and the Historians." *Radical History Review* 78 (Fall 2000): 57–84.

Mee, Jon. *Conversable Worlds: Literature, Contention, and Community 1762 to 1830*. Oxford: Oxford University Press, 2011.

———. "'*The Magician No Conjuror*': Robert Merry and the Political Alchemy of the 1790s." In *Unrespectable Radicals? Popular Politics in the Age of Reform*, edited by Michael T. Davis and Paul Pickering, 41–55. Burlington, VT: Ashgate, 2008.

———. *Print, Publicity, and Popular Radicalism in the 1790s: The Laurel of Liberty*. Cambridge: Cambridge University Press, 2016.

———. "'Reciprocal Expressions of Kindness': Robert Merry, Della Cruscanism, and the Limits of Sociability." In *Romantic Sociability. Social Networks and Literary Culture in Britain 1770–1840*, edited by Gillian Russell and Clara Tuite, 104–122. Cambridge: Cambridge University Press, 2002.

———. "Treason, Seditious Libel, and Literature in the Romantic Period." *Oxford Handbooks Online*. Oxford: Oxford University Press, 2016. https://www.oxfordhandbooks.com/view /10.1093/oxfordhb/9780199935338.001.0001/oxfordhb-9780199935338-e-113?rskey =fvXOZO&result=8, accessed July 18, 2022.

———. "William Godwin's Moment." *Huntington Library Quarterly* 75, no. 1 (March 2012): 123–129.

Menhennet, A. "Drama Between Two Stools: Leisewitz's *Julius von Tarent* and von Gemmingen's *Der deutsche Hausvater*." *Oxford German Studies* 6, no. 1 (1971): 33–49.

Meyer, Stephen. "Terror and Transcendence in the Operatic Prison, 1790–1815." *Journal of the American Musicological Society* 55, no. 3 (Fall 2002): 477–523.

Milhous, Judith. "Reading Theatre History from Account Books." In *Players, Playwrights, Playhouses*, edited by Michael Cordner and Peter Holland, 101–131. Basingstoke: Palgrave Macmillan, 2007.

Moody, Jane. *Illegitimate Theatre in London, 1770–1840*. Cambridge: Cambridge University Press, 2000.

Morris, Marilyn. "Princely Debt, Public Credit, and Commercial Values in Late Georgian Britain." *Journal of British Studies* 43 (July 2004): 339–365.

Mortensen, Peter. "*Robbing the Robbers*: Schiller, Xenophobia, and the Politics of British Romantic Translation." *Literature and History* 11, no. 1 (May 2002): 41–61.

Mulcahy, Matthew. "Weathering the Storms: Hurricanes and Risk in the British Greater Caribbean." *The Business History Review* 78, no. 4 (Winter 2004): 635–663.

Newey, Katherine. "Reform on the London Stage." In *Rethinking the Age of Reform, Britain 1780–1850*, edited by Arthur Burns and Joanna Innes, 238–253. Cambridge: Cambridge University Press, 2003.

Newlyn, Lucy. *William and Dorothy Wordsworth: All in Each Other*. Oxford: Oxford University Press, 2013.

Niall, Brenda. *Georgiana: A Biography of Georgiana McCrae, Painter, Diarist, Pioneer*. Melbourne: Melbourne University Press at the Miegunyah Press, 1994.

Nicoll, Allardyce. *A History of Late Eighteenth-Century Drama, 1750–1800*. Cambridge: Cambridge University Press, 1927.

———. *A History of English Drama: 1660–1900*. Vol. 6. Cambridge: Cambridge University Press, 1952.

Nightingale, Benedict. "The Road to Ruin." *The Times*, 10 September 2002.

Oakley, Warren. *Thomas (Jupiter) Harris: Spinning Dark Intrigue at Covent Garden Theatre, 1767–1820*. Manchester: Manchester University Press, 2018.

O'Halloran, Mieke. "National Discourse or Discord? Transformations of *The Family Legend* by Baillie, Scott and Hogg." In *James Hogg and the Literary Marketplace: Scottish Romanticism and the Working-Class Author*, edited by Sharon-Ruth Alker and Holly Faith Nelson, 43–56. Farnham: Ashgate, 2009.

Oldman, C. B. "Attwood's Dramatic Works." *The Musical Times*. 107 (January 1966): 23–26.

Olivier, Laurence. *Confessions of an Actor*. New York: Simon and Schuster, 1982.

O'Shaughnessy, David. *William Godwin and the Theatre*. London: Routledge, 2015.

Pakenham, Thomas. *The Year of Liberty: The Story of the Great Irish Rebellion of 1798*. 1969. Reprint, London: Panther Books, 1972.

Parrinder, Patrick. "Historical Imagination and Political Reality: A Study in Edwardian Attitudes." *Clio* 4, no. 1 (October 1974): 5–25.

Pascoe, Judith. *Romantic Theatricality: Gender, Poetry, and Spectatorship*. Ithaca and London: Cornell University Press, 1997.

Philp, Mark. "Editor's Introduction." In *Resisting Napoleon: The British Response to the Threat of Invasion, 1797–1815*, edited by Mark Philp, 1–17. Aldershot: Ashgate, 2006.

———. "Godwin, Holcroft, and the Rights of Man." *Enlightenment and Dissent* 1 (1982): 37–42.

———. *Godwin's Political Justice*. London: Duckworth, 1986.

Poole, Steve, ed. *John Thelwall: Radical Romantic and Acquitted Felon*. London: Routledge, 2015.

Prados, John. *Lost Crusader: The Secret Wars of CIA Director William Colby*. Oxford: Oxford University Press, 2003.

Ragussis, Michael. *Theatrical Nation: Jews and Other Outlandish Englishmen in Georgian Britain*. Philadelphia: University of Pennsylvania Press, 2010.

Rigby, Brian. "Stendhal and the English Jacobin Novelist Thomas Holcroft." In *Stendhal en l'Angleterre, Proceedings of the London Colloquium, French Institute*, edited by K. G. McWatters and C. W. Thompson, 191–210. Liverpool: Liverpool University Press, 1983.

Roach, Joseph. *Cities of the Dead: Circum-Atlantic Performance*. New York: Columbia University Press, 1996.

Robinson, Terry F. "Deaf Education and the Rise of English Melodrama." *Essays in Romanticism* 29, no.1 (Spring 2022). 1–31.

Rogers, Nicholas. "Pigott's Private Eye: Radicalism and Sexual Scandal in Eighteenth-Century England." *Journal of the Canadian Historical Association* 4, no. 1 (1993): 247–63.

Rose, Jonathan. *The Intellectual Life of the British Working Classes*. New Haven and London: Yale University Press, 2002.

Rosenthal, Jamie. "From Radical Feminist to Caribbean Slaveowner: Eliza Fenwick's Barbados Letters." *Eighteenth-Century Studies* 52, no. 1 (2018): 47–68.

Rugg, Julie, and Brian Parsons. *Funerary Practices in England and Wales*. Bingley, UK: Emerald Publishing, 2018.

Russell, Gillian. "Burke's Dagger: Theatricality, Politics, and Print Culture in the 1790s." *British Journal for Eighteenth-Century Studies* 20, no. 1 (March 1997): 1–16.

———. *The Playbill and Its People*. Canberra: National Library of Australia, 2011.

———. *The Theatres of War: Performance, Politics, and Society, 1793–1815*. Oxford: Clarendon Press, 1995.

Russell, Gillian, and Clara Tuite, "Introducing Romantic Sociability." In *Romantic Sociability. Social Networks and Literary Culture in Britain 1770–1840*, edited by Gillian Russell and Clara Tuite, 1–23. Cambridge: Cambridge University Press, 2002.

Saglia, Diego. "'I Almost Dread to Tell You': Gothic Melodrama and the Aesthetic of Silence in Thomas Holcroft's *A Tale of Mystery*." *Gothic Studies* 14, no. 1 (May 2012), 93–107.

Semmel, Stuart. *Napoleon and the British*. New Haven and London: Yale University Press, 2004.

Shepherd, Simon. "Melodrama." In *English Drama: A Cultural History*, edited by Simon Shepherd and Peter Womack, 188–218. Oxford: Blackwell, 1996.

———. "The Unacceptable Face of the Theatre." In *English Drama: A Cultural History*, edited by Simon Shepherd and Peter Womack, 219–248. Oxford: Blackwell, 1996.

Shirley, Graham, and Brian Adams. *Australian Cinema, The First Eighty Years*. Canberra: National Library of Australia, 1983.

Sigl, Patricia. "Mrs. Inchbald's *Egyptian Boy*." *Theatre Notebook* 43, no. 2 (1989): 57–68.

Southam, Brian. ed. *Jane Austen: The Critical Heritage*. 2 vols. Vol. 1, 1811–1870. London: Routledge, 1968.

Spencer, Charles. "The Road to Ruin." *The Telegraph*, 10 September 2002.

St. Clair, William. *The Godwins and the Shelleys: A Biography of a Family*. Baltimore: Johns Hopkins University Press, 1989.

Stocking, Marion Kingston. *The Journals of Claire Clairmont*, Cambridge, MA: Harvard University Press, 1968.

Stonefield, John Harrison. *Green Leaves: New Chapters in the Life of Charles Dickens*. London: Piccadilly Press, 1931.

Summerfield, Geoffrey, "The Making of the Home Treasury." *Children's Literature* 8 (1980): 35–52.

Sypher, Wylie. "Aesthetic of Revolution: The Marxist Melodrama." *The Kenyon Review* 10, no. 3 (Summer 1948): 431–444.

Taylor, George. *The French Revolution and the London Stage, 1789–1805*. Cambridge: Cambridge University Press, 2000.

Thale, Mary. "London Debating Societies in the 1790s." *The Historical Journal* 32, no. 1 (June 1989): 57–86.

Thomas, Louisa. "The Art of Biography, 4." Interview with Hermione Lee. *The Paris Review* 205 (Summer 2013): 135–165.

Thompson, E. P. *The Making of the English Working Class*. 1963. Rev. ed. Harmondsworth: Penguin, 1968.

———. *The Romantics: England in a Revolutionary Age*, edited by Dorothy Thompson. 1997. Rpt. New York: The New Press, 1999.

Todd, Barbara J. "The Remarrying Widow: A Stereotype Reconsidered." In *Women in English Society, 1500–1800*, edited by Mary Prior, 25–53. New York: Routledge, 1985.

Todd, Janet. *Daughters of Ireland: The Rebellious Kingsborough Sisters and the Making of a Modern Nation*. New York: Ballantine Books, 2003.

Veitch, G. S. *The Genesis of Parliamentary Reform*. London: Constable & Co., 1913.

Verhoeven, W. M. "Politics for the People: Thomas Holcroft's Proto-Marxism." In *Re-Viewing Thomas Holcroft, 1745–1809: Essays on His Work and Life*, edited by A. A. Markley and Miriam L. Wallace, 197–217. Milton Park, UK: Routledge, 2012.

Vincent, David. *Bread, Knowledge and Freedom: A Study of Nineteenth-Century Working-Class Autobiography*. London: Europa Publications, 1981.

Wallace, Miriam. "Constructing Treason, Narrating Truth: The 1794 Treason Trial of Thomas Holcroft and the Fate of English Jacobinism." *Romanticism on the Net* 45 (February 2007). https://www.erudit.org/en/journals/ron/2007 (accessed July 12, 2022).

———. *Revolutionary Subjects in the English "Jacobin" Novel, 1790–1805*. Lewisburg: Bucknell University Press, 2009.

Wallace, Miriam, and A. A. Markley. "Introduction." *Re-Viewing Thomas Holcroft, 1745–1809 Essays on His Work and Life*, edited by A. A. Markley and Miriam L. Wallace, 1–14. Milton Park, UK: Routledge, 2012.

Ward, Adolphus William, and Alfred Rayney Waller, eds. *The Cambridge History of English Literature*. 15 vols. Cambridge: Cambridge University Press, 1932. Volume 13, "The Nineteenth Century."

Warwick, Lou. *The Mackenzies Called Compton: The Story of the Compton Comedy Company, Incorporated in the History of Northampton Theatre Royal and Opera House, 1884–1927*. Lou Warwick: 1977.

Wearing, J. P. *The London Stage, 1930–1939: A Calendar of Productions, Performances, and Personnel*. Lanham, MD: Rowman and Littlefield, 2014.

Webster, Jeremy W. "Re-Writing Shylock: Thomas Holcroft, Semitic Discourse, and anti-Semitism on the English Stage." In *Re-Viewing Thomas Holcroft, 1745–1809: Essays on His Work and Life*, edited by A. A. Markley and Miriam L. Wallace, 71–85. Milton Park, UK: Routledge, 2012.

Wedd, A. F., ed. *The Fate of the Fenwicks, Letters to Mary Hays (1798–1828)*. London: Methuen, 1927.

Wells, Roger. *Wretched Faces: Famine in Wartime England 1793–1801*. Gloucester: Alan Sutton, 1988.

Werkmeister, Lucyle. *A Newspaper History of England, 1792–1793*. Lincoln, NE: University of Nebraska Press, 1967.

Williams, A. M. "A Group of Revolutionaries." *Saint George: A National Review Dealing with Literature, Art, and Social Questions in a Broad and Progressive Spirit* 8, no. 32 (1905): 296–312.

Wilt, Napier, and Henriette C. Koren Naeseth. "Two Early Norwegian Dramatic Societies in Chicago." NAHA Online. Vol. X. https://www.naha.stolaf.edu/pubs/nas/volume 10/vol10 _2.htm.

Worrall, David. *Celebrity, Performance, Reception: British Georgian Theatre as Social Assemblage.* Cambridge: Cambridge University Press, 2013.

———. *Theatric Revolution: Drama, Censorship, and Romantic Period Subcultures, 1773–1832.* Oxford: Oxford University Press, 2006.

Holcroft, Villiers, 18, 169–170, 204n56, 205–206n93
Holcroft, William, 9, 18, 48, 161, 204n57
Holland, William, 188n78
Holman, Joseph, 55
Hunt, Leigh, 125
Hunter of the Alps, The. See Dimond, William
hurricanes, 75. *See also* plantation economy

Imlay, Fanny, 190n9
Imlay, Gilbert, 90, 189n8, 190n9
"immortal dinner," the, 171
Inchbald, Elizabeth, 4, 17, 41, 43, 51, 52, 69, 85–86, 173n4, 173n10, 181n17, 182n27, 187n49, 205n82; *Every One Has His Fault*, 38, 85
intertheatricality, 36–37, 46
Irish Uprising (1798), 95, 102–104, 105, 192n57
Irving, Henry, 51, 52, 54
Italian, The. See Radcliffe, Ann

Jacobin novel, the, 5
James, Henry, 197n14
James, Louis, 124, 197n15, 197n17, 197n20, 197n21
Jardine, Alexander, 19
Jefferson, Joseph, 54
Jefferson, Thomas, 193n84
Jeffries, Matthew, 195n118
"Jew Bill," the, 42
Jews and Jewishness, 36, 41, 42–44, 148–149, 182n27. *See also* anti-Semitism
Johns, Juliet, 197n23
Johnson, Joseph, 13, 14, 102, 176n4
Johnson, Mr. (theater machinist), 144
Johnston, Kenneth R., 7, 60–61, 66, 96, 102, 166, 174n21, 174n22, 176n4, 185n9, 185n10, 185n11, 186n27, 186n29, 191n45, 192n69, 204n67
Jordan, Dorothy, 150
Jordan, J.S., 13, 15, 176n4
Joyce, Jeremiah, 29
Julius Caesar, 2
Juvenile Library, The, 156–158, 159, 163, 202n25, 202n26

Karr, David, 2, 16, 28, 173n3, 173n7, 176n6, 176n7, 177n24, 177n26, 183n41
Keane, John, 176n10, 196n127
Keats, John, 9, 171
Kegan Paul, Charles, 174n15, 175n1, 189n7, 190n9
Kelly, Gary, 173n11

Kelly, Michael, 131, 198n40
Kemble, John Philip, 17, 73, 107, 127, 128, 129
Kenney, James, 145, 167, 168, 170, 171, 206n96; *Blind Boy of Bohemia, The*, 145
Keogh, Dáire, 193n75
Kilgarriff, Michael, 197n25
King, John ("Jew King"), 182n29
King, Ronald F., 176n3
Klopstock, Friedrich Gottlieb, 116
Knight, Thomas, 112–113, 115
Koenig, Rhoda, 173n1
Koren Naeseth, Henriette C., 183n49
Kotzebue, August von, 123, 128, 198n30
Kyd, Stewart, 29

L'Abbé de L'Epée, 116, 117, 128, 129, 130, 131, 198n28
Lady of the Lake, The, 125
Lake, General Gerard, 103, 106, 193n72
Lamb, Caroline, 205n82
Lamb, Charles, 9, 37, 47, 48, 55, 97, 125, 147, 149–150, 158, 162–163, 165, 166, 167, 169, 170, 171, 172, 181n6, 183n44, 191n36, 196n2, 201n4, 202n26
Lamb, Mary, 55, 90, 147, 162, 167, 169, 170, 171, 172, 202n26
Lane, William. *See* Minerva Press
Laqueur Thomas, 165, 204n60
Larpent, Anna Margaretta, 2
Larpent, John, 2, 45, 46, 61, 65, 80, 133
Larpent Collection of Manuscript Plays, 4. *See* Holcroft, Thomas, plays of (unpublished plays and manuscript versions of published plays)
L'Assommoir. See Zola, Emile
Lavater, Johann Caspar, 69, 71; *Essays on Physiognomy*, 187n47
Lawrence, Sir Thomas, 30
Lee, Hermione, 11, 175n39
Le Maitre, Paul Thomas, 166
Lepaux, Louis Marie de La Révellière, 97, 191n52
Les Deux Journées (libretto), 117, 131, 133, 199n55, 199n60. *See also* Scott, Walter
Les Deux Journées (opera), 133–134
Lessing, Gotthold, 205n79
Lewis, Leopold, 125, 197n20
Lewis, Matthew, 127, 131, 158; *Castle Spectre, The*, 131; *Monk, The*, 108; *Wood Demon, The*, 127
Lewis, William, 37, 54, 55
Licensing Act of 1737, 2, 14

ABOUT THE AUTHOR

AMY GARNAI teaches in the Department of English at the Kibbutzim College of Education in Tel Aviv, Israel. She received her PhD from Tel Aviv University. Her research focuses on the intersections of politics and literature in Britain in the time of the French Revolution. She is the author of *Revolutionary Imaginings in the 1790s: Charlotte Smith, Mary Robinson, Elizabeth Inchbald,* and her essays have appeared in such journals as *Women's Writing, SEL, Eighteenth-Century Studies, The Review of English Studies,* and *The Wordsworth Circle.*